Complete Guide
to the
Maintenance and Repair
of
Band Instruments

Kenneth A. Mueller

Illustrations by Patricia E. Nigl

Parker Publishing Company, Inc.   West Nyack, New York

Library of Congress Cataloging in Publication Data

Mueller, Kenneth A.
  Complete guide to the maintenance and repair
of band instruments.

  Includes index.
  1. Wind instruments—Maintenance and repair.
2. Percussion instruments—Maintenance and repair.
I. Title.
ML930.M83   788′.0028′8   81-16894
ISBN 0-13-160499-6   AACR2

Printed in the United States of America

What This Book Can Do for You

This book is written for the band director who has had little or no instruction in the care or repair of band instruments. By reading it you will learn two important things: (1) how to keep your instruments at school and in use rather than in a repair shop, and (2) how to keep your instruments well adjusted so that your students will play better.

You have probably found that band instruments do not suddenly go out of adjustment or need repair (unless they are dropped or otherwise abused). In most cases, the instrument goes out of adjustment over a long period of time. Corks fall off, pads begin to tear, slides get sticky, keys bend slightly, etc. Because your student is playing regularly as all this is happening, he tends to adapt to the lack of adjustment, not realizing that his instrument is becoming increasingly more difficult to play. Finally it becomes physically impossible to play. At this point there are usually so many things wrong with the instrument that it will need to be repaired at a repair shop.

You can now avoid this problem by knowing how to locate, and how to correct, the small problems *as they occur*. Also, as you teach your students, you will be more effective when you can positively determine if the source of any playing problem is caused by instrument malfunction. With this book you will be capable of solving many of the problems that are the cause of band instruments not playing properly.

Proper care of the band instrument is the first step in a good instrument repair program; with the use of a preventive maintenance plan, you can avoid unnecessary loss of the use of band instruments due to repairs. Each chapter contains detailed explanations on instrument care. This includes proper assembly and storage of the instruments, cleaning and maintenance procedures and a monthly "check list" that can be used quickly by you or your students. I have also explained the basic adjustment used for every woodwind instrument. By following the suggestions in this section of the book you will be able to keep your instruments well adjusted and avoid many repair problems. Properly adjusted instruments will allow your students to play with more ease; therefore, they will play better.

As you check the instrument you will often find that they are in need of minor repairs. This is where you can be of greatest assistance to your students and your band program. Too often instruments are sent needlessly to the repair shop for minor repairs that could have been done by you, the band director. Because many schools must send their repairs to a shop in another city, this usually results in a week or more that your student must wait for the instrument to be returned. You are then faced with the problem of what to do with a student in your band when he or she has to sit through five, ten or more rehearsals without an instrument. This can be avoided with the use of this book and a few minutes of your time.

Each chapter has careful explanations of every minor repair problem that you can expect to encounter with each instrument. By following the detailed instructions, you will be able to correct the problems quickly and easily. Numerous charts are used throughout the book to quickly guide you in regulating any key height or key cork. A comprehensive list of all supplies and tools needed for every repair explained in the book is included in the Appendixes. This list even tells you which supplies and tools should be purchased first and which can be added later. Also included is a list of sources where these materials can be purchased. The tools needed for these repairs are minimal and easily affordable by any school budget. Your savings in money and missed playing time, however, will be tremendous.

There will be times, of course, when an instrument is seriously damaged, or the repairs require the skills of a trained repair technician. Also, some repairs are relatively simple to do, but the cost of the required tools makes these repairs impractical for a school. In these cases I have described the type of work that needs to be done to the instrument when it is sent to the shop. The more knowledgeable you can be on the subject of repairs, the more effective you will be as a director when you explain repair problems to your students and parents.

With this book you can now avoid one of the most frustrating problems that has faced the band director, that of band instruments that do not play properly.

Kenneth A. Mueller

Table of Contents

1

The Flute

Illustration 1-1

Courtesy of Artley Flute Co.; Nogales, Arizona 85621

HOW TO TAKE CARE OF YOUR FLUTE

Taking proper care of the flute should be the first, and most important, step in your flute maintenance plan. By following the suggestions given here you will avoid many problems that cause the flute to play improperly. Although this information might be a review for you, the director, it is a good idea to be sure that your students also have an understanding of proper flute care. When the student understands the *reason* for the maintenance procedures outlined below, there is a better chance that they will be followed.

ASSEMBLE THE FLUTE PROPERLY

Assembling the flute is a relatively simple matter, but care should be taken to avoid disturbing the critical adjustment of the keys.

The flute consists of three sections: The head joint, the main body and the foot joint (see Illustration 1-1). There is no specific order in which these need to be assembled. When inserting the head joint you should hold the main body firmly with one hand near the top, where there are no keys. Insert the head joint into the receiver with a slow back and forth twisting action as you push. Line up the embouchure hole with the top of the keys on the main body.

When inserting the main body into the foot joint, hold the foot joint in the right hand and close the hand firmly around the low C and C# keys. The left hand should be closed firmly around the low F, E and D keys on the main body.

Some sources suggest holding the main body near the top when assembling with the foot joint (as you did when inserting the head joint). I believe it is a much safer policy to

9

to always hold the two sections being assembled as close to the joint as possible. If this is not done, there is a greater tendency to insert the tenon joints at a slight angle. This will bend the tenon so that it is not perfectly round and is the most common reason for a bad fitting tenon joint.

If you hold the keys firmly closed while assembling, you will not damage the key adjustment. It is when you allow your hand to slide over the keys while assembling that you are more likely to bend the keys and cause the adjustment to be disturbed.

Align the rod of the foot joint with the center of the low D key.

The tenon should fit snuggly, but move easily. *Never grease a flute tenon.* Tenons that are difficult to insert need cleaning or straightening, not greasing. (See Maintenance Procedures for the Flute—Tenons, page 11.)

STORE THE FLUTE PROPERLY

Flutes should always be stored in the case. A flute left lying about on a chair, table or music stand is easily bumped or dropped on the floor. This can result in serious and expensive repair problems. I have found the most serious cases of bent flutes or keys are a result of those instruments being left lying on a chair and then being sat upon.

It is a good idea not to keep a pencil with an eraser in the case as this might cause a silver flute to tarnish. Also, if a spring should break, avoid wrapping the key with a rubber band as the rubber will cause the silver to tarnish. Over a long period of time this tarnish can eventually eat through the finish. Whether in or out of the case, the flute should never be stored near radiators or heating ducts. Excessive heat will cause the pads and corks to dry out and shrink. This changes the adjustment of the flute, which is determined somewhat by cork thickness, and will destroy the "seat" in the pads which seal the tone hole.

Flute cases are designed to hold the flute securely in the case. They are not meant to carry music or serve as a display case for contest medals or pins. This overpacking of the case causes excessive pressure on the instrument when the cover is closed and may cause the keys to bend or go out of alignment. In addition, dangling medals will scratch a silver flute, and they can easily catch under the keys and bend them when the case is opened.

You can check to see if the case is holding the flute securely by placing the instrument in the case, closing and latching the cover, then shaking the case. If nothing moves or rattles inside, the instrument is secure. Often you can hear the flute bouncing inside the case. If this happens, there needs to be more padding in the case. Laying a small cloth or towel on top of the flute is the quickest way of providing this padding although care should be taken that the cloth is not too thick. Any other loose objects that you can hear rattling in the case should be removed or secured.

Inspect the case periodically to be sure that it is actually protecting the flute. Prompt attention should be given to broken or loose latches, hinges or handles. Be certain that the lining is not loose as it serves as the protective padding around the flute. Loose linings can easily be repaired with some glue, but the case hardware will usually need to be sent to the repair shop for correcting.

CLEAN THE FLUTE REGULARLY

A few minutes of care in cleaning the flute after each playing session will go a long way in helping maintain the instrument.

First, and most important, is to swab out the inside of the flute (bore) to remove all traces of moisture. Swab out all three sections of the flute using the tuning rod provided with the flute. If your flute does not have a tuning rod, it can be purchased inexpensively from your music dealer. You will need a piece of soft cloth. An old handkerchief works well for this, but you could also use cheesecloth or flannel. Insert the cloth through the "eye" of the tuning rod. Fold the cloth over the top of the rod and twist around the shank, totally covering the rod so that no metal will be exposed inside the flute to scratch the instrument. (See Illustration 1-2.)

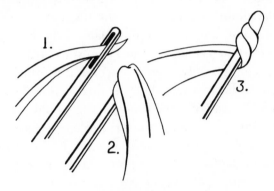

Illustration 1-2

If the flute is put away without swabbing, moisture will accumulate in the pads causing a rapid deterioration of the skin covering. Consistent swabbing, therefore, will greatly increase the life of the pads which is vital to proper instrument performance.

It is also a good idea to carefully wipe the outside of the flute after each playing session. Care should be taken in wiping the flute to avoid wiping sideways across the keys as this could cause them to bend. Use a light stroke on the keys with a cloth, then wipe the body of the instrument. This will remove some of the body oils and will help preserve the flute finish.

MAINTENANCE PROCEDURES FOR THE FLUTE

Tenons—Keeping the flute tenons clean is an often overlooked item which does require regular care. The tenons become dirty through handling and this dirt will also accumulate inside the receivers for each tenon. It does not take much dirt to cause the tenons to fit too tightly. At this point, many band directors think they have to send the flute into a repair shop to have the joint adjusted. In reality, unless the joint has been dented, you will find that the fit will be quite satisfactory after you clean the tenon.

To clean, you will need a piece of canning wax (paraffin), which is available in any grocery store, and a clean cloth. Rub the wax on the tenon then insert the tenon into the receiver, twisting back and forth. When you remove the tenon you will find a black film has accumulated. Wipe the tenon completely with the cloth and then reach inside and wipe the receiver as well. Repeat the process until the black film does not appear (usually twice is sufficient). If the tenon is still too tight after this, it is probably dented or out of round. The flute should be sent to a repair shop to correct this problem. Do not attempt to emery the tenon as this will remove the plating and cause even more difficulty in obtaining a good fit.

Never grease a tenon, as the grease quickly adds to the dirt buildup and only causes the problem to intensify after a few days.

Washing the Bore—If you are swabbing the bore of the flute after each use, the inside should remain quite clean. However, it is a good idea to wash the bore about once a month to be certain that all dirt is removed. To do this, use a swab that is damp (but not dripping wet) and swab out the bore of the main body and foot joint. Follow this immediately with a dry cloth to take up the excess moisture so it will not get into the pads.

Because the head joint is only open at one end, it is usually more difficult to do an effective job of cleaning with the swab. Also, as this section does accumulate the most moisture, it is a good idea to wash out the head joint in a mild soapy water solution about once a month. *(NOTE:* You should never wash the other two sections of the flute as that would destroy the pads.) Before washing the head joint, be sure to remove the head joint stopper cork. (See How to Replace the Head Joint Stopper Cork, p. 26.)

After washing, rinsing and drying the head joint carefully, lightly grease the stopper cork and push back into place. Use the notched guide on the tuning rod to position the stopper cork in the correct place. If the stopper cork does not seal up the head joint, it may have to be replaced.

Cleaning the Flute Body—In time the outside of the flute will begin to accumulate a greasy dirt and lint under the key rods. It is a good idea to take some time to remove this lint before it gets into the rods and slows up the key action. Using a small modeler's paint brush or pipe stem cleaner, reach under the keys and brush away any dirt or lint that has collected there. *Care should be taken to avoid catching any of the springs* as this would change the spring tension and could affect the adjustment. Actually this job is quite easy if done slowly and carefully.

Flutes are most commonly finished in either nickel or silver. Some people have difficulty recognizing the difference between the two finishes, yet it is important to know which is which as they are cared for quite differently.

The nickel finish is darker in color than silver, it is usually more shiny and a little more slippery to handle. The silver finish is a lighter color and will quickly loose its sheen after some use. Silver will tarnish and you can usually see some brownish color under the key rods on the older flutes.

The nickel flute can be kept looking quite nice by simply wiping with a soft, dry cloth. When wear spots begin to appear on the body or keys, they can only be removed by buffing, which should be done in a repair shop.

Silver flutes, on the other hand, can be returned to an almost new appearance with the use of a little silver polish. I suggest a liquid silver polish as it is easier to work with. Your music dealer should be able to recommend a good brand. Apply the polish sparingly with a soft cloth, and avoid getting any polish on the pads or key rods. When the polish is dry wipe off with a clean, dry cloth. You can wipe over the key rods at this time and they will also clean up quite well. Care should be taken to remove all dry polish or it will begin to clog the key rods, slowing down or stopping the key action. If the pads on the flute begin to show signs of wear on the outside edge, this is an indication that they are being rubbed with the polish when being cleaned and will have to be replaced shortly.

Use a soft pipe stem cleaner to remove the dry polish from those hard-to-reach areas. The only way to remove the tarnish which develops under the key rods is to remove all the keys, then polish and replace the keys. I would suggest that you not attempt this job until you feel comfortable with the entire flute mechanism as you will have to check the key regulation when done. (See How to Regulate the Keys, p. 19.) I feel that polishing what you can without removing the keys will produce quite satisfactory results with a lot less time involved.

Sticky Pads—Sticky pads are caused by an accumulation of dirt on the pad seat. A condition which intensifies the problem is that of sugar in the saliva while playing. The student should avoid chewing gum, eating candy or drinking "pop" immediately before or while playing. All these items add lots of sugar to the saliva, some of which will go into the bore and accumulate on the pads. This sticky substance then attracts dirt to the pad causing the stickiness. Swabbing and washing the bore, as described above, will also help reduce the chance of sticky pads.

The whole problem usually begins with an annoying sound as the keys open. As the problem gets worse, the keys will not open promptly and, finally, some keys will stay closed. The problem should be corrected quickly, at the first sound of stickiness, as this is when it is most easy to do. (See How to Clean Dirty and Sticky Pads, p. 24.) It is also a good idea to try to determine the source of the stickiness to avoid further problems.

Oiling the Keys—The keys of the flute should be oiled about once a month to keep them working freely and to prevent the screws and rods from becoming rusted. Key oil is available from your music dealer. Using a pin or toothpick place a *small* drop of key oil at the end of each key rod and between all moveable keys which share the same rod (for example, low D, E, F, and F♯). Move the keys to circulate the oil, then wipe off any excess oil that may be on the rods.

MONTHLY MAINTENANCE CHECK LIST—FLUTE

Chart 1 is a check list that you can use to help in the maintenance procedures of the flute. By following this chart you should be able to keep the instrument well cleaned and be alert to any possible repairs needed before the problems become too severe. With some training, your students should be able to use this check list themselves.

Chart 1
Monthly Maintenance Check List—Flute

INSPECT THE FOLLOWING:

Head Joint _____ Is the stopper cork tight and aligned properly?

_____ Is the tenon clean and fitting correctly?

_____ Are there any dents in the body?

Flute _____ Is the tenon clean and fitting correctly?

_____ Are there any sticky pads?

_____ Are there any torn pads?

_____ Are there any loose pads?

_____ Are all the keys moving freely?

_____ Are there any dents in the body?

_____ Are there any missing screws or rods?

_____ Are there any clicking keys due to missing corks?

Case _____ Are the latches working properly?

_____ Are the hinges tight?

_____ Is the handle secure?

_____ Is the lining tight?

_____ Are there any loose objects in the case?

_____ Is the flute tight in the case when closed?

DO THE FOLLOWING:

1. Check for leaks (see How to Check for Leaks, p. 16).
2. Wash the bore.
3. Polish or wipe the outside of the flute body.
4. Clean dirt and lint from under the key rods.
5. Oil the key rods and screws.

HOW TO REPAIR THE FLUTE

DIAGNOSING INSTRUMENT MALFUNCTIONS

As you look through this section of the book, you probably will have a flute that is not playing properly. Before you can repair the flute, you need to locate the problem. Listed below are some of the more common problems that occur on the flute. For each problem I have suggested some possible causes in the hope that it will help you locate the difficulty. Although this list can hardly be complete, I'm sure that it will serve as a good guideline.

1. *Problem:* Flute blows hard, will not play all the notes.

Possible Causes: Pads are leaking. (Look for torn pads or those not seating level with the tone hole.) Keys are not regulated correctly. Head joint stopper cork is leaking. Embouchure plate is leaking.

2. *Problem:* Flute plays the wrong pitch when key is depressed.

Possible Causes: Check for a broken spring. See if any springs are unhooked from the keys. Keys may not be regulated correctly.

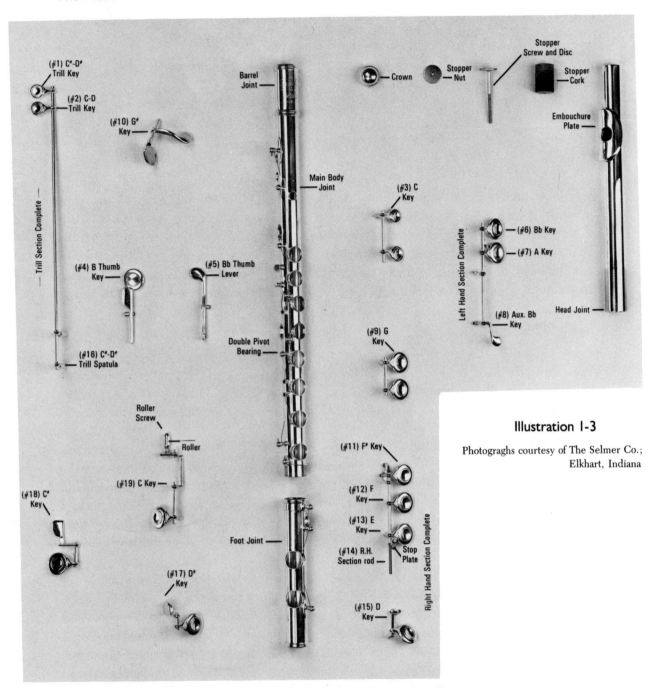

Illustration 1-3

Photograghs courtesy of The Selmer Co.;
Elkhart, Indiana

3. *Problem:* Keys stick.

Possible Causes: Keys or rods may be bent. Spring tension may be too heavy on some keys. The pads or tone holes may be dirty.

4. *Problem:* Some of the notes play out of tune.

Possible Causes: A key cork may be missing, causing the key height to be incorrect. All key heights may be set incorrectly. The stopper cork in the head joint may not be lined up correctly.

5. *Problem:* Keys are not functioning properly.

Possible Causes: Check for broken or unhooked springs. Look for dented or bent key posts, keys or rods. Pivot screws may not be adjusted correctly.

6. *Problem:* Tenons are too tight.

Possible Causes: The tenons are dirty. The tenon is dented or not perfectly round.

HOW TO CHECK FOR LEAKS

When the flute fails to play properly, the first thing you should do is to check the instrument for leaks. When the flute is not leaking, all notes should play with the same amount of ease. (The beginning flute player will usually have difficulty playing all the notes.) Generally speaking, if the player is unable to play down to the low C on the flute, there are some leaking pads. If you encounter this problem but are not sure if the source of the difficulty lies with the student or the flute, have another person play on the same instrument. This will give you a quick indication of whether the suspected problem is in the flute.

Procedure:

1. Check the foot joint. Place your hand over the bottom end of the joint to seal. Press down on the C key lever with normal pressure and blow gently. If there is a leak, you will hear the air escaping and will feel the lack of resistance as you blow into the bore of the joint. (Don't blow too hard as the D♭ key will blow open when your air pressure overcomes the spring tension on that key.)

2. Check the main body. Place the foot joint end of the flute against your leg to seal the end. Press the appropriate keys to close all pads over the tone holes and blow into the other end of the bore. Use the normal light pressure used when playing the flute to hold the keys down. Again, you will be able to hear any escaping air and feel the lack of resistance as you blow into the bore. You may need the help of someone else to determine where the leak is. Be sure to blow gently for if you blow too hard, you will blow open the trill keys or the G♯ key.

3. Check the head joint. The head joint is often overlooked when testing a flute for leaks, but it could be the source of a leak large enough to cause playing problems. Place your thumb over the embouchure hole to seal, and blow into the other end. There should be no escaping air. You probably will not be able to hear a leak in the head joint, because it will be a much smaller quantity of air escaping. You will, however, feel a lack of resistance as you blow into the bore of the head joint. Some people find it easier to check the head joint by sucking on it rather than blowing. When you suck out the air you create a vacuum. If the vacuum disappears quickly, then air is leaking in from some source. (The sucking technique does not work on the other joints, as the vacuum created tends to pull the keys shut and the leaks do not become apparent.)

The head joint can only leak in two places, at the end around the stopper cork or where the embouchure plate is soldered to the head joint. Most often it will leak around the stopper cork, but to be sure place the head joint in a pail or sink of water, seal as indicated above, and blow. Bubbles will appear at the source of the leak. If the stopper cork is leaking it will have to be replaced. (See How to Replace the Head Joint Stopper Cork, p. 26.) If the air is escaping from around the embouchure plate, it should be sent to the repair shop to be resoldered.

You might want to practice this technique of testing for leaks by testing a flute that you know is not leaking. After you experience the resistance produced as you blow through a tight flute, it will be easier for you to recognize a leaking flute.

HOW TO ADJUST THE PAD SEAT

Before you attempt to regulate the keys, you should check the pad seats to be certain they are sealing properly. If the pads do not form a level seat with the tone hole, it will be virtually impossible to regulate the keys.

Tools Needed: Leak light

Key bending tool

Materials Needed: Paper flute pad washers

Small flute pads (optional)

Procedure:

1. Check the seat. Place your leak light under each pad, then close the key very slowly using a light pressure. Using excessive pressure or closing the keys rapidly as you would in normal playing will often hide the problem. It is important to be very critical during this checking procedure. The pad should seat level with the tone hole so that it closes simultaneously around the entire tone hole. Check carefully to be sure the pad is not hitting in the front, back, or on one of the sides before it seals the tone hole. At this point, if you find any torn or loose pads they should be replaced. (See How to Install New Flute Pads, p. 20.)

2. If the pad seat is *not* level with the tone hole, you should do one of the following:

a. Bend the key back to its original position. Chances are that the key has already been bent, thus causing the improper seat. Place your key bending tool (see Appendix A) under the portion of the pad which is hitting the tone hole first and push on the opposite side of the key (see Illustration 1-4). Push gently because it is better to have to repeat the process a number of times than to over-correct. Continue to check and adjust until the pad seat is level. If this does not correct the problem, continue below.

Illustration 1-4

b. If your pad seat continues to have gaps when the key is closed, it is time to use the paper flute pad washers. Make a note of the place or places where the pad is gapping. Remove the key and mark the pad's position in the key (see Illustration 1-5). Remove the pad carefully so as not to tear the skin or disturb the washers already under the pad. Place a small wedge of the paper washer in the key at the places where the gaps occured (see Illustration 1-6). Start with only one paper washer wedge, either thick (.008) or thin (.004) depending on the size of the gap as the wedge will affect the pad position considerably. Replace the pad in its original position in the key according to the marks you made. Remount the key on the flute and repeat step "a" above. If, after steps "a" and "b" the trouble seems impossible to correct, you probably have a bad pad that should be replaced, or you may have a tone hole that is not level. In this case you will have to send the flute to the repair shop to have the tone hole leveled.

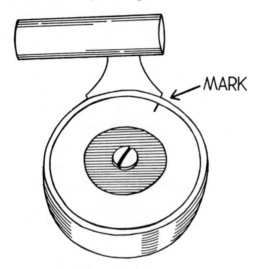

Illustration 1-5

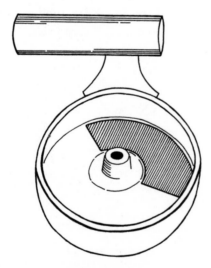

Illustration 1-6

c. If one of the three small pads (trill keys or the C key) are not level, it is best to just replace the pad as the adjustment of the smaller pads is not practical.

HOW TO REGULATE THE KEYS

The proper regulation of the flute keys is of paramount importance. Following is a detailed, step-by-step procedure for this regulation. Although the regulation of the keys is just one step in the complete adjustment process of the flute, it is often all that you will need to do to get a flute playing again. Be sure to check the pads before you begin to regulate the flute. The pads must form a level seat with the tone hole to achieve the proper regulation. (See How to Adjust the Pad Seat, p. 17.)

Tools Needed: Leak light
Small screwdriver
Round nose pliers
Procedure: (Refer to Illustration 1-3 for key names and numbers.)

1. Use a leak light as you check the keys. First press the A key (No. 7). This should close the B♭ key (No. 6) at the same time. If the B♭ key closes first, loosen the adjustment screw which is alongside the top of the A key. If the A key closes first, tighten this screw.

2. Loosen the adjustment screw for the F♯ key (No. 11). This screw is located either alongside the top of the F key (No. 12) or on the foot of the F♯ key.

3. Press down the F key (No. 12). The B♭ key (No. 6) should close at the same time. If it does not, an adjustment needs to be made on the bridge key which is located by the foot of the F key. If the bridge key has an adjustment screw, tightening the screw will cause the B♭ key to close sooner. If your bridge key looks like Illustration 1-7, bending the top bridge key down will cause the B♭ key to close sooner than the F key. If you have any other type of bridge key, you will have to add or take away cork at their point of contact to adjust the bridge. Adding cork will cause the B♭ key to close sooner.

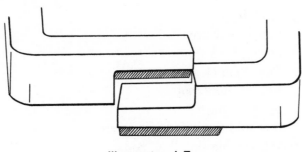

Illustration 1-7

4. After the F key (No. 12) and the B♭ key (No. 6) are closing together, tighten the adjustment screw for the F♯ key (No. 11) until this key closes at the same time as the B♭ key when pushing on the F key. (See step "2" above.)

5. Press down on the E key (No. 13). This should close at the same time as the F♯ key (No. 11). Tightening the adjustment screw alongside the E key will cause the F♯ key to close sooner.

6. Press down the D key (No. 15). This should close at the same time as the F♯ key (No. 11). Tightening the adjustment screw along side the D key will cause the F♯ key to close sooner.

7. Press down on the B♭ thumb lever (No. 5). The B thumb key (No. 4) and the B♭ key (No. 6) should close together. If they do not, check to see if the felt is missing on the B♭ thumb lever where it makes contact with the B thumb key. If so, replace the felt and check again. If the B thumb key closes first, use your round nose pliers and bend the B♭ thumb *lever* up slightly. If the B♭ key (No. 6) is closing first, bend the B♭ thumb *lever* down slightly with the pliers.

8. Secure the adjustment screws. If you found in the process of adjusting the flute that the adjustment screws turned rather easily, it is a good idea to secure them once the adjustment is made. These screws tend to become loose after a while and then will turn with the vibration of the instrument. Even the slightest turn of an adjustment screw will be enough to destroy the regulation you just made. To secure, place a very small drop of one of the new super glues (Zip Grip, Krazy Glue, etc.) on the head of the adjustment screw. The glue will prevent the screw from turning and, if you use a *small enough quantity of glue,* you will be able to break them free when a readjustment is needed.

Replacing the adjustment screws would be another way of correcting this problem. New adjustment screws for many brands of flutes come with a teflon bushing attached to the thread of the screw. This makes the screw more difficult to turn once this bushing is compressed into the screw socket. You could obtain replacement screws from your repair shop.

HOW TO INSTALL NEW FLUTE PADS

A flute pad should be replaced when it begins to show signs of wear. Once the skin covering of the pad is torn the pad will have a tendency to leak. Pads may also have to be replaced if you find it impossible to get them to seat properly or if they are excessively dirty.

Tools Needed: Leak light
                Small screwdriver
                Spring hook
                Pipe stem cleaner
                Key bending tool
                Spring clamps
                Alcohol burner or bunsen burner
Materials Needed: Double skin flute pads
                    Paper flute pad washers
Procedure:

1. Remove the key with the affected pad from the flute. (As some flute keys are connected together on the same rod, you may find yourself removing more than one key to get at the one you need.) Be certain to keep track of any pivot screws or rods that are removed so they are returned to the same position.

2. Remove the pad from the key. Flute pads are not glued in place, but rather are held there by means of a screw and washer or a snap washer. If you have the screw and washer type of key, simply remove the screw and washer and pull out the pad. The snap washer is a clear or white plastic washer which holds the pad in place. If you have this style key, place your screwdriver under the edge of the snap washer and pry off.

There will probably be a number of paper and/or metal washers under the pad. Throw away the paper ones, but save the metal washers.

3. Place one thick (.008) paper washer into the key. Use the largest diameter washer that will fit. If the key has metal washers under the pad, place the metal washer into the key and do not use any paper washer at this time.

4. Select the correct size pad. It should fit *snugly* into the key without any gap between the side of the pad and the key. You should not have to bend the cardboard backing of the pad when putting it in place. If you do, the pad is too large.

5. Replace the washer and screw that hold the pad in place. If your key has a snap washer, simply push the washer down as far as it will go and it will hold the pad in place.

6. The new pad is now in the key and you will notice that it is quite wrinkled. Dip your pipe stem cleaner into some water then rub a coating of water over the pad. When the water dries, the pad will be much smoother. (Don't worry if there are a few wrinkles left.)

7. Return the key to the flute. When in place press the key firmly against the tone hole to push the pad all the way up into the key.

8. Check to see if the pad is level with the tone hole. Using a very light pressure, slowly close the pad while checking with a leak light. If your pad is level you are all set to proceed with step 10. If the pad is not level, continue with step 9 below.

9. Leveling the pad. Place your key bending tool under the portion of the pad which is hitting the tone hole first. Push on the opposite side of the key (see Illustration 1-8). Push gently as it is better to have to repeat the process a number of times than to over-correct. Continue to check and adjust until the pad is level.

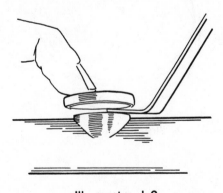

Illustration 1-8

If the above process does not correct the problem, it is then time to use the paper pad washers. Make a note of the place or places where the pad is gapping. Remove the key and mark the pad's position in the key (see Illustration 1-9).

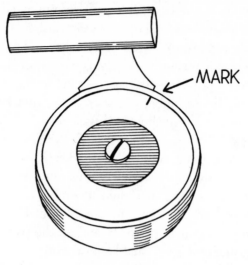

Illustration 1-9

Remove the pad and place a small wedge of paper washer in the key at the places where the gaps occured (see Illustration 1-10). For most gaps you will need only one paper washer wedge. Use a thick washer (.008) for larger gaps and a thin washer (.004) for the smaller gaps.

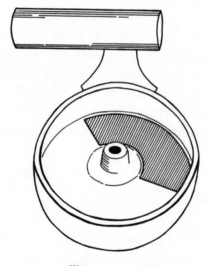

Illustration 1-10

Place the pad into the key in the original position according to the marks you made. Remount the key on the flute and repeat the process with the key bending tool as indicated above.

10. Seating the pad. When the pad is level with the tone hole, wet the skin again with water (using the pipe stem cleaner) and heat the top of the key (see Illustration 1-11) with your flame for about 5 to 10 seconds. (When the key is hot enough, you will not be able to hold your finger on the key.) Clamp the key firmly shut with the spring clamp and

allow it to cool thoroughly. If you do not have a spring clamp you can hold the key down with your fingers but will need something to protect your fingers from the heat. The key should be kept clamped for about 5 minutes for best results.

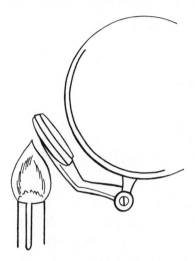

Illustration I-11

11. After the seat has been set, check to see if it is still level with the tone hole. If you find a gap, you will have to add another paper washer wedge. Mark the position of the pad carefully before removing (see Illustration 1-9) so you won't have to reseat the pad after it is replaced.

12. Once the pad is seated and level, regulate the key as needed. See How to Regulate the Keys, p. 19.)

There are some different types of flute pads which you might encounter other than the usual skin pad. If the flute is an open hole model the pads will need to be cut larger in the center to accommodate the open hole key. This requires a special die and it is a more difficult method of mounting the pads. I would suggest you send the open hole model flute to the repair shop for pad work. Of course, the regular keys on the open hole model flute can be changed as indicated above.

Some flutes have been padded with a white rubber type of pad called "Perma-pad." These pads are designed to last a longer time and usually do. Replacement pads are available in kits that include instructions and glue. However, you can also replace a "Perma-pad" with a conventional pad as indicated above.

The Selmer Company has experimented with another type of rubber pad called an "Adjusta-pad." This is a soft rubber pad which floats in the key. Because it moves around freely in the key, it is supposed to seal the tone hole more easily. These pads are mounted on a flexible rubber stem which is glued to the pad cup. Replacement "Adjusta-pads" are available; however, it would not be practical for you to stock these pads unless all of your flutes happen to have them. You cannot substitute a regular pad for the "Adjusta-pad" because the key is missing the nut that holds the pad screw or snap washer in place. Your repair shop can either replace the "Adjusta-pad" or convert the key to accept a regular flute pad. When converting, however, it is best to do all the pads at the same time as the "feel" of the two types of pads is quite different when playing.

HOW TO INSTALL THE FLUTE TRILL KEY PADS

The pads used on the trill keys and the C key are normal clarinet pads and should be installed as follows:

Tools Needed: Leak light
Pad slick
Pipe stem cleaner
Spring clamp
Alcohol burner or bunsen burner

Materials Needed: Double skin clarinet pads
Stick shellac

Procedure:

1. Remove the pad. These three pads are held in place with shellac. You will need to heat the key (see Illustration 1-11) until the shellac softens, then remove the pad.

2. Find the correct size pad as a replacement. The pad should fit snugly into the key. (There are also flute pads made for these keys, but to save on your inventory of supplies, you can easily use a conventional clarinet pad.) Heat the stick shellack and when soft place a drop of shellac on the back of the pad. Place the pad in the key, close the key and heat until the shellac is soft and the pad settles into the key.

3. Level the pad with the tone hole. When the shellac is soft the pad will move freely in the key. At this time, place your pad slick between the pad and the tone hole and rotate back and forth. Remove the pad slick and lightly close the key to see if the pad is level with the tone hole. If the pad hits the back of the tone hole first it is too large and should be replaced with the next smaller size. Likewise, if the pad hits the front of the tone hole first it is too small and should be replaced with the next larger size.

4. Seating the pad. When the pad is level with the tone hole, wet the pad with water (using the pipe stem cleaner), heat the key once again and clamp shut with a spring clamp.

5. After the key has cooled thoroughly, remove the clamp and check with a leak light to see if you have a good level seat on your pad. If not, you will need to repeat step 3 above.

HOW TO CLEAN DIRTY AND STICKY PADS

Tools Needed: Ungummed cigarette paper
Alcohol
Talcum powder

Procedure:

1. Place a sheet of the cigarette paper under the sticky pad, close the key firmly and pull the paper out. You will notice a dirt mark on the paper when removed. Repeat this process a few times always using a clean part of the paper until no mark is noticeable on the paper.

2. If the key still sticks, try placing a small amount of talcum powder on the paper before placing it under the key and repeat the process as outlined in step 1.

3. Still sticking? Place a little alcohol on the paper and try again. (This should be a last resort as the alcohol will damage the skin pad somewhat.)

4. If the problem still persists, you will have no alternative but to remove the key, clean the tone hole with alcohol and change the pad. (See How to Install New Flute Pads, p. 20.)

HOW TO REPLACE KEY CORKS

Most of the corks used on the flute act both to adjust the key heights and to soften the sound of the key hitting the body of the flute. The thickness of the cork used is important. I have listed in Chart 2 the most common size corks to use on each key. In some cases you will have to emery the cork down somewhat to achieve the proper fit. As a general rule, key corks are always glued to the key and never to the body of the flute. Not only does this give a better appearance to the flute but gluing cork to the flute body will eventually destroy the silver finish as the glue is a rubber based product.

Tools Needed: Contact cork cement
Single edge razor blade
Emery paper

Materials Needed: Sheet cork in sizes ⅟₆₄″, ⅟₃₂″, ⅟₁₆″ and ⅛″ as needed

Procedure:

1. Remove any particles of cork which may be left on the key.

2. Select the correct size cork according to Chart 2 and spread contact cement on a small section of the cork.

3. Spread the contact cement on the proper spot of the key.

4. Allow the contact cement to dry thoroughly, then place the cork in position. Trim off excess with a razor blade.

5. Check the adjustment of the key with the other keys and emery the cork if needed to regulate. (See How to Regulate the Keys, p. 19.) To emery the cork, place a small strip of emery paper between the cork and the flute body with the rough side against the cork (see Illustration 1-12). Pull the emery paper while holding the key against it. This will take off cork and shape it to the body of the flute at the same time.

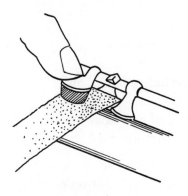

Illustration 1-12

Chart 2
Flute Key Corks

(Refer to Illustration 1-3 for key names and numbers. Those keys not listed do not require any cork.)

Key #	Key Name	Location of cork	Size of cork
3	C key	Under foot	1/32"
5	B♭ thumb lever	Under foot	1/16"
		Under lever	piece of felt
7	A key	Under foot	1/32"
8	Aux. B♭ key	Under foot	1/64"
9	G key	Under foot	1/32"
10	G♯ key	Under lever	1/16"
11	F♯ key	No cork*	—
12	F key	Under foot	1/16"
13	E key	Under foot	1/32"
15	D key	Under foot	1/32"
16	Trill key spatulas	Under spatuala	1/16"**
17	D♯ key	Under lever	1/8" or 1/16"
		Under foot	1/32"
19	C key	Under lever where it contacts C♯ key	1/64"

*If your F♯ key does not have an adjustment screw on the foot you will have to use a piece of cork the correct thickness to allow the F and F♯ keys to close together. (See How to Regulate the keys, p. 19.)

**If the trill key spatula is in a half moon shape, cut a piece of cork off a stopper cork the same width as the key. Cut a wedge about 1/3 the circumference of the cork and glue in place. Trim off excess cork and emery down so trill keys open to correct height. (See How to Check the Intonation of the Flute, p. 30.)

HOW TO REPLACE THE HEAD JOINT STOPPER CORK

If the stopper cork moves easily inside the head joint or turns when you adjust the crown, it is too loose and will probably be leaking. It is then best to replace the stopper cork as follows:

Tools Needed: Pliers
Tuning rod
Rawhide hammer
Old drum stick

Materials Needed: One flute stopper cork
Cork grease
Pad and cork cement

Procedure: (Refer to Illustration 1-3.)

1. Remove the stopper. Loosen the crown and push the stopper out of the tenon end of the head joint. Because the head joint is tapered, you should never attempt to pull the stopper out of the closed end of the head joint. If the cork is dried out, it might be

leaking (see How to Check for Leaks, p. 16) and still be stuck in the head joint. In this case, loosen the crown part way and tap lightly on the crown with a rawhide hammer to free the stopper.

2. Cut a new stopper cork to the same length as the old cork.

3. Remove the stopper nut from the stopper screw and disc. You may have to use a pair of pliers to free this nut as it is often glued in place. Remove the old stopper cork by pulling off with a pair of pliers.

4. Screw the stopper screw into the hole of the new stopper cork until the cork is all the way down to the disc.

5. Place a small drop of pad and cork cement on the top of the stopper cork. The glue will prevent the nut from turning loose while in the head joint. Tighten the nut down firmly with a pair of pliers so that you compress the stopper cork slightly, thus making it expand. Wipe off any glue that may have squeezed out while tightening.

6. Grease the stopper cork with cork grease and place into the tenon end of the head joint.

7. The cork should be quite tight and should only move freely about half way into the head joint. Using an old drum stick, push the cork up to the top of the head joint with the butt end of the stick. Replace the crown. You should not use the tuning rod to push the stopper cork as the metal edge of the rod will damage the stopper disc. Also, as it might require quite a bit of pressure to push the cork in place, the tuning rod could bend.

8. Line up the stopper cork so that the notch on the tuning rod is centered in the embouchure hole. If the stopper cork has been pushed too far up into the head joint, loosen the crown, then use the rawhide hammer and tap the cork back down a bit. Tighten the crown down until it fits against the head joint.

HOW TO REPLACE A FLUTE SPRING

Flute springs do not break often, so you probably will have only a few springs each year that will need to be changed. Flute springs come as a continuous strand of spring wire (Phosphor Bronze) which is then cut to the correct length. The springs come in four sizes and you should have all sizes in stock. The common sizes are: .020″, .025″, .032″, and .035″

Never use a blue needle spring on a flute, even though you will be able to find a spring that fits, as this type of spring provides too much tension on the key. This excessive tension will cause an uneven resistance to finger pressure and sometimes will cause the key to stick.

Tools Needed: Small round nose pliers
Wire cutter
Small hammer
Large blue needle spring
Spring hook

Materials Needed: Flute spring wire

Procedure:

1. Remove keys around the broken spring to make it accessible.
2. Remove the old spring. Usually the spring will break by the post leaving a small

stub in the post. This stub must be pulled out the same end that it went in (see Illustration 1-13). If the flattened end of the spring is extending out from the post, grasp this firmly with the wire cutters and pull out (see Illustration 1-14). If the other end of the spring is extending beyond the post, use the round nose pliers and squeeze the spring out of the post (see Illustration 1-15). If the spring is flush in the post, use a large needle spring (from your supply of saxophone needle springs) as a driver and tap the spring out with a hammer. When doing this it is a good idea to rest the post against some object to prevent the post from bending (see Illustration 1-16). It is also possible that the old spring has already fallen out.

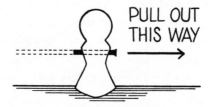

Illustration 1-13

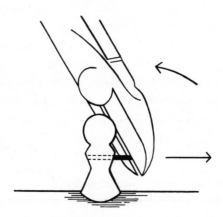

Illustration 1-14

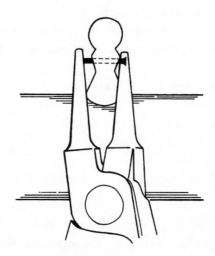

Illustration 1-15

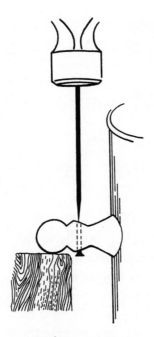

Illustration 1-16

3. Once the old spring is removed, try various sizes of spring wire until you find the thickest wire which will go through the hole in the post. Measure the length of spring needed to reach the spring hook on the key and cut with wire cutters.

4. Hold the spring against a solid metal block (vise, piece of steel, etc.) and with the small hammer tap one end lightly to flatten.

5. Insert the spring into the post so that the flat end will go in last. Squeeze the flat end into the post with your round nose pliers (see Illustration 1-17). This holds the spring in place.

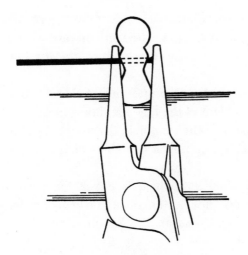

Illustration 1-17

6. Bend the spring slightly in the post to match the other springs in the same area of the flute (see Illustration 1-18). This should make the tension approximately the same.

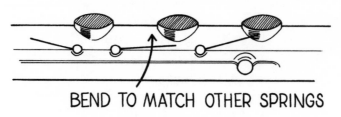

BEND TO MATCH OTHER SPRINGS

Illustration 1-18

7. Remount the key and check the spring tension. (See How to Adjust the Spring Tension, below.)

HOW TO ADJUST THE SPRING TENSION

On the flute, all keys that are usually in the open position should have a light resistance that still allows for a quick, snappy key action. Those keys that are normally in a closed position should be set with a heavier resistance. It is important to keep the tension uniform throughout the flute. That is, all open keys should have the same light tension and all closed keys the same heavier tension. Tension on a key is increased or decreased by bending the spring wire gently in one direction or the other. Be sure to unhook the spring from the key before attempting to bend the spring.

When checking the keys, move only one key at a time. (For example, when checking the tension of the F, E and D keys you must hold the F♯ and B♭ keys closed to get a true feel of the tension of each *individual* key.)

HOW TO CHECK THE INTONATION OF THE FLUTE

The intonation of the flute is determined by a number of factors:

1. The breath support and embouchure of the player.

2. The placement of the head joint into the main body of the flute and its alignment with the main body.

3. The proper placement of the head joint stopper cork. Check this placement by putting the tuning rod into the head joint. The mark on the rod should be centered in the embouchure hole. The distance from the end of the tuning rod to the mark is approximately $^{11}/_{16}''$.

4. The flute keys opening to the proper heights. This is important if the flute is to play in tune with itself. The height of the key opening is measured at the front of the pad and is the distance from the top of the tone hole to the bottom of the pad when the key is fully opened. Chart 3 shows the generally acceptable heights to which flute keys should be set.

If you find an individual key which is not at the correct height, the key has probably lost a cork on the foot. They key heights can usually be corrected by replacing the cork. (See How to Replace Key Corks, p. 25.) You may have to emery down the cork to achieve the correct height as indicated in Chart 3.

If you find that all the key heights are incorrect, it will take a complete adjustment to correct the situation. How successful you can be in doing this will depend somewhat on how comfortable you feel with the complete adjustment of the flute. (See The Complete Adjustment, p. 32.) In any case, whenever you alter the key heights, be sure to check the regulation of the keys afterwards.

Chart 3
Flute Key Heights

(Refer to Illustration 1-3 for key names and numbers)

Key	Number	Height
C♯ -D♯ trill key	1	1⁄16″
C-D trill key	2	1⁄16″
C key	3	1⁄16″
B thumb key	4	3⁄32″*
B♭ key	6	3⁄32″*
A key	7	3⁄32″*
G key	9	3⁄32″
G♯ key	10	3⁄32″
F♯ key	11	3⁄32″*
F key	12	3⁄32″
E key	13	3⁄32*
D key	15	3⁄32″*
D♯ key	17	1⁄8″
C♯ key	18	1⁄8″*
C key	19	1⁄8″

*The heights of these keys will automatically be correct if the flute keys are regulated correctly.

HOW TO CORRECT NON-FUNCTIONING KEYS

A non-functioning key can be defined as any key on the flute which is not operating properly. This includes keys that won't go down or won't come up. When this occurs, you should send the instrument into the repair shop to be corrected as it will take a skilled repair technician to solve and correct the problem. There are, however, a number of things you should check before sending the flute in to be repaired. These are common problems which cause key malfunctions that can be easily corrected by you. Checking these might save you time and money.

1. **Check the spring.**—Is it broken off? Perhaps the spring is just unhooked from the key. If the spring appears O.K., push against it with your spring hook. If there is no tension in the spring, it is broken and will need to be replaced. (See How to Replace Flute Springs, p. 27.) Sometimes the spring will be broken but will appear to be O.K.

2. **Check the pivot screws.**—The screws, which hold the key in place, could be either too tight or too loose. With a small screwdriver, turn the screw both ways and see if the key action improves.

3. **Check the key.**—If the key does not close all the way, use your leak light to see if the pad is still level on the tone hole. If not, your key may have been bent. You then need to re-adjust the pad seat. (See How to Adjust the Pad Seat, p. 17.)

THE COMPLETE ADJUSTMENT— HOW TO MAKE THE ADJUSTMENTS NECESSARY FOR PROPER INSTRUMENT PERFORMANCE

To do a complete adjustment of the flute will seem to be difficult at first. It is, however, quite conceivable that it can be done by you, in the school situation, as it requires very few tools. By following the procedure outlined below you will be able to achieve a well adjusted flute. This task will, most likely, take considerable time the first time you try it but will definitely become easier as you continue to do it.

Tools Needed: Leak light
Round nose pliers
Small screwdriver
Alcohol burner or bunsen burner
Ruler
Key bending tool
Emery paper

Materials Needed: Double skin flute pads
Paper flute pad washers
Sheet cork in sizes 1/64", 1/32" and 1/16"
Stick shellac
Contact cement
Super glue

Procedure: (Refer to Illustration 1-3 for key names and numbers)

1. Using a leak light, check all pads to be certain that they have a level seat which will form a tight seal with the tone hole. (See How to Adjust the Pad Seat, p. 17.) Adjust where necessary. Replace any torn or dried out pads. (See How to Install New Flute Pads, p. 20.)

2. Remove the B thumb key (#4) and the B♭ thumb lever (#5).

3. Adjust the F key (#12) to a height of 3/32". Under the foot of the F key will be a cork which rests against the flute body. Adjust the thickness of the cork to achieve the correct key height. If the cork needs to be replaced, use a piece of 1/16" cork and then emery down to correct height.

4. Adjust the F key (#12) with the F♯ key (#11) so that they close together. Close the keys very slowly using a very light touch. Use a leak light and be very critical as both keys must seat at the same time. The adjustment is made by turning the adjustment screw which is located either alongside the top of the F key or on the foot of the F♯ key (which rests on top of the foot of the F key). On some flutes there is no adjustment screw for this key and the regulation has to be made by adjusting the thickness of the cork on the foot of the F♯ key as it rests on top of the F key foot.

5. Adjust the F key (#12) with the B♭ key (#6) so that they close together. The adjustment for this is made at the point where the foot of the auxilary B♭ key (#8) rests on the foot of the F key. With some flutes that have an adjustment screw at this point, you merely turn the screw in or out to achieve the proper adjustment. If your flute does not have the adjustment screw, it should have a piece of ¹⁄₆₄″ cork under the auxilary B♭ key foot. On most flutes you can easily bend this foot up or down slightly with a round nose pliers to achieve the proper regulation (see Illustration 1-19).

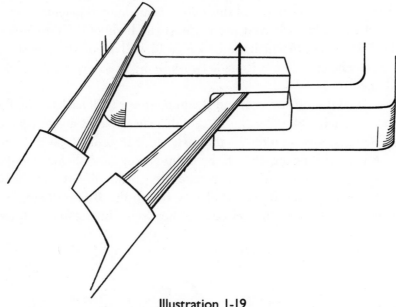

Illustration 1-19

6. Adjust the A key (#7) with the B♭ key (#6) so that they close together. This adjustment is done with the adjustment screw located alongside the top of the A key.

7. Next check the thickness of the cork on the foot of the A key (#7). This cork determines if the keys will move at the same time without any "lost motion" or "play." Press down slowly on the A key (#7) and see if the B♭ key (#6) *starts* to move at the same time. If the A key moves first, you will have to replace the cork on the foot of the A key with a thicker piece until the A and B♭ keys move together.

8. When the A key and B♭ key do move together then press slowly on the F key (#12) and see if the B♭ key starts moving at the same time. If the F key moves first, you will have to emery some cork off the bottom of the A key foot until the F and B♭ keys start moving together.

9. Adjust the E key (#13) with the F♯ key (#11) so that they close together. This is done with the adjustment screw located alongside the top of the E key.

10. Press slowly on the E key to see if the F♯ key begins to move at the same time. If not, you will have to replace the cork on the E key foot with a thicker piece.

11. When the E key and the F♯ key start moving at the same time, press slowly on the F key (#12) to see if it moves at the same time as the F♯ key. If not, you will have to emery some cork off the foot of the E key until they do.

12. Adjust the D key (#15) with the F♯ key (#11) so that they close together. This adjustment is made with the adjustment screw located alongside the top of the D key.

13. Press slowly on the D key to see if the F♯ key (#11) begins to move at the same time. If not, you will have to replace the cork on the D key foot with a thicker piece.

14. When the D and F♯ keys start moving at the same time, press slowly on the E key (#13). If it now moves before the F♯ key (#11) you will have to emery some cork off the foot of the D key.

15. Adjust the height to which the G key (#9) opens. It should be the same as the height of the F key (³⁄₃₂″). Adjustment of this height is made by replacing or emerying the cork on the foot of the G key where it rests against the body of the flute.

16. Adjust the height to which the G♯ key (#10) will open. This key should open to a height of ³⁄₃₂″ also. The adjustment is made by replacing or emerying the cork under the lever of the G♯ key.

17. Place the B thumb key (#4) and B♭ thumb lever (#5) back on the flute. Check to be certain there is a felt pad under the B♭ thumb lever where it makes contact with the B thumb key. Now press slowly on the B♭ thumb lever (#5) to see if the B thumb key (#4) and the B♭ key (#6) are closing together. If the B thumb key closes before the B♭ key, bend the B♭ thumb lever (at the place where it rests on the B thumb key) up a small amount until they close together. If the B♭ key is closing before the B thumb key, bend the B♭ thumb lever down slightly until they close together (see Illustration 1-20). Use a round nose pliers to bend the keys.

BENDING DOWN   BENDING UP

Illustration 1-20

18. The thickness of the cork on the foot of the B♭ thumb lever (#5) must be checked to eliminate "play" in the keys. If the thumb lever moves before the B♭ key (#6), you will have to replace the cork on the foot of the B♭ thumb lever with a thicker piece until they do move together.

19. When the B♭ thumb lever and B♭ key start moving at the same time, press slowly on the F key (#12) to see if it and the B♭ key (#6) still move at the same time. If you now find that the F key moves before the B♭ key you will have to emery some cork off the foot of the B♭ thumb lever until they start moving together.

20. Check the height of the C key (#3). It should open to ¹⁄₁₆″. Adjust this height by the cork under the C key foot.

21. The height of the C♯-D♯ trill key (#1) and the C-D trill key (#2) should open to ¹⁄₁₆″. These trill keys are adjusted by the corks under their levers located between the D, E and F keys.

22. On the foot joint, the D♯ key (#17) should open to a height of ⅛″. Adjust this height by the cork located under the D♯ key lever.

23. Adjust the C♯ key (#18) with the C key (#19) so that they close together when pushing on the C key lever. If the C♯ key closes before the C key, push firmly on the C♯ key lever and bend down slightly. If the C key closes before the C♯ key you will have to bend up on the C♯ key lever slightly. To do this you should hold the pad of the C♯ key firmly closed and gently pull up on the lever. The amount of bending needed for these adjustments is usually so slight that it will take very little bending to achieve the adjustment you desire.

24. The height of the C key (#19) should be ⅛″. Adjust the cork on the foot of the C key to achieve the correct height.

25. Place a small drop of super glue (Zip Grip, Grazy Glue, etc.) on the head of each adjustment screw. This will prevent the screw from turning out due to vibration and, if you use a small enough quantity of glue, you will still be able to break the screws free when a re-adjustment is needed.

REPAIRS TO BE SENT TO THE REPAIR SHOP

In spite of the many repairs that you, the band director, can make on the flute, there are still a number of repairs that will have to be done in the repair shop by a trained repair technician. Some of these repairs require special skills which take time to develop. Others require specialized tools which are too expensive and not practical for school use.

Below is outlined some of the more common flute repairs that will need to be done at a repair shop. I have briefly summarized the work that needs to be done. It is hoped that this will give you a better understanding of the repair procedure.

REMOVING BODY DENTS

Body dents in the flute can usually be removed quite easily in the repair shop. The flute is slipped over a steel rod the diameter of the bore of the flute and then the dents are tapped up with a small dent hammer. Dents that you should consider having removed are: (1) those located by a post, as they will likely destroy the alignment of the keys; (2) those near a tone hole, as they will quite likely cause the tone hole to be uneven, making it impossible to form a level seat with the pad; (3) those that occur on the tenon, as the tenon will not fit as it should. Most small dents do not have to be removed from the flute except for the sake of appearance.

LEVELING UNEVEN TONE HOLES

The tone holes on the flute must be perfectly level across the top or it will be virtually impossible to form a level seat with the pad. You can check the levelness of a tone hole by sighting across its top. If the tone hole is uneven, the repair technician first checks to see if any dents are nearby causing the uneveness. If so, he will lift the dents. Then he will file the tone hole level with a special tone hole file which has a very fine cut. He must use great care to hold the file perfectly flat while filing or the tone hole will not be level. Once the tone hole has been leveled and the keys replaced, it may be necessary for him to change the pad or regulate the keys because the tone hole height has been lowered somewhat.

RE-FITTING THE TENONS

If you have a tight fitting tenon you should first try to clean it. (See Maintenance Procedures for the Flute, Tenons, p. 11.) If this does not correct the problem, the repair technician will have to re-fit it for you. He will use a tenon reducer which compresses the tenon equally around its diameter to shrink its size while maintaining a perfectly round opening.

If the tenon is too loose, he will use a flute tenon expander which is pushed into the bore and actually expands the metal tenon slightly to create a better fit.

TIGHTENING LOOSE KEYS

If your flute has a lot of "play" in the keys, that is, they move sideways on the rod or between the pivot screws, you may have a problem getting the pads to always close on the same spot. The "play" can be caused either by wear or a bent post. If the key is mounted on a rod and slides sideways along the rod, then there is too much room between the posts. In this case the repair technician will have to either stretch the hinge tube to fill the gap (a process called "swedging") or he may cut a small shim out of another piece of hinge tube and place it at the end of the rod to fill in the gap. If the post is bent, he will have to bend the post back into position without breaking it loose from the body of the flute.

It is also possible that the diameter of the key's hinge tube has enlarged through wear and is too large for the diameter of the pivot rod. In this case the repair technician will squeeze the hinge tube slightly to tighten up.

If the key is held in place with a pivot screw and is too loose, the repair technician will first check to see if the posts are still straight. Also, the pivot screw may have worn down and needs replacing. If it is necessary to screw the pivot screw further into the post to create a better fit, the post may have to be drilled out slightly to accommodate the head of the pivot screw.

REPAIRING BROKEN KEYS

If a key on the flute actually breaks in half, this can easily be repaired in the shop. Be certain that you save the pieces and send them along with the entire flute. The repair technician will braze the two pieces together with silver solder. When done correctly, this will bond the two sections together as securely as the original piece. It is important, however, to send the entire instrument so he will be certain that the key is brazed at the correct angle in order to function properly on the flute.

CORRECTING A LEAKING EMBOUCHURE PLATE

As you check the flute head joints for leaks, you may occasionally find that air is escaping from around the embouchure plate. The embouchure plate is soldered in place over a hole drilled into the head joint. Sometimes, especially if the head joint is dropped, the solder will break away a little at this point causing a leak. The repair technician will correct the problem by removing the embouchure plate completely, cleaning up the area to be soldered and re-soldering the plate in the proper position.

REPLATING THE WORN FINISH

Not all repair shops can do this work, although most of them have another company to which they can send this type of work to be done. Replating an instrument requires having the chemicals necessary to strip off the old finish. The flute is completely disassembled and the finish is removed from the body and all of the keys. All parts are then buffed to a high gloss smoothness and then replated using an electroplating process. When the plating is complete, the flute is reassembled using all new pads and corks. Often excess plating must be removed from the keys to insure a proper fit between the posts. The tone holes also need to be carefully checked and leveled as they sometimes wear down slightly in the buffing process. It is customary to have all the dents removed when doing this work as it is convenient to do so while the instrument is apart. When this job is complete, your flute will have a "like new" appearance.

THE COMPLETE REPAD

Even though you do a good job of maintaining the condition of the flutes in your band, there will come a time when most of the pads are old, dry and tearing. Many of the corks become compressed, are dried out and starting to fall off. It is then time for a complete repad. A complete repad consists of replacing all the old pads and corks with new. It should also include re-fitting the tenons, cleaning the body and straightening any posts or tone holes that are strategic to the adjustment of the flute. When re-assembled, all the pads will be re-seated, any loose keys tightened and the springs adjusted for good action. In short, the instrument will *play* like a new flute.

2

The Piccolo

Illustration 2-1

Courtesy of Artley Flute Co.; Nogales, Arizona 85621

HOW TO TAKE CARE OF YOUR PICCOLO

Taking proper care of the piccolo should be the first and most important step in your piccolo maintenance plan. By following the suggestions given here, you will avoid many of the problems which can cause the piccolo to play improperly. Although this information might be a review for many band directors, it is a good idea to be certain that your students also have an understanding of proper piccolo care. When the student understands the reason for the maintenance procedures outlined below, there is a better chance that they will be followed and your repair costs will go down.

ASSEMBLE THE PICCOLO CAREFULLY

Assembling the piccolo is a relatively simple matter, but it should be done carefully to avoid disturbing the critical adjustment of the keys.

The piccolo consists of only two sections, the head joint and the main body. To insert the head joint, hold the body of the piccolo near the top, where there are no keys. If you hold the piccolo by the keys and allow your hand to slide while assembling, you are likely to bend keys and cause the adjustment to be disturbed. Insert the head joint into the receiver with a slow back and forth twisting action as you push. Line up the embouchure hole with the top of the row of keys on the main body.

The tenon should fit snuggly, but move easily. *Never grease a piccolo tenon.* If the tenon is difficult to insert, it needs cleaning or straightening, not greasing. (See Maintenance Procedures for the Piccolo—Tenon, p. 40.)

STORE THE PICCOLO PROPERLY

Piccolos should always be stored in the case. A piccolo left lying about on a chair, table or music stand is easily bumped or dropped on the floor. This can result in serious and expensive repair problems.

38

Whether in or out of the case, the piccolo should *never* be stored near radiators or heating ducts. Excessive heat is one of the contributing factors in causing wood piccolos to crack. Also, heat will cause key corks to dry out and shrink. This changes the adjustment of the piccolo, which is determined somewhat by the cork thickness.

You should also avoid storing your piccolo in subzero weather. Exposure to extreme cold will often cause piccolo pads to loosen and fall out. This is a very common problem that I have seen each winter. Once a pad has shifted in the key it is extremely difficult to relocate its position to the original seat. Most likely you will have to replace the pad with a new one, a difficult task for an untrained person.

Piccolo cases are designed to hold the instrument securely in the case. They are not meant to serve as a display case for contest medals or pins. This overpacking of the case causes excessive pressure on the instrument when the cover is closed and may cause the keys to bend or go out of alignment. In addition, dangling medals will scratch a silver piccolo and they can catch under the keys and bend them when the case is opened. You can check to see if the case is holding the piccolo securely by placing the instrument in the case, closing and latching the cover, then shaking the case. If nothing moves or rattles inside, the instrument is secure. Often you will hear the piccolo bouncing inside the case. If this happens, there needs to be more padding in the case. Laying a small cloth on top of the piccolo is the quickest way of providing this padding, although care should be taken that the cloth is not too thick. If the case cover becomes difficult to close, you have too much padding in the case.

Do not store a pencil with an eraser in the case, as this might cause the silver on the piccolo or keys to tarnish. Also, if a spring should break, avoid wrapping the key with a rubber band because the rubber will cause the silver to tarnish.

Inspect the case periodically to be sure that it is in good condition. Prompt attention should be given to broken or loose latches and hinges. Be certain that the lining is not loose, as it serves as the protective padding around the piccolo. Loose lining can easily be corrected with some glue, but broken case hardware will usually need to be sent to the repair shop for correction.

CLEAN THE PICCOLO REGULARLY

A few minutes of care in cleaning the piccolo after each playing session will go a long way in helping maintain the instrument.

First, and most important, is to swab out the inside of the piccolo (bore) to remove all traces of moisture. Swab out both the body and the head joint using the cleaning rod provided with the piccolo. If your piccolo does not have a cleaning rod, it can be purchased inexpensively from your music dealer. You will need a piece of soft cloth such as cheesecloth or flannel. Insert the cloth through the "eye" of the cleaning rod. Fold the cloth over the top of the rod and twist around the shank, totally covering the rod so that no metal will be exposed inside the piccolo to scratch the instrument (see Illustration 2-2).

If the piccolo is put away without swabbing, moisture will accumulate in the pads causing a rapid deterioration of the skin covering. Consistent swabbing, therefore, will greatly increase the life of the pads which is vital to proper instrument performance.

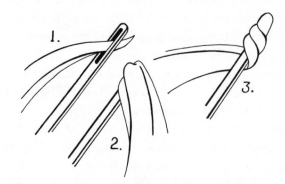

Illustration 2-2

You should also carefully wipe the outside of the piccolo after each playing session. This will remove some of the body oils and will help preserve the finish. Care should be taken in wiping the piccolo to avoid wiping sideways across the keys; this could cause them to bend. Use a light stroke on the keys with a cloth then wipe the body of the instrument. This cleaning should be done whether your piccolo is wood, plastic or metal.

You should not store a damp swabbing cloth in the case. It seems to be a common practice to swab out the piccolo, then lay the wet cloth on top of the instrument and close the case. This will, in essence, trap the moisture in the case. This humidity will cause the pads to stay wet longer, thus deteriorate faster. The excessive moisture will also cause pivot screws and rods to rust which will eventually affect key action.

MAINTENANCE PROCEDURES FOR THE PICCOLO

Tenon—Keeping the piccolo tenon clean is an often overlooked item which does require regular care. The tenon becomes dirty through handling, and this dirt will also accumulate inside the receiver. It does not take much dirt to cause the tenon to fit too tightly. At this point, many band directors think they have to send the piccolo to a repair shop to have the tenon adjusted. In reality, unless the joint has been dented, you will find that the fit will be quite satisfactory after you clean the tenon.

To clean, you will need a piece of canning wax (paraffin), which is available in any grocery store, and a clean cloth. Rub the wax on the tenon, then insert the tenon into the receiver, twisting back and forth. Remove the tenon and you will find the wax has turned black. Wipe the tenon completely with the cloth. Then wrap the cloth around the cleaning rod and reach down into the receiver and wipe out all traces of wax. Repeat the process until the black film does not appear (usually twice is sufficient). If the tenon is still too tight after cleaning, it is probably dented or out of round. The piccolo should be sent to a repair shop to correct this problem.

There is no way that the tenon can become larger or gain extra plating, so do not attempt to emery (or sand) the tenon to reduce its size—this will not solve the proble .

Never grease a tenon because the grease quickly adds to the dirt build up and only causes the tenon to fit tightly again after a few days.

Washing the Bore—If the bore of the piccolo is being swabbed out after each use, the inside should remain quite clean. However, it is a good idea to wash the bore about once a month to be certain that all dirt is removed. To do this, swab out the bore with a swab which is damp (but not dripping wet). Follow this immediately with a dry cloth to take up the excess moisture. Continue swabbing until completely dry. This procedure should be done to wood, plastic or metal piccolos.

Because the head joint is only open at one end, it is usually more difficult to do an effective job of cleaning with the swab. Also, this section accumulates the most moisture and dirt and needs to be thoroughly cleaned each month. It is best, therefore, to remove the head joint stopper cork before washing the bore. (See How to Replace the Head Joint Stopper Cork, p. 51.) Once the stopper cork is removed, you can wash the entire head joint in a solution of mild soapy water. After washing, rinse and dry the head joint carefully. Lightly grease the stopper cork and push back into place. Use the notched guide on the cleaning rod to position the stopper cork in the correct place. If the stopper cork does not seal up the head joint (see How to Check for Leaks, p. 45), it may have to be replaced.

As an added note: you should never wash the main body of the piccolo in the soapy water solution as it would destroy the pads.

Oiling the Bore—If your piccolo has a wood body, it is best to establish a regular schedule for oiling the bore. The use of bore oil slows down the penetration of water into the wood which is one of the major reasons for cracking. It is not necessary, therefore, to oil the bore of a plastic or metal piccolo. Instrument manufacturers recommend that a new instrument should be oiled about once a month for the first six months and then about twice a year.

When oiling the bore, use a commercial bore oil which is available from your music dealer. Use a piece of cloth which is soaked in the bore oil. The cloth should by oily to the touch, but not dripping, as you want to apply the oil very sparingly.

Protect the pads from the oil as it will cause them to dry out and become brittle. Use a thick piece of paper or a piece of plastic between the pads and tone holes so that no oil can soak into the pads. Let the piccolo sit overnight then swab out with a dry cloth before removing the pad protectors. If you have used too much oil, you will find that the oil has soaked up into the tone holes and you will not be able to wipe these off. This oil will eventually get into the pads.

Because the head joint is subjected to the most moisture, you will want to do an effective job of oiling this section. This is best done by removing the head joint stopper cork before oiling.

Cleaning the Piccolo Body—In time the outside of the piccolo will begin to accumulate greasy dirt and lint under the keys and rods. This is particularly true of the wood piccolo because the wood is impregnated with oil by the manufacturer and this tends to attract the dirt. It is a good idea to remove this lint before it gets into the rods and slows up the key action. Using a small paint brush or pipe stem cleaner, reach under the keys and brush away any dirt or lint that has collected. *Take care to avoid catching any of the springs* as this would change the spring tension and could affect the adjustment. This job is quite easy to do if done slowly and carefully.

Metal piccolos are generally silver plated and can be renewed to an almost new appearance with the use of a little silver polish. I suggest a liquid silver polish as it is easier to work with and your music dealer should be able to recommend a good brand. Apply the polish sparingly only to the body with a soft cloth. Avoid getting any polish on the pads, keys or key rods. When the polish is dry, wipe off with a clean, dry cloth. You can then wipe over the keys and rods at this time and they will also clean up quite nicely. Use a soft pipe stem cleaner to remove the dry polish from those hard-to-reach areas. Care should be taken to remove all the dry polish, or it will get into the key rods, slowing down or stopping the key action.

The only way to remove the tarnish which has developed under the key rods is to remove all the keys, then polish and replace the keys. I would not recommend that you do this, for the adjustment and seating of piccolo pads is quite delicate and could be disturbed if the keys are removed. On the wood or plastic piccolo, though the keys are usually silver plated, I advise against polishing the keys. It is too easy to clog up the action in the very small key mechanism of a piccolo.

Sticky Pads—Sticky pads are caused by the accumulation of dirt on the pad seat and/or the tone hole. The student should avoid chewing gum, eating candy or drinking "pop" immediately before or while playing. All these items increase the amount of sugar in the saliva, some of which will travel into the bore and accumulate on the pads. This sticky substance then attracts dirt to the pad, causing the stickiness. Swabbing and washing the bore, as described above, will help reduce the problem.

Another cause of sticky pads is that of the pad being saturated with bore oil. If you have recently oiled the bore, you may have used an excessive amount of oil or you did not protect the pads properly. If the pads do become oil soaked, they will need to be replaced. (See Oiling the Bore, p. 41.)

The stickiness usually begins with an annoying "clicking" sound as the pad opens. As the problem gets worse, the keys will not open promptly and, finally, some keys might even stay closed. The problem should be corrected as soon as noticed, as this is when it is easiest to do. (See How to Clean Dirty and Sticky Pads, p. 49.) It is also a good idea to try to determine the source of the stickiness to avoid further problems.

Oiling the Keys—The keys of the piccolo should be oiled about once a month to keep them working freely and to prevent the screws and rods from becoming rusted. If the rods and screws do rust, the key action can bind up and will require a repair technician to correct. Using a pin or toothpick, place a *small* drop of key oil at the end of each key rod and between all moveable keys which share the same rod (i.e., low D, E, F and F♯). Work the keys to circulate the oil, then wipe off any excess oil that may be on the rods. Key oil is available from your music dealer.

MONTHLY MAINTENANCE CHECK LIST—PICCOLO

Chart 4 is a check list that you can use to help in the maintenance of the piccolo. By following this chart you should be able to keep the instrument well cleaned and be alert to any possible repairs needed before they become too severe. With some training your students should be able to utilize this check list by themselves.

Chart 4
Monthly Maintenance Check List—Piccolo

INSPECT THE FOLLOWING:

Head Joint _____ Is the stopper cork tight and aligned properly?

_____ Is the tenon clean and fitting correctly?

_____ Are there any dents in the head joint?

Piccolo _____ Are there any sticky pads?

_____ Are there any torn pads?

_____ Are there any loose pads?

_____ Are all the keys moving freely?

_____ Are there any dents in the metal body?

_____ Are there any cracks in the wood body?

_____ Are there any missing screws or rods?

Case _____ Are the latches working properly?

_____ Are the hinges tight?

_____ Is the lining tight?

_____ Are there any loose objects in the case?

_____ Is the piccolo held tightly in the case when closed?

DO THE FOLLOWING:
1. Check for leaks (see How to Check for Leaks, p. 45).
2. Wash the bore.
3. Oil the bore (twice a year after first six months).
4. Polish or wipe the outside of the piccolo body.
5. Clean dirt and lint from under the keys and rods.
6. Oil the key rods and screws.

HOW TO REPAIR THE PICCOLO

DIAGNOSING INSTRUMENT MALFUNCTIONS

Before you can repair the piccolo, you must locate the problem. Listed below are some of the more common problems that can occur. For each problem I have suggested some possible causes, in the hope that it will help you locate the difficulty. Although this list can hardly be complete, it should serve as a good guideline in most cases.

1. *Problem:* Piccolo blows hard; will not play all the notes.

Possible Causes: Pads are leaking (look for torn pads or those not seating level with the tone hole). Keys are not regulated correctly. Head joint stopper cork is leaking. Embouchure plate is leaking.

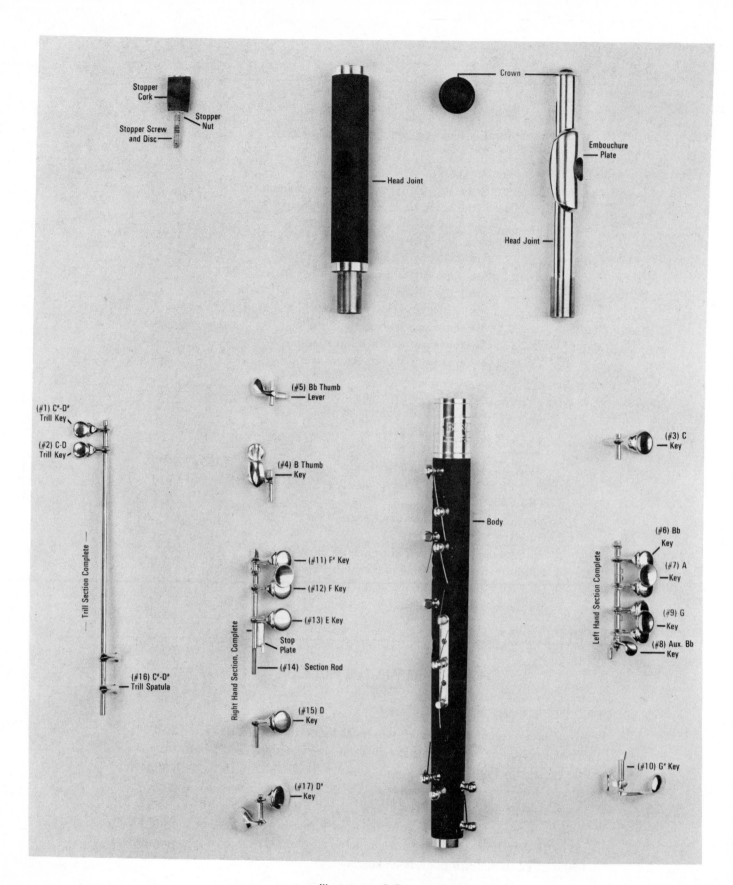

Illustration 2-3

Photograph courtesy of The Selmer Co.; Elkhart, Indiana

2. *Problem:* Piccolo plays the wrong pitch when key is depressed.

Possible Causes: Check for a broken spring. See if any springs are unhooked from the keys. Keys may be regulated incorrectly.

3. *Problem:* Plays out of tune.

Possible Causes: Key corks may be missing, causing the key heights to be incorrect. All key heights may be set incorrectly. The stopper cork in the head joint may not be lined up correctly.

4. *Problem:* Keys are not functioning properly.

Possible Causes: Check for broken or unhooked springs. Look for dented or bent key posts, keys or rods. Pivot screws may be tightened to tightly. Dry silver polish may be in the key rods, clogging the action. Pads or tone holes may be dirty.

5. *Problem:* Tenon is too tight.

Possible Causes: Tenon is dirty, dented or not perfectly round.

HOW TO CHECK FOR LEAKS

When the piccolo fails to play properly, the first thing to do is to check the instrument for leaks. When the instrument is not leaking, all notes should play with the same amount of ease. Generally speaking, if the player is unable to play down to the low D on the piccolo, there are some leaking pads. If you encounter this problem but are not sure if the source of the difficulty lies with the piccolo or the student, have another person play on the same instrument. This will give you a quick indication of whether the suspected problem is in the piccolo. Bear in mind, of course, that often a flute player just switching to the piccolo will have some difficulty in producing these tones on a piccolo.

Procedure:

1. Check the main body. Place the end of the piccolo against your leg as an air seal. Press the appropriate keys to close all pads over the tone holes. Apply the normal light pressure used when playing the instrument to hold the keys down. If there is a leak, you will hear the air escaping and will feel the lack of resistance as you blow into the receiver end of the body. You may need help from someone to determine where the leak is. Be sure to blow gently, for if you blow too hard, you may blow open the trill keys, G♯ key or D♯ key thus giving the impression of a leak. Once you locate the leaking pad or pads you will either have to re-adjust the keys (see How to Regulate the Keys, p. 46) or replace the pad (see How to Install New Piccolo Pads, p. 47).

2. Check the head joint. This section is often overlooked when testing a piccolo, but could be the source of a leak large enough to cause playing problems. Place your thumb over the embouchure hole to seal and blow into the tenon end. There should be no escaping air. It may be more difficult to hear a leak in the head joint because a much smaller quantity of air may be escaping. You should, however, feel the lack of resistance as you blow into the bore of the head joint. Some find it easier to check the head joint by sucking on it rather than blowing. When you suck out the air you create a vacuum. If the vacuum disappears quickly, air is leaking in from some source. (The sucking technique does not work on the other joint of the piccolo as the vacuum created tends to pull the keys shut and the leaks are not as apparent.)

The head jont can only leak in two places, at the end around the stopper cork or, in the case of a metal piccolo head joint, where the embouchure plate is soldered to the head joint. Most often the leak will be around the stopper cork, but to be sure, place the head joint in a pail or sink of water, seal as indicated above and blow into it. Bubbles will appear at the source of the leak. If the stopper cork is leaking, it will have to be replaced. (See How to Replace the Head Joint Stopper Cork, p. 51.) If the air is escaping from around the embouchure plate on the metal piccolo, it should be sent to the repair shop to be resoldered.

HOW TO REGULATE THE KEYS

The proper regulation of the piccolo keys is of paramount importance. Following is a detailed, step-by-step procedure for the regulation. Although the regulation of the keys is just one step in the complete adjustment process of the piccolo, it is sometimes all that you will need to do to get a piccolo playing again.

In general, you will find that piccolo adjustments are much more difficult to do than those on most other instruments. Do not be discouraged if you have difficulty with this. Actually you may find it easier to just send the piccolo into the repair shop for the adjustments needed.

Tools Needed: Leak light (with bulb to fit piccolo bore)

Emery paper

Small screwdriver

Materials Needed: Sheet cork: 1/64″ thick

Contact cork cement

Procedure: (Refer to Illustration 2-3 for key names and numbers.)

1. Check the pad seats. Before you attempt to regulate any keys you should check the pads to be certain that they are sealing properly. If the pads do not form a level seat with the tone holes, it will be virtually impossible to regulate the keys. To check the seat, place your leak light under each pad and close the key very slowly using a very light pressure. It is important to be very critical during this checking procedure. The pad should seat level on the tone hole, that is, it should close simultaneously around the entire tone hole. Often you will find that a pad is hitting the front, back or one of the sides *before* it seals the tone hole. Any pads you find which are torn, loose or not sealing properly will need to be replaced (see How to Install New Piccolo Pads, p. 47). If all pads have a level seat with the tone hole, you are ready to continue with step 2 below.

2. Press the A key (#7). This should close the B♭ key (#6) at the same time. (Use your leak light as you make this check.) There should be a piece of cork under the finger "pan" which is attached to the A key and extends over the B♭ key. It is the thickness of this cork which needs to be adjusted so that both keys will close together. If the B♭ key is closing first, you should emery the cork so it will be slightly thinner. (Do this slowly as it doesn't take much of a change in cork thickness to affect the key adjustment.) If the A key is closing first, you will need to add cork under the finger "pan." Use a piece of 1/64″ sheet cork and glue on with the contact cork cement (see How to Replace Key Corks, p. 50).

Most likely, after the cork is glued in place, it will be too thick, so you will have to reduce the thickness by using a piece of emery paper.

3. Press the F key (#12). The B♭ key (#6) should close at the same time. (Use your leak light as you make this check.) If the F key and B♭ key do not close together, the adjustment is made by the bridge key which is located on the foot of the F key. You will have to add or take away cork at the point where the two overlapping keys make contact. If the B♭ key is closing first, emery down the thickness of this cork. If the F key is closing first, add some cork to the bridge key. Check again and emery this new cork down to the correct thickness.

If you find that *neither* the F key nor the B♭ key will close, you will have to adjust the F♯ key (#11) as indicated in the following step before doing this step.

4. Press down the F key (#12). The F♯ key (#11) should close at the same time. (Again, use your leak light.) If they do not, the adjustment is made in the thickness of the cork under the finger "pan" which is attached to the F key. Adjust this in the same manner as described in step 2.

5. Press the E key (#13). This should close the F♯ key (#11) at the same time. If not, the adjustment is made by adding or removing cork on the stop plate lever which projects under the E key (see Illustration 2-3). If the F♯ key closes first, pull a small piece of emery paper across the cork to reduce its thickness. If the E key is closing first, add a piece of ¹⁄₆₄″ cork to the stop plate arm. It is likely that the added cork will be too thick, so you will have to use emery paper to make it thinner in order to regulate these two keys.

If the F♯ key is closing first and there is *no cork* on the stop plate arm, use a small screwdriver to bend the arm down *slightly*, then add a piece of ¹⁄₆₄″ cork and adjust as indicated above.

6. Press the D key (#15). This should close the F♯ key (#11) at the same time. If not, the adjustment needed is the same as described in step 5 above. After you adjust the D key and F♯ key, the E key/F♯ key adjustment should be rechecked. Sometimes, the stop plate arm will bend slightly as you make adjustments and change previous adjustments.

7. Press the B♭ thumb *lever* (#5). This should close the B thumb key (#4) and the B♭ key (#6) at the same time. If the B♭ key is closing first, add a piece of ¹⁄₆₄″ cork under the B♭ thumb lever (#5) and check again. If the B thumb key (#4) is closing first, emery the cork under the B♭ thumb lever to reduce its thickness until both keys close together.

If the B thumb key (#4) closes first and there is not any cork under the B♭ thumb lever (#5), you will need to add a piece of ¹⁄₆₄″ cork at the point where the foot of the B♭ thumb lever and the foot of the B♭ key contact each other, then check the adjustment as outlined at the beginning of this step.

8. All other keys on the piccolo work independently of each other and do not have to be regulated with other keys.

HOW TO INSTALL NEW PICCOLO PADS

Because of the small size of the piccolo keys and pads, it is extremely difficult to install and level the piccolo pad. This is best done by the experienced repairman. I will, however, outline the procedure below so you can do it yourself if interested.

Tools Needed: Leak light
　　　　　　　　 Pipe stem cleaner
　　　　　　　　 Pad slick
　　　　　　　　 Spring clamp
　　　　　　　　 Alcohol burner or bunsen burner
Tools Needed: Thin, double skin piccolo pads
　　　　　　　　 Stick shellac
Procedure:

1. Remove the old pad. Piccolo pads are held in place with shellac or similar type of substance. You need to heat the key (see Illustration 2-4) to soften the shellac, then remove the old pad. Use this old pad as a sample size for your replacement pad.

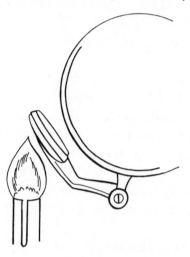

Illustration 2-4

2. Find the correct size pad for a replacement. The pad should fit all the way into the key and fill in the entire space. The thickness of the pad is extremely important. Try the pad in the key before cementing in place. If the pad hits the back of the tone hole first, it is too thick. If you don't have thinner pads, you might try using the next smaller size. Likewise, if the pad is hitting the front of the tone hole first, then it is too thin—try a thicker (or larger) pad. Finding a pad which fits correctly is a difficult part of replacing piccolo pads. Because the keys are so small, there is little space in which you can manuever the pad in the key to make it level with the tone hole.

3. When you feel the pad is the correct size, hold the end of the stick shellac in the flame of your burner and when soft place a small drop on the back of the pad. Place the pad in the key, close the key and heat until the shellac softens and the pad settles into the key.

4. Level the pad with the tone hole by rotating the pad in the key while the shellac is soft. To do this, place the pad slick between the pad and the tone hole and rotate back and forth. Remove the pad slick and *lightly* close the key to see if the pad is level with the tone hole. If it is not level, repeat the process using another size pad.

5. Seat the pad. When you are satisfied that the pad is level with the tone hole, wet the pad with water (using the pipe stem cleaner dipped in water), heat the key once again and clamp shut with a spring clamp.

6. After the key has cooled thoroughly, remove the clamp and check with a leak light to see if the seat on your pad is level with the tone hole. If not, repeat step 2 above.

7. Special care needs to be taken when replacing one of the pads in the double G key (#9) as both pads need to close at the same time. This key is not flexible, so if one pad is closing before the other, the only way to correct the situation is to replace the pad until both are the same thickness. Usually, if one of the double G key pads needs to be replaced, it will be easier and take less time to replace them both. This way you can be certain that both pads will be the same thickness.

Some piccolos use a white rubber type of pad called "Perma-Pad." These pads are designed to last longer. Replacement pads are available in kits which include instructions and glue and will generally be the correct thickness for the piccolo they are designed to fit.

Many experienced repairmen use a process called "floating in." In this method, which is much more difficult than the one described above, the key is filled with a large quantity of shellac and a very thin pad is used. This pad literally floats in the soft shellac, making it easier to level with the tone hole. If you use too much heat, however, your shellac will then leak out around the pad causing a mess on the piccolo. Many new piccolo pads are "floated in" and you should be aware of this if you are attempting to replace a pad. You could have excessive shellac come out when trying to remove the old pad. Before placing the new pad in the key as described in step 2, be sure that all the old shellac is removed from the key.

HOW TO CLEAN DIRTY AND STICKY PADS

Tools Needed: Cigarette paper (ungummed preferred)
Alcohol
Talcum powder

Procedure:

1. Place a sheet of cigarette paper under the sticky pad, close the key firmly and pull the paper out. You will probably notice a dirt mark on the paper when removed. Repeat this process a few times, always using a clean part of the paper until the mark is no longer noticeable on the paper. (If you have difficulty finding ungummed cigarette paper you can use gummed paper, but take care not to place the gummed portion under the pad.)

2. If the key is still sticky, try placing a small amount of talcum powder on the paper before placing it under the key and repeat the process as outlined in step 1.

3. Still sticky? Place a little alcohol on the paper and try again. (This should be a last resort as the alcohol will damage the pad skin somewhat.)

4. If the problem still persists, you will have no alternative but to remove the key, clean the tone hole with alcohol and change the pad. (See How to Install New Piccolo Pads, p. 47.)

HOW TO REPLACE KEY CORKS

Most of the key corks on the piccolo are there to regulate the keys or adjust the key heights. For this reason, the thickness of cork used is extremely important. I have listed in Chart 5 below the most common size cork which is used on each key of the piccolo. In many cases you will also have to use emery paper to reduce the thickness of the cork for a proper fit.

As a rule, key corks are always glued to the key and never to the body of the piccolo. Not only does this give a better appearance to the piccolo, but gluing cork to a silver piccolo will eventually destroy the silver finish as most contact cements have a rubber base.

Tools Needed: Contact cork cement
  Single edge razor blade
  Emery paper

Materials Needed: Sheet cork in sizes ⅟₆₄″, ⅟₃₂″, ⅟₁₆″ and ⅛″ as needed
Procedure:

1. Remove any particles of cork which may be left on the key.
2. Select the correct size cork according to Chart 5 and spread contact cement on a small section of the cork.

Chart 5
Piccolo Key Corks

(Refer to Illustration 2-3 for key names and numbers. Those keys not listed do not require any cork.)

Key #	Key Name	Location of cork	Size of cork*
3	C key	Under foot	⅟₆₄″
5	B♭ thumb lever	Under foot	⅟₃₂″
		Under lever	⅟₁₆″
7	A key	Under finger "pan"	⅟₃₂″
8	Aux. B♭ key	Under foot	⅟₆₄″
9	G key	Under foot	⅟₃₂″
10	G♯ key	Under lever	⅟₃₂″
12	F key	Under foot	⅟₁₆″
		Under finger "pan"	⅟₃₂″
13	E key	Under foot	⅟₃₂″
		On stop plate	⅟₆₄″
15	D key	Under foot	⅟₃₂″
		On stop plate	⅟₆₄″
16	Trill key spatulas	Under each spatula	⅟₃₂″
17	D♯ key	Under lever	⅛″

*In most cases this is the starting size cork to be used. Usually the cork will need to be made thinner by using a piece of emery paper to reduce the size. To determine correct thickness see the following: How to Regulate the Keys, p.46; How to check the Intonation of the Piccolo, p. 55; The Complete Adjustment, p. 57.

3. Spread the contact cement on the proper spot of the key.

4. Allow the contact cement to dry thoroughly, then place the cork in position. Trim off excess with a razor blade.

5. Check the regulation of the key with the other keys and emery the cork if it needs to be thinner. (See How to Regulate the Keys, p. 46.)

6. To emery the cork, place a small strip of emery paper between the cork and the piccolo body or key with the rough side against the cork (see Illustration 2-5). Pull the emery paper while holding the key against it. This will take off a small amount of cork and shape it to the body of the piccolo at the same time.

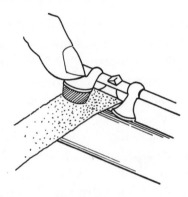

Illustration 2-5

HOW TO REPLACE THE HEAD JOINT STOPPER CORK

If the stopper cork moves easily inside the head joint, turns when you adjust the crown or is leaking when you make the leak check (see How to Check for Leaks, p. 45), it should be replaced as follows:

Tools Needed: Pliers

Cleaning rod

Rawhide hammer

Drum stick or wooden dowel

Materials Needed: One piccolo stopper cork

Cork grease

Pad and cork cement

Procedure: (Refer to Illustration 2-3.)

1. Remove the old stopper cork. Unscrew the crown and push the stopper out of the tenon end of the head joint. Because the head joint is tapered, you should never attempt to pull the stopper out of the closed end of the head joint. If the cork is dried out, it is possible that it can be leaking and still be stuck in the head joint. In this case, loosen the crown only part way and tap lightly on the crown with a rawhide hammer until the stopper begins to move. Then remove the crown and push the rest of the way out. You can use the cleaning rod to push.

2. Cut a new stopper cork to the same length as the old cork.

3. Remove the stopper nut from the stopper screw and disc. You may have to use a pair of pliers to free this nut as it is often glued in place. Remove the old stopper cork by pulling off with a pair of pliers.

4. Screw the stopper screw into the hole of the new stopper cork until the cork is against the disc.

5. Place a small drop of pad and cork cement on the top of the stopper cork. The glue will prevent the stopper nut from turning loose while in the head joint. Tighten the nut down firmly with a pair of pliers so that you compress the stopper cork slightly, thus making it expand. Wipe off any glue which may squeeze out while tightening. (Don't worry if you tear the edge of the stopper cork while tightening with the pliers; this will not affect the seal of the cork in the head joint.)

6. Grease the stopper cork with cork grease and place into the tenon end of the head joint.

7. The cork should be quite tight and should only move freely about halfway into the head joint. Push the cork up to the top of the head joint using an old drum stick or wooden dowel. Replace the crown. Do not use the cleaning rod to push the stopper cork as the metal edge of the rod will damage the stopper disc. Also, as it might require quite a bit of pressure to push the cork in place, the cleaning rod could bend suddenly causing the head joint to slip from your hand.

8. Line up the stopper cork so that the notch on the cleaning rod is centered in the embouchure hole. If the stopper cork has already been pushed too far, loosen the crown then use the rawhide hammer and tap the cork back down a bit. Tighten the crown down until it fits against the head joint. (Be sure that you use a piccolo cleaning rod instead of a flute rod because the placement of the notch is different.)

HOW TO REPLACE A PICCOLO SPRING

Piccolo springs usually do not break because they are short in length and there is little resistance against them. Also, they are not very exposed and cannot easily be caught and bent. If a spring should break you will need to replace it with the flute spring wire. This spring wire is a continuous strand of phosphor bronze wire (it could also be gold wire, although this is considerably more expensive). If you have this wire as part of your supplies for the flute, you should have the following sizes: .020″, .025″, .032″ and .035″. The smallest of these would be most commonly used on the piccolo. If you do not have flute wire, I would not recommend stocking it just for piccolos as there is little need for it.

Never use a blue needle spring (clarinet or saxophone spring) on a piccolo, even though you can find one that fits. This type of spring provides entirely too much tension on the key, and you will get either too much tension or none at all.

Tools Needed: Small round nose pliers
Wire cutter
Small hammer
Large blue needle spring
Spring hook

Materials Needed: Flute spring wire in correct diameter.
Procedure:

1. Remove keys around the broken spring to make it accessible.
2. Remove the old spring. Usually the spring will break by the post leaving a small

stub in the post. This stub must be pulled out the same end that it went in (see Illustration 2-6). If the flattened end of the spring is extending out from the post, grasp this firmly with the wire cutters and pull out (see Illustration 2-7). If the other end of the spring is extending beyond the post, use the round nose pliers to squeeze the flattened end of the spring out of the post (see Illustration 2-8), then pull with the wire cutters. If the spring is flush in the post, use a large needle spring (from your supply of saxophone needle springs) as a driver and tap the spring out with a hammer (see Illustration 2-9). When doing this, it is a good idea to rest the post against some object to prevent it from breaking off the body. There is also the possibility that the old spring has already fallen out, thus eliminating all worry about how to remove the broken stub from the post.

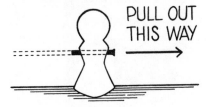

Illustration 2-6

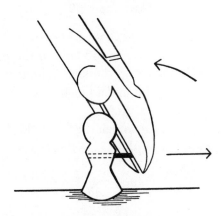

Illustration 2-7

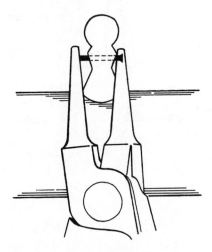

Illustration 2-8

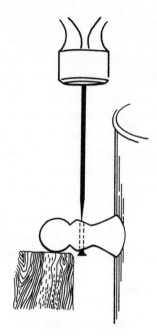

Illustration 2-9

3. Once the old spring is removed, try various sizes of spring wire until you find the thickest wire that will go through the spring hole in the post. Measure the length of spring needed to reach the spring hook on the key and cut with a wire cutter.

4. Hold the spring against a solid metal block (vise, piece of steel, etc.) and with a small tack hammer tap on one end to flatten.

5. Insert the spring into the post so that the flat end will go in last. Squeeze the flat end into the post with your round nose pliers (see Illustration 2-10). This holds the spring in place.

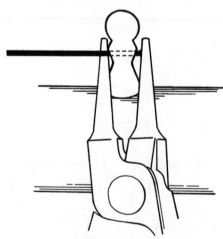

Illustration 2-10

6. Bend the spring slightly in the post to match the other springs in the same area of the piccolo (see Illustration 2-11). This should make the tension approximately the same.

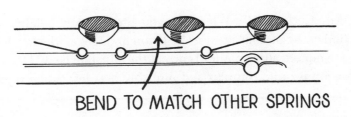

BEND TO MATCH OTHER SPRINGS

Illustration 2-11

7. Remount the key and check the spring tension. (See How to Adjust the Spring Tension, below.)

HOW TO ADJUST THE SPRING TENSION

Spring tension on the piccolo is adjusted in a way similar to that used on the flute. All keys that are usually in the open position should have a light resistance which still allows for a quick, snappy key action. Those keys that are normally in a closed position should be set with a slightly heavier resistance to prevent them from "blowing" open while playing. It is most important that the tension be uniform throughout the entire piccolo. That is, all open keys should have the same light tension and all closed keys the same heavier tension.

Tension on a key is increased or decreased by bending the spring wire gently in one direction or the other. Be sure to unhook the spring from the key before attempting to bend it. Some of the springs will not be readily accessible to bend unless you remove the key first. Care should be taken not to bend the wire too far or it may break.

When checking the tension of the keys, move only one key at a time. (For example, to check the tension of the F, E and D keys, you must hold the F♯ and B♭ keys closed so that only *one* key is moving.) Tension obviously will differ when a key activates one or two additional keys. The uniformity that you try to achieve is for each individual key, not a combination of keys.

HOW TO CHECK THE INTONATION OF THE PICCOLO

The intonation of the piccolo is determined by a number of factors:

1. The breath support and embouchure of the player.
2. The placement of the head joint in the main body of the piccolo and its alignment with the main body.
3. The proper placement of the head joint stopper cork. Check this placement by putting the cleaning rod into the head joint. The mark on the rod should be centered in the embouchure hole. The distance to the mark from the end of the rod should be approximately ¹³⁄₃₂″.
4. The piccolo keys need to be adjusted to the proper open heights. This is very important if the piccolo is to play in tune with itself. The height of the key opening is measured at the front of the pad and is the distance from the top of the tone hole to the bottom of the pad when the key is fully opened. Chart 6 shows the generally acceptable heights to which piccolo keys should be open.

If you find an individual key which is not at the correct height, it may have lost a cork on the foot. These key heights can usually be corrected by replacing the cork (see

How to Replace Key Corks p. 50). Whenever you alter the key heights, you need to recheck the regulation of the piccolo afterwards. If you find that all the key heights are incorrect, it will take a complete adjustment to correct the situation (see The Complete Adjustment, p. 57). This job is quite complex and probably best left to the repair technician.

Chart 6
Piccolo Key Heights

(Refer to Illustration 2-3 for key numbers and names.)

Key	Number	Height
C♯-D♯ trill key	1	1⁄32″
C-D trill key	2	1⁄16″
C key	3	1⁄16″
B thumb key	4	1⁄16″*
B♭ key	6	1⁄16″*
A key	7	1⁄16″*
G key (double)	9	1⁄16″
G♯ key	10	1⁄16″
F♯ key	11	1⁄16″*
F key	12	1⁄16″
E key	13	1⁄16″*
D key	15	1⁄16″*
D♯ key	17	3⁄32″

*The heights of these keys will automatically be correct if the piccolo keys are regulated correctly. Only those keys *not marked* (*) will need to be measured.

HOW TO CORRECT NON-FUNCTIONING KEYS

A non-functioning key can be defined as any key on the piccolo which is not operating properly. This includes keys that won't go down or won't come up. When this occurs you will usually have to send the instrument to the repair shop for a skilled repair technician to find and correct the problem. There are, however, a number of things you should check before sending it in. These are common problems which cause key malfunctions that can easily be corrected by you. Check these and you might save some time and money.

Check the spring—Is it broken off? Perhaps the spring is just unhooked from the spring hook on the key. Sometimes the spring will be broken but will appear to be O.K. If it looks O.K., push against it gently. If there is no tension in the spring, it is broken and will need to be replaced. (See How to Replace a Piccolo Spring, p. 52.)

Check the pivot screws—These screws, located at the ends of the key rods, hold the key in place. Sometimes the pivot screw is turned in too far, thus binding the key. Loosen the screw slightly to see if action improves. Do not loosen the screw too much or it may continue to unscrew as the instrument is played. Sometimes, if the screw is too loose, the key will wiggle around on the instrument causing it to function incorrectly. Try tightening the screw slightly to see if action improves.

Check the key—Look for obvious signs of a bent rod or key. Sometimes the key is bent and the pad no longer seats correctly over the tone hole. Use your leak light to see if the pad is still level on the tone hole. If not, the key may be bent. This needs to be sent to the repair shop for correction.

THE COMPLETE ADJUSTMENT—
HOW TO MAKE THE ADJUSTMENT NECESSARY FOR
PROPER INSTRUMENT PERFORMANCE

The complete adjustment on the piccolo is a very difficult process. Basically, I would recommend that any extensive adjustments on the piccolo be done by a competent repair technician. It is possible that some of you will be able to follow the process outlined below and achieve satisfactory results; however, be prepared for problems. Be sure to read completely through the procedure before beginning.

Tools Needed: Leak light (with small bulb to fit piccolo)
     Spring hook
     Small screwdriver
     Alcohol burner or bunsen burner
     Ruler
     Emery paper
Materials Needed: Thin, double skin piccolo pads (thin clarinet pads will also work)
     Sheet cork in sizes ⅟₆₄″, ⅟₃₂″, ⅟₁₆″ and ⅛″
     Stick shellac
     Contact cement
Procedure: (Refer to Illustration 2-3 for key names and numbers.)

1. Using a leak light, check all pads to be certain that they have a level seat which will form a tight seal with the tone hole. If they do not, they will have to be replaced before you can continue with this adjustment procedure. Also check for, and replace, any loose or torn pads. (See How to Install New Piccolo Pads, p. 47.)

2. Adjust the C key (#3) to an open height of approximately ⅟₁₆″. This is measured from the top of the tone hole to the bottom of the pad at the front of the key. To adjust the height, you must adjust the thickness of the cork which is located under the foot of this key. If the cork needs to be replaced, cement a piece of ⅟₃₂″ sheet cork to the foot and, using emery paper, reduce cork thickness until the correct open height is achieved.

3. Adjust the G key (#9) to an open height of approximately ⅟₁₆″. The adjustment of this height is made by regulating the thickness of the cork under the foot of the G key where it rests against the body of the piccolo. If the cork needs to be replaced, cement a piece of ⅟₃₂″ sheet cork to the foot and, using emery paper, reduce the cork thickness until the correct open height is achieved.

4. Adjust the G♯ key (#10) to an open height of approximately ⅟₁₆″. To adjust this height, you must regulate the thickness of the cork located under the lever of this key. If

the cork needs to be replaced, cement a piece of ⅟₃₂″ sheet cork under the lever and, using emery paper, reduce the thickness of the cork until the correct open height is achieved.

5. Adjust the D♯ key (#17) to an open height of approximately ³⁄₃₂″. To adjust this height, regulate the thickness of the cork located under the lever of the key. If the cork needs to be replaced, cement a piece of ⅛″ sheet cork under the lever and trim down until the proper open height is achieved.

6. Adjust the height of the C♯ -D♯ trill key (#1) to an open height of approximately ⅟₃₂″. This height is adjusted by regulating the thickness of the cork under the trill key lever (spatula) at the point where this lever touches the rod of the lower stack keys. Work carefully as a very small variation in the thickness of the cork will make a big difference in the key opening height.

7. Adjust the height of the C-D trill key (#2) to an open height of ⅟₁₆″. This height is adjusted in the same manner as described in step 6.

8. Remove the B♭ thumb lever (#5) and B thumb key (#4) from the piccolo at this time. (These keys will be replaced at the beginning of step 20.) Adjust the F key (#12) to an open height of approximately ⅟₁₆″. Under the foot of the F key should be a cork which rests against the piccolo body. Regulate the thickness of this cork to achieve the correct key height. If the cork needs to be replaced, cement a piece of ⅟₁₆″ sheet cork and emery this down until the key opens to the correct height.

9. Adjust the F key (#12) with the F♯ key (#11) so that they close together. When checking, close the keys very slowly and use a very light touch. Use a leak light and be very critical, as both keys must seat at *exactly* the same time without using any excessive pressure. The adjustment for these two keys is made by regulating the thickness of the cork under the spatula of the F key. If the F♯ key is closing first, use a piece of emery paper and sand down the thickness of this cork. Sand a little at a time and check often so that you do not over-correct. If the F key is closing first, then more cork must be added. Cement a piece of ⅟₆₄″ sheet cork under the spatula and over any existing cork. It is most likely that this additional cork will be too thick, so you will then need to sand it down·with emery paper until the keys close together.

10. Adjust the F key (#12) with the B♭ key (#6) so that they close together. Again, check carefully as described in step 9. This adjustment is made at the point where the foot of the auxiliary B♭ key (#8) rests on the foot of the F key. There should be a piece of ⅟₆₄″ cork under the auxiliary B♭ key foot at this point. On most piccolos you can easily bend the B♭ auxiliary foot up or down slightly with a round nose pliers to achieve the proper regulation. If the F key is closing before the B♭ key, then bend the auxiliary B♭ foot *down slightly* toward the F foot. If the B♭ key closes before the F key then bend the auxiliary B♭ foot *up slightly*. (See Illustration 2-12.)

11. Adjust the A key (#7) with the B♭ key (#6) so that they close together. Check with a leak light. This adjustment is made by regulating the thickness of the cork under the spatula of the A key. Regulate this in the same manner as you did the F/F♯ adjustment described in step 9.

12. Next check the thickness of the cork on the foot of the A key (#7). This cork determines if the keys will move at the same time without any "lost motion" or "play." Press down slowly on the A key (#7) to see if the B♭ key (#6) *starts* to move at the same time. If

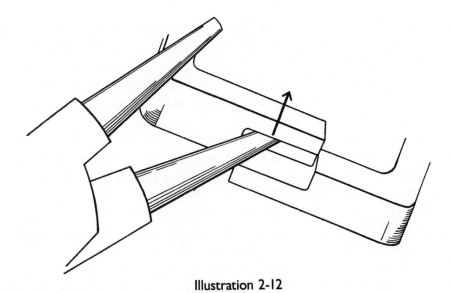

Illustration 2-12

the A key moves first, you will have to replace the cork on the foot of the A key with a thicker piece (usually a piece of 1/32" will work) until the A and B♭ keys move together as one key.

13. When the A key and the B♭ key are moving together, press slowly on the F key (#12) to see if the B♭ key *starts* moving at the same time. If the F key moves first, you will have to emery some cork off the bottom of the A *key foot* until the F and B♭ keys start moving at the same time. *(Caution:* If you reduce the cork too much, the A and B♭ keys will go out of adjustment again and you will have to repeat steps 12 and 13.)

14. Adjust the E key (#13) with the F♯ key (#11) so that they close together. Check with a leak light. Under the arm of the E key you will see a small metal tab as a part of the stop plate which moves with the F♯ key (see Illustration 2-3). There should be a small piece of cork either under the E key arm or on the tab. Adjusting the thickness of this cork will regulate the two keys. If the F♯ key is closing before the E key, some cork must be removed. If the E key is closing before the F♯ key, add a piece of 1/64" cork, then emery the cork down until the keys close together.

15. Now press slowly on the E key (#13) to see if the F♯ key (#11) *starts* moving at the same time. If not, replace the cork on the E key foot with a thicker piece (usually a 1/32" piece will work).

16. When the E key and the F♯ key are moving at the same time, press slowly on the F key (#12) to see if it *starts* to move at the same time as the F♯ key. If not, emery some cork off the foot of the E *key* until they do.

17. Adjust the D key (#15) with the F♯ key (#11) so that they close together. Check with a leak light. This adjustment is made in the same manner as that in step 14.

18. Now press slowly on the D key (#15) to see if the F♯ key (#11) *starts* to move at the same time. If not, replace the cork on the D key foot with a thicker piece (usually a 1/32" piece will work).

19. When the D and F♯ keys are moving at the same time, press slowly on the E key (#13). If it moves before the F♯ key (#11), emery some cork off the foot of the D *key*.

20. Replace the B♭ thumb lever (#5) and B thumb key (#4). Press slowly on the B♭ thumb lever and check to see if the B thumb key and the B♭ key (#6) are closing together. Check with a leak light. If the B thumb closes before the B♭ key, emery off some of the cork located under the B♭ thumb lever. If the B♭ key is closing before the B thumb key, replace the cork under the B♭ thumb key with a thicker piece and then emery this new piece until the keys close together.

21. The thickness of the cork on the foot of the B♭ thumb lever (#5) must be checked to eliminate "play" in the keys. If the thumb lever moves before the B♭ key (#6), replace the cork on the foot of the B♭ thumb lever with a thicker piece, then emery this cork until the keys *start* moving together.

22. When the B♭ thumb lever and the B♭ key *start* moving at the same time, press slowly on the F key (#12) to see if it and the B♭ key (#6) still *start* to move at the same time. If you now find that the F key moves before the B♭ key, emery some cork off the foot of the B♭ *thumb lever* until the F and B♭ keys move together. (*Caution:* Do not emery too much cork or you will create "play" between the B♭ thumb lever and the B♭ key and will then have to repeat steps 21 and 22.)

23. This should complete the adjustment of the piccolo. Play test the instrument to check the adjustment. It is best to play the low range down to the bottom note. If a note blows hard, look at the pad above the last closed pad for a possible leak.

REPAIRS TO BE SENT TO THE REPAIR SHOP

As I have mentioned throughout this chapter, the piccolo is an extremely difficult instrument on which to do any type of work. I have found that it takes much experience to be able to successfully repair a piccolo. For this reason I would suspect that all but the most talented of you will be sending your piccolos to the repair shop for repairs. In addition, some repairs require specialized tools which are too expensive and not practical for school use, while others require special skills that take time to develop.

Below I have outlined some of the more common piccolo repairs that will need to be done at a repair shop. I have also briefly summarized the work that needs to be done. It is hoped that this will give you a better understanding of the repair procedures.

REMOVING BODY DENTS

Obviously, this is only done on the silver piccolo. The dents can be removed quite easily in the repair shop. The piccolo is slipped over a steel rod which has the same diameter as the bore of the piccolo, then the dents are tapped up with a small dent hammer. The skill is in removing these dents with a minimum of marks on the body of the piccolo. Dents that you should consider having removed are (1) those located by a post, as they can destroy the alignment of the keys; (2) those near a tone hole, as they can cause the tone hole to become uneven making it impossible to form a level seat with the pad; and (3) those on the tenon of the head joint, as they will affect the fit of the head joint. Most other dents, unless extremely deep, do not have to be removed from the piccolo except for appearance' sake.

LEVELING UNEVEN TONE HOLES

The tone holes on the piccolo must be perfectly level across the top or it will be virtually impossible to form a level seat with the pad. You can check this by sighting across the top of the tone hole. If the tone hole is uneven on a metal piccolo, the repair technician will first check to see if there are any dents in the area causing the problem. If so, he will lift the dents first, then he will file the tone hole flat with a special tone hole file which has a very fine cut. He uses great care to hold the file perfectly flat while filing so that the tone hole is not filed at an angle.

If the piccolo is made of wood or plastic, the tone holes will usually remain level. The problem that may occur is a chip in the edge of the tone hole. In this case the repair technician will use a tone hole reamer to level off the tone hole once again. Once the tone hole has been leveled and any chipped areas removed, it may be necessary to replace and reseat the pad, then regulate the key as the repaired tone hole may be a little lower than the original.

RE-FITTING THE TENON

If the tenon of your piccolo is tight fitting, you should first try to clean it. (See Maintenance Procedures of the Piccolo, Tenon, p. 40.) If this does not correct the problem, the repair technician will have to re-fit the tenon for you. He will use a tenon reducer which compresses the tenon equally around its diameter to shrink its size while maintaining a perfectly round opening.

If the tenon is too loose, he will use a tenon expander which is pushed into the bore of the tenon and actually expands the metal slightly to create a better fit.

TIGHTENING LOOSE KEYS

If your piccolo has a lot of "play" in the keys (that is, they move sideways on the rod or between the pivot screws), you may have a problem getting the pads to always close on the seat. This "play" can be caused either by wear or a bent post. If the key is mounted on a *rod* and slides sideways along the rod, then there is too much room between the posts. In this case the repair technician will have to stretch the hinge tube of the key to fill the gap (a process called "swedging"). If the post is bent, he will have to bend the post back into position without breaking it loose from the body of the piccolo.

It is also possible that the diameter of the key's hinge tube has enlarged through wear and is now bigger than the diameter of the pivot rod. In this case the repair technician will squeeze the hinge tube slightly to tighten, but not so much as to bind the key action.

If the loose key is held in place with pivot screws, the repair technician will check to see if the posts are straight. Also, the pivot screws may have worn and need to be replaced.

REPAIRING BROKEN KEYS

If the piccolo key actually breaks in half, this can be repaired in the shop. Be certain that you save the pieces and send them along with the entire piccolo. The repair technician will braze the two pieces together with silver solder. When done correctly, this will bond the two sections together as securely as the original piece. Also, the mend will not be too noticeable and should function like the original key. It is important to send the entire instrument in, so the repair technician can be certain that the key is brazed at the correct angle and readjusted to the instrument.

If you should lose one of the broken pieces, most repair shops will be able to either order a new key, or fashion a key from an old part from another piccolo. In either case, this is usually more expensive.

CORRECTING A LEAKING EMBOUCHURE PLATE

Only the metal piccolo head joint will have an embouchure plate. As you check the piccolo head joint for leaks, you may occasionally find that air is escaping from around the embouchure plate. The embouchure plate is soldered in place over a hole in the head joint. Sometimes, especially if the head joint is dropped, the solder will break away a little and at this point cause a leak. The repair technician will correct the problem by removing the embouchure plate completely, cleaning up the area to be soldered, and re-soldering the plate in the proper position.

REPLATING THE WORN FINISH

Most metal piccolos are finished in silver and most wood and plastic piccolos will have silver plated keys. In time the finish will wear off, giving a rather poor appearance to the instrument. Not all repair shops can do replating, although most of them have another company to which they can send this type of work to be done. Replating an instrument requires having the chemicals necessary to strip off the old finish and the equipment for electroplating. The piccolo is completely disassembled and the finish removed from the body and/or keys. All parts are then buffed to a high gloss smoothness and then replated using an electroplating process. When the plating is complete, the piccolo is re-assembled using all new pads and corks. Often excess plating must be removed from the keys to insure a proper fit between the posts. The tone holes of the metal piccolo also need to be carefully checked and leveled, as they sometimes are worn down accidentally in the buffing process. It is customary to have all dents removed from the metal body when doing this work because it is convenient to do so while the instrument is apart and does not add much to the cost. When this job is complete, your piccolo will have a "like new" appearance and playability.

THE COMPLETE REPAD

Even though you may do a good job of maintaining the playing condition of the piccolos in your band, there will come a time when most of the pads are starting to tear and dry out. Many of the corks will be depressed, dried out or missing altogether. This is the time to consider having the piccolo completely repadded. A complete repad in most shops will consist of replacing all the old pads and corks with new. It should also include re-fitting the tenon, cleaning the body, straightening posts and leveling tone holes where needed. Loose keys are usually tightened in this job. When re-assembled, all the pads would be seated and the springs would be adjusted for good action. In short, the instrument should *play* like a new piccolo.

3

The Oboe

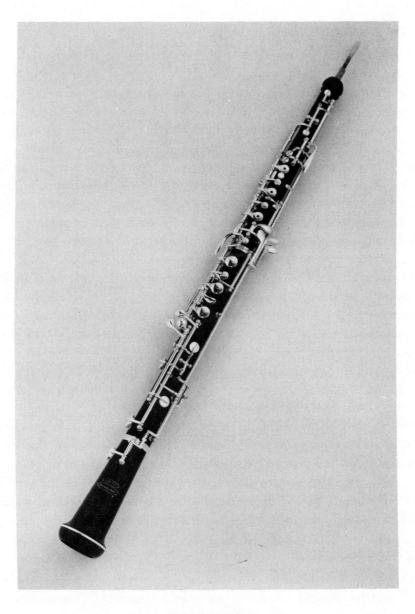

Illustration 3-1

Photograph courtesy of The Selmer Co.; Elhart, Indiana

HOW TO TAKE CARE OF YOUR OBOE

Taking proper care of the oboe should be the first, and most important step in your oboe maintenance plan. By following the suggestions given here, you will avoid many of the problems which can cause the oboe to malfunction or not play properly. Although this might be a review for many band directors, it would be a good idea to share this information with your oboe players, so they will have an understanding of proper oboe care. When the student understands the reasons for the maintenance procedures outlined below, there is a better chance that they will be followed. As most oboes are school owned, this should help lower your repair costs.

ASSEMBLE THE OBOE CAREFULLY

The oboe consists of three sections which need to be assembled: the upper joint, the lower joint and the bell. Because of the delicate nature of the keys, and the complexity of the key adjustments, great care must be taken to avoid bending or putting any sort of stress on the keys while assembling the oboe.

Before assembling it is extremely important that the tenon corks be greased so that they work freely. If the corks are dry or fit tightly, this can cause difficulty in assembling the sections which, in turn, may cause the player to damage the keys. In addition, it can also be the source of broken tenons because the excess pressure required, plus any "angling" of the sections when putting together or taking apart, will put too much stress on the tenon. The cork tenon should go into the receiver smoothly but not be so loose that the joint is likely to come apart or "wiggle" when the sections are together.

To assemble, start with the upper and lower joints. The upper joint will have two bridge keys which extend over the tenon. It is very important that these bridge keys are not damaged or bent in any way while assembling. Special care should be taken that the cork on these keys is not scraped off, as that can destroy the bridge key adjustment. Grasp the upper joint firmly around the keys and check to be certain that the G♯ key (bottom key on the upper joint) remains closed. Grasp the lower joint so that the two lower bridge keys (which line up with the upper keys) remain in the down position. In so doing there will be no damage to the bridge keys as you assemble. Push the two joints together with a slight twisting action. Line up the bridge keys.

To attach the bell section, hold the bell key closed (so that the bridge key will be up). Hold the lower section so the corresponding bridge key remains in the down position. Push the bell in place with a slight twisting action and line up the bridge keys. Care must be taken so the bridge keys are not damaged or the cork scraped off the keys, as this will destroy the adjustment. Some oboes do not have a key on the bell, in which case it is simply pushed on the lower joint with a slight twisting action.

STORE THE OBOE PROPERLY

The oboe should always be stored in the case. An oboe left lying about on a chair, table or music stand is easily bumped or dropped on the floor. This can result in serious and expensive repairs.

The oboe should *never* be stored near a radiator or heating duct. Excessive heat is one of the contributing factors in causing wood oboes to crack. In addition, as the wood dries out, the posts will loosen on the instrument, often turning and binding the key action.

One should also avoid storing the oboe in extremely cold conditions. Having the oboe in sub-zero weather can cause the pads to loosen. Once the pad has loosened or fallen out it will be necessary for you to replace it with a new pad as it is almost impossible to re-locate the pad seat in the same position. As quick temperature changes can contribute to the wood instrument cracking, always avoid playing a cold oboe. Let the instrument warm up to room temperature before playing it.

Oboe cases are designed to hold the instrument securely in the case. Most cases usually have a small storage section to hold reeds and swabs. The case is not designed to serve as a display area for medals and pins or to carry lesson books and music. This overpacking of the case can cause excessive pressure on the instrument when the cover is closed and may cause the keys to bend or go out of alignment. Dangling medals can also catch under the keys of the oboe when the case is closed and then bend them when the case is opened.

Check to be certain that the case is holding the oboe securely. Place the oboe in the case, close the cover and latch it, then shake the case (hold the handle down when shaking). If you hear the oboe bouncing inside the case, it is not providing the protection that it should and there needs to be more padding in the case. Lay a small cloth on the top of the oboe. Usually a piece of towel works well. This is the quickest and cheapest way to correct the problem. This cloth will take up some of the room inside the case and yet will not damage the instrument. Check again and add more cloth if needed. If the cover becomes hard to close, you know you have added too much cloth.

You could also remove the lining from the cover of the case, add more padding and then re-glue. This will take more time, but will look better when completed.

Inspect the case periodically to be certain that it is in good condition. Prompt attention should be given to broken or loose latches, hinges or handles. Be certain that the lining is not loose. Loose lining can easily be corrected with some glue, but broken case hardware will usually need to be sent to the repair shop for correction.

Many oboes are supplied with tenon protectors. These are not essential as the primary function of the protector is to help prevent cork grease from getting on the case lining. On some oboes I have found that the protector is smaller than the comparable receiver. Therefore, in order to allow the protector to fit over the tenon, the cork had to be too thin for a good fit when assembling the oboe. If this has happened to you, it is best to discard the protector and recork the tenon for a good fit. If your tenons are fitting well, then you can continue to use the tenon protectors.

It is not advisable to store damp swabs or cloths in the oboe case. Trapping this moisture in the case will cause the oboe pads to remain wet for a longer period of time, thus decreasing the life span. Also, excessive moisture or humidity will contribute to rust forming on the pivot screws and rods. This will eventually cause the key action to slow up or stop.

CLEAN THE OBOE REGULARLY

A few minutes of care in cleaning the oboe after each playing session will go a long way in helping to maintain the instrument. First, and most important, is to swab out the bore of the oboe after each playing session in order to remove all traces of moisture. The oboe bore is tapered and extremely small at the top end and, therefore, is difficult to dry effectively. As a result, many students are tempted to only swab out the lower joint and skip the upper joint even though it will have much more moisture in it. If the oboe is not dried after each playing, the water will soak into the wood of the oboe and may cause cracking to occur. In addition, excess moisture left in the bore will seep into the pads, causing them to deteriorate much more rapidly than normal. This, in turn, will increase the amount of work or money that you will have to put into the oboe to maintain its good playing condition.

An old method of swabbing out the oboe bore, using either a turkey or pheasant tail feather, is not the best method. The feather is not absorbant and, therefore, only distributes the moisture and does not remove it. You can now find swabs that are designed for the oboe and do an effective job of drying out the bore. Some oboe swabs are small and designed to be pulled through the upper joint without getting stuck. Other, larger swabs are designed to pull only part way through the upper joint and then have to be pulled back out the same end. Be sure you understand how the oboe swabs you have are supposed to work.

The oboe has two octave vents in the upper joint which consist of small tubes that extend into the bore. Because the amount of moisture in the upper joint is usually quite heavy, some of the saliva will flow into the octave vents. As you play and open one of the octave keys, the tone will actually "gurgle." The best way to remove this excess water is to blow into the octave tone hole. A short, hard burst of air will usually blow out any of the accumulated moisture. This should be followed with a careful and thorough swabbing as soon as possible.

Although the oboe keys are usually silver plated, you should not attempt to polish them. The keys on the oboe are extremely small and the adjustment mechanisms quite complex. Even a small amount of dry polish can get into the key mechanism and cause the keys to bind up and not function properly. You willl find that you can maintain the appearance of the oboe keys for quite a long time if you have the player wipe the keys with a soft cloth after each playing session. Wiping off all the body oil that accumulates from the fingers will go a long way in preventing tarnish.

In time the outside of the oboe will begin to accumulate a greasy dirt and lint under the keys and rods. This is particularly true of the wood oboe because the wood is impregnated with oil by the manufacturer and this tends to attract the dirt. It is a good idea to remove this lint before it gets into the rods and slows up the key action. Using a small modeler's paint brush or pipe stem cleaner, reach under the keys and brush away any dirt or lint that has collected. *Care should be taken to avoid catching any of the springs* as this might change the spring tension and could affect the adjustment and function of some keys. This job is quite easy if you just do it slowly and carefully.

MAINTENANCE PROCEDURES FOR THE OBOE

Tenons—When the tenon cork is new, it is fitted correctly for the receiver and then a light coating of cork grease is applied to ease the assembling of the sections. The cork grease attracts dirt which begins to build up on the cork tenon, thus making the tenon fit tighter. Usually the player will then add more cork grease. This cycle continues with layers of grease and dirt slowly building up on the tenon cork. I have seen oboes that had so much grease that it was all over the tenon, the body of the oboe and the keys and pads near the tenon joint.

The cork tenons of the oboe should be kept *clean* to insure a good fit. The best procedure to follow is to wipe them completely dry about once a month. Use a strip of cloth which is cut to a width of about 1½″. Have someone hold the oboe section for you and wipe the tenon with the cloth strip (see Illustration 3-2). Slowly rotate the oboe section as you wipe. After the tenon cork is completely clean and dry, apply a *small* amount of cork grease.

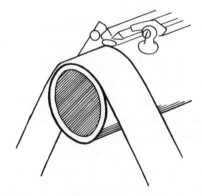

Illustration 3-2

By following this procedure, you will not only lengthen the life of the tenon cork and avoid having excessive grease on the tenon and instrument, but will also prevent a tight-fitting tenon which is one of the chief reasons for broken tenons.

As the tenon cork gets older, it will begin to dry out (cork grease helps prevent this) and will shrink in size. When the cork is too small for the receiver, a loose fit results and the two sections will "wiggle" when they are together. When this happens it is time to replace the tenon cork (See How to Re-cork the Tenons, p. 81). In an emergency you can expand the cork *temporarily* by holding it over some heat. Use a match, alcohol lamp or bunsen burner and rotate the tenon over the flame. Care should be taken to avoid getting it too hot as the cork will burn quite easily. This is not a permanent solution because the cork will quickly compress again after it is used.

Oiling the Bore—A lot of water accumulates in the bore while the oboe is being played. To prevent this moisture from soaking into the wood of the oboe, you should oil the bore regularly. Of course, this only needs to be done to a wood oboe; plastic oboes do not absorb moisture. Most instrument manufacturers recommend that a new instrument should be oiled about once a month for the first six months and then about twice a year.

Oil the bore with a commercial bore oil which is available from your music dealer. The oil will cause the skin pads to dry out quite rapidly, so protect the pads by placing a thick piece of absorbent paper between each pad and tone hole. Any excess oil will then soak into the paper rather than the pad.

When oiling, hold the oboe section at a 45° angle with no tone holes on the bottom side of the bore. Then place a *few* drops of bore oil at the top of the bore and allow the oil to flow down the length of the bore. Once the oil has run the length of the bore distribute the oil throughout the bore by using a turkey or pheasant tail feather. (Save this feather and you can use it again.) If you don't have access to a feather, you can use a commercial oboe swab that will fit through the top opening. Plan to use this swab only for oiling and save for future use. Let the oboe sit overnight, then swab out again with a clean feather or swab to remove any excess oil. You may then remove the pad protectors. If you have used too much oil, the oil will soak into the pads even after the protectors are removed. It is better to start with too little oil the first few times (until you get used to the correct amount) rather than too much and ruin the pads.

Sticky Pads—Sticky pads are caused by the accumulation of dirt on the pad seat or tone hole. The student should avoid chewing gum, eating candy or drinking "pop" immediately before or while playing. All these items increase the amount of sugar in the saliva, some of which will travel into the bore and accumulate on the pads. This sticky substance then attracts dirt to the pad causing the stickiness. In addition, of course, the excess sugar in the saliva will also accumulate in the oboe reed. Swabbing the bore will help this problem, but not after the moisture has reached the pads.

Another cause of sticky pads is that of the pad being saturated with bore oil. If you have recently oiled the bore, you may have used an excessive amount of oil or did not protect the pads properly. If the pads do become oil soaked, they will need to be replaced. You can tell if the pads are oil soaked by looking at them. (See Oiling the Bore, p. 67.)

The stickiness in the pads usually begins with an annoying "clicking" sound as the pad opens from the tone hole. As the problem gets worse, the keys will not open promptly and the key action will be slowed down. The problem should be corrected as soon as it is noticed, as this is when it is easiest to do. (See How to Clean Dirty and Sticky Pads, p.78.) If possible, try to determine the source of the sticky pads to avoid future problems.

Oiling the Keys—The keys of the oboe should be oiled about once a month to keep them working freely and to prevent the screws and rods from becoming rusted. If the rods and screws do rust, the key action can bind up and will require a repair technician to correct. Key oil is available from your music dealer. Using a pin or toothpick, place a *small* drop of key oil at the end of each key and between all moveable keys which share the same rod. Work the keys to circulate the oil then wipe off any excess oil that may be on the rod. Care should be taken to avoid using too much key oil. If there is excess oil left on the keys, this will attract dirt which will mix with the oil to slow down the key action.

MONTHLY MAINTENANCE CHECK LIST—OBOE

Chart 7 is a check list that you can use to help in the maintenance procedures of the oboe. By following this chart you should be able to keep the instrument well cleaned and be alert to any possible repairs needed before they become too severe. With some training, your students should be able to utilize this check list by themselves.

Chart 7
Monthly Maintenance Check List—Oboe

INSPECT THE FOLLOWING:

Oboe
- _____ Are the tenon corks clean, intact and lightly greased?
- _____ Do the sections of the oboe fit securely together?
- _____ Are there any sticky pads?
- _____ Are there any worn pads?
- _____ Are there any loose pads?
- _____ Are all the keys moving freely?
- _____ Are there any cracks in the wood body?
- _____ Are there any missing screws or rods?
- _____ Are the bridge keys between each section working properly?

Case
- _____ Are the latches working properly?
- _____ Are the hinges tight?
- _____ Is the handle secure?
- _____ Is the lining in place?
- _____ Are there any loose objects in the case?
- _____ Are there any pins or medals attached to the lining?
- _____ Is the oboe held tightly in the case when closed?
- _____ Is there a swab with the oboe? Where is it stored when damp?

DO THE FOLLOWING:
1. Check for leaks (See How to Check for Leaks, p. 71).
2. Oil the bore (twice a year after first six months).
3. Clean dirt and lint from under the keys and rods.
4. Oil the key rods and screws.
5. Clean the tenon corks and lightly grease.

HOW TO REPAIR THE OBOE

DIAGNOSING INSTRUMENT MALFUNCTIONS

Before you can repair the oboe you need to understand the problem. Listed below are some of the more common problems that occur with the oboe. For each problem I have suggested some possible causes in hopes that it will help you locate the difficulty. Although this list can hardly be complete, it should serve as a good guideline in many cases.

1. *Problem:* Oboe blows hard, will not play all notes clearly.
Possible Causes: Pads are leaking. (Look for torn pads, missing pads or those not seating properly.) Keys are not regulated properly (particularly check the bridge keys and G♯ key). Reed problems.

2. *Problem:* Oboe will not play upper register notes.
Possible Causes: Octave key tone holes are plugged. Keys are not regulated correctly. Pads are leaking.

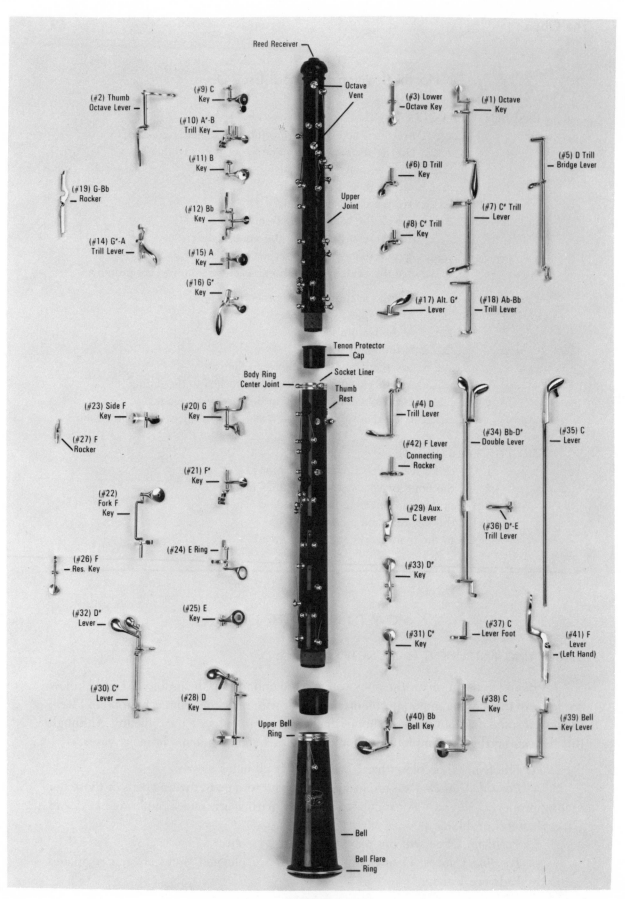

Illustration 3-3

Photograph courtesy of The Selmer Co.; Elkhart, Indiana

3. *Problem:* Oboe plays the wrong pitch for the fingering used.

Possible Causes: Springs are unhooked from keys. Broken springs. Keys may not be regulated correctly.

4. *Problem:* Oboe plays out of tune.

Possible Causes: Key corks may be missing, causing incorrect key heights. All key heights may be set incorrectly. Player's embouchure and/or reed may need attention.

5. *Problem:* Keys are not functioning properly.

Possible Causes: Broken or unhooked springs. Bridge keys not correctly aligned. Bent keys, rods or posts. Pivot screws may be too tight or rusted. Keys and rods may be dirty or rusted.

6. *Problem:* Bridge keys do not stay aligned.

Possible Causes: Tenon corks too loose causing sections to "wiggle," thus changing bridge key alignment. Bridge key may be broken.

HOW TO CHECK FOR LEAKS

When your oboe does not seem to play properly, the first thing you should do is check for leaks. Leaks in the oboe can by the result of a missing, torn or worn pad, bent keys, loose adjustment screws or cracks in the body. Finding the leak is necessary if you wish to correct the problem.

Generally speaking, all the notes on the oboe should produce the same quality of tone. If you have a note or notes that sound "stuffy" or are hard to blow, you probably have a leak. Also, if the upper or lower register notes do not play correctly, you may have a leak. Bear in mind, however, that many beginning oboe players will have trouble playing these notes.

Tools Needed: Leak testing cork

Leak light (with small bulb)

Procedure:

1.Check the upper joint. Using the appropriate size leak testing cork, plug the bottom end of this joint. Close all the keys in this joint. Apply the normal pressure used when playing the instrument to hold these keys down. Blow gently into the top of the joint. Do not blow too hard as you may blow open some keys that would normally remain closed. If there is a leak, you will hear the air escaping and feel the lack of resistance as you blow into the joint. Be very critical when listening for the escaping air as it will not be a very loud sound. Because the keys of the oboe are small, the amount of air escaping could be quite minimal yet cause serious playing problems. You can double-check for leaks by sucking the air out of the joint. If there is a leak, the vacuum that you create will not last. *Caution:* The sucking method cannot be used as the only test for leaks. When the vacuum is created in the bore it will tend to pull the pads against the tone hole, thus hiding some leaks.

Once you have located the leaking pad or pads you will have to readjust the keys (see How to Regulate the Keys, p.72), replace the skin oboe pad (see How to Install New Skin Oboe Pads, p.75) or adjust the cork oboe pad (see How to Level the Cork Oboe Pad, p.77).

2. Check the lower joint. Using the appropriate size leak testing cork, plug the *top* end of the lower joint. When checking this section you will need to blow into the bottom of the joint as you will not be able to get your mouth around the receiver because of the bridge keys. This is a little harder to check until you get used to it because of being upside down. Close all the keys of this joint. Not only will you have to close the stack keys that the right hand normally operates, but you will also have to depress the left hand side lever which closes the low C key. With a little experimenting, you will find the correct levers to close all the keys. (Never close the low C key by just pressing on the key, always use the proper key lever.) Apply the normal light pressure used when playing the instrument to hold the keys down. Place your mouth around the entire lower tenon and blow gently into the joint. Follow the same procedure as described in step 1.

3. Check the bell. If your oboe has a key on the bell this should also be checked for leaks. The easiest way of doing this is to use a leak light. Close the key *lightly* and with the leak light inside, check all around the pad to be certain that there is no gap in the seal with the tone hole.

4. Check the bridge key alignment. Once you have checked each of the oboe joints individually, assemble the oboe to be certain that a leak is not being created by the faulty alignment of the bridge keys. Assemble the upper and lower joints. There are three bridge keys that span this joint. The bridge keys should line up and the arm on the G key (#20) should extend over the G♯ key (#16). Both the D trill lever (#4) and the foot of the G key (#20) should be able to move slightly *before* activating the bridge key of the upper joint. That arm of the G key (#20) should touch the G♯ key (#16) at the *same time* that the G key seals the tone hole on the lower joint. Use the leak light to check this.

Between the bell section and the lower joint the bridge key should line up and when you press the side B♭ lever (#34) both the bell key and the low C key (#38) should close. If any of the above adjustments are not correct, see How to Regulate the Keys, below.

HOW TO REGULATE THE KEYS

The correct regulation of the oboe keys is of utmost importance for proper instrument performance. The oboe, along with the piccolo, is an extremely difficult instrument to regulate. Do not become discouraged if you have trouble. I present this information because I know that some of you will have enough knowledge of the oboe to be able to follow the step-by-step instructions. Many of you will find that it is best to leave the regulation of the oboe to a qualified repair technician.

In many cases, however, the oboe may not be playing correctly because of a simple adjustment screw or key adjustment. If you follow the instructions given below, you may be able to locate the problem and correct it. Although the regulation of the keys is just one step in the complete adjustment process of the oboe, it is sometimes all that you will need to do to get an oboe playing again.

Tools Needed: Leak light (with small bulb)
　　　　　　　　Small screwdriver
　　　　　　　　Emery paper

Materials Needed: Sheet cork as needed in sizes ⅟₆₄″,
⅟₃₂″ and ⅟₁₆″
Contact cork cement
Procedure: (Refer to Illustration 3-3 for key names and numbers.)

1. Check the pad seats. Before you attempt to regulate any keys, check all the pads to be certain that they are sealing properly. If the pads do not form a level seat with the tone holes, it will be virtually impossible to regulate the keys. To check the seat, place your leak light under each pad and close the key slowly using a very light pressure. It is important to be very critical during this checking procedure. The pad should seat level on the tone hole, that is, it should close simultaneously around the entire tone hole. Often you will find that a pad is hitting the front, back or one of the sides *before* it seals the tone hole. Any pads you find which are torn, loose or not sealing properly will need to be replaced. If the pad is a skin pad, see How to Install New Skin Oboe Pads, p. 75. If the pad is a cork pad see How to Level Cork Oboe Pads, p.77. If *none* of the pad touches the tone hole, check the adjustment screws or levers around the key as they are probably holding the key open and need to be adjusted to allow the key to close all the way. When all the pads have a level seat with the tone hole, you are ready to continue with step 2 below.

2. Start with the upper joint. Place a small wedge of wood or cork under the G-B♭ rocker (#19) to hold the lower portion of the key up. This will allow both the A♯-B trill key (#10) and the B♭ key (#12) to open.

3. Press the B♭ key (#12). This should close the A♯-B trill key (#10) at the same time. Use your leak light to check. If they do not close together, adjust the screw on the arm of the A♯-B trill key which extends over the arm of the B♭ key. Turning the screw down will cause the A♯-B trill key to close sooner.

4. Press the B key (#11). This should close the A♯-B trill key (#10) at the same time. Use your leak light as you check. If they do not close together, adjust the *other* screw on the arm of the A♯-B trill key which extends over the foot of the B key. Turning the screw down will cause the A♯-B trill key to close sooner.

5. Press the A key (#15). This should close at the same time as both the A♯-B trill key (#10) and the B♭ key (#12). Use a leak light to make this check. If they do not close together (remember that the A♯-B trill key and the B♭ key have already been adjusted to close together) you must make the adjustment with the screw located on the arm of the B♭ key (#12). Turning this screw down will cause the A♯-B trill key and the B♭ key to close sooner. You can now remove the wedge from under the G-B♭ rocker (#19).

6. Press the lever of the C♯ trill lever (#7) to be certain that it will open the C♯ trill key (#8). If not, you will need to add cork under the arm of the C♯ trill lever where it extends over the foot of the C♯ trill key.

7. Lift the bridge key end of the D trill bridge lever key, (#5) to be certain that it will open the D trill key (#6). If not, you will need to add cork under the arm of the D trill key lever where it extends over the foot of the D trill key.

8. Press the Thumb Octave lever (#2). This will open the lower octave key (#3). The back of the lower octave key (#3) should touch the arm of the octave key (#1) *at the same time* that the bottom of the thumb octave lever (#2) touches the body of the oboe. If

they are not touching at the same time, and the gap is small, most oboes will have an adjustment screw at the back of the lower octave key (#3) which can be turned to achieve the correct adjustment. If there is no adjustment screw, or the gap is too large to correct by the screw, you will need to adjust this by the thickness of cork under the bottom of the thumb octave lever (#2). If the thumb octave lever hits the body of the oboe *before* the lower octave key (#3) touches the octave key (#1), then you must make the cork thinner by emerying away some of the cork. If the opposite is true, add a piece of cork to make it thicker. Check various thicknesses of cork to see which works best before gluing in place.

9. Continue by checking the lower joint. Press the Fork F key (#22). This should close at the same time as the F♯ key (#21). Use a leak light as you check. If they do not, the adjustment is made with the screw located on the arm of the F♯ key which extends over the foot of the Fork F key. Turning the screw down will cause the F♯ key to close sooner. *NOTE:* It is sometimes very difficult to see whether these keys are closing together because your vision will be blocked by other keys. You may find it easier to check if you remove the D trill lever (#4), the B♭-D♯ double lever (#34) and the C lever (#35) before you make the check.

10. Press the E ring (#24) or the E key (#25). Your oboe will have one or the other of these keys, but not both. This should close at the same time as the F♯ key (#21). Use a leak light as you make this check. If you have the E ring, you will not have to worry about the E pad sealing the tone hole, but must be certain that the E ring, when pressed all the way down, will close the F♯ key. If the two keys do not close together, the adjustment is made with the screw which is located on the arm of the F♯ key (#21) which extends over the foot of the E ring or key. Turning the screw down will cause the F♯ key to close sooner. After you complete this step, you can replace the D trill lever (#4), the B♭-D♯ double lever (#34) and the C lever (#35) if they were removed in step 9.

11. Press the D key (#28). The pad should seal the tone hole at the *same time* that the top of its foot touches the adjustment screw of the D♯ key (#33). If not, adjust this screw until they do. Also, the D key should close at the *same time* as the Fork F key (#22) and the F♯ key (#21). Use your leak light to make this check. If they do not close together, the adjustment is made at the point where the lever of the D key extends over the arm of the Fork F key. On some oboes there will be an adjustment screw located alongside the lever of the D key for this purpose. Turning the adjustment screw down will cause the Fork F key and the F♯ key to close sooner. If you do not have a screw, the adjustment will need to be made with a piece of cork at this point. Thicker cork will cause the Fork F and F♯ key to close sooner, thinner cork will have the opposite effect.

12. Press the C♯ lever (#30) which is located right next to the D♯ lever (#32). This should open the C♯ key (#31) and at the same time close the D key (#28), the Fork F key (#22) and the F♯ key (#21). Remember that you have already adjusted these last three keys to close together in step 11. If the three keys do not close all the way when the C♯ key is opened, you will need to add cork to the top of the arm which extends from the D key lever (#28) under the C♯ key lever until they do work properly.

13. Check the B♭ D♯ double lever (#34). At the end of this lever are two arms, each of which should have an adjustment screw. You must eliminate any play in this key by adjusting the screws to contact the spring and the bell key lever (#39) without pushing either one. The adjustment screw should be just touching each point.

14. Now check the bridge keys. Insert the upper joint tenon into the lower joint receiver and line up the two sections properly. Press the G key (#20). This key should seal the tone hole at the *same time* that the arm extending over the G♯ key (#16) touches the top of the G♯ key. If it does not do this, the adjustment will be made by turning the adjustment screw located in the arm of the G key. If the gap is too large, and the adjustment screw cannot make the adjustment, you will have to bend the arm *slightly*, then adjust the screw.

15. Check the G-B♭ rocker (#19) at the point where it extends over the foot of the G key (#20). The G key should move *very slightly* before it touches the G-B♭ rocker. If the foot of the G key is already in contact with the G-B♭ rocker you will need to emery some cork off the foot of the G key until there is a slight gap at the bridge. If the gap at the bridge is too much, add a piece of 1/64″ cork to reduce the gap.

16. Check the bridge between the D trill lever (#4) and the D trill bridge lever (#5). The D trill lever should move *very slightly* before making contact with the D trill bridge lever. If the D trill bridge lever is already making contact with the D trill lever, it will be necessary to emery off some of the cork located on the under side of the D trill foot. If there is too much of a gap, you should add a piece of 1/64″ sheet cork to this point to reduce the gap.

17. If your oboe has a bell key, continue with this step. If there is no bell key, proceed to step 18 below. Attach the bell to the lower joint of the oboe and line up the bridge keys. Press the B♭ D♯ double lever (#34). This should close the B♭ bell key (#40) at the *same time* as the C key (#38). If they do not, the adjustment is made by the thickness of cork under the bridge of the B♭ bell key (#40) where it extends over the bell key lever (#39). More cork will cause the B♭ bell key to close sooner.

18. The adjustment of the oboe is now complete. All other keys on the oboe are independent of each other and do not have to be regulated to work with other keys. To adjust the key heights or regulation of these other keys, see The Complete Adjustment, p. 89.

HOW TO INSTALL NEW SKIN OBOE PADS

Oboe pads, like those of the piccolo, can be difficult to install. Many of them are quite small and, therefore, cause difficulty in obtaining a good level seat with the tone hole. Whenever you install any pad, the primary objective is to get a good level seat with the tone hole. In addition, a new pad will often be thicker or thinner than the pad being replaced, and as a result the key adjustment will be off. It will probably be necessary, therefore, to adjust the key so that it is regulated correctly with the other keys.

There are two basic types of pads on the oboe and most oboes will have both types: the skin pad, similar to those used on the clarinet or piccolo, and the cork pad (on some oboes the cork has been replaced with a rubber-like material). This section will deal with the installation of skin pads only. If you need to replace or adjust a cork pad, see How to Level the Cork Oboe Pad, p.77.

Tools Needed: Leak light (with small bulb)
Pipe stem cleaner
Pad slick
Spring clamp

Alcohol burner or bunsen burner
Thin needle spring
Flat nose pliers
Materials Needed: Double skin clarinet pads
Stick shellac
Procedure:

1. Remove the old pad. Skin oboe pads are held in place with shellac or a similar type of substance. In some cases you may need to remove the key in order to get at the pad. Heat the key as shown in Illustration 3-4. Always heat the key at an angle so that the main concentration of heat will not burn or melt the body of the oboe. When the shellac is soft, remove the old pad.

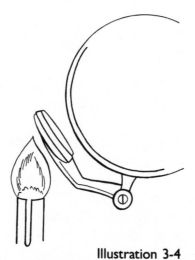

Illustration 3-4

2. Find the correct size replacement pad using your old pad as a sample. Particularly important is finding a pad which has the same thickness, as this will make the final adjustment much easier. Some oboe pads are "floated in" at the factory. In this method there is a large quantity of shellac placed in the pad cup, then a very thin pad is "floated in" on top of this shellac. If you are replacing a pad that has been "floated in," the new pad will need to be thicker. There should be no problem in replacing a "floated in" pad with a pad mounted in the method described here.

Before placing the pad into the key, be sure that all the old shellac is out of the key cup. This is especially true if the pad has been "floated in." If there is a small piece of hard shellac in the key, the pad will not fit squarely into the key. Use your needle spring to scratch out any excess shellac. Place the pad into the key, then slowly close the key over the tone hole. Using your leak light, check the following. If the pad hits the back of the tone hole first, it is either too thick or too large. Likewise, if the pad is hitting the front of the tone hole first, it is too thin or too small. Finding the correct size pad is important for the oboe, especially on those keys with smaller pads. There is little room in the key to manuever the pad to make it level with the tone hole. With the larger (lower) pads of the oboe, you can usually slide the pad slightly to help level it with the tone hole when seating.

3. When you feel that the pad is the correct size, hold the end of the stick shellac in the flame of your burner and, when soft, place a small drop of the shellac on the back of the pad. (The back of the pad is the cardboard side.) Place the pad into the key, close the key and heat until the shellac softens and the pad settles into the key cup.

4. Level the pad with the tone hole by rotating the pad in the key while the shellac is soft. To do this, place the pad slick between the pad and the tone hole and rotate back and forth. Remove the pad slick and *lightly* close the key to see if the pad is level with the tone hole. Use your leak light to make this check. If it is not level, repeat the process using either a larger or smaller pad depending on whether the pad tends to hit the front or back of the tone hole. If the pad has a tendency to hit either side of the tone hole first, check the *key* to see if it is level with the tone hole. Sometimes the key will bend, causing it to be uneven. If this is the case, use a large flat nose pliers and *gently* bend the key back to a level position.

5. Seat the pad. When you are satisfied that the pad is level with the tone hole, wet the pad with water (using the pipe stem cleaner dipped in water), heat the key once again and clamp shut with a spring clamp.

6. After the key has cooled thoroughly, remove the clamp and check with a leak light to see if the seat on the pad is level with the tone hole. If not, repeat the process starting with step 2.

7. Adjust the key. If the key in which you have replaced the pad works in conjunction with other keys of the oboe, it will be necessary to readjust the key. (See How to Regulate the Keys, p. 72.)

HOW TO LEVEL THE CORK OBOE PAD

As mentioned above, some of the pads on the oboe will be made of cork. These are usually found on the "articulated" keys, that is, those keys which have a small hole in the key that must remain open. These pads cannot be replaced with skin pads.

If you find that a cork pad is leaking at one point, it may be possible to correct this problem without having to replace the pad. If the following procedure does not work, the pad will need to be replaced. The procedures and supplies needed to make a cork pad dictate that it is best to send the oboe to the repair shop when new cork pads are needed.

Tools Needed: Emery paper
                        Leak light (with small bulb)

Procedure:

1. Check the pad for leaks. Using the leak light, check the pad carefully for leaks. Close the key lightly with your finger. If there is any light showing through, there is a leak at that point.

2. Emery the pad. Tear a piece of emery paper to the width of the cork pad. Place the emery paper between the pad and the tone hole with the rough side up against the pad. Close the key lightly and pull the emery paper. Repeat this a few times and then check the pad with the leak light again. This procedure will emery the cork pad so that it will again be level with the tone hole. After the pad is level, tap the key closed a number of times with a firm tap to help set a new seat in the pad.

3. Some oboes now have a rubber type of pad in place of the cork pad. This pad is designed to last longer and generally serves well on the oboe. If you have this type of pad, it will usually be a gray or white colored pad as opposed to the light brown of the cork pad. The above adjustment procedure will not work on this type of pad. If the pad is rough or worn, it should be replaced by a repair technician. If the pad appears smooth, you may be able to correct the leak by heating the key gently to loosen the pad. When it is loose, rotate the pad slightly while holding the key closed lightly over the tone hole. This should level the pad with the tone hole. Hold the key while the shellac sets. If this does not work, the pad will need to be replaced.

HOW TO CLEAN OUT TONE HOLES

All woodwind instruments collect dirt in the tone holes over a period of time. On the oboe, however, this dirt is critical and could plug the tone hole enough to cause playing difficulty, especially in the upper register. It is a good idea to clean the tone holes at least once a year, and to check more often if a problem arises.

Tools Needed: Pipe stem cleaner

Small needle spring

Procedure:

1. On all tone holes that are open, you can see whether there is any dirt in the tone hole. The dirt will build up most in those tone holes where the fingers seal the tone hole rather than a pad. Bend the pipe stem cleaner in half and use to swab out the tone hole.

2. The two octave tone holes near the top of the upper joint often become plugged because they have an octave vent (tube) which extends into the bore of the oboe. As the instrument is swabbed, dirt is often forced into this tube. To clean, remove the two octave keys and find a needle spring which will *slide easily* into the octave tone hole. Push the needle spring up and down a number of times in the tone hole to free it of any dirt. Blow through the octave tone hole, then swab out the upper joint. Repeat the process to be certain that everything is clean.

3. Replace the keys.

HOW TO CLEAN DIRTY AND STICKY PADS

Tools Needed: Cigarette paper (ungummed preferred)

Alcohol

Talcum powder

Emery paper

Procedure: (The first three steps can be used on either skin or cork pads.)

1. Place a sheet of cigarette paper under the sticky pad, close the key firmly and pull the paper out. You will probably notice a dirt mark on the paper when removed. Repeat this process a few times, always using a clean part of the paper until the mark is no longer noticeable on the paper. (If you have difficulty finding ungummed cigarette paper you can use gummed paper but take care not to place the gummed portion under the pad.)

2. If the key is still sticky, try placing a small amount of talcum powder on the paper before placing it under the key and repeat the process as outlined in step 1.

3. Still sticky? Place a little alcohol on the paper and try again. (This should be a last resort on the skin pads as the alcohol will dry out the skin.)

4. If the problem still persists on the cork pad, place a strip of emery paper which is the width of the cork pad between the tone hole and the pad. Close the key lightly on the emery paper with the rough side against the pad and draw the emery paper out. This will lightly sand off any dirt still on the pad.

5. If the problem still persists with the skin pad you will have no alternative but to remove the key, clean the tone hole with alcohol and pipe stem cleaner, and change the pad. (See How to Install New Skin Oboe Pads, p.75.)

HOW TO REPLACE KEY CORKS

Key corks on the oboe are used to regulate the keys, adjust the key heights or provide for quiet key action. For this reason, the thickness of the cork used on each key is extremely important. I have listed in Chart 8 below the most common size cork which is used on each key of the oboe. In many cases, you will have to use emery paper to reduce the thickness of the cork after applied to achieve the proper key adjustment or height.

As a general rule, key corks are always glued to the key and never to the body of the oboe.

Tools Needed: Single edge razor blade

Emery paper

Materials Needed: Sheet cork as needed in sizes $\frac{1}{64}''$, $\frac{1}{32}''$ and $\frac{1}{16}''$

Contact cork cement

Procedure:

1. Remove any particles of cork which may be left on the key.

2. Select the correct size cork according to Chart 8 (p.80) and spread contact cement on a small section of the cork.

3. Spread the contact cement on the proper spot of the key.

4. Allow the contact cement to dry thoroughly, then place the cork in position. Trim off excess with a razor blade.

5. Check the regulation of the key with the other keys of the oboe and emery the cork if needed. (See How to Regulate the Keys, p.72.)

6. To emery the cork, place a small strip of emery paper between the cork and the oboe body or key with the rough side against the cork (see Illustration 3-5). Pull the emery paper while holding the key and cork against it. This will take off a small amount of cork and shape it to the body or key of the oboe at the same time.

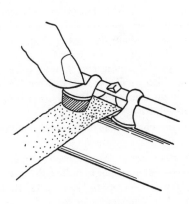

Illustration 3-5

Chart 8
Oboe Key Corks

Refer to Illustration 3-3 for key names and numbers.* Those keys not listed do not require any cork.

Key	Key Name	Location of Cork**	Size of Cork‡
1	Octave key	Top of bar under lower octave key	¹⁄₆₄″
2	Thumb octave lever	Under lever	¹⁄₃₂″
		Under arm of lower oct. key	¹⁄₆₄″
4	D trill lever	Under arm	¹⁄₃₂″
		Under bridge	¹⁄₆₄″
5	D trill bridge lever	Under arm	¹⁄₆₄″
		Under bridge	¹⁄₆₄″
6	D trill key	Under foot	¹⁄₃₂″
7	C♯ trill lever	Under arm	¹⁄₆₄″
		In valley of lever	¹⁄₆₄″
8	C♯ trill key	Under foot	¹⁄₃₂″
9	C key	Under foot	¹⁄₃₂″
11	B key	Under foot	¹⁄₃₂″
12	B♭ key	Under arm (without adjustment screw)	¹⁄₆₄″
14	G♯-A trill lever	Under foot	¹⁄₆₄″
		On arm	¹⁄₆₄″
15	A key	Under foot	¹⁄₃₂″
17	Alt. G♯ lever	Under both arms	¹⁄₆₄″
18	A♭ B♭ trill lever	Under long arm	¹⁄₆₄″
19	G-B♭ rocker	Under bridge portion (both ends)	¹⁄₆₄″
20	G key	Under bridge portion	¹⁄₃₂″
		Under arm (if no adj. screw)	¹⁄₆₄″
22	Fork F key	Under foot	¹⁄₆₄″
23	Side F key	Under lever	¹⁄₁₆″

*There are many keys on the oboe and any diagram of oboe keys is bound to be confusing. I'm sure that the Illustration 3-3 will prove to be confusing at first glance. Hopefully you will be able to identify a key by the picture and then find the cork location through the description in the chart. Many oboes will also have different key systems, so that many of the keys pictured may not be on your oboe. This chart is complete with the maximum number of keys that an oboe will have.

**The term "lever" as used in this chart refers to the portion of the key which is touched by the fingers while playing.

‡In most cases this is the starting size cork to be used. Usually the cork will need to be made thinner by using a piece of emery paper to reduce the size. To determine the correct thickness see the following: How to Regulate the Keys, p.72; How to Check the Intonation of the Oboe, p. 87; The Complete Adjustment, p. 89.

Key	Key Name	Location of Cork**	Size of Cork‡
24	E ring	Under foot	1/32″
25	E key	Under foot	1/32″
27	F rocker	Under both ends	1/64″
28	D key	Under foot	1/64″
		Top of arm extending from lever	1/32″
29	Aux. C lever	Under arm	1/32″
30	C♯ lever	Under arm	1/64″
32	D♯ lever	Under foot	1/64″
33	D♯ key	Under bridge (without adjustment screw)	1/64″
35	C lever	Top of arm on lever	1/64″
36	D♯ -E trill lever	Under end	1/64″
37	C lever foot	Under lever foot	1/16″
38	C key	Under foot	1/64″
39	Bell lever key	Bottom of bridge	1/16″
		Top of other end	1/64″
40	B♭ bell key	Under bridge	1/64″
		Under foot	1/32″

HOW TO RE-CORK THE TENONS

When the tenon cork of the oboe tears, falls off or the fit becomes too loose, it should be replaced. To determine if the fit is too loose, insert the tenon into the receiver. After the sections are together, try to wiggle them. If they do wiggle, then the joint should be re-corked in order to maintain the critical adjustment between the bridge keys. Torn or missing tenon corks should be replaced as they will not only cause a loose fitting joint, but may also have a tendency to leak air, causing playing problems.

If your tenon is beginning to fit too tightly, it is time to clean and regrease it. Wipe the tenon with a clean cloth to remove all dirt and old grease. Then grease lightly with cork grease. (See Maintenance Procedures for the Oboe: Tenons, p. 67.) If, after cleaning, the tenon fit is too loose, it should be replaced.

Tools Needed: Ruler
Small screwdriver
Razor blade
Pliers (or scraper)
Emery paper

Materials Needed: Sheet cork (1/16″ thick)
Contact cork cement
Cork grease

Procedure:

1. Remove any keys which extend over the joint cork. (This will make it easier to do the job.) On the upper oboe joint this would include the G-B♭ rocker (#19), the A♭ -B♭

trill lever (#18) and the G♯ key (#16). On most oboes the first two keys will be relatively easy to remove. The G♯ key, however, may require taking off all of the stack keys. If this is the case, leave the G♯ key on the oboe and work around it.

On the lower oboe joint there usually are no keys extending over the tenon cork.

2. Remove all particles of the old tenon cork. This is most easily done with a regular pair of pliers. Open the pliers to the extended position and grip the tenon cork loosely. Turn the pliers back and forth around the tenon to tear off all the cork on the tenon. Do this thoroughly and carefully to be certain that all cork is gone and all traces of either cement or shellac holding the cork in place is removed. It is essential that the tenon be *completely clean* before proceeding if the job is to be successful. Do not worry if the pliers scrape the wood or plastic of the oboe tenon. This will not hurt the instrument and will be covered with the new cork when the job is completed.

3. Measure the size cork needed for the tenon. Measure the width of the recessed portion of the tenon once it is clean (see Illustration 3-6).

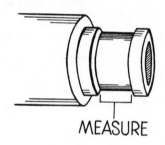

MEASURE

Illustration 3-6

4. Cut the new cork. Cut the new tenon cork from a sheet of ¹⁄₁₆″ sheet cork. This cork is usually available in 4″ x 12″ sheets. The joint cork can be cut across the narrow portion of the sheet so the final piece will be 4″ long and the width you measured in step 3. Cut this piece with a bevel for a better fit. The measurement you took in step 3 will be the bottom of the cork and it should bevel to a larger size at the top (see Illustration 3-7).

|← MEASURED →|
DISTANCE

Illustration 3-7

5. Cut a beveled edge on one end of the cork strip. Be sure that the cut is made so that the bevel starts at the top (which is wider) and thins out toward the bottom of the cork strip (see Illustration 3-8).

BEVEL

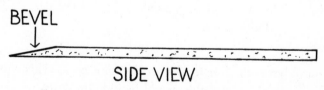

SIDE VIEW

Illustration 3-8

6. Apply the cork cement. The contact cement should completely cover the recessed area of the tenon. Also apply the cement to the entire bottom of the tenon cork *and* to the top portion of the cork which is beveled (see Illustration 3-9).

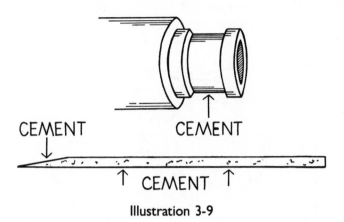

Illustration 3-9

7. Allow the cement to dry thoroughly as indicated in directions on can. Usually about 10 minutes.

8. Glue the new cork on tenon. When the glue is dry, place the bottom of the beveled end of the cork on the tenon. Care should be taken that this is done so the cork is on straight. Once you make contact with the cement, you cannot remove it without pulling the cement off. Work around the tenon carefully pressing the cork to make good contact and avoid any gaps in the cork. When you have completed the circle around the tenon the cork should lap on top of the bevel end already in place (see Illustration 3-10).

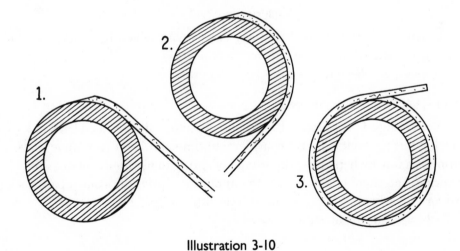

Illustration 3-10

9. Cut the excess length of tenon cork off with a razor blade as shown in Illustration 3-11.

10. Emery the cork joint. Using a strip of emery paper which is the same width as the tenon cork, first emery the overlap in the joint cork so that it is level with the rest of the cork. Then slowly emery around the cork taking care to remove equal portions of the cork from around the circumference of the tenon. Use the strip of emery paper as shown in

Illustration 3-12. *Stop emerying* when the cork tenon just *begins* to fit into the receiver but is still rather difficult to push in. Apply some cork grease to the cork and this will help the tenon fit into the receiver. The cork will compress at this point and give you a good fit. (*NOTE:* if you emery until you get a good fit with the dry cork, the fit will be too loose once the cork grease has been applied and the tenon cork is compressed.)

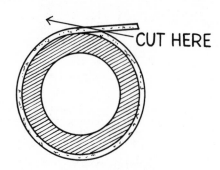

CUT HERE

Illustration 3-11

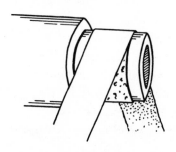

Illustration 3-12

11. Trim with your razor blade any excess cork which has come loose or rough edges which formed while fitting the two sections together. The job is now complete, except to replace any keys which have been removed.

HOW TO REPLACE AN OBOE SPRING

Oboe springs do not usually break, but when they do it is not a hard task to replace them. Doing this yourself can save considerable time and keep your oboe playing rather than sitting in a repair shop. The proper type of spring to use on the oboe is the blue steel needle spring. You should have an assortment of these springs in your repair stock as they are used for all woodwind instruments except flute and piccolo.

Tools Needed: Small round nose pliers
Wire cutter
Small hammer
Alcohol burner or bunsen burner
Steel or metal block
Large blue steel needle spring
Spring hook

Materials Needed: Blue steel needle springs
Procedure:

1. Remove the keys from around the broken spring to make it accessible.

2. Remove the old spring. Usually the spring will break, leaving a small stub in the post. This stub must be pulled out the same end that it went in (see Illustration 3-13). If the flattened end of the spring is extending out from the post, grasp this firmly with the wire cutter and pull out (see Illustration 3-14). If the other end of the spring is extending beyond this post, use the round nose pliers and squeeze the spring out of the post (see Illustration 3-15). If the spring is flush in the post, use a large needle spring as a driver and tap the spring out with a hammer. When doing this be sure to rest the post against some object to prevent the post from bending or breaking (see Illustration 3-16). It is also possible that the old spring has already fallen out of the post.

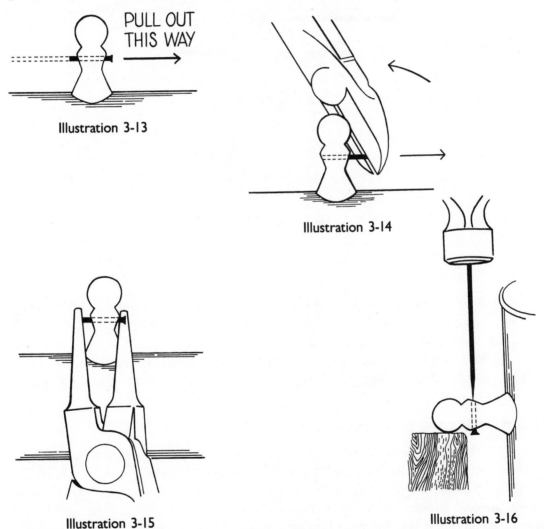

Illustration 3-13

Illustration 3-14

Illustration 3-15

Illustration 3-16

3. When the old spring is removed, find the correct size needle spring which will fit snuggly into the post but will still slide all the way through. Slide the spring into the post so that the correct length will extend beyond the post allowing the point of the spring to catch in the spring hook on the key. Mark the length of spring needed. Remove and cut the spring with a wire cutter to the correct length as marked.

4. Hold the spring with a pair of pliers and heat the butt end of the spring in the flame of the burner until the end starts to turn red. Take care that only the very *end* of the spring turns red, for if too much of the spring is heated it will loose its "spring." When the

end is red, hold the spring against a solid metal block (vice, piece of steel, etc.) and with the small hammer tap the end to flatten slightly. Allow to cool.

5. Insert the spring into the post with the pointed end going in first. Squeeze the flat end into the post with your round nose pliers (see Illustration 3-17). This should hold the spring in place. If the spring does not go in far enough, this means you have flattened the end too much and must try again with another spring. If the spring goes in easily and is not tight, repeat step 4 again to flatten the end a little more.

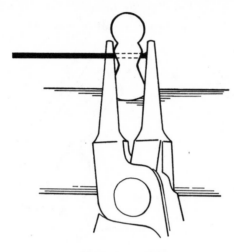

Illustration 3-17

6. Bend the spring slightly in the post. If the key affected is normally in the open position, then the spring should be bent *toward* the tone hole. If the key is usually closed, the spring should be bent *away* from the tone hole.

7. Remount the key and check the spring tension. (See How to Adjust the Spring Tension, below.) Replace any other keys which were removed to make the spring accessible.

HOW TO ADJUST THE SPRING TENSION

On the oboe, all keys that are usually in the open position should have a light resistance which still allows for a quick, snappy key action. Those keys which are normally in a closed position should be set with a heavier resistance. It is important to keep the tension uniform throughout the oboe. That is, all open keys should have the same light tension and all closed keys the same heavier tension. When checking the keys, move only one key at a time. (For example, when checking the tension of the A key (#15) you will need to hold the B♭ key (#12) and the A#-B trill key (#10) closed to get a true feel of the tension of just the A key.)

Tension on a key is increased or decreased by bending the spring gently in one direction or the other. Bending the spring too far will cause it to break, so only do a little at a time. Use a spring hook for this process. Those keys that are normally open need to have the spring bent *toward* the tone hole to *increase* the tension. Those keys that are normally closed need to have the spring bent *away* from the tone hole to *increase* the tension. Be sure to unhook the spring from the key before attempting to bend the spring.

HOW TO CHECK THE INTONATION OF THE OBOE

The intonation of the oboe is determined by a number of factors:

1. The breath support and embouchure of the player.
2. The placement and hardness of the reed used.
3. The oboe keys opening to the proper height. This is important if the oboe is to play in tune with itself. The height of the key openings is measured at the front of the pad and is the distance from the top of the tone hole to the bottom of the pad when the key is fully opened. Chart 9 shows the acceptable open heights to which oboe keys should be set.

If you find an individual key that is not at the correct height, the key has probably lost a cork on the foot or some other point on the key. These individual key heights can usually be corrected by replacing the cork. (See How to Replace Key Corks, p. 79.) Also, whenever you add a cork you will have to re-check the adjustment of the key with any other keys that are activated at the same time. (See How to Regulate the Keys, p. 72.)

If, in checking the oboe heights, you find that all the key heights are incorrect, it will take a complete adjustment to correct the situation. How successful you can be in doing this will depend somewhat on how comfortable you feel with the complete adjustment of the oboe as described later in this chapter. In any case, whenever you alter key heights, be sure to check the regulation of the keys afterwards.

Chart 9
Oboe Key Heights

(Refer to Illustration 3-3 for key numbers and names.)

Key	Number	Height
Octave key	1	$\frac{1}{32}''$
Lower octave key	3	$\frac{1}{32}''$
D trill key	6	$\frac{1}{32}''$
C♯ trill key	8	$\frac{1}{32}''$
C key	9	$\frac{1}{32}''$
A♯-B trill key	10	$\frac{1}{32}''$*
B key	11	$\frac{1}{32}''$
B♭ key	12	$\frac{1}{32}''$*
A key	15	$\frac{1}{32}''$
G♯ key	16	$\frac{1}{16}''$
G key	20	$\frac{1}{16}''$
F♯ key	21	$\frac{1}{16}''$*
Fork F key	22	$\frac{1}{16}''$
Side F key	23	$\frac{1}{16}''$
E key	25	$\frac{1}{16}''$
F. res. key	26	$\frac{1}{16}''$*
D key	28	$\frac{3}{32}''$
C♯ key	31	$\frac{1}{16}''$*
D♯ key	33	$\frac{1}{16}''$*
C key	38	$\frac{3}{32}''$
B♭ bell key	40	$\frac{3}{32}''$*

*The heights of these keys will automatically be correct if the oboe is regulated correctly. Only those keys *not marked* (*) will need to be measured. Only those keys listed above have pads which seal the tone holes.

HOW TO CORRECT NON-FUNCTIONING KEYS

A non-functioning key can be defined as any key on the oboe which is not operating properly. This includes keys that won't go down or won't go up. For the most part, when this occurs you are going to have to send the instrument to the repair shop to be corrected. It usually will take a skilled repair technician to solve and correct the problem. There are, however, a number of things which you can check before sending the oboe in to be repaired. These are common problems which cause key malfunctions that can easily be corrected by you. Check this first and you might save time and money.

1. **Check the spring**—Is it broken off? Perhaps the spring is just unhooked from the key. If the spring appears O.K. push against it with your spring hook. If there is no tension in the spring, it is broken and will need to be replaced. (See How to Replace an Oboe Spring, p. 84.)

2. **Check the pivot screws**—These screws, which are located at the ends of the keys, go through the post and hold the key in place. It is possible that the screw could be tightened down too far and might be binding the key action. On the other hand, if the pivot screw is not tight enough, it will allow extra motion in the keys. This will cause the key adjustment to be inaccurate and the pads to seat poorly over the tone holes. Use a small screwdriver and move the pivot screw both ways to see if the action of the key improves.

3. **Check the key**—If the key does not close all the way, use your leak light to see if the pad is still level on the tone hole. If not, your key may have been bent. You will then need to bend the key back to a level position and probably replace the pad. (See How to Install New Skin Oboe Pads, p. 75.) Another possibility, if you find that the key is not closing over the tone hole, is that an adjustment screw has become out of adjustment and is holding the key open. Check all adjustment screws which might affect the key in question.

HOW TO REMOVE A STUCK OBOE SWAB

Because the bore of the oboe is tapered, and gets quite narrow at the top of the upper joint, it is not uncommon to occasionally get a swab stuck in the joint.

The most important thing to remember if the swab gets stuck is *not* to try to force it through the reed receiver at the top of the joint or through the tone holes. The swab will have to be removed from the bottom end of the joint.

Tools Needed: Crochet hook, Long thin screwdriver or Piece of firm bent wire.
Procedure:

1. Push one of the recommended tools up into the swab and turn. The swab will eventually begin to wrap around the sharp edge of the tool. As it wraps around, the swab will tighten up around the tool and become loose in the bore. It can then be pulled out.

2. It is also possible that the swab will tear apart which will also aid in removing the swab. Pull out the torn pieces as they become loose and repeat the process. It is likely that this procedure will need to be repeated several times until the swab is removed.

THE COMPLETE ADJUSTMENT—
HOW TO MAKE THE ADJUSTMENTS NECESSARY FOR
PROPER INSTRUMENT PERFORMANCE

The complete adjustment of an oboe is a very difficult process. Most oboes will have up to 40 keys, and the relationship of these keys to each other is very complex. I recommend that any extensive adjustments to the oboe be done by a competent repair technician. Some of you will be able to follow the process outlined below and achieve satisfactory results; however, be prepared for problems. Be sure to read completely through the procedure before beginning.

As you refer to Illustration 3-3 for key names and numbers, you will find the picture confusing. When there are 40 keys on an instrument it is difficult to diagram each key. By carefully examining the picture and your oboe I am confident that you will be able to locate the keys you wish to refer to. Remember also that all oboes do not employ the same system of keys. The oboe shown in Illustration 3-3 is probably the most common and has the most keys. Your oboe could have fewer keys than are shown here.

Tools Needed: Leak light (with small bulb)
Small screwdriver
Spring hook
Alcohol burner or bunsen burner
Ruler
Emery paper
Materials Needed: Double skin clarinet pads
Sheet cork in sizes 1/64″, 1/32″
and 1/16″
Stick shellac
Contact cork cement

Procedure: (Refer to Illustration 3-3 for key names and numbers.)

1. Using a leak light, check all pads to be certain that they have a level seat which will form a tight seal with the tone hole. You can check each pad as you adjust it in the procedure to follow, or check them all at once before you continue with step 2. If any of the skin pads are uneven, loose or torn, they will have to be replaced before you can continue with this adjustment. (See How to Install New Skin Oboe Pads, p. 75.) If the cork pads are not sealing the tone hole properly, they should be leveled before continuing. (See How to Level the Cork Oboe Pad, p. 77.) If the cork pad cannot be made to seat properly on the tone hole after leveling, send the oboe to the repair shop to have the cork pad replaced. At the same time you might just as well have the repair technician adjust the oboe for you.

2. Starting with the upper joint, check the open height of the D trill key (#6) and the C♯ trill key (#8). When all the way open, they should measure 1/32″ from the pad to the tone hole. To adjust this height, you must adjust the thickness of the cork on the foot of each key. If the cork needs to be replaced, cement a piece of 1/32″ cork in place and then emery lightly until the correct open height is achieved.

3. Check the C♯ trill lever (#7). This key should have a *slight* amount of play before activating the C♯ trill key. If there is too much play, more cork must be added to the C♯ trill lever (#7), if there is no play, some cork must be made thinner. There should be a piece of cork on both the arm which extends over the C♯ trill key (#8) and on the portion of the lever which extends under the D trill bridge lever (#5) and the A♭-B♭ trill lever (#18).

4. Press the octave key (#1). The pad should open to a height of ⅟₃₂″. If it does not, you adjust the height to which it opens at the back of the lower octave key (#3) which extends over the octave key (#1). On some oboes the lower octave key (#3) will have an adjustment screw at this point. Simply turn this screw until the octave key (#1) opens to a height of ⅟₃₂″. If your oboe does not have the adjustment screw, you must regulate this height by the thickness of the cork at this point on the lower octave key (#3).

5. Press the thumb octave lever (#2). This will open the lower octave key (#3) and should allow the back of the lower octave key to touch the arm of the octave key (#1) at the same time that the thumb lever touches the body of the oboe. If they do not, the adjustment is made by the thickness of the cork on the bottom of the thumb octave lever (#2). Less cork will allow the lower octave key (#3) to open further. More cork will allow the thumb lever to stop moving sooner.

6. Check the height of the C key (#9). It should open to a distance of ⅟₃₂″. This height is adjusted by the thickness of the cork on the foot of this key. If the corks needs to be replaced, start by cementing a piece of ⅟₃₂″ cork to the key, then use emery paper to reduce the cork thickness if necessary until the proper height of the C key is achieved.

7. Check the height of the B key (#11). It should open to a distance of ⅟₃₂″. This height is adjusted by the thickness of the cork on the foot of this key. If the cork needs to be replaced, start by cementing a piece of ⅟₃₂″ cork to the key foot, then use emery paper to reduce the cork thickness if necessary until the proper open height of the B key is achieved.

8. When the B key (#11) is open to a height of ⅟₃₂″, the lever attached to the key should just be touching the arm of the A♭-B♭ trill lever (#18), and the foot of the B key should be touching the body of the oboe. If it is not, check the lever to be certain that it has cork under the arm which reaches out over the B key. Also check the Alt. G♯ lever (#17) to be certain that it has cork under both ends of the arm. All cork should be ⅟₆₄″ thick. Replace any cork which is missing. If the A♭-B♭ trill lever (#18) now holds the B key (#11) down somewhat, you must emery the cork which is on the Alt. G♯ lever (#17) thinner (emery both pieces equally) until the A♭-B♭ trill lever (#18) allows the B key (#11) to open to the proper height. If, for some reason, the A♭-B♭ trill lever (#18) has play in it before touching the B key, then extra cork must be added under the arms of the Alt. G♯ lever (#17).

9. Check the height of the A key (#15). It should open to a distance of ⅟₃₂″. This height is adjusted by the thickness of the cork on the foot of this key. If the cork needs to be replaced, start by cementing a piece of ⅟₃₂″ cork to the key foot, then use emery paper to reduce the cork thickness if necessary until the proper open height of the A key is achieved.

10. Lift the bottom of the G-B♭ rocker (#19) up as far as possible. This will allow the A♯-B trill key (#10) and B♭ key (#12) to open up. A small wedge of cork will work quite neatly to hold the rocker in this position while the following checks are made.

11. Press the B♭ key (#12). This should close at the same time as the A♯-B trill key (#10). Check this with a leak light. If they do not close together the adjustment is made with the screw located on the arm of the A♯-B trill key which extends over the arm of the B♭ key. Tightening the screw will cause the A♯-B trill key to close sooner.

12. Press on the B key (#11). This should close the A♯-B trill key (#10) at the same time. Check this with a leak light. If they do not close together, the adjustment is made with the screw located on the arm of the A♯-B trill key which extends over the foot of the B key. Tightening this screw will cause the A♯-B trill key to close sooner.

13. Press on the A key (#15). This should close the A♯-B trill key (#10) and the B♭ key (#12) at the same time. Check this with a leak light. If these three keys do not close together, the adjustment is made by the screw on the arm of the B♭ key (#12) which extends over the foot of the A key (#15). Tightening this screw will cause the A♯-B trill key and B♭ key to close sooner. Remember that the A♯-B trill key and the B♭ key have been adjusted to close together in step 11 above. You may now remove the wedge holding the G-B♭ rocker (#19).

14. The height of the G♯ key (#16) should be correct providing you took all play from the A♭-B♭ trill lever (#18) as described in step 8 above. This ends the adjustments needed on the upper joint. Continue in step 15 below with the lower joint adjustments.

15. Check the height of the side F key (#23). It should open to a distance of 1/16″. This height is adjusted by the thickness of the cork under the lever of this key. If the cork needs to be replaced, cement a piece of 1/16″ cork under this lever, then use a piece of emery paper to reduce the thickness of the cork if necessary until the proper open key height is achieved.

16. Check the height of the G key (#20). This key should open to a distance of 1/16″. This height is adjusted by the thickness of the cork located under the foot of this key. If the cork needs to be replaced, cement a piece of 1/16″ cork under the foot, then use a piece of emery paper to reduce the thickness of the cork if necessary until the proper open key height is achieved.

17. Check the height of the Fork F key (#22). It should open to a distance of 1/16″. This height adjustment is made by the thickness of the cork located under the foot of the key. If the cork needs to be replaced, cement a piece of 1/32″ cork under the foot, then use a piece of emery paper to reduce the thickness of the cork if necessary until the proper open key height is achieved.

If the Fork F key will not open far enough to allow the foot to touch the body of the oboe, check the point where the Fork F arm extends under the D key (#28). The adjustment screw at this point may need to be loosened to allow the Fork F key to open all the way. If there is no screw at this point, you will need to reduce the thickness of the cork to allow the Fork F to open.

18. Check the height of the E key (#25) or the E ring (#24). Your oboe will have one of these keys but not both. They should open to a distance of 1/16″. This height adjustment is made by the thickness of the cork located under the foot of the key. If the cork needs to be replaced, cement a piece of 1/32″ cork under the foot, then use a piece of emery paper to reduce the thickness of the cork if necessary until the proper open key height is achieved.

19. Press the Fork F key (#22). This should close the F♯ key (#21) at the same time. If it does not, the adjustment is made with the screw located on the arm of the F♯ key where it extends over the foot of the Fork F key. Tightening the screw will cause the F♯ key to close sooner. If there is no screw at this point, then the adjustment must be made by adding or subtracting cork at the point of contact between these two keys.

20. Press the E key (#25) or the E ring (#24). The E key should close at the same time as the F♯ key (#21). The E ring should close the F♯ key. If they do not, the adjustment is made with the screw which is located on the arm of the F♯ key where it extends over the foot of the E key or ring. Tightening the screw will cause the F♯ key to close sooner. If there is no screw at this point, then the adjustment must be made by adding or subtracting cork at the point of contact between these two keys.

21. Press the D key (#28). This should close the D key at the same time that it closes the Fork F key (#22). If the Fork F does not close, then the adjustment must be made with the screw which is located alongside the lever of the D key extending over the arm of the Fork F key. Tightening the screw will cause the Fork F to close sooner. If the D key (#28) does not close, loosen the screw. If this does not correct the problem, loosen the screw which is located on the D♯ key (#33) where it extends over the foot of the D key, then check for adjustment with the Fork F again. If there isn't any screw at this point, the adjustment must be made by regulating the thickness of the cork at the point where these two keys make contact.

22. After the above regulation is complete, there should be no play in the D key, i.e., the key should not move before activating the Fork F key (#22). If there is play you must add cork to the foot of the D key (#28).

23. Check the arm of the D key (#28) which extends under the C♯ lever (#30) which is located next to the D♯ lever (#32). This arm should be in contact with the C♯ lever. If it is not, add cork to the arm until it makes contact. If there is too much cork at this point, it will not allow the Fork F (#22) to open all the way.

24. Press the D♯ lever (#32). This should open the D♯ key (#33). There should be no play in this lever, i.e., no motion before it activates the D♯ key. If there is play, you will need to add cork to the foot of the D♯ lever. If there is too much cork, the D♯ key (#33) will not close and seal the tone hole. If you need to replace this cork, cement a piece of $\frac{1}{32}$" cork to the foot of the D♯ lever (#32) and emery for a correct fit. (*Note:* Be certain that there is a piece of $\frac{1}{64}$" cork on the *top* of this foot before adjusting as described.)

25. Check the B♭-D♯ double lever (#34). There should not be any play in this lever. At the other end of the lever you will find two arms, each of which will have an adjustment screw. Adjust the screws so that one is in contact with the spring located under the D♯ key (#33) and the other is in contact with the bell key lever (#39). This should eliminate the play in the lever.

26. Check the height of the C key (#38). This key should open to a distance of $\frac{3}{32}$". The height of the key is regulated by the thickness of the cork under the foot of the C lever (#37). Before regulating the thickness of this cork, check to be certain that there is a piece of $\frac{1}{64}$" cork under the arm of the C key (#38) where it extends over the foot of the C lever foot (#37).

27. Check the arm which extends from the C lever (#35) under the B♭ lever (#34). This arm should be in contact with the B♭ lever. If not, add cork until contact is made. If

there is too much cork at this point, the foot of the C lever (#37) will not be able to rest against the body of the oboe, thus holding the C key (#38) somewhat closed.

28. Attach the bell to the lower joint and do the following adjustment of the bell key. (If your oboe does not have a bell key, proceed to step 31 below.) Line up the bridge keys of the B♭ bell key (#40) and the bell key lever (#39).

29. Press the B♭ lever of the B♭-D♯ double lever (#34). This should close both the B♭ bell key (#40) and the C key (#38) at the same time. If they do not close together, the adjustment is made by the thickness of the cork under the foot of the B♭ bell key where it extends over the bell key lever (#39). Adding more cork to this bridge will cause the B♭ bell key to close sooner.

30. Press again on the B♭ lever of the B♭-D♯ double lever (#34). Both the B♭ bell key (#40) and the C key (#38) should *start* moving at the same time. If they do not, the adjustment is made in the thickness of the cork located *under* the bridge of the bell key lever (#39). Adding cork to this point will cause the C key to move before the B♭ bell key.

31. Assemble the upper and lower joints of the oboe, being certain to line up the bridge keys properly. Check to see that there is a piece of ¹⁄₆₄″ cork located under the bridge key of the G-B♭ rocker (#19) and the D trill bridge lever (#5).

32. Press down on the D trill lever (#4) which is located on the lower joint. This lever should activate the D trill key (#6) so that it opens all the way. If not, there may be a cork missing in the mechanism. Remember, there should always be a piece of ¹⁄₆₄″ cork located at any point where two keys make contact. The D trill lever (#4) *should* have a small amount of motion in it before it makes contact with the D trill bridge lever (#5). If it does not have any play, you will have to reduce the thickness of the cork located under the foot of the D trill lever (#4). If there is too much play, add some cork at this point.

33. Press lightly on the G key (#20). There should be a small amount of motion in this key before it makes contact with the G-B♭ rocker (#19). If there is no motion, you must add cork to the arm of the B♭ key (#12) which extends over the G-B♭ rocker (#19) until there is a small amount of play between the G key (#20) and the G-B♭ rocker.

34. Press the G key (#20) all the way down. This key should seal the tone hole at the same time that the arm extending over the G♯ key (#16) contacts that key. If they do not, there is a screw in the arm of the G key which should be adjusted so that the contact is correct. If your oboe does not have a screw at this point, the adjustment is made by adding or subtracting cork. If the adjustment is off more than can be corrected with the adjustment screw, you will have to bend the arm of the G key (#20) *slightly*, then adjust with the screw.

35. This should complete the adjustment of the oboe. Play test the instrument to check. Play all the way down to the bottom note of the instrument's range. Any notes which seem to blow harder or sound stuffy could still be out of adjustment.

REPAIRS TO BE SENT TO THE REPAIR SHOP

As I have mentioned throughout this chapter, the oboe is an extremely difficult instrument on which to do any type of work. I have found that experience is essential to be able to successfully repair an oboe. In addition, there are some repairs which will require specialized tools, while others require special skills that take time to develop. For this reason I would suspect that most of you will be sending your oboes to the repair shop for repairs. You can best determine what repairs you feel capable of doing as you read through this chapter. A good rule to follow is: "When in doubt, send it out."

Below I have outlined some of the more common oboe repairs that *will* need to be done at a repair shop. It is hoped that this will give you a better understanding of the repair procedures.

REPAIRING CRACKS IN THE BODY

Only wood oboes will have the potential for cracking. Following a careful maintenance plan as outlined in the beginning of this chapter will help greatly to reduce the possibility of cracking. If the oboe should crack, it is best to have it repaired as soon as possible before the crack increases. The larger the crack, the more difficult and expensive the repair. If the crack becomes too large, the joint will need to be replaced. A quick visual check each month can reveal developing cracks before they become serious. Cracks always develop along the grain of the wood, so look for them to run up and down along the length of the joint. Before sending in for repair, *mark the crack with a pencil* to help the repair technician find it. Because of temperature changes, cracks will sometimes close up before the repair technician has a chance to work on it.

The most common method of repairing a crack is to pin it. The repair technician will determine the length of the crack by scratching it open further with a fine pick. This also gives a good base for the filler which is added later. To pin the crack, the repair technician starts by drilling a hole through the body (but not the bore) of the oboe. The hole is drilled perpendicular to the crack at an interval of about one per inch for the length of the crack. A piece of threaded rod, which is slightly larger than the hole is then heated at the tip. When the rod is red hot, it is screwed into the hole. When cool, this threaded rod will hold the sections together and prevent the crack from spreading any further. The pins *do not* pull the sections of the crack back together.

After the pins are in place, a filler is used (usually a hard epoxy) to fill the crack, and the holes left from the pins. If the crack runs through the tone hole, it must be filled carefully so that the tone hole will not leak when the job is complete. After the epoxy is dry, it is filed and sanded smooth and then a black die is used to color the epoxy to match the body of the oboe. If pinned correctly, the oboe should not crack further and the epoxy filler will seal the crack.

REPAIRING BROKEN TENONS

A broken tenon can occur on either a wood or plastic oboe. This is not a common occurence, but when it does happen it is almost always on the tenon of the upper joint. This is because the break usually occurs when assembling or disassembling the sections. If the player does not insert the sections carefully, with the slight twisting action, there will be a tendency to pull or push the sections at an angle. When this angle becomes great enough the tenon will break. Tenons will also break if the section of the oboe is dropped.

A broken tenon is not the end of your oboe. It can be replaced and, although the job will be expensive, it should be less than the cost of buying a new section. When repaired correctly, the replacement tenon should be as strong as the original.

The repair technician will first cut off the remains of the old tenon. He then drills up into the body of the oboe with a special cutting tool which enlarged the bore diameter about ⅜″ to ¼″. The hole is drilled up about ½″ to ¾″ into the body. A tenon plug, which has already been cut so that it will fit into the receiver of the other section, is then inserted into this new hole and epoxied in place. After the epoxy has set, the new plug will be bonded firmly to the body of the oboe. It is then necessary to redrill any tone holes and post holes which have been blocked by the tenon plug. Also, the repair technician will have to ream out the bore of the plug so that it matches that of the oboe body. The tenon is then corked and fitted to the receiver.

The procedure is the same for replacing either tenon of the oboe. Only the size of the tenon plug and the cutting tools have to be different to accomodate the difference in bore size between the two tenons.

REPAIRING BROKEN KEYS

If an oboe key actually breaks in half, this can be repaired in the shop. Be certain that you save the pieces and send them along with the entire oboe. The repair technician will braze the two pieces together with silver solder. When done correctly, this will bond the two sections of the key together as securely as the original piece. Also, the mend will not be too noticeable and should function like the original key. It is important to send the entire instrument in so the repair technician can be certain that the key is brazed at the correct angle and re-adjusted to the instrument.

If you should loose one of the broken pieces, most repair shops will be able to either order a new key, or fashion a key from an old part off a discarded oboe. In either case, this is usually more expensive and time consuming.

TIGHTENING LOOSE KEYS

If your oboe had a lot of "play" in the keys (that is, they move sideways on the rod or between the pivot screws) you may have a problem getting the pads to always close on the seat. This "play" is usually found on older oboes, as the metal of the key will eventually wear off through use. If the key is mounted on a *rod* and slides sideways along the rod, then there is too much room between the posts. The repair technician will have to stretch the hinge tube of the key to fill the gap (a process called "swedging").

It is also possible that the diameter of the key's hinge tube has enlarged through wear and is now bigger than the diameter of the pivot rod. In this case, the repair technician will squeeze the hinge tube slightly to tighten, but not so much as to bind the key action.

If the loose key is held in place with pivot screws, the repair technician will check to see if the screws have backed out or are worn. Sometimes, on older oboes, the screws will be worn down on the ends and cannot hold the key firmly in place. In this case the screw can be replaced with a new screw for the same brand oboe. It is also possible that the hole in the post will be worn causing the screw to be loose. It will then be necessary to re-fit the post with a different style pivot screw that can be adapted to the oboe.

TIGHTENING LOOSE POSTS

On the wood oboe it is possible for the post to loosen up in the body. When this happens the post will begin to turn and the pivot screws will no longer be aligned with the key. This will usually cause the key to bind. Any time there is a loose post, it should be tightened.

There are two ways to correct this problem. One is to epoxy the loose post in place. This will hold the post permanently in place but has the disadvantage of making it impossible to remove the post should this ever become necessary.

Another, more common correction, is to use a post locking screw. With a special drill the repair technician will drill a small hole alongside the base of the post into the body of the oboe. This drill will also countersink a small bevel into the edge of the post base at the same time. The repair technician then screws a small flat head screw into the hole. As the screw is tightened down, the head goes into the countersunk portion in the post and prevents the post from turning. With this method, the post locking screw can always be removed if it becomes necessary to remove the post for some future repair.

REPLATING THE KEYS—THE COMPLETE OVERHAUL

Most oboe keys are silver plated, and in time this plating can begin to wear off. Although this in no way affects the playability of the oboe, it does tend to give it a shabby appearance. The keys can be replated to look like new, but this procedure should only be done as a part of a complete overhaul of the oboe. In order to replate the keys, it is obviously necessary to remove all the pads and corks. Also, all the posts will have to be removed as they cannot be plated while on the instrument.

Not all repair shops can do replating, although most of them have another company to whom they send this type of work. Replating any type of instrument or key requires having the chemicals necessary to strip off the old finish and the equipment for electroplating. The oboe keys and posts are all removed and the old finish removed. All parts are then buffed to a high gloss smoothness and then replated using an electroplating process. When the plating is complete, the oboe is re-assembled using all new pads and corks. Often excess plating must be removed from the keys to insure a proper fit between the posts.

When this job is complete your oboe will have a "like new" appearance and playability.

THE COMPLETE REPAD

Even though you may do a good job of maintaining the playing condition of the oboes in your band, there will come a time when most of the pads are starting to tear and dry out. Many of the corks will be depressed, dried out or missing altogether. This is the time to consider having the oboe completely repadded. A complete repad in most shops will consist of replacing all the old pads and corks with new, installing new tenon corks, and cleaning the body of the oboe. Loose keys are usually tightened as a part of this job. When re-assembled, all the pads are seated and the springs adjusted to a good action. In short, the instrument should *play* like a new oboe.

4

The Clarinet Family

HOW TO TAKE CARE OF YOUR CLARINET

Taking proper care of the instrument should be the first, and most important, step in your clarinet maintenance plan. By following the suggestions given here, you will avoid many of the problems which can cause the clarinet to malfunction or not play properly. These suggestions apply to all types of clarinets. Although much of this might be a review for you, it would be a good idea to share this information with your students as well. When the student understands the reasons for the maintenance procedures outlined below, there is a better chance that he or she will follow them. This information can help each student maintain an instrument in good playing condition. This will improve their playing ability and at the same time reduce repair costs to the student and the school.

ASSEMBLE THE CLARINET CAREFULLY

The assembling of the clarinet is a relatively simple matter. There are many pieces involved but not difficult to assemble. The clarinet consists of upper joint, lower joint, barrel or neck, mouthpiece and bell. There is one bridge key located between the upper and lower joints, and that is the only place that you must be concerned about alignment.

Before assembling, it is extremely important to grease the tenon corks so that they work freely. If the corks are dry or fit tightly, this can cause difficulty in assembling the sections which, in turn, may cause the player to bend the keys. Also, the excess pressure required, plus any "angling" of the sections when they are being put together or taken apart, may put too much stress on the tenon causing it to break. The cork tenon should go into the receiver smoothly but not be so loose that the joint is likely to come apart or "wiggle" when the sections are together. It is especially important that the barrel or neck section be secure on the upper joint, as this is where most of the tuning is done. If the fit is not good, the player may find that the mouthpiece and barrel together will wiggle as they play.

To assemble, start with the upper and lower joints. (Some alto and bass clarinets have one-piece bodies.) Always hold the two pieces being assembled as close to the point of joining as possible. This will help prevent breaking the tenons. Grasp the upper section near the bottom so that the fingers will press the ring keys. This will "lift" the bridge key which extends over the lower tenon of this section. Grasp the lower joint near the top, but

98

Illustration 4-1: B♭ Clarinet

Courtesy of Artley Inc.; Elkhart, Indiana 46516

Illustration 4-2: Alto Clarinet

Photograph courtesy of The Selmer Co.; Elhart, Indiana

Illustration 4-3: Bass Clarinet

Photograph courtesy of G. Leblanc Corporation

avoid pressing the ring keys to allow the bridge key to remain in the down position. Push the two joints together with a slight twisting action. Line up the bridge key.

To attach the bell, grasp the lower joint near the bottom. On the alto and bass clarinet, grasp the bell so that the key is closed on the bell. This will raise the bridge lever and will prevent it from being bent when being assembled. Push the bell into place with a slight twisting action. Line up the bell so that it will be to the front of the instrument. The bridge key should then extend over the bridge key lever on the lower joint. There isn't any lining up needed for the soprano clarinet bell.

The barrel or neck is attached in a similar manner. Hold the upper joint near the top and assemble with a slight twisting action. The alto and bass clarinet neck should be attached so that the neck is angled toward the back of the instrument. The bass clarinet may have an octave key. Care must be taken to avoid bending this octave key. Some alto and bass clarinets have necks which do not have a cork tenon but rather fit into a receiver that is tightened by a screw.

Remove the reed and ligature from the mouthpiece, then place the mouthpiece into the barrel or neck of the clarinet. If you leave the reed and ligature in place while assembling, they often become loose with the twisting action and can break or bend.

Some bass clarinets have a floor peg to attach or adjust at this time.

STORE THE CLARINET PROPERLY

The storage procedure is the same for any type of clarinet. Careful attention to this kind of detail can prolong the life of your instrument.

The clarinet should always be stored in its case. An instrument left lying about on a chair, table or music stand is easily bumped or dropped on the floor. This can result in serious, expensive repairs.

The clarinet should never be stored near a radiator or heating duct. Excessive heat is one of the contributing factors in causing wood clarinets to crack. Also, as the wood dries out, the posts will loosen on the instrument, causing them to turn and bind the key action. You should also avoid storing the clarinet in extremely cold conditions. Cold weather can cause the pads to loosen and fall out. Once this happens, it will be necessary to replace the pad, as it is almost impossible to re-locate the pad seat. Quick temperature changes can contribute to the wood instrument's cracking, therefore, you should avoid playing on a cold clarinet. Let the instrument warm to room temperature before playing.

Clarinet cases are designed to hold the instrument securely. Most cases will usually have a small storage section to hold reeds, lyres, swabs and sometimes small pieces of music. The case is not designed as a display area for medals and pins. Music and lesson books should only be carried in the case if there is an appropriate place for them. Overpacking of the case can cause excessive pressure on the instrument when the cover is closed and may cause the keys to bend or go out of alignment. Dangling medals can also slide under the keys of the clarinet when the case is closed and bend them when the case is opened.

Always use the mouthpiece cap on the mouthpiece when storing. This cap is designed to protect the mouthpiece in storage. The prevention of a broken or chipped mouthpiece (or reed) is well worth the time needed to put the cap in place when packing up the clarinet.

Check the case to be certain that it is holding the clarinet securely. My experience has shown that many cases do not provide adequate protection. Place the instrument in the case, remove all extra pieces from the storage compartments, close the cover and latch. Shake the case (hold the handle down when shaking). If you hear the clarinet bouncing inside the case, it is not providing the protection that it should and there needs to be more padding added. The quickest and cheapest way to correct this problem is to lay a piece of towel on top of the instrument. This towel will take up the excess room inside the case and will not damage the instrument. If the cover becomes hard to close, you know you have added too much toweling. Shake the case again to check the security of the clarinet in the case. Extra padding in the case can also be added by removing the lining from the cover of the case, adding more padding and then re-gluing. This takes more time, but looks better when completed.

Inspect the case periodically to be certain that it is in good condition. Prompt attention should be given to broken or loose latches, hinges and handles. Storage compartments should also be secure and covers, if any, tight. Be sure that the lining is not loose. Loose lining can easily be corrected with some glue, but broken case hardware will need to be sent to the repair shop for correction.

Clarinet swabs can be stored in the case but they should be kept in the storage compartment of the case and not alongside the instrument. Having a damp cloth in the case alongside the instrument will promote rusting of the rods and pivot screws. Never store the wet swab in a bag, box or tube in which it was purchased. Damp swabs that cannot dry will mildew, causing an unpleasant smell in the case and instrument. The swab should be left loose in the storage compartment thus allowing it to dry adequately.

CLEAN THE CLARINET REGULARLY

The Bore—A few minutes of care in cleaning the clarinet will go a long way in helping maintain the instrument. First, and most important, is to swab out the bore of the instrument after each playing session in order to remove all traces of moisture. Use a good quality swab which is designed for the soprano, alto or bass clarinet. This is not the place to economize; the cheaper and smaller swabs do a less effective job of drying out the bore. It is important to remove *all* moisture. Pull the swab through *every* piece of the clarinet. This includes removing the reed and drying the mouthpiece.

Water that is left in the bore of the wood clarinet will soak into the wood and may cause cracking. In addition, excess moisture left in the bore of any clarinet will seep into the pads causing them to deteriorate much more rapidly than normal.

The Tone Holes—The tone holes which the fingers contact directly will, in time, accumulate a greasy substance around the inside. If this substance is allowed to remain, it reduces the size of the opening thus producing tuning discrepancy and possibly some playing problems. When you notice some dirt in a tone hole, remove it at once by using a piece of pipe stem cleaner. Fold the pipe stem cleaner in half and swab out the tone hole until clean. Those tone holes located under the pads will not accumulate this type of substance.

The Body and Keys—Most clarinet keys are nickel plated and will remain quite clean by simply being wiped with a soft cloth. These keys should never be cleaned with silver polish as the polish will gum up the key mechanisms. After a period of time, the plating will wear off the keys of the clarinet. Not much can be done to improve this short of replating (an expensive job), although a repair shop may be able to buff the keys to provide a temporary improvement in appearance.

In time the outside of the clarinet will begin to accumulate greasy dirt and lint under the keys and rods. This is particularly true of the wood clarinet, as the wood is impregnated with oil by the manufacturer and this tends to attract the dirt. It is a good idea to remove this lint before it gets into the rods and slows the key action. Use a small modeler's paint brush or pipe stem cleaner and reach under the keys to brush away any dirt or lint that has collected. Take care to avoid catching any of the springs; this might change the spring tension and affect the adjustment and function of some keys. This job is easy if done slowly and carefully.

The Mouthpiece—I have found through experience that the most neglected and dirtiest part of the clarinet is the mouthpiece. The reason is that students often do not remove the reed from the mouthpiece and therefore never see how dirty the mouthpiece actually is. The number of mouthpieces that I have seen that are loaded with mineral deposits and scum is unbelievable. It is hard to believe that anyone would want to place such an object in his or her mouth. All students should be taught that the reed is never to be stored on the mouthpiece. When finished playing, the reed should be removed, the mouthpiece swabbed out, and the ligature and cap placed over the mouthpiece.

As a matter of routine, the mouthpiece should be washed out in warm soapy water about once a week, using a reed mouthpiece brush to clean it thoroughly. Swabbing and washing will keep the mouthpiece clean indefinitely.

If you have some mouthpieces that are already crusted with minerals, washing will not remove this material. In order to clean these mouthpieces see How to Clean the Clarinet Mouthpiece, p. 135.

MAINTENANCE PROCEDURES FOR THE CLARINET

Tenons—A new tenon cork is fitted tightly to the receiver and a light coating of cork grease applied to ease the assembling of the sections. This cork grease attracts dirt which begins to build up on the tenon cork, thus making the tenon fit tighter. Usually the player will then add more cork grease. This cycle continues with layers of grease and dirt slowly building up on the tenon cork.

The tenon corks of all clarinets should be kept clean to insure a good fit. Once a month use a clean cloth and wipe each tenon cork until it is free from all grease and dirt. After it is completely clean and dry, apply a *small* amount of cork grease. By following this procedure you will not only lengthen the life of the tenon cork, but will also avoid having excessive grease and dirt on the tenon and instrument.

As the tenon cork gets older, it will begin to dry out and shrink (cork grease helps slow down this process). When the cork is too small for the receiver a loose fit results; the two sections will "wiggle" when they are together. When this happens it is time to replace the tenon cork (See How to Re-Cork a Tenon, p. 124). In an emergency you can expand the cork *temporarily* by holding it over some heat. Use a match, alcohol lamp or bunsen burner and rotate the tenon over the heat. Care should be taken to avoid getting it too hot as the cork will burn quite easily. This is not a permanent solution because the cork will quickly compress again after it is used.

Some alto and bass clarinets have a clamp around the center joint which is tightened with a small bolt. This joint should be loosened and taken apart on occasion. Some clarinets have a cork tenon at this joint while others do not. Grease this tenon cork and lightly and replace when it becomes loose.

Some alto and bass clarinets have a metal tenon which is tightened down in the receiver by means of a screw. These need to be cleaned just like the flute head joint. Dirt will accumulate on the tenon and can be kept clean by using a piece of paraffin (canning wax) which is available at any grocery store. Rub the paraffin on the tenon, then insert into the receiver and twist back and forth. When you take it apart you will notice that a black film has formed. Wipe this off with a dry cloth and repeat the process until no more film appears. Wipe both the tenon and receiver dry each time. This joint should have no lubrication as then the screw will not be able to hold the neck firmly in place.

Oiling The Bore—There is a lot of saliva which accumulates in the bore of any clarinet. To prevent this moisture from soaking into the wood clarinet, the manufacturer has impregnated the instrument with oil. It is up to you to maintain this oil or subject the instrument to possible cracking. This only needs to be done to wood clarinets. Most instrument manufacturers recommend that a new instrument should be oiled about once a month for the first six months and then about twice a year. Use a commercial bore oil which is available from your music dealer. This oil will cause the skin or leather pads to dry out quite rapidly, so protect the pads by placing a thick piece of absorbent paper between each pad and tone hole. Any excess oil will then soak into the paper rather than the pad.

After the pads are protected, place some oil on an old swab (the Chamois type works best) that you will use only for oiling. Try not to saturate the swab because too much oil in the bore will cause problems. Pull this swab through each section of the instrument until all sections have a light coating of oil in the bore. (You can look into the clarinet to see if the oil has coated the bore.) Let the clarinet sit overnight, then swab out again with a clean swab to remove any excess oil. Remove the pad protectors. If you have used too much oil you will find that the oil has soaked the pad protectors and may also have soaked the pads. It is better to start with too little oil the first few times you do this rather than too much and ruin the pads.

Sticky Pads—Sticky pads are caused by the accumulation of dirt on the pad seat or tone hole. The student should avoid chewing gum, eating candy or drinking "pop" immediately before or while playing. All these items increase the amount of sugar in the saliva, some of which will travel into the bore and accumulate on the pads. Those pads most frequently affected are the ones near the top of the instrument which collect the most moisture while playing. This sticky substance on the pad then attracts dirt, causing the stickiness. In addition, the excess sugar in the saliva will also accumulate in the clarinet reed, slowing down its vibrating ability.

Pads saturated with bore oil will also be sticky. If you have recently oiled the bore, you may have used an excessive amount of oil or did not protect the pads properly. If the pads do become oil soaked, they will need to be replaced. (See How to Install New Skin Pads, p.117 or How to Install New Leather Pads, p.118.)

The stickiness in the pads usually begins with an annoying "clicking" sound as the pad opens from the tone hole. As the problem gets worse, the keys will not open promptly and the key action will be slowed down. The problem should be corrected as soon as noticed, as this is when it is easiest to correct. (See How to Clean Dirty and Sticky Pads, p. 120.) If possible, try to determine the source of the sticky pads to avoid future problems.

Oiling the Keys—The keys of the clarinet should be oiled about once a month to keep them working freely and to prevent the screws and rods from becoming rusted. If the rods and screws do rust, the key action can bind up and will require a repair technician to correct. Key oil is available from your music dealer. Using a pin or toothpick, place a small drop of key oil at the end of each key and between all moveable keys which share the same rod. Work the keys to circulate the oil then wipe off any excess oil that may be on the rod. Care should be taken to avoid using too much key oil. If there is oil left on the keys, it will attract dirt which will mix with the oil to slow down the key action.

MONTHLY MAINTENANCE CHECK LIST—CLARINET FAMILY

Chart 10 is a check list that you can use to help maintain the clarinet. By following this chart, you can keep the instrument in good playing shape and be alert to any possible repairs needed before they become too severe. With some training, your students should be able to utilize this check list also.

HOW TO REPAIR THE CLARINET

DIAGNOSING INSTRUMENT MALFUNCTIONS

Before you can begin to repair the clarinet, you need to understand the problems. Listed are some of the common problems that occur with the clarinet, also some possible causes to help you locate the difficulty. Although this list is not complete, it will serve as a guideline in many cases.

1. *Problem:* Clarinet blows hard, will not play all notes clearly.
   Possible Causes: Pads are leaking (look for torn pads, missing pads or those not seating properly). Keys are not regulated properly (particularly check the bridge key and the lever under the low F-C key). Old or broken reed.

2. *Problem.* Clarinet squeaks.
   Possible Causes: Leaking pads, especially in the upper joint. Poor reed.

3. *Problem:* Alto and base clarinets will not play in the upper register.
   Possible Causes: Keys are not regulated properly. Leaks in some pads will allow instrument to play the low register but not the upper register.

4. *Problem:* Clarinet plays the wrong pitch for the fingering used.
   Possible Causes: Springs are unhooked from the keys. Broken springs. Keys may not be regulated correctly (particularly check the bridge key).

5. *Problem:* Clarinet plays out of tune.
   Possible Causes: Key corks may be missing causing incorrect key heights. All key heights may be set incorrectly. Player's embouchure and/or reed may need attention.

6. *Problem:* Keys are not functioning properly.
   Possible Causes: Broken or unhooked springs. Bridge key not correctly aligned.

Bent keys, rods or posts. Pivot screws may be too tight or rusted. Keys and rods may be dirty or rusted.

     7. *Problem:* Parts of the instrument "wiggle," will not stay securely together.
        Possible Cause: Tenon corks are too loose.

(Text continues on p. 110.)

Chart 10
Monthly Maintenance Check List—Clarinet Family

INSPECT THE FOLLOWING:

Clarinet
- _____ Are the tenon corks clean, intact and lightly greased?
- _____ Are any metal tenons clean and fitting properly?
- _____ Do the sections of the clarinet fit securely together?
- _____ Are there any sticky pads?
- _____ Are there any worn pads?
- _____ Are there any loose pads?
- _____ Are the tone holes clean and free from dirt buildup?
- _____ Are all the keys moving freely?
- _____ Are there any cracks in the wood body?
- _____ Are there any missing screws or rods?
- _____ Are the bridge keys between each section working properly?
- _____ Is there a mouthpiece cap?

Case
- _____ Are the latches working properly?
- _____ Are the hinges tight?
- _____ Is the handle secure?
- _____ Is the lining in place?
- _____ Are there any loose objects in the case?
- _____ Are there any pins or medals which will lay against the instrument when the case is closed?
- _____ Is the instrument held tightly in the case when closed?
- _____ Is there a swab with the instrument? Where is it stored when damp?
- _____ Where is the wet reed stored?

DO THE FOLLOWING:

1. Check for leaks (see How to Check for Leaks, p.105).
2. Oil the Bore on wood instruments (twice a year after first six months).
3. Clean dirt and lint from under the keys and rods.
4. Clean dirt from exposed tone holes.
5. Clean the tenon corks and grease lightly.
6. Oil the key rods and screws.
7. Clean the mouthpiece to remove any scale which has built up.

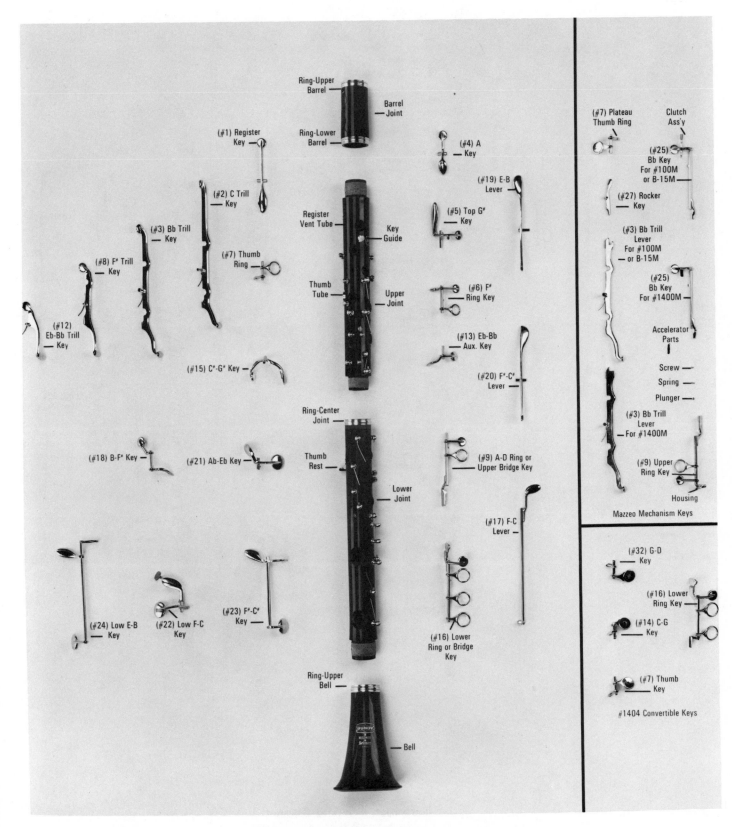

Illustration 4-4: B♭ Clarinet

Photograph courtesy of The Selmer Co.; Elkhart, Indiana

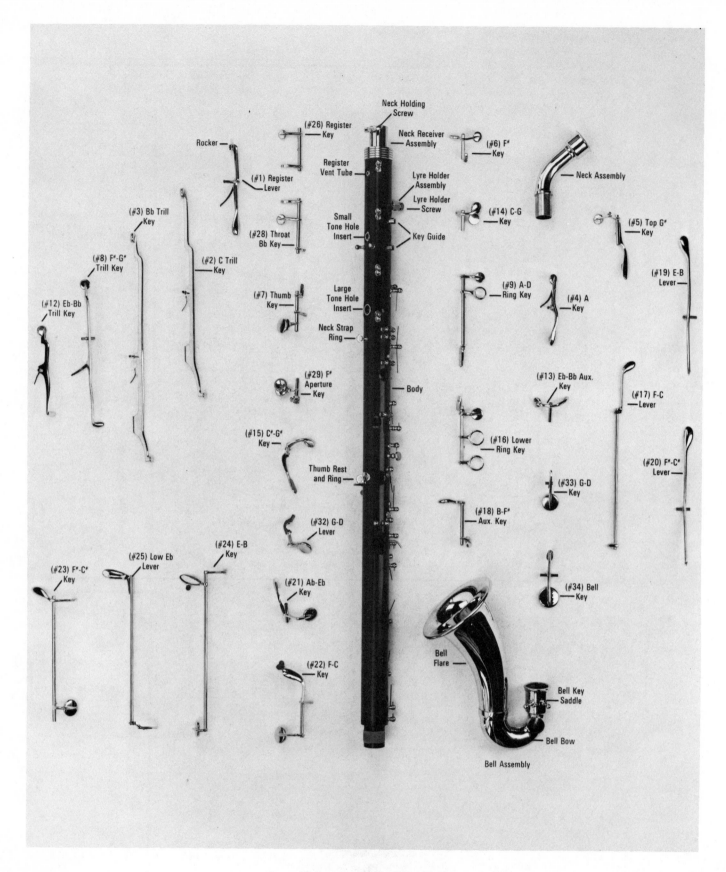

Illustration 4-5: Alto Clarinet

Photograph courtsey of The Selmer Co.; Elkhart, Indiana

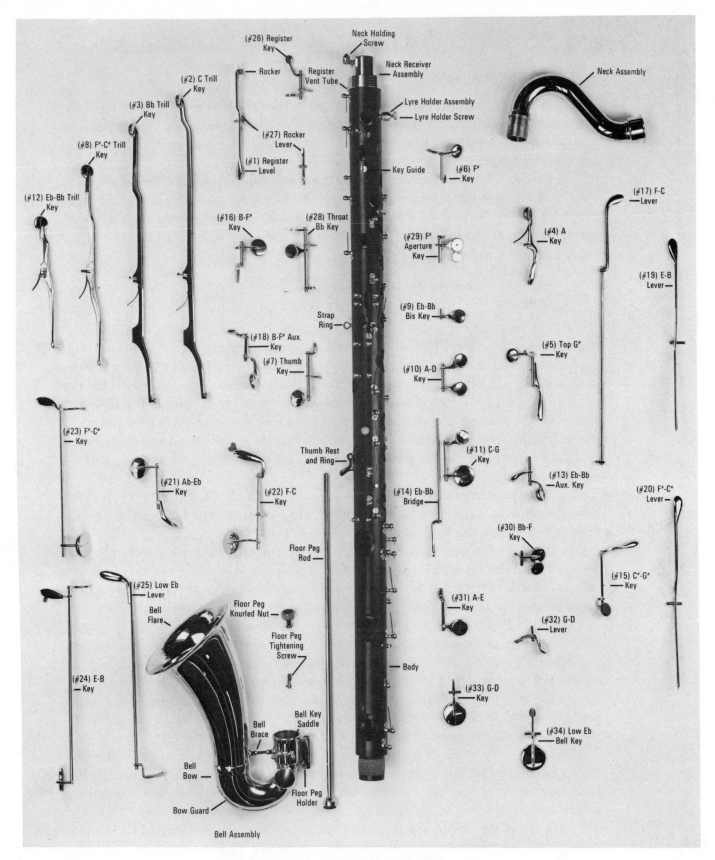

Illustration 4-6: Bass Clarinet

Photograph courtesy of The Selmer Co.; Elkhart, Indiana

109

HOW TO CHECK FOR LEAKS

When your clarinet does not play properly, the first thing to do is check for leaks. Leaks in the clarinet can be the result of a missing, torn or worn pad, bent keys, loose adjustment screws or a crack in the body. Finding the leak is necessary if you wish to correct the problem.

Generally speaking, all the notes on the clarinet should produce the same quality of tone. If you have a note or notes that sound "stuffy" or are hard to blow, you probably have a leak. Also, if the upper or lower register notes do not play correctly, you may have a leak. However, a poor reed can also cause this problem, so check the reed first.

Tools Needed: Leak testing cork
Leak light
Procedure:

1. Check the upper joint. Using an appropriate size leak testing cork, plug the bottom end of this joint. Close all the keys in this joint using the normal finger pressure used when playing the instrument to hold these keys down. Blow gently into the top of the joint. (For alto and bass clarinets that have a neck holding screw in the receiver at the top of the joint, put your mouth around the *outside* of the receiver in order to cover the slot which is in the receiver.) Do not blow too hard as you may blow open some keys that would normally remain closed. If there is a leak, you will hear the air escaping and feel the lack of resistance as you blow. Be very critical when listening for the escaping air as it may not be a very loud sound.

Once you have located the leaking pad or pads, replace the pad or readjust the keys. (See How to Install New Skin Pads, p.117; How to Install New Leather Pads, p.118; or How to Regulate the Keys, p.111, p.112 or p.114.)

2. Check the lower joint. Using an appropriate size leak testing cork, plug the bottom end of the lower joint. Close all the keys of this joint using the normal finger pressure used when playing the instrument. Special care should be taken to use a light finger pressure on the low E♭ key. Place your mouth around the receiver and blow gently into the joint. Follow the same procedures as described in step 1 above.

3. To check the one piece clarinet body (as on some alto and bass clarinets) the procedure is essentially the same, except that the entire instrument must be checked at once. Find the appropriate size leak testing cork and place in the bottom of the section. Blow into the top of the section as described in step 1 above, while using a light finger pressure to hold all of the keys closed. Because both hands will be used while checking, you may need the assistance of somebody else to help you locate the leak.

4. Check the bell. The alto and bass clarinet will have a key on the bell which should be checked for leaks. The best way to do this is to use a leak light. Close the key *lightly* and, with the leak light inside, check all around the pad to be certain that there is no gap in the seal with the tone hole.

5. Check the bridge key alignment. Once you have checked each of the clarinet joints individually, assemble the clarinet to be certain that a leak is not being created by the faulty alignment of the bridge keys. Assemble the upper and lower joint. There is one bridge key that spans this joint and it should line up. Press the B♭/F key or ring key with the first finger on the lower joint. This should close at the same time as the A-D Ring key

(#9) on the soprano and alto clarinet or the E♭-B♭ Bis key (#9) on the bass clarinet (see Illustrations 4-4, 4-5, or 4-6).

On the alto and bass clarinet, pressing the low E-B lever should activate the bell key. This key should close at the same time as the Low F-C key (#22). On some alto and bass clarinets, there is an extra key on the instrument which plays a low E♭. In this case the low E♭ lever must be pressed to activate the bell key. If any of the above adjustments are not correct see: How to Regulate the Keys below.

HOW TO REGULATE THE KEYS—SOPRANO CLARINET

The correct regulation of the clarinet keys is of utmost importance for proper instrument performance. The clarinet, fortunately, is one of the easier instruments to regulate. If you follow the instructions given below you should be able to locate a problem and correct it. Although the regulation of the keys is just one step in the complete adjustment process of the clarinet, it sometimes is all that you will need to do to get the clarinet playing again.

Tools Needed: Leak light

Small round nose or duck bill pliers

Small screwdriver

Emery paper

Materials Needed: Sheet cork as needed in sizes ⅟₆₄″, ⅟₃₂″ or ⅟₁₆″

Contact cork cement

Procedure: (Refer to Illustration 4-4 for key names and numbers.)

1. Check the pad seats. Before you attempt to regulate any keys, check all the pads to be certain that they are sealing properly. In many cases, this alone will reveal the problem of the clarinet. If the pads do not form a level seal with the tone holes, it will be virtually impossible to regulate the keys. To check the seat, place your leak light under each pad and close the key slowly using a very light pressure. It is important to be very critical during this checking procedure. The pad should seat level on the tone hole, that is, it should close simultaneoulsy around the entire tone hole. Often you will find that a pad is hitting the front, back or one of the sides *before* it seals the tone hole. If this is happening, visually check to see if the *key* is level with the tone hole. Sometimes, a key will be bent, causing one side of the pad to strike the tone hole before the other. If this is the case, use a large duck bill pliers and gently bend the key back to a level position and check again. Any pads you find which are torn, loose or not sealing properly will need to be replaced. (See How to Install New Skin Pads, p.117.) When all the pads have a level seat with the tone hole, continue with step 2 below.

2. Start with the upper joint. Press the Thumb ring (#7). This should close the F♯ ring key (#6) at the same time. Use your leak light as you check. If they do not close at the same time, the most common fault will be that the thumb will seal the tone hole before the F♯ ring key closes. If this happens, add a piece of ⅟₆₄″ cork to the arm of the F♯ ring key (#6) where it extends over the arm of the Thumb ring (#7). If the F♯ ring key now closes too soon, emery this cork thinner until they close together.

3. Check the top G♯ key (#5). This key should be closed firmly over the tone hole. Use your leak light to check. If not, loosen the screw located on the arm of the key until the pad rests firmly on the tone hole.

4. Press the A key (#4). This key should *start* to move at the same time as the top G♯ key (#5). If the A key moves first, tighten the screw on the arm of the top G♯ key until the two keys move at the same time. *Caution:* Do not tighten the screw too far as this will lift the G♯ pad off the tone hole (see step 3 above).

5. Check the lower joint. Press the Low E-B key (#24) *very lightly*. This key should seal the tone hole at the same time as the low F-C key (#22). Use your leak light to make this check. If they are not closing at the same time, you can adjust by bending the arm of the low F-C key (#22) which extends *under* the lever of the low E-B key (#24). Before bending, be sure that this arm has a piece of ¹⁄₆₄″ cork on the top of the spatula which will contact the E-B key lever. If the E-B key is closing first, bend the arm *up* slightly. If the F-C key is closing first, bend the arm *down* slightly. Check again until they close at the same time.

6. Check the bridge key. Assemble the upper and lower joints and line up the bridge key. If the two bridge keys do not line up properly when the tone holes of the two sections are lined up correctly, bend the key back into position with a small pair of pliers. Check to be certain that there is a piece of ¹⁄₆₄″ cork on the under side of the upper bridge key bridge (#9). If not, cement a piece on before continuing with step 7.

7. Press the lower ring or bridge key (#16). The *pad* on this key should close at the same time as the pad on the A-D ring (#9). Use your leak light to make this check. If they do not close together, adjust by bending the extension of the upper bridge key. If the A-D ring key is closing first, then you must bend this extension *up* slightly. If the lower bridge key pad is closing first, bend the extension *down* slightly. Recheck until the two keys close at the same time.

8. The adjustment of the clarinet is now complete. All other keys on the clarinet are independent and do not have to be regulated to work with other keys.

HOW TO REGULATE THE KEYS—ALTO CLARINET

In order for the alto clarinet to play correctly, it is important that the keys be regulated properly. One key out of adjustment can cause the instrument to squeak or, perhaps, not play at all. The alto clarinet is not difficult to regulate if you follow the outline below. Although the regulation of the keys is just one step in the complete adjustment process, it is sometimes all that needs to be done to get the alto clarinet playing again.

Tools Needed: Leak light
Small round nose or duck bill pliers
Emery paper
Small screwdriver
Materials Needed: Sheet cork as needed in sizes ¹⁄₆₄″, ¹⁄₃₂″ and ¹⁄₁₆″
Contact cork cement
Double skin or leather pads as needed
Procedure: (Refer to Illustration 4-5 for key names and numbers.)

1. Check the pad seats. Before you attempt to regulate the instrument, you must check all the pads to be certain that they are sealing properly. In many cases, this alone will reveal the source of the playing difficulty. If the pads do not form a level seat with each

tone hole, it will be virtually impossible to regulate the keys. To check the seat, place the leak light under each pad and close the key slowly using a very light pressure. It is important to be very critical during this checking procedure. The pad should seat level on the tone hole, that is, it should close simultaneoulsy around the entire tone hole. Often you will find that a pad is hitting the front, back or one of the sides *before* it seals the tone hole. If this happens, visually check to see if the *key* is level with the tone hole. Sometimes, a key will be bent, causing one side of the pad to strike the tone hole before the rest of the pad. If this is the case, use large duck bill pliers to gently bend the key back to a level position and check again. Replace any pads that are torn, loose or not sealing properly. (See How to Install New Skin Pads, p.117 or How to Install New Leather Pads, p.118.) When all pads are seated correctly, continue with step 2.

2. Start at the top of the instrument. Press the Thumb key (#7). This should close the F♯ key (#6) at the same time. Use the leak light as you check. If they do not close at the same time, the most common fault will be that the cork on the foot of the F♯ key will be missing or torn. This causes the Thumb key (#7) to close before the F♯ key (#6). Remove any old cork from under the foot of the F♯ key and cement a piece of 1/64" cork in place. If the F♯ key still does not close, add another piece of cork. If the F♯ key closes before the Thumb key, then use a piece of emery paper to thin the cork until they do close together.

3. Use your leak light to check the Top G♯ key (#5). This key should rest firmly on the tone hole. If it does not, loosen the screw located on the arm of the key until the pad rests firmly on the tone hole.

4. Press the A key (#4). This key should *start* to move at the same time as the Top G♯ key (#5). If the A key moves first, tighten the screw on the arm of the Top G♯ key until the two keys move at the same time. *Caution:* Do not tighten the screw too far, as this will lift the top G♯ key pad off the tone hole (see step 3 above).

5. Press the F♯ Aperture key (#29). This pad should close at the same time as the F♯ key (#6). Use your leak light to check. If the two keys do not close together, the adjustment is made where the two small tabs (one on each key) overlap. On some models, there will be a small adjusting screw located here. Tightening the screw will cause the F♯ key (#6) to close sooner. If there isn't any screw, the thickness of the cork located between these two tabs will need to be regulated. The thicker the cork, the sooner the F♯ key (#6) will close.

6. Now check the octave mechanism. Press down the Register lever (#1). This should open the Throat B♭ key (#28). While holding the Register lever (#1) down also press the Thumb key (#7). This should open the Register key (#26) while at the same time close the Throat B♭ key (#28). Both the Throat B♭ key and the Thumb key should close at the same time. Use your leak light to make this check. If they do not close together, then make the adjustment in the thickness of the cork on the tab which connects these two keys. (Some models have an adjustment screw here in place of the cork.

7. Press the Low E-B key (#24) very lightly. This key should seal the tone hole at the same time as the Low F-C key (#22). Use your leak light to make this check. If they are not closing together, adjust by bending the arm of the Low F-C key (#22) which extends under the lever of the Low E-B key (#24). Before bending, be sure that there is a piece of 1/64" cork on the top of the spatula which will contact the Low E-B key lever. If the

Low E-B key is closing first, bend the arm *up* slightly. If the F-C key is closing first, bend the arm *down* slightly. Check again until they close at the same time. *Note:* If your Low E-B key is located on the bell of the instrument, be certain that the arm of the bell key has a piece of ⅟₆₄″ cork on the underside where it makes contact with the Low E-B lever (#24).

8. Check the bridge key. If the alto clarinet has a two piece body, assemble the upper and lower sections and line up the bridge keys. If the two bridge keys do not line up properly when the tone holes of the two sections are lined up correctly, bend the bridge back into position with a small pair of pliers. Check to be certain that there is a piece of ⅟₆₄″ cork on the under side of the upper bridge on the A-D Ring key (#9). If not, glue a piece on before continuing with step 9.

9. Press the Lower ring key (#16). The pad on this key should close at the same time as the pad on the A-D ring key (#9). Use your leak light to make this check. If they do not close together, adjust by bending the extension of the upper bridge key. If the A-D Ring key is closing first, bend this extension *up* slightly. If the Lower ring key (#16) pad is closing first, then bend the extension *down* slightly. Recheck until the two keys close at the same time.

10. The adjustment of the alto clarinet is now complete. All other keys on the instrument are independent of each other, so they do not have to be regulated to work with other keys. On some model alto clarinets, the Lower ring key (#16) will be replaced with a number of independent keys which are similar to those of the bass clarinet. If your alto clarinet has such a key system, read below on how to regulate the bass clarinet for an explanation of how to adjust these additional keys.

HOW TO REGULATE THE KEYS—BASS CLARINET

In order for the bass clarinet to play correctly it is important that the keys be regulated properly. One key out of adjustment can cause the instrument to squeak or, perhaps, not play at all. The bass clarinet is not difficult to regulate if you follow the instructions given below. Although regulating the keys is just one step in the complete adjustment process, it is sometimes all that needs to be done to get the instrument playing again.

Tools Needed: Leak light
Pad slick
Small round nose or duck bill pliers
Emery paper
Small screwdriver

Materials Needed: Sheet cork as needed in sizes ⅟₆₄″, ⅟₃₂″ and ⅟₁₆″
Contact cork cement
Double skin or leather pads as needed

Procedure: (Refer to Illustration 4-6 for key names and numbers.)

1. Check the pad seats. Before you attempt to regulate the instrument, you must check all the pads to be certain that they are sealing properly. In many cases, this alone will reveal the source of the playing difficulty you are searching for on the bass clarinet. If the pads do not form a level seat with each tone hole, it will be virtually impossible to regulate the keys. To check the seat, place your leak light under each pad and close the key

slowly using a very light pressure. It is important to be very critical during this checking procedure. The pad should seat level on the tone hole, that is, it should close simultaneously around the entire tone hole. Often a pad hits the front, back, or one of the sides *before* it seals the tone hole. If this is happening, visually check to see if the *key* is level with the tone hole. Sometimes, a key will be bent causing one side of the pad to strike the tone hole before the rest of the pad. If this is the case, use large duck bill pliers and gently bend the key back to a level position and check again. Any pads you find that are torn, loose or not sealing properly will need to be replaced. (See How to Install New Skin Pads, p.117 or How to Install New Leather Pads, p.118.) When all pads are seated correctly, continue with step 2.

2. Start at the top of the instrument. Press the Thumb key (#7). This should close the F♯ key (#6) at the same time. Use your leak light to check. If they do not close at the same time, the most common fault will be that the cork on the foot of the F♯ key is missing or torn. This causes the Thumb key (#7) to close before the F♯ key (#6). Remove any old cork from under the foot of the F♯ key and cement a piece of ¹⁄₆₄″ cork in place. If the F♯ key still does not close, add another piece of cork. If the F♯ key closes before the Thumb key, use a piece of emery paper to thin the cork until they do close together.

3. Check the Top G♯ key (#5). This key should rest firmly on the tone hole. Use the leak light to check. If it does not, loosen the screw located on the arm of the key until the pad rests firmly on the tone hole.

4. Press the A key (#4). This key should *start* to move at the same time as the Top G♯ key (#5). If the A key moves first, tighten the screw on the arm of the Top G♯ key until the two keys move at the same time. *Caution:* Do not tighten the screw too far as this will lift the Top G♯ key pad off the tone hole (see step 3 above).

5. Press the F♯ Aperture key (#29). This pad should close at the same time as the F♯ key (#6). Use the leak light to check. If the two keys do not close together, the adjustment is made where two small tabs (one on each key) overlap. On some models, there will be a small adjusting screw located here. Tightening the screw will cause the F♯ key (#6) to close sooner. If there isn't any screw, the thickness of the cork located between these two tabs will need to be regulated. The thicker the cork, the sooner the F♯ key (#6) will close.

6. Press the A-D key (#10). The pad of this key should close at the same time as the E♭-B♭ Bis key (#9). Use the leak light as you make this check. If the keys do not close together, check for a piece of flat felt under the lever of the A-D key. If there is none, cement a piece of felt in place, then check the adjustment again. If the two keys still do not close together, the adjustment is made by bending the lever of the A-D key (#10). If the E♭-B♭ Bis key (#9) is *not closing*, place a pad slick under the pad of the A-D key (#10). Hold the pad against the slick and bend *down* slightly on the lever of the A-D key. If the E♭-B♭ Bis key is closing *before* the A-D key, you will need to bend this lever *up* slightly. Do this by holding the pad of the A-D key firmly against the tone hole and gently lift up on the lever of the A-D key.

7. Press down on the C-G key (#11). This key should close at the same time as the A-D key (#10). If they do not, check for a piece of felt under the lever of the C-G key. If there is none, cement a piece of flat felt in place, then check the adjustment again. If the

two keys still do not close together, the correction is made by gently bending the lever of the C-G key (#11). If the A-D key (#10) is *not closing*, bend the lever *down* slightly. If the A-D key is closing *before* the C-G key (#11) bend this lever *up* slightly. Be sure to use a leak light as you check this adjustment. This lever is bent in the same manner as described in step 6 above.

8. Now check the octave mechanism. Press down the Register lever (#1). This should open the Throat B♭ key (#28). While holding the Register lever (#1) down also press the Thumb key (#7). This should open the Register key (#26) while at the same time close the Throat B♭ key (#28). Both the Throat B♭ key and the Thumb key should close at the same time. Use your leak light to make this check. If they do not close together, the adjustment is made in the thickness of the cork on the tab which connects these two keys. (Some models may have an adjustment screw here in place of the cork.)

9. Press the Low E-B key (#24) very lightly. This key should seal the tone hole at the same time as the Low F-C key (#22). Use the leak light to make this check. If they are not closing together, adjust by bending the arm of the Low F-C key (#22) which extends under the lever of the Low E-B key (#24). Before bending, be sure that there is a piece of ¹⁄₆₄" cork on the top of the spatula which will contact the Low E-B key lever. If the Low E-B key is closing first, bend the arm *up* slightly. If the F-C key is closing first, bend the arm *down* lightly. Check again until they close at the same time. *Note:* If your Low E-B key is located on the bell of the instrument, be certain that the arm of the bell key has a piece of ¹⁄₆₄" cork on the underside where it makes contact with the Low E-B lever (#24).

10. Press the Low E♭ key lever (#25). This should close the Low E♭ bell key (#34) at the same time as the E-B key (#24). Use the leak light to make this check. If they do not close at the same time, the adjustment is made at the tab between the levers of the E-B key and the E♭-B♭ key. There should be a piece of ¹⁄₆₄" cork on this tab. An adjustment can also be made on the Low E♭ bell key (#34). There should be a piece of ¹⁄₆₄" cork under the arm of this key. If not, add a piece then check again. If the keys still do not close together, bend the lever of the Low E♭ lever to correct. Hold the Low E♭ bell key (#34) down against the tone hole and bend the lever up or down for the correct adjustment.

11. Press the B♭-F key (#30). This key should close at the same time as the B-F♯ key (#16). Use the leak light to make the check. If they do not close together, the adjustment is made where the arm of each key contacts the other. Regulating the thickness of the cork will correct the problem. A thicker cork will result in the B-F♯ key closing sooner.

12. Press the A-E key (#31). This key should close at the same time as the B-F♯ key (#16). Use your leak light to make the check. If they do not close together, the adjustment is made where the arm of each key contacts the other. Regulating the thickness of the cork will correct the problem. A thicker cork will result in the B-F♯ key closing sooner.

13. Check the bridge key. If the two bridge keys do not line up properly when the instrument is assembled, bend the appropriate key with a small pair of pliers until they are aligned. Check to be certain that there is a piece of ¹⁄₆₄" cork under the E♭-B♭ bridge (#14) which is a part of the E♭-B♭ Bis key (#9). If the cork is missing or torn, cement a piece on before continuing with step 14 below.

14. Press the B♭-F key (#30). This key should close at the same time as the E♭-B♭ Bis key (#9). Use the leak light to make this check. If they do not close together, adjust by

bending the E♭-B♭ bridge (#14). If the E♭-B♭ Bis key (#9) is closing first you must bend the bridge *up* slightly. If the B♭-F key (#30) is closing first you must bend the bridge *down* slightly.

15. The adjustment of the bass clarinet is now complete. All other keys on the instrument are independent of each other and do not have to be regulated to work with other keys.

HOW TO INSTALL NEW SKIN PADS

The clarinet pad is relatively easy to install. With a little bit of practice, anybody will be able to accomplish this job.

Tools Needed: Leak light
Pipe stem cleaner
Pad slick
Spring clamp
Alcohol burner or bunsen burner
Thin needle spring
Small screwdriver

Material needed: Double skin clarinet pads (medium or thick style)
Stick shellac

Procedure:

1. Remove the old pad. Skin pads are held in place with shellac or similar type of substance. You may need to remove the key in order to get at the pad. Use the small screwdriver to remove any pivot screws or rods needed to free the key, but be certain that you remember which screws go where. Heat the key as shown in Illustration 4-7. Always heat the key at an angle so that the main concentration of heat will not burn or melt the body of the clarinet. When the shellac is soft, remove the old pad.

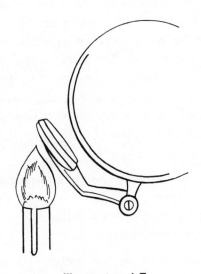

Illustration 4-7

2. Find the correct size replacement pad. Use the empty key cup as a guide. Be certain that all the old shellac is out of the cup (use the needle spring to scratch out any excess shellac), then place the new pad into the cup. The pad shoud fit snuggly into the key cup. If the pad is too large, it will not go all the way into the cup. If the pad is too small, it will move around in the cup when in place.

3. When you have the correct size pad, hold the end of the stick shellac in the flame of the burner and, when soft, place a small drop of the shellac on the back of the pad (the cardboard side). Place the pad into the key.

4. With the needle spring, make a small hole in the side of the pad. This will allow the expanding air to escape when you heat the pad and prevent the skin from "bloating."

5. Seat the pad. Heat the key as shown in Illustration 4-7 until the shellac softens and the pad settles into the key cup. Place the pad slick between the pad and the tone hole. Close the key over the pad slick and rotate the pad slick slightly. This will level the pad with the tone hole while the shellac is still warm. Remove the pad slick, wet the pad with water (using the pipe stem cleaner dipped in water) and close the key firmly over the tone hole. Hold in place with a spring clamp until cool.

6. After the key has cooled thoroughly, remove the clamp and check with a leak light to be certain the pad is level with the tone hole. If not, repeat the process starting with step 2.

7. Adjust the key. If the key in which you have replaced the pad works in conjunction with other keys of the clarinet, it will be necessary to re-adjust the key. (See How to Regulate the Keys, p. 111, p. 112 or p. 114.)

HOW TO INSTALL NEW LEATHER PADS

Some alto and bass clarinets have leather pads instead of the skin clarinet pads. This type of pad usually works better when the tone holes become larger and the diameter of the pad increases. You may replace any skin pad on the alto or bass clarinet with a leather pad. This is a common procedure for you to follow, as the leather pads used are the same as the saxophone pads that you may already have in stock. By doing this you will not have to keep a stock of the larger skin pads which are not often used.

The F♯ aperature key (#29) on the alto and bass clarinet has a small opening in the center of the key. The pad of this key must be either leather or cork and will have to have a hole cut into the center of the pad to allow for correct functioning of this key. *Do not* replace this pad with an ordinary skin or leather pad. The special tools required to make a replacement pad dictates that it should be sent to the repair shop for replacement.

Installing a leather pad is a relatively simple task and you will find little difficulty with it once you have done it a few times.

Tools Needed: Leak light
Pad slick (size corresponding to tone hole)
Spring clamp
Alcohol burner or bunsen burner
Small screwdriver

Materials Needed: Tan leather sax pad (either plain or riveted)
Stick shellac

Procedure:

1. Remove the old pad. Leather pads are held in place with shellac or similar type of substance. In some cases you may need to remove the key in order to get at the pad. Use a small screwdriver to remove any pivot screws or rods needed to free the key, but be certain that you remember where the screws belong when you reassemble the key. Heat the key as shown in Illustration 4-8. Always heat the key at an angle so that the main concentration of heat will not burn or melt the body of the clarinet. When the shellac is soft, remove the old pad.

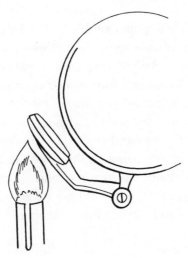

Illustration 4-8

2. Find the correct size replacement pad. The pad should fit snuggly into the empty key cup. If it is too large, the pad will not go all the way into the cup or will bend, thus wrinkling the leather. If the pad is too small, a space between the pad and the side of the key cup will allow the pad to slide around in the key cup.

3. When you have the correct size pad, hold the end of the stick shellac in the flame of the burner and, when soft, place a small drop of the shellac on the back of the pad. Place the pad into the key.

4. Seat the pad. Heat the key as shown in Illustration 4-8 until the shellac softens and the pad settles into the key cup. Place the pad slick between the pad and tone hole. Close the key over the pad slick and rotate the pad slick slightly. This will spread the shellac and level the pad with the tone hole (this must be done while the shellac is soft). Remove the pad slick and close the key firmly over the tone hole. Hold in place with a spring clamp until cool.

5. After the key has cooled thoroughly, remove the clamp and check the pad with a leak light. Be certain that the pad is level with the tone hole and that there are no gaps between the pad and the tone hole. If the seat is not tight, repeat the process starting with step 2.

6. Adjust the key. If the key in which you have replaced the pad works in conjunction with other keys of the clarinet, it will be necessary to re-adjust the keys. (See How to Regulate the Keys—Alto Clarinet, p. 112 or How to Regulate the Keys—Bass Clarinet, p. 114.)

HOW TO CLEAN DIRTY AND STICKY PADS

Skin clarinet pads may be cleaned as described below. If you have leather pads which have become dirty and sticky, they cannot effectively be cleaned and will need to be replaced (see How to Install New Leather Pads, p. 118).

Tools Needed: Cigarette paper (ungummed preferred)

Alcohol

Talcum powder

Emery paper

Procedure:

1. Place a sheet of cigarette paper under the sticky pad, close the key firmly and pull the paper out. You will probably notice a dirt mark on the paper when removed. Repeat this process a few times, always using a clean paper until the mark is no longer noticeable. (If you have difficulty finding ungummed cigarette paper, use gummed paper but be careful not to place the gummed portion under the pad.)

2. If the key is still sticky, try placing a small amount of talcum powder on the paper before placing it under the key and repeat the process as outlined in Step 1.

3. Still sticky? Place a little alcohol on the paper and try again. (This should be a last resort as the alcohol will dry out the skin pad and shorten its life.)

4. If the problem still persists, you will have no alternative but to remove the key, clean the tone hole with alcohol and a pipe stem cleaner, and change the pad. (See How to Install New Skin Pads, p. 117.)

HOW TO REPLACE KEY CORKS

Key corks on the clarinet are used to regulate the keys, adjust the key heights and provide for quiet key action. For this reason the thickness of the cork used on each key is extremely important. I have listed in Charts 11, 12 and 13 the most common size cork used on each key of the clarinet, alto clarinet and bass clarinet. In many cases, you will have to use emery paper to reduce the thickness of the cork to achieve the proper key adjustment or height.

As a general rule, key corks are always glued to the key and never to the body of the clarinet. Also, where there is a choice, the cork is always glued to the under side of the key.

Tools Needed: Single edge razor blade

Emery paper

Materials Needed: Sheet cork as needed in sizes $\frac{1}{64}''$,

$\frac{1}{32}''$, $\frac{1}{16}''$ and $\frac{3}{32}''$

Contact cork cement

Procedure:

1. Remove any old cork that is left on the key.

2. Select the correct size cork according to Charts 11, 12 or 13 (pp. 121-124) and spread contact cement on a small section of the cork.

(Text continues on p. 124.)

Chart 11
Soprano Clarinet Key Corks

(Refer to Illustration 4-4 for key names and numbers. Only those keys listed require cork.)

Key #	Key Name	Location of Cork*	Size of Cork**
1	Register key	Under lever	1/32″
2	C trill key	Under key (end opposite pad)	1/16″
3	B♭ trill key	Under key (end opposite pad)	1/16″
4	A key	Under lever	1/32″ or 3/32″
5	Top G♯ key	Under lever	1/32″ or 3/32″
6	F♯ ring key	Under foot	1/64″
7	Thumb ring	Under foot	1/64″
8	F♯ trill key	Under key (end opposite pad)	1/16″
9	A-D ring key	Under bridge	1/64″
12	E♭-B♭ trill key	Under lever	3/32″
13	E♭-B♭ aux. key	Under lever	1/16″
15	Curved C♯-G♯ key	Under lever	1/16″
16	Lower ring key	Under bridge	1/16″
17	F-C lever	Under foot	1/32″
18	B-F♯ key	Under lever	1/16″
19	E-B lever	Under key	1/16″
		Top of key	1/64″
20	F♯-C♯ lever	Under key	1/16″
		Top of key	1/64″
21	A♭-E♭ key	Under lever	1/32″
22	Low F-C key	Under foot	1/64″
		Top of arm	1/64″
	Right hand thumb rest	Under rest	1/32″

*The term "lever" as used in this chart refers to the portion of the key which is touched by the finger while playing.

**In most cases this is the starting size cork to be used. Usually the cork will need to be made thinner by using a piece of emery paper to reduce the size. To determine the correct thickness see the following: How to Regulate the Keys—Soprano Clarinet, p. 111; How to Check the Intonation of the Clarinet, p. 131; The Complete Adjustment—Soprano Clarinet, p. 136.

Chart 12
Alto Clarinet Key Corks

(Refer to Illustration 4-5 for key names and numbers.* Only those keys listed require cork.)

Key #	Key Name	Location of Cork**	Size of Cork°
1	Register key	Under lever	1/32″
2	C trill key	Under key (end opposite pad)	1/16″
3	B♭ trill key	Under key (end opposite pad)	1/16″
4	A key	Under lever	3/32″
5	Top G♯ key	Under lever	3/32″
6	F♯ key	Under foot	1/64″
		On adj. screw plateau	1/64″
7	Thumb key	Under foot	1/16″
		On bridge	1/64″
8	F♯ -G♯ trill key	Under key (end opposite pad)	1/16″
9	A-D ring key	Under bridge	1/64″
12	E♭ -B♭ trill key	Under lever	3/32″
13	E♭ -B♭ aux. key	Under lever	1/16″
14	C-G key	Under foot	1/16″
15	C♯ -G♯ key	Under lever	1/16″
16	Lower ring key	Under bridge	1/16″
17	F-C lever	Under foot	1/32″
18	B-F♯ aux. key	Under lever	1/16″
19	E-B lever	Around peg	small circle of plastic‡
20	F♯ -C♯ lever	Around peg	small circle of plastic‡
21	A♭ -E♭ key	Under lever	1/32″
22	F-C key	Under foot	1/64″
		Top of arm	1/64″
24	E-B key	Under foot	1/16″
		Top of tab	1/64″
25	Low E♭ lever	Under arm	1/16″
26	Register key	Top of arm	1/64″
28	Throat B♭ key	Top of arm	1/64″
29	F♯ aperture key	Under foot	1/16″
32	G-D lever	Under foot	1/16″
33	G-D key	Under arm	1/64″
34	Bell key	Under arm	1/64″

*There are many keys on the alto clarinet and Illustration 4-5 may prove confusing. Identify a key in the illustration; find the cork location through the description in this chart. Some alto clarinets have different key systems. The system described here is most common.

**The term "lever" refers to the portion of the key touched by the finger while playing.

°In most cases this is the starting size cork to be used. Usually the cork will need to be made thinner by using a piece of emery paper to reduce the size. To determine the correct thickness see the following: How to Regulate the Keys—Alto Clarinet, p. 112; How to Check the Intonation, p. 131; The Complete Adjustment—Alto Clarinet, p. 139.

‡The peg on the lever will insert into the hole in the corresponding key. Cut a small circle (about ¼″ in diameter) of plastic from a plastic bag, glue this to the lever and insert into the key. This will quiet the action and remove most of the "play" in the key.

Chart 13
Bass Clarinet Key Corks

(Refer to Illustration 4-6 for key names and numbers.* Only those keys listed require cork.)

Key #	Key Name	Location of Cork**	Size of Cork°
1	Register key	Under lever	$\frac{1}{32}''$
2	C trill key	Under key (end opposite pad)	$\frac{1}{16}''$
3	B♭ trill key	Under key (end opposite pad)	$\frac{1}{16}''$
4	A key	Under lever	$\frac{3}{32}''$
5	Top G♯ key	Under lever	$\frac{3}{32}''$
6	F♯ key	Under foot	$\frac{1}{64}''$
7	Thumb key	Under foot	$\frac{1}{16}''$
		On bridge	$\frac{1}{64}''$
8	F♯ -C♯ trill key	Under key (end opposite pad)	$\frac{1}{16}''$
10	A-D key	Under lever	Piece of felt‡
11	C-G key	Under lever	Piece of felt‡
12	E♭ -B♭ trill key	Under lever	$\frac{3}{32}''$
13	E♭ -B♭ aux. key	Under lever	$\frac{1}{16}''$
14	E♭ -B♭ bridge	Under bridge	$\frac{1}{64}''$
15	C♯ -G♯ key	Under lever	$\frac{1}{16}''$
16	B-F♯ key	Under bridge	$\frac{1}{64}''$
17	F-C lever	Under foot	$\frac{1}{32}''$
18	B-F♯ aux. key	Under lever	$\frac{1}{16}''$
19	E-B lever	Around peg	Small circle of plastic‡
20	F♯ -C♯ lever	Around peg	Small circle of plastic‡‡
21	A♭ -E♭ key	Under lever	$\frac{1}{32}''$
22	F-C key	Under foot	$\frac{1}{64}''$
		Top of arm	$\frac{1}{64}''$

*There are many keys on the bass clarinet, and Illustration 4-6 will prove confusing at first glance. Identify the key in the picture, then find the cork location through the description in this chart. Some bass clarinets have different key systems. The system described here is the most common.

**The term "lever" as used in this chart refers to the portion of the key which is touched by the finger while playing.

°In most cases this is the starting size cork to be used. Usually the cork will need to be made thinner by using a piece of emery paper to reduce the size. To determine the correct thickness, see the following: How to Regulate the Keys—Bass Clarinet, p. 114; How to Check the Intonation of the Clarinet, p. 113; The Complete Adjustment— Bass Clarinet, p. 139.

‡Cut a small piece of flat felt to fit the key and glue in place with contact cement.

‡‡The peg on the lever will insert into the hole in the corresponding key. Cut a small circle (about ¼″ in diameter) of plastic from a plastic bag. Glue this to the lever and insert into the key. This will quiet the action and remove most of the "play" in the key.

Key #	Key Name	Location of Cork**	Size of Cork°
24	E-B key	Under foot	1/16″
		Top of tab	1/64″
25	Low E♭ lever	Under arm	1/16″
26	Register key	Under foot	1/64″
		Top of arm	1/64″
28	Throat B♭ key	Under foot	1/64″
		Top of arm	1/64″
29	F♯ aperture key	Under foot	1/16″
30	B♭ -F key	Under foot	1/16″
31	A-E key	Under foot	1/16″
32	G-D lever	Under foot	1/16″
33	G-D key	Under arm	1/64″
34	Low E♭ bell key	Under arm	1/64″

3. Spread contact cement on the proper place of the key.

4. Allow the contact cement to dry thoroughly, then place the cork in position. Trim off excess with a razor blade.

5. Check the height and regulation of the key with the other keys on the clarinet and emery the cork if needed. (See How to Regulate the Keys, pp. 111-117 or How to Check the Intonation, p. 131.)

6. To emery the cork, place a small strip of emery paper between the cork and the clarinet body or key with the rough side against the cork (see Illustration 4-9). Pull the emery paper while holding the key and cork against it. This will take off a small amount of cork and shape it to the body or key of the clarinet at the same time.

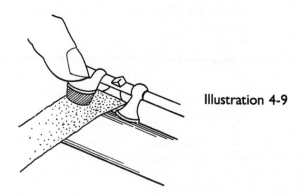

Illustration 4-9

HOW TO RE-CORK THE TENONS

When a tenon cork of the clarinet tears, falls off, or becomes too loose, it should be replaced. To determine if the fit is too loose, insert the tenon into the receiver. After the sections are together, try to wiggle them. If they do wiggle, then the joint should be re-corked. Torn or missing tenon corks should be replaced; they not only cause a loose fitting joint, but also may leak air, causing playing problems.

If your tenon is beginning to fit too tightly, it is time to clean and regrease it. Wipe the tenon with a clean cloth to remove all dirt and old grease. Then grease lightly with cork grease. (See Maintenance Procedures for the Clarinet—Tenons, p. 103.) If, after cleaning, the tenon fit is too loose, it should be replaced.

Tools Needed: Ruler
Small screwdriver
Razor blade
Pliers or scraper
Emery paper
Materials Needed: Sheet cork (1/16″ thick)
Contact cork cement
Cork grease

Procedure:

1. Remove any keys which extend over the joint cork. This will make it easier to do the job. On the upper clarinet joint this includes the C trill key (#2), B♭ trill key (#3), F♯ trill key (#8), E♭-B♭ trill key (#12) and the A-D ring or upper bridge key (#9). All of these keys are easy to remove.

2. Remove all particles of the old tenon cork. This is most easily done with a regular pair of pliers. Open the pliers to the extended position and grip the tenon cork loosely. Turn the pliers back and forth around the tenon to tear off all the cork. Do this thoroughly and carefully to be certain that all cork is gone and all traces of either cement or shellac which was holding the cork in place are removed. It is essential that the tenon be *completely clean* before proceeding if the job is to be successful. Do not worry if the pliers scrape the wood or plastic of the clarinet tenon. This will not hurt the instrument and will be covered with the new cork when the job is completed.

3. Measure the width of the recessed portion of the tenon once it is clean to determine the size cork needed (see Illustration 4-10).

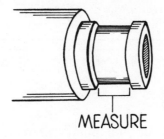

MEASURE

Illustration 4-10

4. Cut the new tenon cork from a sheet of 1/16″ cork. This cork is usually available in 4″ x 12″ sheets. The joint cork can be cut across the narrow portion of the sheet so that the final piece will be 4″ long and the width that you measured in step 3. On the lower tenon of the alto and bass clarinet you will need a longer strip of cork to go around the circumference of the tenon. The piece should be cut with a bevel for a better fit. The

measurement you took in step 3 will be the bottom of the cork and it should bevel to a larger size at the top (see Illustration 4-11).

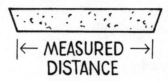

|← MEASURED →|
DISTANCE

Illustration 4-11

5. Cut a beveled edge on one end of the cork strip. Be sure that the cut is made so that the bevel starts at the top (which is wider) and thins out toward the bottom of the cork strip (see Illustration 4-12).

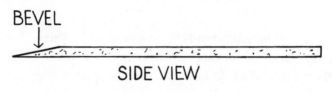

BEVEL
↓

SIDE VIEW

Illustration 4-12

6. Apply the cork cement. The contact cement should completely cover the recessed area of the tenon. Also apply the cement to the entire bottom of the tenon cork *and* to the top portion of the cork which is beveled (see Illustration 4-13).

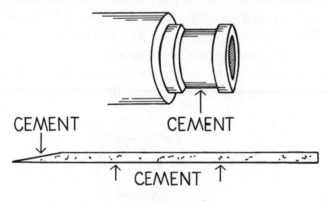

CEMENT   CEMENT
↓   ↑

↑ CEMENT ↑

Illustration 4-13

7. Allow the cement to dry thoroughly as indicated in the directions on the container, usually about 10 minutes.

8. Glue the new cork on the tenon. When the glue is dry, place the bottom of the beveled end of the cork on the tenon. Take care that the cork is on straight. Once you make contact with the cement, you cannot remove it without pulling the cement off. Work around the tenon, carefully pressing the cork to make good contact and avoid any gaps in the cork. When you have completed the circle around the tenon, the cork should lap on top of the bevel end which is already in place (see Illustration 4-14).

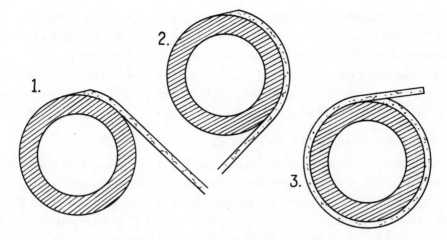

Illustration 4-14

9. Cut the excess length of tenon cork off with a razor blade as shown in Illustration 4-15.

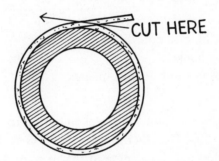

Illustration 4-15

10. Emery the cork joint. Using a strip of emery paper which is the same width as the tenon cork, first emery the overlap in the joint cork so that it is level with the rest of the cork. Then slowly emery around the cork taking care to remove equal portions of the cork from around the circumference of the tenon. Use the strip of emery paper as shown in Illustration 4-16. *Stop emerying* when the cork tenon just *begins* to fit into the receiver but is still rather difficult to push in. Apply some cork grease to the cork and this will help the

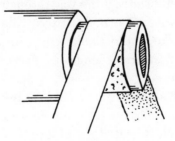

Illustration 4-16

tenon fit into the receiver. The cork will compress at this point and give you a good fit. (*NOTE:* If you emery until you get a good fit with a dry cork, the fit will be too loose once the cork grease has been applied and the tenon cork is compressed.)

11. With the razor blade, trim any excess cork which has come loose or rough edges which formed while fitting the two sections together. The job is now complete, except to replace any keys that were removed.

HOW TO REPLACE A CLARINET NEEDLE SPRING

Occasionally a clarinet needle spring may break. Such a spring is not difficult to replace, and by doing it yourself you can save considerable time and keep your clarinet playing rather than sitting in a repair shop. The proper type of spring to use on the clarinet is the blue needle spring. Keep an assortment of these springs in your repair stock because they are also used for all woodwind instruments except flute and piccolo.

Tools Needed: Small round nose pliers
                   Wire cutter
                   Small hammer
                   Alcohol burner or bunsen burner
                   Steel or metal block
                   Large blue needle spring
                   Spring hook
Materials Needed: Blue steel needle springs
Procedure:

1. Remove the keys from around the broken spring to make it accessible.

2. Remove the old spring. Usually the spring will break, leaving a small stub in the post. This stub must be pulled out the same end that it went in (see Illustration 4-17). If the flattened end of the spring is extending out from the post, grasp this firmly with the wire cutter and pull out (see Illustration 4-18). If the other end of the spring is extending beyond the post, use the round nose pliers and squeeze the spring out of the post (see Illustration 4-19). If the spring is flush in the post, use a large needle spring as a driver and tap the spring out with a hammer. When doing this be sure to rest the post against some object to prevent the post from bending or breaking (see Illustration 4-20). It is also possible that the old spring has already fallen out of the post.

3. Once the old spring is removed, find the correct size needle spring which will fit snuggly into the post but will still slide all the way through. Slide the spring into the post so that the correct length will extend beyond the post, allowing the point of the spring to catch in the spring hook on the key. Mark the length of spring needed. Remove the spring and cut with a wire cutter to the correct length as marked. Be sure that you cut off the "butt end" and not the pointed end.

4. Hold the spring with a pair of pliers and heat the "butt end" of the spring in the flame of the burner until the *end* starts to turn red. Take care that only the very *end* of the spring turns red, for if too much is heated it will lose it's "spring." When the end is red, hold the spring against a solid metal block (vice, piece of steel, etc.) and with the small hammer tap the end to flatten slightly. Allow to cool.

5. Insert the spring into the post with the pointed end going in first. Squeeze the flat end into the post with the round nose pliers (see Illustration 4-21). This should hold

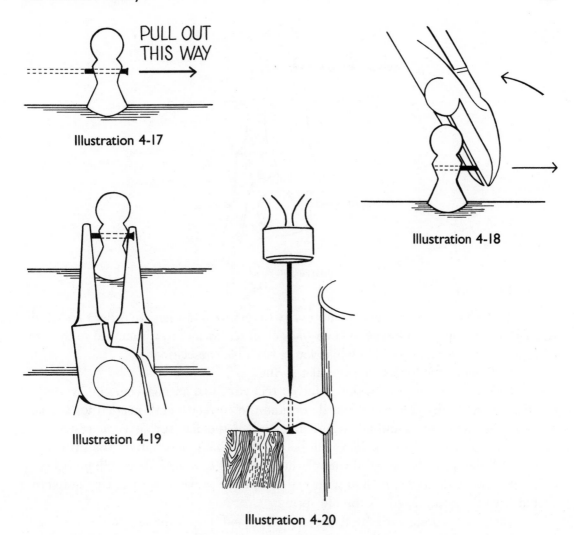

Illustration 4-17

Illustration 4-18

Illustration 4-19

Illustration 4-20

the spring in place. If the spring does not go in far enough, this means you have flattened the end too much and must try again with another spring. If the spring goes in easily and is not tight, repeat step 4 to flatten the end a little more.

6. Bend the spring slightly in the post. If the key affected is normally in the open position, then the spring should be bent *toward* the tone hole. If the key is usually closed, the spring should be bent *away* from the tone hole.

7. Remount the key and check the spring tension. (See How to Adjust the Spring Tension, p. 130) Replace all keys which were removed to make the spring accessible.

HOW TO REPLACE A CLARINET FLAT SPRING

If the clarinet key does not have a needle spring, it will most likely have a flat spring. Unlike the needle spring, the flat spring is attached directly to the key rather than to a post. All flat springs are held in place with a small screw and, therefore, are relatively easy to replace. Your main problem will be in finding the correct size replacement.

Tools Needed: Small screwdriver
             Wirecutter
Materials Needed: Correct size flat spring
             Flat spring screw (if missing)

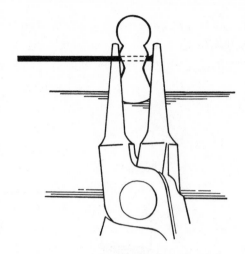

Illustration 4-21

Procedure:

1. Remove the key. It may be necessary to remove other keys in order to reach the key with the flat spring. Be sure to keep track of all screws and rods removed so they will be replaced in the same position when you reassemble the clarinet.

2. Remove the broken piece of flat spring.

3. Select a new spring which is the correct size. Flat springs come in a variety of lengths and strengths. You must first determine the correct length needed for the key. This can be done by examining where the end of the flat spring is to rest on the instrument. On most clarinets there will be a little metal box or tab on the instrument upon which the spring is to rest. If your clarinet does not have this, there will probably be either a groove in the instrument or wear marks from the previous spring. The new spring should have the same length as the old spring.

Install the spring with the flat spring screw and mount the key to test for length and strength. If the flat spring screw is missing, replace with a new screw. (These screws are uniform in size and you should have a small supply of them in the repair stock.) If the key pushes too hard or too easily, replace this spring with another of the same length which will be either thinner or thicker.

It is not a good idea to cut the length of the flat spring to make it the right length as the end of most flat springs are usually slightly curved so that the spring will slide easily on the instrument. If you *must* cut the end, be sure to use your round nose pliers to curve the end of the spring slightly.

4. Mount the spring back on the key and replace the key in the proper position. Return any other keys that had to be removed.

HOW TO ADJUST THE SPRING TENSION

All keys on the clarinet that are usually in the *open* position should have a light resistance which still allows for a quick, snappy key action. Those keys which are normally in a *closed* position would be set with a heavier resistance to prevent the key from being blown open while playing. In order to give the player a more consistent "feel" of the instrument, it is important to keep the spring tension uniform throughout. That is, all open keys should have the same light tension and all closed keys the same heavier tension. When checking the keys, move only one key at a time. (For example, when checking the tension of the A key (#4), hold the Top G♯ key (#5) open so that you feel only the tension of the A key.)

Tension on a key is increased or decreased by bending the needle spring gently in one direction or the other. Bending the spring too far will cause it to break, so only do a little at a time. Use a spring hook for this job. Those keys that are normally open need to have the spring bent *toward* the tone hole to *increase* the tension. Those keys that are normally closed need to have the spring bent *away* from the tone hole to *increase* the tension. Be sure to unhook the spring from the key before attempting to bend it.

If you need to adjust the tension of a flat spring, remove the key first so that you can have better access to the key. Use small round nose pliers to bend about half the spring. If you wish to *increase* the tension of this spring, bend the end *away* from the key and toward the body of the instrument. If you wish to *decrease* the tension, bend the spring *toward* the key and away from the body of the instrument. After the spring has been bent, replace the key and check the tension. If this bending action does not solve the spring tension problem, you may have to replace the flat spring with a different strength spring. (See How to Replace a Clarinet Flat Spring, p.129.)

HOW TO CHECK THE INTONATION OF THE CLARINET

The intonation of the clarinet is determined by a number of factors:

1. The breath support and embouchure of the player.
2. The hardness of the reed used.
3. The placement of the barrel and middle joints as the instrument is assembled.
4. The open heights of the clarinet keys.

Item 4 above is important if the clarinet is to play in tune with itself. The height of the key openings is measured at the front of the pad and is the distance from the top of the tone hole to the bottom of the pad when the key is fully opened. Charts 14, 15 and 16 show the acceptable open heights to which the soprano clarinet, alto clarinet and bass clarinet keys should be set.

An individual key which is not at the correct height has probably lost a cork on the foot or some other point on the key. These individual key heights can usually be corrected by replacing the cork. (See How to Replace Key Corks, p.120.) Also, whenever you add a cork you will have to re-check the adjustment of the key with any other keys that are activated at the same time. (See How to Regulate the Keys, pp. 111-117.)

If, in checking the clarinet key heights, you find that all the key heights are incorrect, it will take a complete adjustment to correct the problem. This will be relatively simple to adjust on the soprano clarinet but can become more difficult on the alto and bass clarinet. The complete adjustment of each of these instruments is described later in the chapter. (See pp.139-145.)

HOW TO CORRECT NON-FUNCTIONING KEYS

A non-functioning key can be defined as any key on the clarinet which is not operating properly. For the most part, when this occurs, you should send the instrument

Chart 14
Soprano Clarinet Key Heights

(Refer to Illustration 4-4 for key numbers and names.)

Key	Number	Height
Register key	1	$\frac{1}{16}''$
C trill key	2	$\frac{1}{16}''$
B♭ trill key	3	$\frac{1}{16}''$
A key	4	$\frac{1}{16}''$
Top G♯ key	5	$\frac{1}{16}''$
F♯ ring key	6	$\frac{1}{16}''$
F♯ trill key	8	$\frac{1}{16}''$
A-D ring key	9	$\frac{1}{16}''$*
E♭ -B♭ trill key	12	$\frac{1}{16}''$
E♭ -B♭ aux. key	13	$\frac{1}{16}''$
C♯ -G♯ key	15	$\frac{1}{16}''$
Lower ring or bridge key	16	$\frac{5}{64}''$
B-F♯ key	18	$\frac{5}{64}''$
A♭ -B♭ key	21	$\frac{3}{32}''$
Low F-C key	22	$\frac{3}{32}''$
F♯ -C♯ key	23	$\frac{3}{32}''$*
Low E-B key	24	$\frac{3}{32}''$*

Chart 15
Alto Clarinet Key Heights

(Refer to Illustration 4-5 for key numbers and names.)

Key	Number	Height
C trill key	2	$\frac{1}{16}''$
B♭ trill key	3	$\frac{1}{16}''$
A key	4	$\frac{1}{16}''$
Top G♯ key	5	$\frac{1}{16}''$
F♯ key	6	$\frac{1}{16}''$*
Thumb key	7	$\frac{1}{16}''$
F♯ -G♯ trill key	8	$\frac{1}{16}''$
A-D ring key	9	$\frac{1}{16}''$*
E♭ -B♭ trill key	12	$\frac{1}{16}''$
E♭ -B♭ aux. key	13	$\frac{1}{16}''$
C-G key	14	$\frac{1}{16}''$
C♯ -G♯ key	15	$\frac{1}{16}''$
Lower ring key	16	$\frac{3}{32}''$
B-F♯ aux. key	18	$\frac{3}{32}''$
A♭ -E♭ key	21	$\frac{1}{8}''$
F-C key	22	$\frac{1}{8}''$
F♯ -C♯ key	23	$\frac{1}{8}''$*
E-B key	24	$\frac{1}{8}''$*
Register key	26	$\frac{1}{16}''$*
Throat B♭ key	28	$\frac{1}{16}''$*
F♯ aperture key	29	$\frac{1}{16}''$*
G-D key	33	$\frac{1}{8}''$
Bell key	34	$\frac{1}{8}''$*

*The heights of these keys will automatically be correct if the clarinet is regulated correctly.

Chart 16
Bass Clarinet Key Heights

(Refer to Illustration 4-6 for key numbers and names.)

Key	Number	Height
C trill key	2	³⁄₃₂″
B♭ trill key	3	³⁄₃₂″
A key	4	³⁄₃₂″
Top G♯ key	5	³⁄₃₂″
F♯ key	6	³⁄₃₂″*
Thumb key	7	³⁄₃₂″
F♯ -C♯ trill key	8	³⁄₃₂″
E♭ -B♭ bis key	9	³⁄₃₂″*
A-D key	10	³⁄₃₂″*
C-G key	11	³⁄₃₂″
E♭ -B♭ trill key	12	³⁄₃₂″
E♭ -B♭ aux. key	13	³⁄₃₂″
C♯ -G♯ key	15	³⁄₃₂″
B-F♯ key	16	⅛″*
B-F♯ aux. key	18	⅛″
A♭ -E♭ key	21	⅛″
F-C key	22	⅛″
F♯ -C♯ key	23	⅛″*
E-B key	24	⅛″*
Register key	26	¹⁄₁₆″*
Throat B♭ key	28	¹⁄₁₆″*
F♯ aperture key	29	¹⁄₁₆″*
B♭ -F key	30	⅛″*
A-E key	31	⅛″*
G-D key	33	⅛″
Low E♭ bell key	34	⅛″*

*The heights of these keys will automatically be correct if the bass clarinet is regulated correctly.

---

into the repair shop to be corrected by a skilled repair technician. There are, however, a number of things you can check before sending the clarinet to be repaired. These are common problems that can be easily corrected by you. Check this first and you might save time and money.

1. **Check the spring**—Is it broken off? Perhaps the spring is just unhooked from the key. If the spring appears O.K. push against it with your spring hook. If there is no tension in the spring, it is broken and will need to be replaced. (See How to Replace a Clarinet Needle Spring, p.128 or How to Replace a Clarinet Flat Spring, p.129.)

2. **Check the pivot screws**—These screws, which are located at the ends of the keys, go through the post and hold the key in place. It is possible that the screw could be tightened down too far and might be binding the key action. On the other hand, if the pivot screw is not tight enough, it will permit extra motion in the keys. This will cause the

key adjustment to be inaccurate and the pads to seat poorly over the tone holes. Use a small screwdriver to move the pivot screw both ways to see if the action of the key improves.

3. **Check the key**—If the key does not close all the way, use the leak light to see if the pad is still level on the tone hole. If not, your key may have been bent. You will then need to bend the key back to a level position and probably replace the pad. (See How to Install New Skin Pads, p.117 or How to Install New Leather Pads, p.118.) Another possibility is that an adjustment screw has gone out of adjustment (this would especially be true on the alto and bass clarinets) and is holding the key open. Check all adjustment screws which might affect the key in question.

HOW TO TIGHTEN LOOSE RINGS ON THE CLARINET BODY

On each receiver of a wood clarinet there will be a metal ring around the edge. This ring is placed to strengthen the thin walls of the receiver and help prevent breaking. In dry weather (winter) the wood will shrink a little and occasionally this ring will loosen up. When the ring is loose it can no longer protect the receiver so breakage or cracking may occur. It is a simple matter to tighten a loose ring.

Tools Needed: Rawhide hammer
Screwdriver (with larger, thin blade)
Single edge razor blade
Materials Needed: Large saxophone pad (may be a used pad)
Procedure:

1. Remove the loose ring from the clarinet body. In most cases it will just lift off. If it is loose but will not come off, use the screwdriver as a wedge and tap the ring off with the rawhide hammer. Work around the ring as you tap.

2. Find a new or used saxophone pad whose diameter is about one inch larger than that of the clarinet ring. Cut a leather circle from the pad with the razor blade. (There may be a hole in the leather due to the rivot in the pad, but this is not a problem for this repair.)

3. Check the fit of the ring on the receiver. Some rings are beveled and will only fit correctly one way. Be sure to determine which side will go on first.

4. Place the piece of leather over the receiver then place the ring on top of the leather. With the rawhide hammer, tap the ring halfway into place. (See Illustration 4-22.)

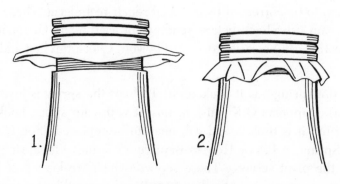

Illustration 4-22

Illustration 4-23

5. Trim the excess leather from around the bottom of the ring. (See Illustration 4-23.)

6. Tap the ring all the way into place and trim all leather from around the ring with the razor blade.

This same procedure can be used on plastic body clarinets as well, although those instruments will not have loose rings nearly as often.

HOW TO CLEAN THE CLARINET MOUTHPIECE

If the clarinet mouthpiece is cleaned regularly as described at the beginning of this chapter, you will not need to do anything further. The regular cleaning with soap and water, using a mouthpiece brush, will remove all dirt and traces of minerals which begin to gather on the mouthpiece.

In reality, however, we often find a mouthpiece that has not been cleaned and is coated with a hard crust of mineral deposit. This unslightly and distasteful mouthpiece can be cleaned quite easily. (Normal washing in warm soapy water will not remove the formed crust.)

Tools Needed: Mouthpiece brush

Small hook made from piece of wire

Muriatic Acid (available from druggist)

Baking soda (mixed in water)

Procedure:

1. Place the dirty mouthpiece in a jar of acid so that it is completely submerged. (Store the muriatic acid in a wide mouth jar which is large enough to hold the largest woodwind mouthpiece.) Leave in the acid about 10-15 minutes. (No harm will come to the mouthpiece if left in the acid too long.)

2. Lift the mouthpiece out of the acid with the hook you made from the wire so that your hands do not contact the acid. Immediately place the mouthpiece into the solution of baking soda and water. This will neutralize the acid. (You will notice a bubbling action when the mouthpiece is placed in the soda solution.)

3. Remove the mouthpiece from the baking soda solution and rinse thoroughly under clear running water. Brush out all loose material with the mouthpiece brush. The mouthpiece will now be clean. (*Notice:* If the mouthpiece is made of hard rubber, you may notice a slight green tinge has developed. This discoloration is the result of the acid and water, but does not harm the mouthpiece.)

THE COMPLETE ADJUSTMENT—
HOW TO MAKE THE ADJUSTMENTS NECESSARY FOR PROPER
PERFORMANCE OF THE SOPRANO CLARINET

The complete adjustment of the soprano clarinet is a relatively simple procedure. The job is easy because the soprano clarinet has very few keys which need to be regulated with other keys. Be certain to read completely through the procedure before beginning.

Tools Needed: Leak light
Small screwdriver
Spring hook
Alcohol burner or bunsen burner
Pad slick
Ruler
Emery Paper
Small round nose pliers
Razor blade

Materials Needed: Double skin clarinet pads
Sheet cork in sizes 1/64″, 1/32″ and 1/16″
Stick shellac
Contact cork cement

Procedure: (Refer to Illustration 4-4 for key names and numbers.)

1. Using a leak light, check all pads to be certain that they have a level seat which will form a tight seal with the tone hole. You can check each pad as you adjust it in the procedure to follow or check them all at once before you begin the adjustment. If any of the pads are uneven, loose or torn, they will have to be replaced before you can continue with this adjustment. (See How to Install New Skin Pads, p.117.)

2. Starting with the upper joint, check the height of the register key (#1). When open all the way, this key should measure 1/16″ from the bottom of the pad to the top of the tone hole. If it does not, it is corrected by changing the thickness of the cork under the lever of this key. If the key needs to open further, emery the cork to make it thinner until the correct height is achieved. If the key is opening too far, remove all the old cork and replace with a piece of 1/32″ cork. Adjust the thickness of the cork until the proper height is achieved.

3. Check the height of the C trill key (#2). When open all the way, this key should measure 1/16″ from the bottom of the pad to the top of the tone hole. If it does not, it is corrected by changing the thickness of the cork under the lever of the key. Emery the cork to allow the key to open more. If the key is opening too far, remove all old cork and replace with a piece of 1/16″ cork. Adjust the thickness of the cork until the proper height is achieved.

4. Check the open height of the B♭ trill key (#3). When open all the way, this key should measure 1/16″ from the bottom of the pad to the top of the tone hole. If it does not, the adjustment is made the same as indicated in step 3 above.

5. Check the open height of the F♯ trill key (#8). When open all the way, this key should measure ⅟₁₆″ from the bottom of the pad to the top of the tone hole. If it does not, the adjustment is made the same as in step 3 above.

6. Check the height of the E♭-B♭ trill key (#12). It should open to ⅟₁₆″ from the pad to the tone hole. If it does not, it is corrected by changing the thickness of the cork under the lever of this key. If the cork needs to be replaced, cement a piece of ³⁄₃₂″ cork under the lever, then check the height again. This cork can be trimmed to achieve the correct height by cutting thin pieces off with the single edge razor blade, then using emery paper for the finer adjustment. You will need to assemble the upper and lower joints before checking, as the key lever touches against a portion of the lower joint in actual operation.

7. Check the height of the Top G♯ key (#5). This key should open to a height of ⅟₁₆″. If it does not, the adjustment is made by changing the thickness of cork under the lever of the key. If the cork needs replacing, cement a piece of ⅟₃₂″ cork under the lever of the key (some model clarinets will require a piece of ³⁄₃₂″ cork at this point). Emery the cork if necessary to achieve the proper key height opening.

8. Press the A key (#4). This key should activate the Top G♯ key (#5) at the same time that it starts to move. If it does not, adjust the screw located where the arm of the Top G♯ key extends over the A key. If the A key moves before the Top G♯ key, turn the screw down slightly. Check with a leak light to be certain that this adjustment screw is not holding the Top G♯ key open.

9. Press the A key (#4). This key should open so that the cork under the lever touches the body of the clarinet at the same time that the cork under the lever of the Top G♯ key (#5) touches the body of the instrument. If the A key cork touches first, emery the cork thinner until they touch at the same time. If the Top G♯ key cork touches first, remove all the old cork and replace with a piece of ⅟₃₂″ cork. (On some model clarinets you will have to add a piece of ³⁄₃₂″ cork instead.) Emery this cork until the two keys touch at the same time.

10. Press the Thumb ring (#7). Your thumb should cover the hole of the thumb key at the same time that the F♯ ring key (#6) closes the tone hole. If the F♯ ring key does not close all the way, add a piece of ⅟₆₄″ cork under the foot of this key where it rests on top of the foot of the Thumb ring (#7).

11. Check the open height of the F♯ ring key (#6). This should open to a height of ⅟₁₆″. If it does not, the height is corrected by changing the thickness of the cork under the foot of the Thumb ring (#7). If the F♯ ring key is open too far, add a piece of ⅟₆₄″ cork under the foot of the *Thumb ring* (#7). Check the open height again and emery the cork if the F♯ ring key does not open far enough.

12. Check the bridge of the A-D ring key (#9). Be certain that there is a piece of ⅟₆₄″ cork under this bridge where it will rest on top of the lower bridge key.

13. Check the open height of the E♭-B♭ aux. key (#13). This key should open to a height of ⅟₁₆″. If it does not, the height is corrected by changing the thickness of the cork located under the lever of this key. Emery the cork to allow the key to open further. If the key opens too far, replace the cork with a piece of ⅟₁₆″ cork. Emery this new cork until the proper open height for the key is achieved.

14. Check the open height of the Curved C♯-G♯ key (#15). This key should open to a height of ¹⁄₁₆″. If it does not, it can be adjusted by regulating the thickness of the cork under the lever of this key. Emery the cork to permit the key to open further. If the key opens too far, replace the cork with a piece of ¹⁄₁₆″ cork. Emery this new cork until the proper open height for the key is achieved.

15. Continue with the lower joint. Check the open height of the B-F♯ key (#18). This key should open to a height of ⁵⁄₆₄″. If it does not, it can be adjusted by regulating the thickness of the cork on the lever of the key. Emery the cork to permit the key to open further. If the key opens too far, remove the cork and replace with a piece of ¹⁄₁₆″ cork. Emery this new cork in order to achieve the correct open key height.

16. Check the open height of the Lower ring key (#16). This key should open to a height of ⁵⁄₆₄″. If it does not, it can be adjusted by regulating the thickness of the cork under the lower bridge. If the key does not open far enough, emery this cork until the proper height is reached. If the key opens too far, remove the old cork and replace with a piece of ¹⁄₁₆″ cork. Emery the new cork until the proper open height is achieved.

17. Check the open height of the A♭ -E♭ key (#21). This key should open to a height of ³⁄₃₂″. If it does not, regulate the thickness of the cork under the lever of this key. If the pad does not open far enough, emery this cork until the correct height is achieved. If the key is opening too far, remove the old cork and replace with a piece of ¹⁄₃₂″ cork. Emery this cork if necessary until the proper open height is achieved.

18. Remove the E♯-B lever (#19) and the F♯-C♯ lever (#20) before continuing with the following adjustment.

19. Check the open height of the Low F-C key (#22). This key should open to a height of ³⁄₃₂″. If it does not, the adjustment is made by bending the foot on the Low F-C key (#22) which extends under the lever of the F♯-C♯ key (#23). First check to be certain that there is a piece of ¹⁄₆₄″ cork on the top of this foot. If the Low F-C key is open too far, bend this foot up slightly with round nose pliers. If the Low F-C key needs to open further, bend this foot down slightly and check again. Care should be taken in bending this foot that it remains level under the keys. Once the F-C key is adjusted to the correct height, the F♯ -C♯ key (#23) will also be at the correct height.

20. Press the lever of the Low E-B key (#24). Using a light pressure, this key should close at the same time as the Low F-C key (#22). Use your leak light to check this. If they do not close at the same time, the adjustment is made by bending the lever of the Low E-B key (#24). If the Low E-B key is closing before the Low F-C key, bend the lever of the Low E-B key down slightly. Place a pad slick under the pad when doing this. If the Low F-C key is closing first, bend the lever of the Low E-B key up slightly while holding the pad against the tone hole.

21. Replace the E-B lever (#19). Be certain that there is a piece of ¹⁄₆₄″ cork located between the lever and the arm of the Low E-B key, (This cork might be either on the top of the lever or the bottom of the arm.) There should not be any excessive "play" in the E-B lever. Pressing the lever should immediately activate the Low E-B key. If the E-B lever (#19) moves before it activates the E-B key (#24), add cork *under* this lever. Remove any old cork and replace with a piece of ¹⁄₁₆″ cork. This cork may be too thick. If it is, the Low E-B key (#24) will hold the Low F-C key (#22) down so that the foot of this key will not be

touching the lever of the F#-C# key (#23). Emery the cork under the E-B lever (#19) until the foot of the Low F-C key will make contact with the lever of the F#-C# key. (*Caution:* If you emery too much, "play" will develop in the E-B lever (#19) and you will have to start over.)

22. Replace the F#-C# lever (#20). Be certain that there is a piece of ¹⁄₆₄″ cork located between this lever and the arm of the F#-C# key (#23). This cork may be either on the top of the F#-C# lever (#20) or the bottom of the arm of the F#-C# key (#23). There should not be any excess "play" in the F#-C# lever (#20). If there is, add cork to the *bottom* of this lever. Remove the old cork and replace with a piece of ¹⁄₁₆″ cork. If this cork is too thick, the F#-C# key (#23) will be holding the Low F-C key (#22) down so that its foot will not make contact with the Low E-B key (#24). Emery the cork under the F#-C# lever (#20) until contact is made between the foot of the Low F-C key (#22) and the lever of the Low E-B key (#24). (*Caution:* If you emery too much, "play" will develop in the F#-C# lever (#20) and you will have to start over.

23. Assemble the upper and lower sections. Press the Lower ring key (#16). This should close the pad at the same time as the A-D ring key (#9). If they do not, make the adjustment by bending the upper bridge of the A-D ring key (#9). If the A-D ring key is closing first, bend the upper bridge *up* slightly. If the Lower ring key (#16) is closing first, bend the upper bridge key *down* slightly.

24. To finish the job, check the thumb rest. If there is no padding under the thumb rest, cement a piece of ¹⁄₃₂″ cork to act as a cushion for the player's thumb. The adjustment of the soprano clarinet is now complete.

THE COMPLETE ADJUSTMENT— HOW TO MAKE THE ADJUSTMENTS NECESSARY FOR PROPER PERFORMANCE OF THE ALTO OR BASS CLARINET

The complete adjustment of the alto or bass clarinet is more complex than that of the soprano clarinet. Although the procedure is basically the same, key mechanisms are more complex and, therefore, require more skill to adjust. By carefully following the instructions below you should be able to do a thorough job of adjusting either the alto or bass clarinet. If, however, you are not sure of the procedures described, you might do more damage than good in attempting to repair or adjust the instrument. In this case a good rule to follow is "When in doubt, send it out." Be sure to read completely through the procedure before beginning.

Tools Needed: Leak light
Small screwdriver
Spring hook
Alcohol burner or bunsen burner
Ruler
Pad slick
Emery paper
Small round nose pliers
Razor blade

Materials Needed: Double skin clarinet pads and/or
leather saxophone pads
Sheet cork in sizes ¹⁄₆₄″, ¹⁄₃₂″ & ¹⁄₁₆″
Stick shellac
Contact cork cement

Procedure: (Refer to Illustration 4-5 for alto clarinet key names and numbers or
Illustration 4-6 for bass clarinet key names and numbers.)

1. Using a leak light, check all pads to be certain that they have a level seat which will form a tight seal with the tone hole. You can check each pad as you adjust it in the procedure to follow or check them all at once before you begin the adjustment. If any of the pads are uneven, loose or torn, they will have to be replaced before you can continue with this adjustment. (See How to Install New Skin Pads, p.117 or How to Install New Leather Pads, p.118.)

2. Starting with the upper joint (or top part of the one piece section), check the open height of the C trill key (#2). When open all the way, this key on the alto clarinet should measure ¹⁄₁₆″ from the bottom of the pad to the top of the tone hole. On the bass clarinet the measurement should be ³⁄₃₂″. If the open height is not correct, change the thickness of the cork under the lever of the key. Emery the cork to allow the key to open more. If the key is opening too far, remove all old cork and replace with a piece of ¹⁄₁₆″ cork. Adjust the thickness of this cork until the proper open key height is achieved.

3. Check the open height of the B♭ trill key (#3). When open all the way, this key on the alto clarinet should measure ¹⁄₁₆″ from the bottom of the pad to the top of the tone hole. On the bass clarinet the measurement should be ³⁄₃₂″. If the open height is not correct, change the thickness of the cork under the lever of the key. Emery the cork to allow the key to open more. If the key is opening too far, remove all old cork and replace with a piece of ¹⁄₁₆″ cork. Adjust the thickness of this cork until the proper open key height is achieved.

4. Check the open height of the F♯-C♯ trill key (#8). When open all the way, this key on the alto clarinet should measure ¹⁄₁₆″ from the bottom of the pad to the top of the tone hole. On the bass clarinet the measurement should be ³⁄₃₂″. If the open height is not correct, change the thickness of the cork under the lever of the key. Emery the cork to allow the key to open more. If the key is opening too far, remove all old cork and replace with a piece of ¹⁄₁₆″ cork. Adjust the thickness of this cork until the proper open key height is achieved.

5. Check the open height of the E♭-B♭ trill key (#12). When open all the way, this key on the alto clarinet should measure ¹⁄₁₆″ from the bottom of the pad to the top of the tone hole. On the bass clarinet the measurement should be ³⁄₃₂″. If the open height is not correct, change the thickness of the cork under the lever of the key. If the cork needs to be replaced, remove all the old cork, then cement a piece of ³⁄₃₂″ cork under the lever. This cork can be trimmed to achieve the correct open key height by cutting thin pieces off with a single edge razor blade, then using emery paper for the final adjustment. If you have an instrument with separate upper and lower sections, you will need to assemble these sections before you can make the height adjustment for this key.

6. Check the open height of the Top G♯ key (#5). This key should open to a height

of $\frac{1}{16}$" on the alto clarinet, and $\frac{3}{32}$" on the bass clarinet. If the open height is not correct, change the thickness of cork under the lever of the key. If the cork needs replacing, remove all the old cork and cement a piece of $\frac{1}{32}$" cork under the lever of the key. (Some clarinets may require a piece of $\frac{3}{32}$" cork at this point.) Emery the cork as necessary to achieve the proper open key height.

7. Press the A key (#4). This key should move the Top G♯ key (#5) at the same time that it starts to move. If it does not, adjust the screw located where the arm of the Top G♯ key extends over the A key. If the A key moves before the Top G♯ key, turn the screw down slightly. Check with a leak light to be certain that the adjustment screw is not holding the Top G♯ key open.

8. Check the A key (#4). This key should open so that the cork under the lever touches the body of the clarinet at the same time that the cork under the lever of the Top G♯ key (#5) touches the body of the instrument. If the A key cork touches first, emery the cork thinner until they touch at the same time. If the Top G♯ key cork touches first, remove all the old cork on the A key and replace with a piece of $\frac{1}{32}$" cork. (Some model clarinets will need a piece of $\frac{3}{32}$" cork instead.) Emery the cork as necessary to achieve the correct adjustment.

9. Press the Thumb key (#7). This key should close at the same time as the F♯ key (#6). Use a leak light to make this check. If the F♯ key does not close all the way, add a piece of $\frac{1}{64}$" cork under the foot of this key where it rests on the top of the foot of the Thumb key (#7). If the F♯ key closes *before* the Thumb key (#7), emery this cork a little thinner. If this does not solve the problem, us small round nose pliers to bend the foot of the F♯ key (#6) up slightly, then re-adjust the cork as described in the above.

10. Now check the open height of the F♯ key (#6). On the alto clarinet it should measure $\frac{1}{16}$" from the bottom of the pad to the top of the tone hole. On the bass clarinet this measurement should be $\frac{3}{32}$". If the open height is not correct, change the thickness of the cork under the foot of the *Thumb key* (#7). If the F♯ key is open too far, add a piece of $\frac{1}{64}$" cork under the foot of the Thumb key. Check the open key height again and emery the cork if the F♯ key does not open far enough.

11. Press the F♯ Aperture key (#29). This key should close at the same time as the F♯ key (#6). Use a leak light to make this check. If these two keys do not close at the same time, the adjustment is made by a small screw which is located on the F♯ Aperture key. (Some models will have a small tab with a piece of cork between these two keys.) If the F♯ key (#6) is closing before the F♯ Aperture key (#29) then loosen the screw slightly (or thin down the cork with a piece of emery paper). If the F♯ key (#6) does not close all the way, tighten the screw slightly (or remove all the old cork from the tab and replace with a piece of $\frac{1}{64}$" cork, then emery for proper adjustment).

12. Check the open height of the E♭-B♭ Aux. key (#13). On the alto clarinet this key should open to a height of $\frac{1}{16}$". On the bass clarinet this measurement should be $\frac{3}{32}$". If the open height is not correct, change the thickness of the cork located under the lever of this key. Emery the cork to allow the key to open further. If the key opens too far, the cork will need to be replaced with a piece of $\frac{1}{16}$" cork. Emery this new cork until the proper open key height is achieved.

13. Check the open height of the C♯-G♯ key (#15). On the alto clarinet this key should open to a height of $\frac{1}{16}$". On the bass clarinet this measurement should be $\frac{3}{32}$". If the

open height is not correct, change the thickness of the cork under the lever of this key. Emery the cork to permit the key to open farther. If the key opens too far, the cork will need to be replaced with a piece of ¹⁄₁₆″ cork. You will need to emery this new cork until the proper open key height is achieved.

14. Press the Register key lever (#1). This should open the Throat B♭ key (#28). While holding the Register key lever (#1) down also press the Thumb key (#7). This should open the Register key (#26) while at the same time closing the Throat B♭ key (#28). At this point, both the Throat B♭ key (#28) and the Thumb key (#7) should close at the same time. Use a leak light to make this check. If they do not close together, make the adjustment in the thickness of the cork on the tab which connects these two keys. (Some models will have an adjustment screw at this point.) If the Throat B♭ key (#28) is not closing all the way, add a small piece of cork to this tab (or tighten the screw). If the Thumb key (#7) does not close all the way, emery this cork thinner (or loosen the screw) until the correct adjustment is achieved.

15. Press the Register lever (#1) to open the Throat B♭ key (#28). This key should open far enough so that it will touch the tab on the Thumb key (#7) mentioned above. If it does not, you will need to remove some of the cork under the lever of the Register lever (#1). If the Register lever lifts higher than the Throat B♭ key (#28), remove all the old cork from under the Register lever and replace with a piece of ¹⁄₃₂″ cork then check again.

16. **Bass Clarinet Only**—Press the A-D key (#10). The pad on the key should close at the same time as the E♭-B♭ bis key (#9). Use a leak light to make this check. If they do not close together, first check under the lever of the A-D key (#10). There should be a piece of felt under this key. If not, glue a piece of flat felt under this lever using contact cement, then check again. If the keys are still not in adjustment, correct by bending the lever of the A-D key slightly. If the E♭-B♭ bis key (#9) is closing before the A-D key, hold the pad of this key against the tone hole and bend the lever *up* slightly. If the E♭-B♭ bis key (#9) is not closing, place a pad slick between the pad and tone hole of the A-D key and bend the lever *down* slightly. Check regularly until the adjustment is correct.

17. **Bass Clarinet Only**—Press the C-G key (#11). The pad in this key should close at the same time as the A-D key (#10) and the E♭-B♭ bis key (#9) if step 16 has been completed correctly. Use a leak light to make this check. If they do not close together, first check under the lever of the C-G key (#11). There should be a piece of felt under the key. If not, glue a piece of flat felt under this lever using contact cement, then check again. If the keys are still not in adjustment, correct by bending the lever of the C-G key slightly. If the A-D key is closing ahead of the C-G key, hold the pad of this key against the tone hole and bend the lever *up* slightly. If the A-D key is not closing, place a pad slick between the pad and tone hole of the C-G key and bend the lever *down* slightly. Check regularly until the adjustment is correct.

18. Continue with the lower joint or the lower portion of the single section clarinet. Check the open height of the B-F♯ aux. key (#18). On the alto clarinet this key should open to a height of ³⁄₃₂″. On the bass clarinet the measurement should be ¹⁄₈″. If the open height is not correct, change the thickness of the cork under the lever of the key. If the key does not open far enough, emery this cork until the proper height is achieved. If

the key opens too far, remove the old cork and replace with a piece of ⅟₁₆″ cork. Emery this new cork until the proper open key height is achieved.

19. **Alto Clarinet Only**—Check the open height of the Lower ring key (#16). This key should open to a height of ³⁄₃₂″. If the open height is not correct, it can be adjusted by regulating the thickness of the cork under the lower bridge. If the key does not open far enough, emery this cork until the proper height is reached. If the key opens too far, remove the old cork and replace with a piece of ⅟₁₆″ cork. Emery this new cork until the proper open key height achieved.

20. **Bass Clarinet Only**—Check the open height of the B♭-F 12-key (#30). This key should open to a height of ⅛″. If this height is not correct, it can be adjusted by regulating the thickness of the cork under the foot of the key. If the pad does not open far enough, emery the cork thinner until the correct height is achieved. If the key opens too far, remove all the old cork and cement a new piece of ⅟₁₆″ cork in place. Adjust this cork until the correct open key height is achieved.

21. **Bass Clarinet Only**—Press the B♭-F key (#30). This key should close at the same time as the B-F♯ key (#16). Use a leak light as you check. If they do not close together, the adjustment is made where the foot of the B♭-F key (#30) goes under the arm of the B-F♯ key (#16). Usually there is a thin piece of cork located between these keys at this point; however, some models have an adjustment screw. If the B♭-F(#30) is closing before the B-F♯ key (#16), add a thin piece of cork (probably ⅟₆₄″). This will probably cause the B-F♯ key to close too soon so then emery this new piece of cork until the adjustment is correct.

22. **Bass Clarinet Only**—Press the A-E key (#31). This key should close at the same time as the B-F♯ key (#16). Use a leak light as you check. If they do not close together, the adjustment is made where the foot of the A-E key (#31) goes under the arm of the B-F♯ (#16). Usually there is a thin piece of cork located between these keys at this point; however, some models have an adjustment screw. If the A-E key (#31) is closing before the B-F♯ key (#16), add a thin piece of cork (probably ⅟₆₄″). If this causes the B-F♯ key to close too soon, emery this new piece of cork until the adjustment is correct.

23. Check the open height of the G-D key (#33). This key should open to a height of ⅛″. If it is not correct, the adjustment is made by regulating the thickness of the cork under the foot of the G-D *lever* (#32). Adding more cork will lower the open key height, removing cork will raise the key. Be certain that there is a piece of ⅟₆₄″ cork located under the arm of the G-D key (#33) before adjusting.

24. Check the open height of the A♭-E♭ key (#21). This key should open to a height of ⅛″. If the key height is not correct, adjust by regulating the thickness of the cork under the lever of this key. If the pad does not open far enough, emery this cork until the correct height is achieved. If the key is opening too far, remove all the old cork and replace with a piece of ⅟₃₂″ cork. Emery this cork, if necessary, to achieve the proper open height.

25. Remove the E-B lever (#19) and the F♯-C♯ lever (#20) before continuing with the following adjustment.

26. Check the open height of the F-C key (#22). This key should open to a height of ⅛″. If it does not, an adjustment is made by bending the foot of the F-C key (#22) which extends under the lever of the F♯-C♯ key (#23). First check to be certain that there is a

piece of ¹⁄₆₄" cork on the top of this foot. If the F-C key is open too far, bend this foot *up* slightly, with round nose pliers. If the F-C key needs to open further, bend this foot *down* slightly. Care should be taken while bending this foot that it remains level under the keys. Once the F-C key is adjusted to the correct height, the F♯-C♯ key (#23) will also open to the correct height.

27. Press on the lever of the E-B key (#24). Using a light pressure, this key should close at the same time as the F-C key (#22). Use a leak light to check this. If they do not close together, adjust by bending the lever of the E-B key (#24). If the E-B key is closing before the F-C key, bend the lever of the E-B key down slightly. (Place a pad slick under the pad of the E-B key before bending.) If the F-C key is closing first, bend the lever of the E-B key up slightly while holding the pad against the tone hole. (*NOTE:* If your clarinet has the low E-B key located on the bell of the instrument, disregard this step and proceed to step 28.

28. If your clarinet has the Low E-B key located on the bell of the instrument, press the E-B key lever (#24). Using a light pressure, this key should close at the same time as the F-C key (#22). Use a leak light to check this. If they do not close at the same time, adjust the cork under the arm of the Bell key (#34). If the Bell key is closing before the F-C key, emery this cork thinner until the proper adjustment is achieved. If the F-C key is closing first, add a piece of cork under this arm. Remove all the old cork and replace with a piece of ¹⁄₃₂" cork. Emery this new cork until the proper adjustment is achieved.

29. If your clarinet has the additional Low E♭ key, follow the same adjustment procedures as described in step 28.

30. Replace the E-B lever (#19). Be certain that there is a piece of ¹⁄₆₄" cork located between the lever and the arm of the E-B key (#24). There should not be any excess "play" in the E-B lever. On some instruments the E-B lever has a small pin on the end which inserts into a hole in the arm of the E-B key. If this is the case, wrap a small circle of plastic (cut from a plastic bag) around this pin before inserting into the hole.

31. Press the E-B lever (#19). This should immediately activate the Low E-B key. If the E-B lever (#19) moves before it activates the E-B key, add cork under the *lever*. Remove any old cork and replace with a piece of ¹⁄₁₆" cork. This new cork will probably be too thick. If it is, the Low E-B key (#24) will hold the F-C key (#22) down so that the foot of this key will not be touching the lever of the F♯-C♯ key (#23). Emery the cork under the E-B lever (#19) until the foot of the E-B key makes contact with the lever of the F♯-C♯ key. (*Caution:* If you emery too much, "play" will develop in the E-B lever (#19) and you will have to start over.)

32. Replace the F♯-C♯ lever (#20). Be certain that there is a piece of ¹⁄₆₄" cork located between this lever and the arm of the F♯-C♯ key (#23). There should not be any excessive "play" in the F♯-C♯ lever (#20). On some instruments the F♯-C♯ lever has a small pin on the end which inserts into the hole in the arm of the F♯-C♯ key. If this is the case, wrap a small circle of plastic (cut from a plastic bag) around this pin before inserting into the hole.

33. Check the F♯-C♯ lever (#20). If there is any "play" in this lever, add cork to the bottom of this lever. Remove the old cork and replace with a piece of ¹⁄₁₆" cork. If this new cork is too thick, the F♯-C♯ key (#23) will hold the F-C key (#22) down so that its foot will not make contact with the Low E-B key (#24). Emery the cork under the F♯-C♯ lever

(#20) until contact is made between the foot of the F-C key (#22) and the lever of the E-B key (#24). (*Caution:* If you emery too much, "play" will develop in the F#-C# lever (#20), and you will have to start over.)

34. **Alto Clarinet Only**—If you have a two piece instrument, assemble the upper and lower sections. Press the Lower ring key (#16). This should close the pad at the same time as the A-D ring key (#9). Use a leak light to make this check. If they do not close together, the adjustment is made by bending the upper bridge of the A-D ring key (#9). If the A-D ring key is closing first, bend the upper bridge *up* slightly. If the Lower ring key (#16) is closing first, bend the upper bridge key *down* slightly. Before bending, be certain that the upper bridge key has a piece of 1/64" cork under it where it makes contact with the lower bridge.

35. **Bass Clarinet Only**—If you have a two piece instrument, assemble the upper and lower sections. Press the Bb-F key (#30). This should close the pad at the same time as the Eb -Bb bis key (#9). Use your leak light to make this check. If they do not close together, the adjustment is made by bending the upper bridge of the Eb-Bb bis key (#9). If the Eb-Bb bis key is closing first, bend the upper bridge *up* slightly. If the Bb-F key (#30) is closing first, bend the upper bridge key *down* slightly. Before bending, be certain that the upper bridge key has a piece of 1/64" cork under it where it makes contact with the lower bridge.

36. The adjustment of the alto or bass clarinet is now complete.

REPAIRS TO BE SENT TO THE REPAIR SHOP

The clarinet is a relatively easy instrument to repair, with the alto and bass clarinet being somewhat more difficult. I feel that most of the adjustments and work listed in this chapter can be done by you with a minimum of tools and supplies. You can best determine after reading this chapter which repairs you feel capable of doing and which you feel should be sent to the repair shop. A good rule to follow is: "When in doubt, send it out."

There are some repairs, however, which require specialized tools or special skills that take time to develop. Below I have outlined some of the more common clarinet repairs that will need to be done at a repair shop. It is hoped that this will give you a better understanding of the repair procedures.

REPAIRING CRACKS IN THE BODY

Only wood clarinets will have the potential for cracking. Following a careful maintenance plan as outlined in the beginning of this chapter will help greatly to reduce this possibility. If the clarinet should crack, it is best to have it repaired as soon as possible before the crack increases in size. The larger the crack, the more difficult and expensive the repair. A quick visual check each month can reveal developing cracks before they become serious. Cracks always develop along the grain of the wood, so look for them to run along the length of the joint. Before sending in for repair, mark the crack with a pencil. Because of temperature changes, cracks sometimes close up before the repair technician has a chance to work on it. The pencil mark will help the repair technician find the crack.

The most common method of repairing a crack is to pin it. The repair technician will determine the length of the crack by scratching it open further with a fine pick. This also gives a good base for the filler which is added later. To pin the crack the repair technician starts by drilling a hole through the body (but not the bore) of the clarinet. The hole is drilled perpendicular to the crack at intervals of about one per inch for the length of the crack. A piece of threaded rod, which is slightly larger than the hole, is heated at the tip. When the rod is red hot, it is threaded into the hole. When cool, this threaded rod will hold the sections together and prevent the crack from spreading any further. The pins do not pull the sections of crack back together; they just prevent the crack from spreading further.

After the pins are in place, a filler is used (usually a hard epoxy) to fill the crack and the hole left from the pins. If the crack runs through the tone hole, it must be filled carefully so that the tone hole will not leak when the job is complete. After the epoxy is dry, it is filed and sanded smooth and then a black die is used to color the epoxy to match the body of the clarinet. If pinned correctly, the clarinet should not crack further, and the epoxy filler will seal the crack.

REPAIRING BROKEN TENONS

A broken tenon can occur on either a wood or plastic clarinet. This is not a common occurence, but when it does happen it is almost always on the tenon of the upper joint. This is because the break usually occurs when assembling or disassembling this section. If the player does not insert the sections carefully, with the slight twisting action, there will be a tendency to pull or push the sections at an angle. When this angle becomes great enough, the tenon will break. Tenons can also break if the section of the clarinet is dropped.

A broken tenon is not the end of your clarinet. It can be replaced and, although the job will be expensive, it should be less than the cost of buying a new section. When repaired correctly, the replacement tenon should be as strong as the original.

The repair technician will first cut off the remains of the old tenon. He then drills up into the body of the clarinet with a special cutting tool which enlarges the bore diameter about ⅜″ to ¼″. The hole is drilled up about ½″ to ¾″ into the body. A tenon plug, which has already been cut so that it will fit into the receiver of the other section, is then inserted into this new hole and epoxyed in place. After the epoxy has set, the new plug will be bonded firmly to the body of the clarinet. It is then necessary to re-drill any tone holes and post holes that have been blocked by the tenon plug. Also, the repair technician will have to ream out the bore of the plug so that it matches that of the clarinet body. The tenon is then corked and fitted to the receiver.

The procedure is the same for replacing either tenon of the clarinet. Only the size of the tenon plug and the cutting tools have to be different to accommodate the difference in bore size between the two tenons.

REPAIRING BROKEN KEYS

If a clarinet key actually breaks in half this can be repaired in the shop. Be certain that you save the pieces and send them along with the entire clarinet. The repair technician will braze the two pieces together with silver solder. When done correctly, this will bond the two sections of the key together as securely as the original piece. Also, the mend will not be too noticeable and should function like the original key. It is important to send the entire instrument, so the repair technician can be certain that the key is brazed at the correct angle and re-adjusted to the instrument.

If you should lose one of the broken pieces, most repair shops will be able to either order a new key, or fashion a key from an old part of a discarded clarinet. In either case, this is usually more expensive and time consuming.

TIGHTENING LOOSE KEYS

If your clarinet has a lot of "play" in the keys (that is, they move sideways on the rod or between the pivot screws) you may have a problem getting the pads to always close on the seat. This "play" is usually found on older clarinets, as the metal of the key will eventually wear off through use. If the key is mounted on a *rod* and slides sideways along the rod, then there is too much room between the posts. The repair technician will have to stretch the hinge tube of the key to fill the gap (a process called "swedging").

It is also possible that the diameter of the key's hinge tube has enlarged through wear and is now bigger than the diameter of the pivot rod. In this case the repair technician will squeeze the hinge tube slightly to tighten, but not so much as to bind the key action.

If the loose key is held in place with pivot screws, the repair technician will check to see if the screws have backed out or are worn. Sometimes on older clarinets, the screws will be worn down on the ends and cannot hold the key firmly in place. In this case the screw can be replaced with a new screw for the same brand clarinet. It is also possible that the hole in the post will be worn causing the screw to be loose. It will then be necessary to re-fit the post with a different style pivot screw that can be adapted to the clarinet.

TIGHTENING LOOSE POSTS

On the wood clarinet it is possible for the post to loosen up in the body. When this happens, the post will begin to turn and the pivot screws will no longer be aligned with the key. This will usually cause the key to bind. A loose post should be tightened.

There are two ways to correct this problem. One is to epoxy the loose post in place. This will hold the post permanently in place but has the disadvantage of making it impossible to remove the post if this ever becomes necessary.

Another more common correction is to use a post locking screw. With a special drill the repair technician will drill a small hole alongside the base of the post into the body of the clarinet. This drill will also countersink a small bevel into the edge of the post base at the same time. The technician then screws a small flat head screw into the hole. As the screw is tightened down, the head goes into the counter sunk portion in the post and prevents the post from turning. With this method, the post locking screw can always be removed if it becomes necessary for future repair.

REPLATING THE KEYS—THE COMPLETE OVERHAUL

Most clarinet keys are silver plated or nickel plated, and in time this plating can begin to wear off. Although this in no way affects the playability of the clarinet, it does give it a shabby appearance. The keys can be replated to look like new, but this should only be done as a part of a complete overhaul of the clarinet. In order to replate the keys, it is obviously necessary to remove all the pads and corks. Also, all the posts will have to be removed as they cannot be plated while on the instrument.

Not all repair shops can do replating, although most can send this type of work to another company. Replating any type of instrument or key requires having the chemicals necessary to strip off the old finish and the equipment for electroplating. The keys and posts are all removed and the old finish removed. All parts are then buffed to a high gloss smoothness and then replated using an electroplating process. When the plating is complete, the clarinet is re-assembled using all new pads and corks. Often excess plating must be removed from the keys to insure a proper fit between the posts.

When this job is complete, your clarinet will have a "like new" appearance and playability.

THE COMPLETE REPAD

Even though you may do a good job of maintaining the playing condition of the clarinets in your band, there will come a time when most of the pads start to tear and dry out. Many of the corks will be depressed, dried out or missing altogether. This is the time to have the clarinet completely repadded. A complete repad in most shops will consist of replacing all the old pads and corks with new, installing new tenon corks, and cleaning the body of the clarinet. Loose keys are usually tightened as a part of this job. When re-assembling, all the pads will be seated and the springs will be adjusted to a good action. In short, the instrument should *play* like a new clarinet.

5

The Bassoon

Illustration 5-1

Photograph courtesy of The Selmer Co.; Elkhart, Indiana

HOW TO TAKE CARE OF YOUR BASSOON

Taking proper care of the bassoon should be the first, and most important step in your bassoon maintenance plan. By following the suggestions given here, you can avoid many of the problems which cause the bassoon to play improperly. Although this might be a review for many band directors, it is suggested that you share this information with your bassoon players so they will also have an understanding of proper bassoon care. When the student understands the reasons for the maintenance procedures outlined below, there is a better chance that he or she will follow them.

ASSEMBLE THE BASSOON CAREFULLY

The bassoon consists of five sections that need to be assembled: the bocal, the wing (or tenor) joint, the boot joint, the bass joint and the bell. (See Illustration 5-2, page 155, for a picture of each joint.) The bassoon key mechanism is quite intricate and, therefore, great care must be taken in putting the instrument together. If it is done carelessly, bent keys could result.

Before assembling it is extremely important to be sure that the tenons work freely. If they are cork and are dry or tight fitting, they need some cork grease to avoid difficulty in assembling the sections. If they are string wound tenons, apply a slight amount of wax to help free the fit. The tenon should go into the receiver smoothly but not be so loose that the joint is likely to come apart or wiggle when the sections are together.

Begin by inserting the wing joint into the boot joint. Line these two sections up so that the Whisper key bridge lever (#16) on the wing joint will extend over the Low E key (#17) on the boot joint. Next insert the bass joint into the boot joint. This section will fit into the "groove" of the wing joint. You will need to push with a steady pressure and rotate the bass joint slightly as you push to get this section in. Almost all bassoons have a joint locking mechanism of some sort located near the top of the bass and wing joint. Line up the two locking pieces and secure the lock. This will automatically line up these two sections of the bassoon. Many players attempt to insert both the wing and bass joints into the boot joint at the same time. This is a poor practice because it requires that the tenons fit much looser. This, in turn, could cause air leaks or even permit the boot joint to fall off while playing.

Next add the bell to the bass joint. Assemble this with a slight twisting action and line up the bridge keys.

Finally insert the bocal into the receiver located on the top of the wing joint. The bocal should be lined up so that the bocal vent (small hole in the side of the bocal) is lined up with the Whisper key (#13). Some bassoons have a hand rest located on the boot joint which can be attached at this time.

STORE THE BASSOON PROPERLY

The bassoon should always be stored in the case. A bassoon left lying about on a chair, table or music stand is easily bumped or dropped on the floor. This can result in serious and expensive repairs. *Never* store the bassoon near a radiator or heating duct. Excessive heat is a contributing factor in causing wood to crack (an expensive repair on the bassoon). In addition, as the wood dries out, the posts will loosen, permitting them to turn and bind the key action. This is a common problem on the bassoon.

One should also avoid storing the bassoon in extremely cold conditions. Having the bassoon in sub-zero weather can cause the pads to loosen. Once the pad has loosened or fallen out it will be necessary for you to replace it with a new pad as it is very difficult to relocate the pad seat in the same position.

Quick temperature changes can contribute to a wood instrument cracking, so avoid playing on a cold bassoon. Let the instrument warm up to room temperature before playing it.

Bassoon cases should be designed to hold the instrument securely in the case. Most cases have a small storage section to hold reeds, swabs, hand rests, etc. The case is not designed to serve as a display area for medals and pins or to carry lesson books and music. This overpacking of the case can cause excessive pressure on the instrument when the cover is closed and may cause the keys to bend or go out of alignment. Dangling medals can catch under the keys of the bassoon when the case is closed, bending them when the case is opened.

Many bassoon cases do not protect the instrument very well. This, I feel, is one of the major causes of bassoon damage. Check your bassoon cases to be certain that they are holding the instrument securely. Place the bassoon in the case, remove all accessories stored in the storage compartment, close the cover and latch it. Hold the handle down and shake the case. If you hear the bassoon bouncing inside, the case is not providing the protection that it should and there needs to be padding added to the case.

The quickest and cheapest way to correct the problem is to lay a piece of towel on top of the bassoon. This cloth will fill up the excess space inside the case yet will not damage the instrument. Shake again and add more cloth if needed. If the cover becomes hard to close, you have added too much cloth. You could also remove the lining from the cover of the case, add more padding and then reglue. This will take more time and skill but will look better when completed.

Inspect the case periodically to be certain that it is in good condition. Prompt attention should be given to broken or loose latches, hinges or handles. Be certain that the lining is not loose. Loose lining can easily be corrected with some glue, but broken case hardware will need to be sent to the repair shop for correction.

Do not store damp swabs or cloths in the bassoon case. Trapping this moisture in the case will cause the bassoon pads to remain wet for a longer period of time, thus decreasing the life span. Also, excessive moisture or humidity will contribute to rust forming on the pivot screws and rods. This will eventually cause the key action to slow or stop.

CLEAN THE BASSOON REGULARLY

A few minutes of care in cleaning the bassoon after each playing session will go a long way in helping maintain the instrument. Most important is to swab out the bore of the bassoon after each playing session in order to remove all traces of moisture. The bassoon is a large instrument and the diameter of the bore varies considerably from the bocal to the bell. For this reason it is important that the player have a set of various sized bassoon swabs to accommodate all the different sections of the instrument. This is a bother and, as a result, many students are tempted not to swab the bassoon. If the bassoon is not dried after each playing session the water will seep into the pads, causing them to deteriorate much more rapidly than normal.

Use a swab that fits each section of the instrument and dry thoroughly. This is especially important in the wing and boot joints, as this is where most of the moisture accumulates. It is also important to clean out the bocal. Use a piece of pipe stem cleaner for this task; it is small enough to go into the small openings. You will have to swab this from both ends in order to reach the entire length of the bocal.

The octave vent in the bocal should be cleaned out periodically. Use a piece of broom straw or a small needle spring and work around the hold to be sure that it is free from dirt. Care should be taken, however, that the hole is not enlarged in any way while being cleaned.

Most bassoon keys are nickel plated, so there is no need to polish the keys. Wipe the keys regularly with a soft cloth to remove any body oils that collect on the keys. This will help maintain a good appearance.

The outside of the bassoon will eventually begin to accumulate dirt under the keys and rods. It is a good idea to remove this lint before it gets into the rods and slows up the key action. Using a small modeler's paint brush or pipe stem cleaner, reach under the keys and brush away any dirt or lint that has collected. *Care should be taken to avoid catching any of the springs*. This might change the spring tension and could affect the adjustment and function of some of the keys.

MAINTENANCE PROCEDURES FOR THE BASSOON

Cork Tenons—When the tenon cork is new, it is fitted correctly for the receiver and then a light coating of cork grease is applied to ease the assembling of the section. The cork grease attracts dirt which begins to build up on the cork tenon, thus making the tenon fit tighter. The player will then add more cork grease. This cycle continues with layers of grease and dirt slowly building up on the tenon cork.

The cork tenons of the bassoon should be kept clean to insure a good fit. The best procedure to follow is to wipe them completely dry about once a month. Use a piece of cloth and rub vigorously as you rotate the tenon. After the tenon cork is completely clean and dry, apply a *small* amount of cork grease. By following this procedure you will not only lengthen the life of the tenon cork, but you will also avoid tight fitting tenons which can be one of the chief causes of bent bassoon keys.

As the tenon cork gets older, it will begin to dry out (cork grease helps prevent this) and will shrink in size. When the cork is too small for the receiver, a loose fit results and the two sections will "wiggle" when they are together. When this happens, it is time to replace the tenon cork (See How to Re-cork the Tenons, p. 162).

String Tenons—Many bassoons are supplied with string wound tenons instead of cork tenons. There is nothing mysterious about this type of tenon and it can easily be cared for by the student. As with the cork tenon, the new tenon is fitted so that a tight fit will result with the corresponding receiver. You *should not apply cork grease* to a string tenon as it has a coating of beeswax on the string to help hold the string in place. If your tenon is too tight, apply a light coating of beeswax to help ease the assembling process.

If the tenon fit has become too loose, it can be repaired easily (see How to Restring the Tenons, p.000). The string tenon also needs to be cleaned periodically. Wipe the tenon with a clean dry cloth to remove all traces of dirt, then coat lightly with beeswax. This will act both to keep the string intact and as a lubricant for the tenon and receiver.

Oiling the Bore—It is important to note here that you should NEVER OIL THE BORE OF THE BASSOON. Bassoons are usually made from maple, not grenadilla, and are less likely to crack. In addition, the outside of the instrument is varnished and the inside is usually coated (or lined with another material) to protect the bore against absorbing any moisture.

Sticky Pads—Sticky pads are caused by the accumulation of dirt on the pad seat or tone hole. The student should avoid chewing gum, eating candy or drinking "pop" immediately before or during playing. All these items increase the amount of sugar in the saliva, some of which will travel through the bore and accumulate on the pads. This sticky substance then attracts dirt to the pad, causing the stickiness. Swabbing the bore will help prevent this, but not after the moisture has reached the pads.

Sticky pads are usually first noticed by an annoying "clicking" sound as the pad opens from the tone hole. As the problem gets worse, the key will not open promptly and the key action will be slowed down. The problem should be corrected as soon as it is noticed, as this is when it is easiest to do. If possible, try to determine the source of the sticky pads to avoid future problems.

Oiling the Keys—The keys of the bassoon should be oiled about once a month to keep them working freely and to prevent the screws and rods from rusting. If the rods and screws do rust, the key action can bind up and will require a repair technician to correct. Key oil is available from your music dealer. Use a pin or toothpick and place a small drop of key oil at the end of each key rod. Work the keys to circulate the oil, then wipe off any excess oil that may be on the rod. Care should be taken to avoid using too much key oil. Excess oil on the keys will attract dirt which, will mix with the oil to slow the key action.

MONTHLY MAINTENANCE CHECK LIST—BASSOON

Chart 17 is a check list that can be used to help in the maintenance of the bassoon. Following this chart should keep the instrument clean, and alert you to any repairs needed before they become too severe. With some training, your students should be able to utilize this check list by themselves.

HOW TO REPAIR THE BASSOON

DIAGNOSING INSTRUMENT MALFUNCTIONS

Before you can repair the bassoon, you need to diagnose the problem. Listed below are some of the more common problems that can occur with the bassoon. For each problem I have suggested some possible causes in hopes that it will help you locate the

Chart 17
Monthly Maintenance Check List—Bassoon

INSPECT THE FOLLOWING:

Bassoon
- _____ Are the tenon corks or string clean, intact and lightly greased or waxed?
- _____ Do the sections of the bassoon fit easily together, yet remain secure while playing?
- _____ Are there any sticky pads?
- _____ Are there any worn pads?
- _____ Are there any loose pads?
- _____ Are all the keys moving freely?
- _____ Are there any missing screws or rods?
- _____ Are all the posts tight in the body of the bassoon?
- _____ Are the bridge keys between each section working properly?

Case
- _____ Are the latches working properly?
- _____ Are the hinges tight?
- _____ Is the handle secure?
- _____ Is the lining in place?
- _____ Are there any loose objects in the case?
- _____ Are there any pins or medals attached to the lining?
- _____ Is the bassoon held tightly in the case when closed?
- _____ Is the bassoon supplied with a swab?

DO THE FOLLOWING:
1. Check for leaks (see How to Check for Leaks, p.156).
2. Clean dirt and lint from under the keys and rods.
3. Oil the key rods and screws.
4. Clean the tenon corks and grease lightly (or)
5. Clean the string tenons and wax lightly.

difficulty. Although this list can hardly be complete, it should serve as a good beginning guideline.

1. _Problem:_ Bassoon blows hard, will not play all notes clearly.

Possible Causes: Pads are leaking (look for torn pads, missing pads or those not seating properly). Keys are not regulated properly (particularly check the bridge keys). Leak in the boot gasket. Reed problems.

2. _Problem:_ Bassoon plays wrong note.

Possible Causes: Spring may be unhooked from key. Broken spring. Keys may not be regulated correctly. Loose pad remains closed when key is opened.

3. _Problem:_ Bassoon plays out of tune.

Possible Causes: Player's embouchure and/or reed may need attention. Key corks may be missing, causing incorrect key heights. All keys may be set incorrectly.

4. _Problem:_ Keys are not functioning properly.

Possible Causes: Broken or unhooked springs. Bridge keys not correctly aligned. Bent key rod or posts. Loose post in body of bassoon. Pivot screws may be too tight or rusted. Keys and rods may be dirty or rusted.

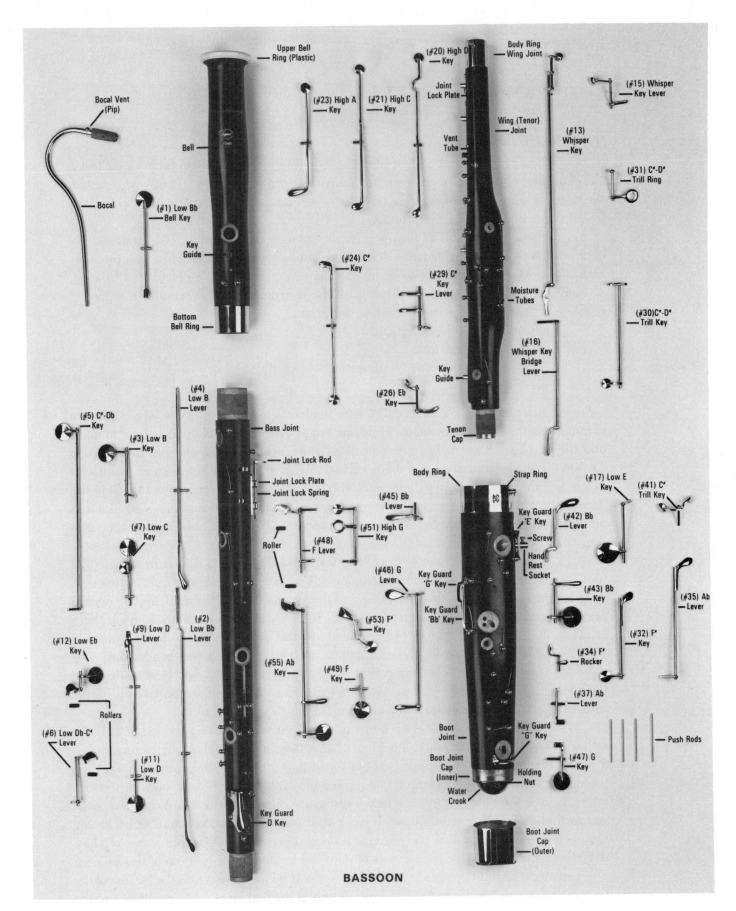

BASSOON

Illustration 5-2

Photograph courtesy of The Selmer Co.; Elkhart, Indiana

5. *Problem:* Bassoon sections do not stay aligned.
   Possible Causes: Joint lock broken. Tenons too loose.

HOW TO CHECK FOR LEAKS

When your basson does not play properly, the first thing to do is check for leaks. Leaks in the bassoon can be the result of a missing, torn or worn pad, bent keys, crack in the bocal, leaking boot gasket, loose posts or rusted screws and rods. You need to find the leak if you wish to correct the problem.

Generally speaking, all the notes on the bassoon should produce the same quality of tone. If you have a note or notes that sound "stuffy," or are hard to blow, you probably have a leak. Many beginning bassoon players, however, have trouble playing the bassoon, so I suggest that an experienced player play the instrument to determine if the playing problem is the fault of the instrument or the player.

Tools Needed: Leak testing corks
                Leak light
                Sink or pail with water

Procedure:

1. Start by checking the bocal. A very small leak in this section can be a big source of trouble on the entire instrument. Hold one finger over the end of the bocal and another over the vent hole. Blow in the other end. You should be able to hear and feel any escaping air. You might also try sucking on the bocal rather than blowing to see if it can maintain a vacuum. If the vacuum rapidly disappears, then there is a leak. If you suspect a leak in the bocal, fill a pail with water and submerge the entire bocal in the water and blow into it as indicated above. Any leak will become readily apparent by the air bubbles that appear in the water.

2. Check the wing (tenor) joint. The testing of this joint is similar to the method used in testing the other woodwind instruments. Use an appropriate size leak testing cork and plug the bottom end of this joint. Close all the keys in the joint by applying the normal pressure used when playing the instrument. Blow *gently* into the top of the joint. If there is a leak, you should hear the air escaping and feel the lack of resistance as you blow. Be very critical when listening for the escaping air, as it will not be a very loud sound.

After you locate the leaking pad or pads, re-adjust the keys (see How to Regulate the Keys, p.157), replace the pad (see How to Install New Leather Bassoon Pads, p.158) or adjust the key mechanism (see How to Regulate the Keys, p.157).

3. Check the boot joint. This is the most difficult section to test because of its being rather awkward. As above, you will need to close all keys in order to seal all the tone holes. Seal the smaller of the two openings at the top of this joint with a leak testing cork, then place your mouth around the larger opening and blow into this end. Keep normal pressure on the keys as you blow. If there is a lack of resistance, there is a leak. Have someone assist you in finding this leak as you blow. It can either be located by the sound or by having someone press lightly on each pad until the leaking stops. Another possible source of a leak is the boot gasket. Remove the outer boot joint cap located on the bottom of this section. This cap might be tight but can be worked off with a little patience. Place the bottom of the boot joint in enough water to cover the metal parts at the bottom of the joint. Blow into the

joint as described above, holding all keys closed. If the gasket is leaking, air bubbles will appear at the source (see How to Replace the Boot Gasket, p. 171).

4. Check the bass joint in the same manner as described under step 2.

5. To check the bell, it is easier to use a leak testing light. As there is only one key on this section, simply place the light under the pad and close *lightly*. Check all around the pad; if no light is visible it is sealing properly.

6. Check the bridge key alignment. Assemble the bassoon then press the Low E key (#17) located on the boot joint. This key will activate the bridge lever which, in turn, will close the whisper key (#15) at the vent hole on the bocal. If this key is not closing, or the Low E key is not closing, you will need to bend the Whisper Key bridge lever (#16) slightly to achieve the correct alignment.

Now press lightly on the Low B♭ lever (#2) located on the bass joint. This key should close the Low B♭ key (#1), the Low C key (#7) and the Low D key (#9). If not, these will have to be regulated as indicated in the section below (How to Regulate the Keys).

HOW TO REGULATE THE KEYS

Correctly regulating the basson keys is important for proper instrument performance. The bassoon, contrary to how it appears, is not really very difficult to regulate. By following the instructions below you will be able to regulate your bassoon and keep it in good playing condition.

In many cases, only a simple adjustment will be needed to keep the bassoon playing correctly. The difficulty comes in locating this simple adjustment. The following steps should help you.

Tools Needed: Leak light (with small and large bulbs)

Small screwdriver

Flat nosed pliers

Emery paper

Scraper

Materials Needed: Sheet cork in sizes as needed (1/64″, 1/16″, 3/32″ or 1/8″)

Contact cork cement

Procedure: (Refer to Illustration 5-2 for key names and numbers.)

1. Check the pad seats. Before you attempt to regulate any keys you must check all the pads to be certain that they are sealing properly. If the pads do not form a level seat with the tone holes, it will be virtually impossible to regulate the keys. To check the seat, place a leak light under each pad and close the key slowly, using a very light pressure. It is important that the pad be closed in the normal playing way, that is, pressing on the key lever, not on the pad cup itself. Be very critical during this checking procedure. The pad should seat level to the tone hole, that is, it should close simultaneously around the entire tone hole. Often a pad hits the front, back or one of the sides before it seals the tone hole. Any pads you find which are torn, loose or not sealing properly will need to be replaced. (See How to Install New Leather Bassoon Pads, p. 158.) When all pads have a level seat with the tone hole, continue with step 2.

2. Start with the bell joint. Join the bell and bass joints together so that the Low B♭ lever (#2) is lined up properly with the Low B♭ key (#1). Pressing on the Low B♭ lever should close the Low B♭ key. If the key does not close before the lever hits another key, be certain that there is a piece of ¹⁄₆₄″ cork under the bridge of the Low B♭ key. If this doesn't solve the problem, either the key or lever is bent and will need to be bent back to position using flat nosed pliers.

3. Check the keys on the bass joint. Press the Low D lever (#9). This should close the Low D key (#11). On some bassoons there is a key guard around this key, making it difficult to see if the pad is seating correctly. If this is the case, remove the guard (usually three small screws) and check. If the pad is closing properly, continue with the next step.

4. Press the Low C key (#7). As this key closes so should the Low D key (#11). If they do not close together, an adjustment is made by bending the small tab at the end of the Low D lever (#9). If the Low C key (#7) is closing first, bend the tab on the Low D lever *up*. If the Low D key (#11) is closing first, bend the tab on the Low D lever (#9) *down*.

5. Press the Low B lever (#4). This should close the Low B key (#3) at the same time it closes the Low C key (#7) and Low D key (#11). (Be sure that you have done the adjustment in step 4 before continuing with this step.) If the Low B *does not* close, check to be certain that there is a piece of ¹⁄₆₄″ cork under the arm of the Low B key where it extends over the Low B lever (#4). If not, replace the cork and check again. If the key still does not close, emery some cork from the piece located under the end of the lever which extends over the Low C key (#7). If the Low C key (#7) does not close, then add cork to the Low B lever (#4), at the place where it extends over the Low C key, until they do close together.

6. Check the keys on the boot joint. Press the F lever (#48). This should close the F key (#49). If it does not, adjust by adding cork to the end of the F key where it extends over the F lever.

7. Insert the wing joint into the boot joint and line up correctly. Place the bocal in the receiver of the wing joint and line up correctly. Now press the Low E key (#17) on the boot joint. This key should close at the same time as the Whisper key (#13) closes over the tone hole in the bocal. If they do not close together, the adjustment can be made on the end of the Whisper key bridge lever (#16) which extends over the Low E key (#17). Bend this lever *toward* the Low E key to have the Whisper key close sooner and *away* from the Low E key to have the Whisper key close later.

8. Check the keys on the wing joint. Press the C♯ key (#24). This will open both the C♯ key and the C♯-D♯ trill key (#30). While holding this key down, press the C♯-D♯ trill ring (#31). This should close the C♯-D♯ trill key. If it does not, check the thickness of the cork between the arm of the C♯-D♯ trill ring and the arm of the C♯-D♯ trill key where they overlap. Add small amounts of cork here until the C♯-D♯ trill key closes.

9. The regulation of the bassoon is now complete. All other keys on the bassoon are independent of each other and will not need to be regulated to have them work properly. To adjust the key heights or regulate the other keys, see The Complete Adjustment, p.173.

HOW TO INSTALL NEW LEATHER BASSOON PADS

Most bassoons require the use of a special medium-thin leather bassoon pad which can be obtained in either white or tan. In many cases a regular riveted or unriveted saxophone pad will work just as well in the key. If the sax pad is too thick you can determine this as soon as you start.

Tools Needed: Leak light

Pad slick (size corresponding to tone hole)

Spring clamp or wooden wedge

Alcohol or bunsen burner

Small screwdriver

Materials Needed: Tan or white leather bassoon pads (saxophone

pads may be substituted)

Stick shellac

Procedure:

1. Remove the old pad. Leather pads are held in place with shellac or a similar type of substance. In some cases you may need to remove the key in order to get at the pad. Heat the key as shown in Illustration 5-3 to soften the shellac. Always heat the key at an angle so that the main concentration of heat will not burn or melt the body of the bassoon. When the shellac is soft, remove the old pad.

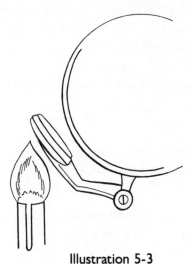

Illustration 5-3

2. Find the correct size replacement pad. The pad should fit snuggly into the empty key cup. If it is too large, the pad will not go all the way into the cup or will bend, thus wrinkling the leather. If the pad is too small, there will be a space between the pad and the side of the key cup permitting the pad to slide around in the key cup. (*NOTE:* If you are substituting a sax pad for a bassoon pad, it may be *necessary* that the pad be slightly smaller than the key in order for it to work. See step 4 below.)

3. When you have the correct size pad, hold the end of the stick shellac in the flame of your burner, and when soft place a few small drops of the shellac on the back of the pad. Place the pad into the key.

4. Seat the pad. Heat the key as shown in Illustration 5-3 until the shellac softens and the pad settles into the key cup. Place a pad slick between the pad and the tone hole. Close the key over the pad slick and rotate the pad slick slightly. This will spread the shellac and level the pad with the tone hole (this must be done while the shellac is soft). Remove the pad slick and close the key gently over the tone hole. With a leak light, check

to see if the pad is level with the tone hole. If the back of the pad is striking the tone hole first, then the pad was too thick and needs to be replaced with a smaller pad (this might happen if you are substituting a sax pad). If the front of the pad is striking the tone hole first, the pad might be too thin or small and needs to be replaced. When the pad is level with the tone hole, heat again and close the key firmly over the tone hole. Hold in place with a spring clamp or a small wooden wedge under the key lever until it is cool.

5. After the key has cooled thoroughly, remove the clamp and check again with a leak light. Be certain that the pad is level with the tone hole and that there are no gaps between the pad and the tone hole. If the seal is not tight, you will need to repeat the process starting with step 2.

6. Adjust the key. If the key in which you have replaced the pad works in conjunction with other keys of the bassoon, it will be necessary to re-adjust the keys. (See How to Regulate the Keys, p.157.)

HOW TO REPLACE THE KEY CORKS

Key corks on the bassoon are used to regulate the keys, adjust the key heights or provide for quiet key action. For this reason, the thickness of the cork used on each key is extremely important. Listed in Chart 18 is the most common size cork used on each key of the bassoon. In many cases, you will have to use emery paper to reduce the thickness of the cork after it has been applied to achieve the proper key adjustment or height. Key corks are always glued to the key and never to the body of the bassoon.

Tools Needed: Single edge razor blade

Emery paper

Materials Needed: Sheet cork as needed in sizes $\frac{1}{64}''$, $\frac{1}{16}''$, $\frac{3}{32}''$ and $\frac{1}{8}''$

Contact cork cement

Procedure:

1. Remove any particles of cork which may be on the key.

2. Select the correct size cork according to Chart 18 and spread contact cement on a small section of the cork.

3. Spread the contact cement on the proper spot of the key.

4. Allow the contact cement to dry thoroughly, then place the cork in position. Trim off excess cork with a razor blade.

5. Check the regulation of the key with other keys of the bassoon and emery the cork if needed. (See How to Regulate the Keys, p.157.)

6. To emery the cork, place a small strip of emery paper between the cork and the bassoon body or key with the rough side against the cork (see Illustration 5-4). Pull the emery paper while holding the key and cork against it. This will take off a small amount of cork and at the same time shape it to the body or the key of the bassoon.

Chart 18
Bassoon Key Corks

(Refer to Illustration 5-2 for key names and numbers.* Those keys not listed do not require any cork.)

Key #	Key Name	Location of Cork**	Size of Cork†
1	Low B♭ bell key	Under bridge	1/64″
2	Low B♭ lever	Under each end of key	1/64″
3	Low B key	Under arm	1/64″
4	Low B lever	Under both ends of key	1/64″
5	C♯-D♭ key	Under arm	1/64″
		Under foot	1/16″
6	Low C♯-D♭ lever	Under foot	1/64″
		Under arm	1/8″
7	Low C key	Under lever	1/64″
		Under foot	1/64″
9	Low D lever	Under end of key	1/64″
11	Low D key	Under bridge	1/64″
12	Low E♭ key	Under lever or	1/8″
		Under foot	1/16″
13	Whisper key	Under end of key	1/64″
15	Whisper key lever	Under foot	1/64″
		Under lever	1/16″
16	Whisper key bridge lever	Under each end of key	1/64″
17	Low E key	Under foot	1/16″
20	High D key	Under lever	1/16″
21	High C key	Under lever	1/64″
23	High A key	Under lever	1/16″
24	C♯ key	Under lever	1/64″
26	E♭ key	Under lever	1/16″
29	C♯ key lever	Under each arm	3/32″
		Under foot	1/64″
30	C♯-D♯ trill key	Under each foot	1/64″
31	C♯-D♯ trill ring	Under foot	1/64″

*There are many keys on the bassoon, so any diagram is bound to be confusing. I'm sure that Illustration 5-2 will prove to be confusing at first glance. Hopefully you will be able to identify a key by the picture, then find the cork location through the description in the chart. Many bassoons also have different key systems, so that many of the keys pictured may not be exactly the same as on your bassoon. This chart contains the most common keys found on most bassoons.

**The term "lever" as used in this chart refers to the portion of the key which is touched by the fingers while playing.

†In most cases this is the starting size cork to be used. Usually the cork will need to be made thinner by using a piece of emery paper to reduce the size. To determine the correct thickness see the following: How to Regulate the Keys, p.157; How to Check the Intonation of the Bassoon, p.169; The Complete Adjustment, p.173.

Key #	Key Name	Location of Cork**	Size of Cork†
32	F♯ key	Under lever	1/16″
34	F♯ rocker	Under each arm	1/64″
35	A♭ lever	Under foot	1/16″
37	A♭ lever	Under each end	1/64″
42	B♭ lever	Under lever	1/16″
		Under foot	1/64″
43	B♭ key	Under arm	1/64″
		Under foot	1/16″
45	B♭ lever	Under lever	1/64″
		Under foot	1/16″
46	G lever	Under lever	1/64″
		Under arm	1/16″
47	G key	Under key end	1/64″
48	F lever	Under each arm	1/64″
49	F key	Under end	1/64″
53	F♯ key	Under lever	1/16″
55	A♭ key	Under arm	1/64″
		Under foot (or lever)	1/16″

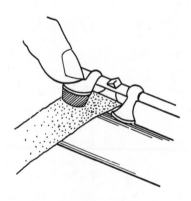

Illustration 5-4

HOW TO RE-CORK THE TENONS

Torn or missing tenon corks should be replaced; they not only result in a loose fitting joint, but also have a tendency to leak air, causing playing problems.

Tools Needed: Ruler

Small screwdriver

Razor blade

Scraper or small knife

Emery paper

Materials Needed: Sheet cork (1/32″ or 1/16″ thick)

Contact cork cement

Cork grease

Procedure:

1. If there are any keys which extend over the cork tenon, they should be removed first. Some bassoon keys are held in place with pivot screws or roads. Other bassoons have keys held in place with small rods that are removed by pulling them out with pliers. This style rod will have an end sticking out from the post which is bent in a "U" shape and can be grasped with the pliers.

2. Remove all particles of the old tenon cork. This is most easily done with a scraper or small knife. Scrape thoroughly and carefully to be certain that all cork is gone and all traces of either cement or shellac holding the cork in place is removed. Don't worry if the scraper also scrapes the wood slightly. This does not hurt the instrument and will be completely covered with new cork when the job is complete. It is essential that the tenon be *completely clean* before proceeding if the job is to be successful. If there is grease or dirt on the tenon, the new cork will come off soon after applied as the glue will not hold.

3. Measure the size cork needed for the tenon. Measure the width of the recessed portion of the tenon once it is clean. On the bocal, measure the width of the old cork. (see Illustration 5-5). Also measure the length of cork needed to cover the circumference of the tenon.

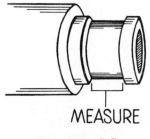

MEASURE

Illustration 5-5

|← MEASURED →|
DISTANCE

Illustration 5-6

4. Cut the new cork from a sheet of ⅟₃₂″ sheet cork (use ⅟₁₆″ sheet cork for bocal tenons). This cork is usually available in 4″ x 12″ sheets. When cutting the width of the cork, use a beveled cut for a better fit. The measurement you took in step 3 would be the width of the bottom of the cork as shown in Illustration 5-6 and it will be slightly larger on the top. If the cork is for the bocal, it will not be beveled.

5. Cut a beveled edge on one *end* of the cork strip. Be sure that the cut is made so that the bevel starts at the top (which is wider) and thins out toward the bottom of the cork strip (see Illustration 5-7).

BEVEL

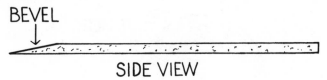

SIDE VIEW

Illustration 5-7

6. Apply the cork cement. The contact cement should completely cover the recessed area to be corked. Also apply the cement to the entire bottom of the tenon cork and to the top portion of the cork which is beveled (see Illustration 5-8).

7. Allow the cement to dry thoroughly as indicated in the directions for the glue.

8. Cement the new cork on the tenon. When the cement is dry, place the bottom of the beveled end of the cork on the tenon. Care should be taken that this is done so the cork is on straight. Once you make contact with the cement, you cannot remove it without pulling the cement off. Work around the tenon carefully, pressing the cork firmly to make good contact and avoid gaps in the cork. When you have completed the circle around the tenon, the cork should lap on top of the beveled end already in place (see Illustration 5-9).

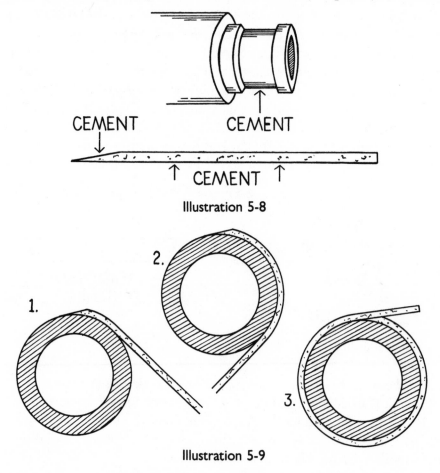

Illustration 5-8

Illustration 5-9

9. Cut the excess length of tenon cork off with a razor blade as shown in Illustration 5-10.

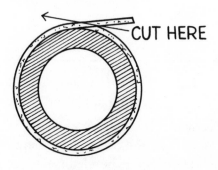

Illustration 5-10

10. Emery the cork joint. Using a strip of emery paper which is the same width as the tenon cork, first emery the overlap of the joint cork so that it is level with the rest of the cork. Then check and slowly emery around the cork, taking care to remove equal portions of the cork from around the circumference of the tenon. Use the strip of emery paper as shown in Illustration 5-11. Stop emerying when the cork tenon just *begins* to fit into the receiver but is still rather difficult to push in. Apply some cork grease to the cork to help the tenon fit into the receiver. The cork will compress at this point and give you a good fit.

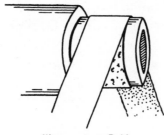

Illustration 5-11

11. Trim any excess cork that came loose or any rough edges that formed while fitting the two sections together. Use the single edge razor blade for this job. Replace any keys which were removed.

HOW TO RE-STRING THE TENONS

If your bassoon has string wound tenons that are showing signs of wear or are loose, you have three options available to you as you repair these tenons:

1. You can replace all the string with new string
2. You can replace the string with a conventional cork tenon
3. You can repair the string tenon.

If you are uncertain about working with the string tenon, I would suggest that you replace the tenon with a cork tenon. This type of work is described in the section above and is relatively easy to do.

The procedure for re-stringing or repairing a string tenon is basically the same and is described below.

Tools Needed: Scraper or knife

Beeswax

Materials Needed: Heavy duty thread (usually red)

Procedure:

1. Examine the thread tenon carefully. If it is in need of being completely replaced, remove all of the old thread from the tenon. If the condition of the thread is good, but just the fit is loose, you only need to add new thread on top of the old.

2. Remove any keys that extend over the tenon to make the tenon more accessible.

3. Obtain a heavy duty thread which is the same approximate size as that which is already on the bassoon. This thread can usually be obtained at any fabric store. There also is a commercial thread sold for bassoon tenons, but this tends to be more expensive. The thread is usually red in color, but obtain a color that will match the other tenons.

4. Coat the end of the thread with beeswax and tie this end around the bassoon tenon. Then wind the thread around the tenon to form an even layer. As you wind be sure to continue to coat the thread with beeswax. In a repair shop, it is common to have the bassoon joint mounted on a lathe for this process. With the lathe turning at a slow speed, the repairman is able to apply an even layer of thread on the tenon. By yourself this can be a slow job. It will be easier if you have someone turn the bassoon joint for you as you apply the thread. Continue to wind the tenon with an even layer of thread until there is enough on the tenon to form a good fit with the receiver. String tenons do not compress as much as cork tenons, so continue to wind until you have a good fit.

5. As you check the tenon for a correct fit, do not cut the thread until you are satisfied with the fit. Then cut the thread and tie this end in a knot around the tenon. Coat the end of the thread with beeswax. This will help hold the thread in place and prevent it from unraveling.

6. Return any keys which were removed and the job is complete.

HOW TO REPLACE A NEEDLE SPRING

Occasionally a bassoon needle spring will break. Such a spring is not difficult to replace, and by doing it yourself you can save considerable time and keep your bassoon playing rather than sitting in a repair shop. The proper type of spring to use on the bassoon is a blue steel needle spring. You should have an assortment of these springs in your repair stock; they are used for all woodwind instruments except the flute and the piccolo.

Tools Needed: Small round nose pliers
Wire cutter
Small hammer
Alcohol or bunsen burner
Steel or metal block
Large blue steel needle spring
Spring hook

Materials Needed: Blue steel needle spring
Procedure:

1. Remove the keys from around the broken spring to make it accessible.

2. Remove the old spring if necessary. Usually the broken spring will leave a small stub in the post. This stub must be pulled out the same end that it went in (see Illustration 5-12). If the flattened end of the spring is extending out from the post, grasp this firmly with the wire cutter and pull out (see Illustration 5-13). If the other end of the spring is extending beyond the post, use the round nose pliers and squeeze the spring out of the post (see Illustration 5-14). If the spring is flush in the post, use a large needle spring as a driver and tap the spring out with a hammer. When doing this be sure to rest the post against some object to prevent it from bending or breaking (see Illustration 5-15).

3. When the old spring is removed, find the correct size needle spring which will fit snuggly into the post but will slide all the way through. Slide the spring into the post so

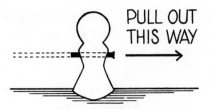

PULL OUT
THIS WAY

Illustration 5-12

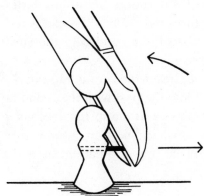

Illustration 5-13

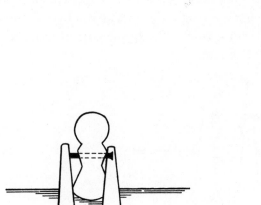

Illustration 5-14

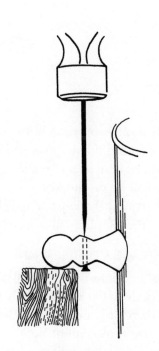

Illustration 5-15

that the correct length will extend beyond the post permitting the *point* of the spring to catch in the spring hook on the key. Mark the length of spring needed. Remove the spring and cut with a wire cutter to the correct length as marked. (Be sure that you cut off the "butt" end and not the pointed end of the spring.)

4. Hold the spring with a pair of pliers and heat the "butt" end of the spring in the flame of the burner until the *end* starts to turn red. (Take care that only the very end of the spring turns red.) When the end is red, hold the spring against a solid metal block (vice, piece of steel, etc.) and with the small hammer tap the end to flatten slightly. Let the spring cool.

5. Insert the spring into the post with the pointed end going in first. Squeeze the flat end into the post with the round nose pliers (see Illustration 5-16). This will hold the spring in place. If the spring does not go in far enough, this means you have flattened the end too much and must try again with another spring. If the spring goes in easily and is not tight, repeat step 4 to flatten the end a little more.

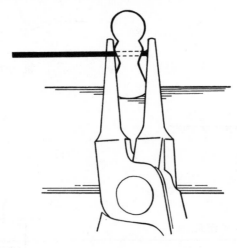

Illustration 5-16

6. Bend the spring slightly in the post. If the key affected is normally in the open position, the spring should be bent *toward* the tone hole. If the key is usually closed, the spring should be bent *away* from the tone hole. The more you bend the spring, the greater the tension will be on the key.

7. Remount the key and check the spring tension. (See How to Adjust the Spring Tension, p. 169.) Replace all keys which were removed to make the spring accessible.

HOW TO REPLACE A FLAT SPRING

Most bassoons have a few flat springs. Unlike the needle spring, the flat spring is attached directly to the key rather than to a post. Flat springs are held in place with a small screw and, therefore, are relatively easy to replace. Your main difficulty will be in finding the correct size replacement.

   Tools Needed: Small screwdriver
          Wirecutter
          Small round nose pliers
  Materials Needed: Correct size flat spring
          Flat spring screw (if missing)

Procedure:

1. Remove the key. Be sure to keep track of all screws and rods so they can be replaced in the same position when you re-assemble the bassoon.

2. Remove the broken piece of flat spring.

3. Select a new spring which is the correct size. Flat springs come in a variety of lengths and strengths. You must first determine the correct length needed for the key. This can be done by examining where the end of the flat spring is to rest on the instrument. On most bassoons there will be a little groove or metal box on the instrument in which the spring is to rest. If your bassoon does not have this, there will probably be some type of wear mark on the instrument from the previous spring. The new spring should have the same length as the old spring.

After you have selected a spring, install it with the flat spring screw and mount the key to test for length and strength. If the key pushes too hard or too easily, replace this spring with another of the same length which will be either thinner or thicker.

It is not a good idea to cut a flat spring to the correct length as the end of most flat springs are usually slightly curved so that the spring will slide easily on the instrument. If you must cut the end, be sure to use your round nose pliers to curve the end of the spring slightly.

4. Return any other keys that had to be removed.

HOW TO ADJUST THE SPRING TENSION

All bassoon keys that are usually in the open position should have a light resistance which still allows for a quick, snappy key action. Those keys which are normally in a closed position should be set with a heavier resistance. It is important to keep the tension uniform throughout the bassoon. That is, all open keys should have the same light tension and all closed keys the same heavier tension. When checking the keys, move only one key at a time. When more than one key moves when pressing a lever the tension will, of course, be greater.

The tension on a key is increased or decreased by bending the spring gently in one direction or the other. Bending the spring too far will cause it to break, so only do a little at a time. Use a spring hook for this process. Those keys that are normally *open* need to have the needle spring bent *toward* the tone hole to increase the tension. Those that are normally *closed* need to have the spring bent *away* from the tone hole to increase the tension. Be sure to unhook the spring from the key before attempting to bend it.

On flat springs the tension is adjusted in a similar way. To *increase* the tension use round nose pliers and bend the spring *away* from the key. To *decrease* the tension, bend the spring *toward* the key. In most cases you will need to remove the key while bending the spring.

HOW TO CHECK THE INTONATION OF THE BASSOON

The intonation of the bassoon is determined by a number of factors:

1. The breath support and embouchure of the player.
2. The placement and hardness of the reed used.
3. The size of the bocal used.
4. The bassoon keys opening to the proper height. This is important if the bassoon

is to play in tune with itself. The height of the key openings is measured at the front of the pad and is the distance from the top of the tone hole to the bottom of the pad when the key is fully opened. Chart 19, below, shows the normal open heights to which bassoon keys should be set.

If you find an individual key which is not at the correct height, the key has probably lost a cork on the foot or some other point on the key. These individual key heights can usually be corrected by replacing the cork (see How to Replace Key Corks, p. 160). Also, whenever you add a cork you will have to re-check the adjustment of the key with any other keys that are activated at the same time. (See How to Regulate the Keys, p. 157.)

If, in checking the bassoon heights, you find that all the keys are incorrect, it will take a complete adjustment to correct the situation. How successful you can be in doing this will depend somewhat on how comfortable you feel with the complete adjustment of the bassoon as described later in this chapter.

Chart 19
Bassoon Key Heights

(Refer to Illustration 5-2 for key numbers and names.)

Key*	Number	Height
Low B♭ bell key	1	¼″
Low B key	3	7/32″
C♯ -D♭ key	5	3/16″
Low C key	7	7/32″
Low D key	11	7/32″
Low E♭ key	12	7/32″
Whisper key	13	5/32″
Low E key	17	7/32″
High D key	20	5/32″
High C key	21	5/32″
High A key	23	5/32″
C♯ key	24	5/32″
E♭ key	26	5/32″
C♯ -D♯ trill key	30	5/32″
F♯ key	32	5/32″
B♭ key	43	5/32″
G key	47	7/32″
F key	49	7/32″
F♯ key	53	5/32″
A♭ key	55	7/32″

*Only those keys which have tone hole pads are listed here.

HOW TO CORRECT NON-FUNCTIONING KEYS

A non-functioning key can be defined as any key which is not operating properly. This includes keys that won't go down or won't go up. For the most part, when this occurs you are going to have to send the instrument into the repair shop to be corrected. It will take a skilled repair technician to solve and correct the problem. There are, however, a number of things which you can check before sending the bassoon in to be repaired. These are common problems which cause key malfunctions that can easily be corrected by you. Check this first and you might save time and money.

1. **Check the spring**—Perhaps the spring is just unhooked from the key. Push against the spring with your spring hook. If there is no tension in the spring, it is broken and will need to be replaced. (see How to Replace a Needle Spring, p.166 or How to Replace a Flat Spring, p.168.)

2. **Check the pivot screws**—These screws, which are located at the ends of the keys, go through the post and hold the key in place. The screw might be tightened too much and might be binding the key action. On the other hand, if the pivot screw is not tight enough, it will allow extra motion in the keys. This will cause the key adjustment to be inaccurate and the pads to seat poorly over the tone holes. Using a small screwdriver, move the pivot screw both ways to see if the action of the key improves.

3. **Check the key**—If the key does not close all the way, use a leak light to see if the pad is still level on the tone hole. If not, your key may have been bent. You will then need to bend the key back to a level position and probably replace the pad. (See How to Install New Leather Bassoon Pads, p.158.) If the key is not closing over the tone hole, it is also possible that the key is out of adjustment with another key. Check this possibility by using the section on "How to Regulate the Keys" (p.157) as a guide.

HOW TO REPLACE THE BOOT GASKET

If you have determined that there is a leak in the boot gasket of the bassoon, you will need to replace this gasket. (See How to Check for Leaks, p.156, to determine if the gasket is leaking.)

Tools Needed: Screwdriver
Small hammer (rawhide)
Razor blade
Scraper
Materials Needed: Sheet cork (1/16")
Contact cement
Procedure:

1. Remove the outer boot joint cap. This is the metal cap which is located at the bottom of the boot joint and is used to cover the water crook and boot gasket (see Illustration 5-2). Usually this cap will simply pull off. It has a snug fit so it may take a bit of "wiggling" to free it. If the cap refuses to move, use the small screwdriver as a driver and tap lightly around the edge of the cap with the rawhide hammer until free.

2. Loosen the two holding nuts on the water crook. These can be freed with a small screwdriver, a pair of pliers or even by hand. (*NOTE:* If your bassoon does not have any holding nut, then this model does not have a separate water crook and also will not have a boot gasket.)

3. Remove the water crook. This crook is usually glued into place so you may have to pry it off with the screwdriver. Do not worry about damaging the cork as all of this will be replaced.

4. Clean the water crook and inner boot joint cap. With the scraper, remove all traces of cork and residue glue. These pieces need to be completely clean so that the new glue will adhere properly.

5. Cut a piece of ¹⁄₁₆″ sheet cork in a size which is larger than the water crook. Apply a coating of contact cement to one side of this cork. Also apply a coating of contact cement to the underside of the water crook. Allow the glue to dry, then cement the cork in place on the water crook (see Illustration 5-17).

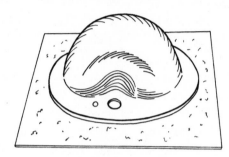

Illustration 5-17

6. Trim the cork to fit the water crook. Trim around the outside edge of the water crook and cut the two holes in the middle which are part of the inner bore of the crook. Two small holes need also be made at the point where the holding nuts go through the water crook (see Illustration 5-18). When all holes are made and the cork is completely trimmed, apply a coating of contact cement to the exposed side of the cork and the inner boot cap. Allow the glue to dry.

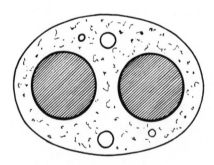

Illustration 5-18

7. Place the water crook in place on the boot joint and the contact cement will form a tight seal. Replace the holding nuts. Test the seal as indicated in the section "How to Check for Leaks, p.156. If the seal is tight, replace the outer boot joint cap. This cap will probably need to be tapped in place with a rawhide hammer.

THE COMPLETE ADJUSTMENT—
HOW TO MAKE THE ADJUSTMENTS NECESSARY FOR
PROPER INSTRUMENT PERFORMANCE

The complete adjustment of a bassoon is difficult. There are a large number of keys which work with the aid of many levers. Basically I recommend that any extensive adjustment of the bassoon be done by a competent repair technician. It is possible that you will be able to follow the process outlined below and achieve satisfactory results; however, be prepared for some problems. Be sure to read completely through the procedure before beginning.

As you refer to Illustration 5-2 for key names and numbers, you will find the picture confusing. When there are this many keys on an instrument, it is difficult to diagram each key. By carefully examining the picture and your bassoon, you will be able to locate the key you wish to find. Remember also that all bassoons do not employ the same system of keys. Your bassoon may have fewer keys than shown here, but those shown should work in the same way.

> *Tools Needed:* Leak light (with small bulb)
> Flat nose pliers
> Spring hook
> Alcohol or bunsen burner
> Ruler
> Emery paper
>
> *Materials Needed:* Tan or white leather bassoon pads
> (leather saxophone
> pads may be substituted)
> Sheet cork in sizes ¹⁄₆₄″, ¹⁄₁₆″ ³⁄₃₂″ & ⅛″
> Stick shellac
> Contact cork cement
>
> *Procedure:* (Refer to Illustration 5-2 for key names and numbers.)

1. Using a leak light, check all pads to be certain that they have a level seat which will form a tight seal with the tone hole. You can check each pad as you adjust it in the procedure to follow or check them all at once before you continue with step 2. If any of the pads are uneven, loose or torn, they will have to be replaced before you can continue with this adjustment (see How to Install New Leather Bassoon Pads, p. 158).

2. Start with the bell and bass joints. Attach the bell to the bass joint and line up the bridge key. Check the Low B♭ key (#1) to be certain that there is a piece of ¹⁄₆₄″ cork located under the bridge portion of this key. Check the height. When open all the way it should measure ¼″ from the pad to the tone hole. To adjust this height, adjust the thickness of the cork located on the bottom of the Low B♭ lever (#2). More cork will lower the key.

3. Check the open height of the Low C key (#7). This should measure $\frac{7}{32}''$ from the pad to the tone hole. If the height is not correct, the adjustment is made by regulating the thickness of the cork located on the foot of this key. More cork will lower the height of the key.

4. Press on the Low C key lever (#7). This should close the Low C key and the Low D key at the same time. If they do not close together, make the adjustment by bending the small tab located on the end of the Low D lever (#9) where it extends under the Low C key. Bending the tab *up* will cause the Low D key to close sooner. Once these two keys are regulated correctly, the open height of the Low D key will be correct.

5. Check the Low B lever (#4). One end of the key should rest against the body of the bassoon and the other end against the Low C key (#7). There should be a piece of $\frac{1}{64}''$ cork under both ends and no "play" in this key. If there is "play," add some cork under the foot end of the key until the correct contact is made.

6. Press the Low B lever (#4). This should close the Low C key (#7) and the Low B key (#3) at the same time. If they do not close together, this is regulated by adjusting the thickness of the cork on the foot of the Low B key. More cork here will permit the Low B key to close sooner. When regulated correctly, the open height of this key will be correct.

7. Press the Low D♭-C♯ lever (#6). This should open the C♯-D♭ key (#5) to a height of $\frac{3}{16}''$. If this height is not correct, make the adjustment by regulating the thickness of the cork on the foot of the C♯-D♭ key. On some models, this key does not have a foot and, therefore, the regulating needs to be done on the underside of the D♭-C♯ lever (#6). In either case, more cork will prevent the key from opening as far.

8. Check the open height of the Low E♭ key (#12). When all the way open, this height should measure $\frac{7}{32}''$ from pad to tone hole. If this height is incorrect, it can be adjusted by regulating the thickness of the cork on the foot of this key. Some models do not have a foot and the cork is located under the lever of this key. More cork will prevent the key from opening as far.

9. Now proceed by checking the keys on the boot joint. Check the open height of the Low E key (#17). This should measure $\frac{7}{32}''$ from pad to tone hole. If the height is incorrect, adjust it by regulating the thickness of the cork located on the foot of this key. More cork will prevent the key from opening as far.

10. Press the C♯ trill key (#41) open. This should open to a height of $\frac{5}{32}''$. If this height is incorrect, adjust it by regulating the thickness of the cork under the lever of this key. More cork will prevent the key from opening as far.

11. Press the B♭ lever (#42). This will open the B♭ key (#43) to a height of $\frac{5}{32}''$. If the open height is not correct, correct it by regulating the thickness of the cork under the foot of the B♭ key (#43). More cork will prevent the key from opening as far. Before making this check, be certain that there is a piece of $\frac{1}{64}''$ cork located under the arm of the B♭ key (#43) where the B♭ lever makes contact. The B♭ lever should open the B♭ key *all* the way. If it is not able to do this, bend the arm of the B♭ lever up slightly where it extends under the arm of the B♭ key. Now check the B♭ lever (#45). It should have cork under the lever where it makes contact with the push rod that goes through the body of the bassoon. When this lever is pushed, the B♭ key (#43) should open all the way.

12. Check the open height of the G key (#47). This key should be open to a height of $\frac{7}{32}''$. If it is not, make the adjustment by regulating the thickness of cork located under

the foot of this key. More cork will prevent the key from opening as far. Now check to be certain that there is a piece of 1/64″ cork located under the foot of this key at the point where the push rod will make contact with the key.

13. Check the G lever (#46). Be certain that there is a piece of 1/64″ cork located under the arm of this lever, where it will make contact with the push rod that extends through the body of the bassoon. Pressing the G lever should close the G key. There should not be any "play" at this point if the length of the push rod is correct. If there is "play," either replace the push rod or add a slight amount of cork to the under side of the arm of the G lever (#46).

14. Check the High G key (#51). This key should be completely closed. If it is not, more cork needs to be added under the arm of the F lever (#48) where it extends over the arm of the High G key (#51) until the High G key is completely closed. The open height of the High G key will be correct when the regulation explained in step 15 is completed.

15. Check the open height of the F key (#49). This should measure 7/32″ from the pad to the tone hole. If the height is not correct, make the adjustment by regulating the thickness of the cork under the foot of the F key (#49) where it extends over the arm of the F lever (#48). More cork at this point will prevent the key from opening as far. When this height adjustment is correct, pressing the F lever will close the F key and open the High G key to the correct height.

16. Press the F♯ key (#53). There should not be any "play" in the key before it begins to activate the F lever (#48). If there is "play," some cork needs to be added under the F♯ key lever to eliminate this "play." Too much cork at this point will prevent the F♯ key (#53) from closing all the way.

17. Press the A♭ key (#55). This key should open to a height of 7/32″. If the open height is not correct, it can be regulated by changing the thickness of the cork under the foot of this key. More cork will prevent the key from opening as far.

18. Press the A♭ lever (#35). This lever should open the A♭ key (#55) all the way. If it does not, check each contact point between keys, levers and push rods to be certain that there is a piece of 1/64″ cork. This cork both quiets the key action and gives the proper regulation for the keys.

19. Press the F♯ key (#32). This key should open and close the F key (49) at the same time. There should not be any "play" between this key, the F♯ rocker (#34), the push rods and the F key (#49). If there is, check all points of contact to be certain that there is a piece of 1/64″ cork cemented to one of the pieces at each point of contact.

20. Press the F♯ key (#32). There should not be any "play" in this key before it activates the F♯ rocker (#34). If there is play, and you have corked all the pieces of this key mechanism as described in step 19, then bend the tab of the F♯ rocker *down* slightly toward the F♯ key (#32) until the play is removed. If there is no play in the F♯ key (#32), check the High G key (#51) to be certain that it is still closed tightly over the tone hole. If it is no longer closed (as adjusted in step 14 above), bend the tab of the F♯ rocker (#34) *up* slightly to allow the High G key to close all the way.

21. Now check the keys on the Wing joint. Press the E♭ key (#26). This key should open to a height of 5/32″. If the height is not correct, it can be adjusted by regulating the thickness of the cork located under the lever of this key. More cork will prevent the key from opening as far.

22. Check the C♯-D♯ trill ring key (#31). Be certain that there is a piece of 1/64" cork located on both the top and bottom of the foot of this key. Check the C♯-D♯ trill key (#30). Be certain that there is a piece of 1/64" cork located on both the top and bottom of the foot of this key which is on the same side of the rod as the pad. Now press the C♯ key lever (#29) which is located *under* some other keys. Pressing this lever should open the C♯-D♯ trill key (#30). While this is down, press the C♯-D♯ trill ring (#31). This should close the C♯-D♯ trill key. All points of contact between these keys should have cork between them for proper and quiet action.

23. Check the open height of the C♯-D♯ trill key (#30). This key should open to a height of 5/32". If the height is not correct, it can be adjusted by regulating the thickness of the cork located *under* the foot of the C♯-D♯ trill ring (#31). More cork at this point will prevent the key from opening as far.

24. Press the C♯ key (#24). There should be just a *slight* amount of "play" in this key before it activates the C♯ key lever (#29) which is located under the lever of the C♯ key. Adjust the thickness of the cork under the C♯ key (#24) until the slight "play" does exist. The open height of this key will be correct when adjusted correctly.

25. Press the High C key (#21). The regulation of this key shoud be the same as described in step 24 for the C♯ key.

26. Check the open height of the High A key (#23). This should measure 5/32" from the pad to the tone hole. If this opening is not correct, adjust it by regulating the thickness of the cork located under the lever of this key. More cork will prevent the key from opening as far.

27. Assemble the wing joint, boot joint and bocal. Press the Low E key (#17). This should close at the same time the Whisper key (#13) closes on the bocal tone hole. If they do not, first check all points of contact for these keys to be certain that there is a piece of 1/64" cork between each moving part. If the regulation is still not correct, bend the arm of the Whisper key bridge lever (#16) slightly with a flat nose pliers. Bending the arm *toward* the Low E key will allow the Whisper key (#13) to close sooner.

28. This should complete the adjustment of the bassoon. Play test the instrument to check. Play all the way down to the bottom note of the instrument's range. Any notes which seem to blow harder or sound stuffy could still be out of adjustment.

REPAIRS TO BE SENT TO THE REPAIR SHOP

The bassoon is an instrument which is quiet complex in its mechanical operation and, therefore, can prove to be difficult to repair. I have explained throughout this chapter many of the repairs that you can make which are relatively easy to accomplish. Experience always helps when trying to fix the bassoon and, because you are not going to have that many opportunities to repair the bassoon, you will not gain much experience. Also, some repairs require specialized tools while others require special skills that take time to develop. For this reason I suspect that you will be sending your bassoons to the repair shop for any major repairs. You can best determine what repairs you feel capable of doing as you read through this chapter. A good rule to follow is: "When in doubt, send it out."

Below I have outlined some of the more common bassoon repairs that *will* need to be done at a repair shop. It is hoped that this will give you a better understanding of the repair procedures.

REPAIRING CRACKS IN THE BODY

Only wood bassoons have the potential for cracking. This is rather rare as the instrument is usually made of maple and there is less tendency for this wood to crack. Many bassoons also will have a liner inside the bore of the instrument to protect the wood from cracking. If the bassoon should crack, it is best to have it repaired as soon as possible before the crack increases. The larger the crack, the more difficult and expensive to repair. If the crack becomes too large, the joint will need to be replaced. A quick visual check each month can reveal developing cracks before they become serious. Cracks always develop along the grain of the wood, so look for them to run up and down along the length of the joint. Before sending the instrument for repair, mark the crack with a pencil to help the repair technician find it. Because of temperature changes, cracks will sometimes close up before the repair technician has a chance to work on it.

The most common method of repairing a crack is to pin it. The repair technician will determine the length of the crack by scratching it open further with a fine pick. This also gives a good base for the filler which is added later. To pin the crack, the technician drills a hole through the body (but not the bore) of the bassoon. The hole is drilled perpendicular to the crack at an interval of about one per inch for the length of the crack. A piece of threaded rod, slightly larger than the hole, is then heated at the tip. When the rod is red hot, it is screwed into the hole. When cool, this rod will hold the sections together and prevent the crack from spreading further. The pins *do not* pull the sections of the crack back together.

After the pins are in place, a filler is used (usually a hard epoxy) in the crack and the holes left from the pins. If the crack runs through a tone hole, it must be filled carefully so that the tone hole will not leak when the job is completed. After the epoxy is dry, it is filed and sanded smooth. If possible, the epoxy is colored to approximate the color of the bassoon.

On the bell, bass joint and portions of the boot joint, the walls of the instrument are so thin that they cannot be pinned. In these places, only the epoxy filler can be used.

REPAIRING DENTS OR CRACKS IN THE BOCAL

The bocal, being made of metal, is very susceptible to denting or cracking. When the bocal is not swabbed out after playing, there is a high quantity of moisture left inside. The acids in the saliva begin to deteriorate the metal inside of the bocal. In time this will eat through the walls of the bocal causing a crack. As the walls are deteriorating, they become weaker so the student is more likely to bend the bocal when assembling the bassoon.

To remove dents from the bocal, the repair technician will use a very small steel or brass ball attached to a fine wire. These balls come in various sizes, and he can pull the ball under the dent and tap on the outside of the bocal (where the dent is) with a small dent hammer to raise the dent. Usually to do this he will have to remove the vent tube first by unsoldering so that he can pull the ball through the bore of the bocal. When the dents are removed, it is necessary to replace the vent and solder back in place to avoid any leaks. It is usually worthwhile to have an old bocal repaired if it is not severely damaged because the cost of a new bocal is quite high.

If the walls of the bocal are cracked, the repair technician will need to patch this crack by soldering a small piece of metal over the top of the crack. This piece needs to be cut and fitted to the shape of the bocal (not an easy task, depending on where the crack is located). It then must be soldered in place so that it is completely sealed. This does give the appearance of a patched bocal, but still will probably be desirable over the cost of replacing. Your repair technician can best determine whether it is advisable to repair or replace a damaged bocal.

REPAIRING BROKEN TENONS

A broken tenon can occur on either a wood or plastic bassoon. This is not a common occurence, but when it does happen it is almost always on the wing joint or bass joint where they fit into the boot joint. This usually occurs in the process of assembling the instrument, although the tenon can also break if the instrument is dropped.

A broken tenon on these joints can be repaired and save you considerable expense over replacing the section (although the repair job itself will also be expensive). When repaired correctly, the replacement tenon will be as strong as the original.

The repair technician first cuts off the remaining portion of the old tenon. He then drills up into the body of the bassoon with a special cutting tool which enlarges the bore diameter. The hole is drilled about ½″ to ¾″ into the body. A tenon plug, which has already been cut so that it will fit into the receiver on the other section, is then inserted into this new hole and expoxyed in place. After the epoxy has set, the new plug will be bonded firmly to the body of the bassoon. It is then necessary to re-drill any tone holes and post holes which have been blocked by the tenon plug. Also, the repair technician will ream out the bore of the plug so that it matches that of the bassoon body. The tenon is then corked or wrapped with string and fitted to the receiver.

The procedure is the same for replacing either tenon of the bassoon. Only the size of the tenon plug and the cutting tools have to be different to accommodate the difference in bore size.

REPAIRING BROKEN KEYS

If a bassoon key actually breaks in half it can be repaired in the shop. Be certain that you save the pieces and send them along with the entire bassoon. The repair technician will braze the two pieces together with silver solder. When done correctly, this will bond the two sections of the key together as securely as the original piece. Also, the mend will not be too noticeable and should function like the original key. It is important to send in the entire instrument so the technician can be certain that the key is brazed at the correct angle and re-adjusted to the instrument.

If you should lose one of the broken pieces, most repair shops will be able to either order a new key or fashion a key from an old part of a discarded bassoon. In either case, this is usually more expensive and time consuming. Check with your repair shop for the best value on either replacing or repairing broken keys.

TIGHTENING LOOSE KEYS

If your bassoon has a lot of "play" in the keys (that is, they move sideways on the rod or between the pivot screws) you may have a problem getting the pads to always close on the seat. The "play" is usually found on older bassoons, as the metal of the key eventually wears. If the key is mounted on a *rod* and slides sideways along the rod, then there is too much room between the posts. The repair technician will stretch the hinge tube of the key to fill the gap (a process called "swedging"). If there is a great deal of space between the posts, he can make a small shim from another key rod and place it at the end of the key to fill in the gap.

It is also possible that the diameter of the key's hinge tube has enlarged through wear and is now bigger than the diameter of the pivot rod. In this case, the repair technician will squeeze the hinge tube slightly to tighten, but not so much as to bind the key action.

If the loose key is held in place with pivot screws, the technician checks to see if the screws have backed out or are worn. Sometimes, on an older bassoon, the screws will be worn down and cannot hold the key firmly in place. In this case, the screw can be replaced with a new screw for the same brand bassoon. It is also possible that the hole in the post will be worn, causing the screw to "wiggle" in the post. It will then be necessary to re-fit the post with a larger style pivot screw, then adapt this screw to the bassoon key.

TIGHTENING LOOSE POSTS

On the wood bassoon, loose posts are a very common problem. When this happens, the post begins to turn and the pivot screws will no longer be aligned with the key. This usually causes the key to bind and stop functioning. Any time there is a loose post, it should be corrected.

There are three ways to correct this problem. One is to epoxy the loose post in place. This will hold the post permanently in place but has the disadvantage of making it nearly impossible to remove the post should that ever become a necessity.

Another means of tightening the post is to remove the post, wrap it with a small quantity of thread to give a tighter fit, and glue the post back into the hole with pad cement. This cementing is not permanent, thus it is possible to remove the post at a later date if necessary. Unfortunately, this also makes the repair less permanent.

The repair technician will most likely correct the problem by using a post locking screw. With a special drill he drills a small hole alongside the base of the post into the body of the bassoon. This drill will also countersink a small bevel into the end of the post at the same time. Care must be taken not to drill too deeply as this could cause a leak in the instrument. The repair technician then screws a small flat head screw into the hole. As the screw is tightened down, the head goes into the countersunk portion in the post and prevents the post from turning. With this method, the post locking screw can always be removed if it becomes necessary for some future repair.

REPLATING THE KEYS—THE COMPLETE OVERHAUL

Most bassoon keys are nickel plated. This is a durable finish and will take a long time to wear off. In fact, by time most bassoon keys are worn to the point that you might want to restore them, the instrument itself is also worn out and not worth the expense. However, the keys can be replated to give a "like new" look. This should only be done as a part of a complete overhaul of the bassoon. In order to replate the keys, it is obviously necessary to remove all the pads and corks. Also, all the posts will have to be removed as they cannot be plated while on the instrument.

Replating any type of instrument or key requires having the chemicals necessary to strip off the old finish and the equipment for electroplating. The keys and posts are all removed and the old finish is removed. All parts are then buffed to a high gloss smoothness and then replated using an electroplating process. When the plating is complete, the bassoon is re-assembled, using all new pads and corks. Often excess plating must be removed from the keys to insure a proper fit between the posts.

When this job is complete your bassoon will have a "like-new" appearance and playability.

THE COMPLETE RE-PAD

Even though you may do a good job of maintaining the playing condition of the bassoons in your band, there will come a time when most of the pads start to tear and dry out. Many of the corks will be depressed, dried or missing altogether. This is the time to have the bassoon completely repadded. A complete re-pad in most shops consists of replacing all the old pads and corks with new, installing new tenon corks and cleaning the body of the bassoon (check with your shop to be certain what is included). Loose keys are usually tightened as a part of this job. When re-assembled, all the pads will be seated and the springs adjusted for good action. In short, the instrument should *play* like a new bassoon.

6

The Saxophone Family

Illustration 6-1

Photograph courtesy of G. Leblanc Corporation

HOW TO TAKE CARE OF YOUR SAXOPHONE

Taking proper care of the saxophone should be the first, and most important step in your saxophone maintenance plan. By following the suggestions given here, you can avoid many of the problems which may cause the saxophone to malfunction. Although this might be a review, it is suggested that you share this information with your saxophone players so they will understand proper saxophone care. When the student understands the reasons for the maintenance procedures outlined below, there is a better chance that he or she will follow them.

ASSEMBLE THE SAXOPHONE CAREFULLY

The saxophone is a relatively easy instrument to assemble, although care must be taken to avoid bending any keys. Bent keys are a very common problem because they are large, often made of a soft metal and exposed on the instrument.

Begin by inserting the neck into the receiver on the top of the body of the instrument. Take care when assembling this part that you do not bend the upper octave key located on the neck as this key is very easily bent. Line up the neck so that the mouthpiece will comfortably face the player when held. If this fit is too loose or too tight, see "Maintenance Procedures for the Saxophone—The Neck Tenon," p.185.

After the neck is in place, add the mouthpiece. This should be placed at the point which will have the instrument relatively in tune. (*NOTE:* If the mouthpiece is placed in a position which causes the saxophone to be out of tune, the players will experience difficulty in playing the very low notes on the instrument. These low notes will tend to "warble" when played.) Once the mouthpiece is in place, add the reed and ligature. It is a poor habit to put the mouthpiece on with the reed and ligature already in place as the assembling process can cause the read to twist, changing its alignment and sometimes even causing it to break.

A neck strap should always be used when playing the saxophone.

STORE THE SAXOPHONE PROPERLY

The saxophone should always be stored in the case when not in use. A saxophone left lying about on a chair, table or stand is easily bumped or dropped to the floor. This can result in serious and expensive repairs.

Never store the saxophone near a radiator or heating duct. Excessive heat will tend to dry out the leather pads more quickly, requiring that they be replaced. Also avoid storing the saxophone in extremely cold conditions; this may cause the shellac holding the pads in place to freeze and crack, thus loosening the pads. When a pad has loosened or fallen out, you should replace it with a new pad as it is very difficult to relocate an old pad in the same position.

All saxophones should use a neck plug when being stored. Unfortunately, this piece is often ignored when putting the instrument away. The plug fits into the receiver of the saxophone and serves to protect the octave floating lever on the instrument. If the plug is not in place, this lever can bend as the instrument shifts around in the case. Once bent, this lever will cause the octave mechanism to malfunction. In some cases, this plug is also necessary to hold the instrument securely in the case.

It is a good idea to always place the mouthpiece cap on the mouthpiece when storing it. This cap is designed to protect the mouthpiece; the cost of replacing a broken or chipped mouthpiece is well worth the time needed to put the cap in place when finished playing. Never store the mouthpiece without first taking off the reed and ligature, drying out the mouthpiece thoroughly and wiping off the reed. Doing this will extend the life of each reed plus reduce the amount of mineral scale which will build up on the mouthpiece.

When storing the saxophone, never leave the neck strap attached to the instrument. The strap should *always* be removed, wound up and placed in the storage compartment. When the strap is left in the case around the instrument, the player often bends the keys when removing the instrument to play.

Do not store damp swabs or cloths in the saxophone case. Trapping this moisture in the case will cause the pads to remain wet for a longer period of time, thus decreasing their life span. Also, excessive moisture or humidity will contribute to rust forming on the pivot screws and rods. This will eventually cause the key action to slow or stop.

Saxophone cases are designed to hold the instrument securely. Most cases have a small storage section to hold reeds, swabs, mouthpiece, etc. Also, many cases have a separate section to hold the neck to protect it from the other parts of the saxophone. The saxophone case is not designed to serve as a display area for medals and pins or to carry lesson books and music. This overpacking of the case can cause excessive pressure on the instrument when the cover is closed and may cause the keys to bend and go out of alignment. Dangling medals can catch under the keys when the case is closed, bending them quite easily when the case is opened.

Many cases do not protect the instrument very well. Check your saxophone case to be certain that it is holding the instrument securely. Place the saxophone in the case (be sure that the neck plug is in place), remove all accessories, mouthpiece and neck from the case storage compartments, close the cover and latch it. Hold the case handle down and shake the case. If you hear the saxophone bouncing inside, the case is not providing the protection that it should and there needs to be padding added to the case.

The quickest, cheapest way to correct the problem is to lay a piece of towel on top of the saxophone to fill up the excess space inside the case. Shake again and add more towel if necessary. If the cover becomes hard to close, you have added too much. You can also remove the lining from the cover of the case, add more padding and then re-glue. This will take more time and skill but will look better when finished.

Inspect the case periodically to be certain that it is in good condition. Prompt attention should be given to broken or loose latches, hinges or handles. Be certain that the lining is not loose. Loose lining can easily be corrected with some glue, but broken case hardware will need to be sent to the repair shop for correction.

CLEAN THE SAXOPHONE REGULARLY

The Bore—A few minutes of care in cleaning the saxophone after each playing session will go a long way in helping to maintain the instrument. Most important is to swab out the *entire* instrument after each playing session in order to remove all traces of moisture. For some reason, saxophone players seldom take the time to do this. Of course, these players get just as much saliva in the instrument as do other players, but they make little or no attempt to remove any of it.

Failure to remove this moisture results in rotting reeds, a dirty, crusty mouthpiece, hard dried out pads (especially in the side palm keys) and a generally smelly instrument. For these reasons it is important that each player have a set of saxophone swabs. These do tend to be expensive and, I suspect, the reason why many players do not bother. However, the savings in repair and replacement of pads and reeds is well worth the investment.

A body swab for the saxophone is used to clean all the moisture from the main body of the instrument. A smaller neck swab should be used to dry out the neck of the instrument. This is particularly important because the neck becomes quite wet while playing. The player should also use a small piece of cloth to dry out the inside of the mouthpiece.

The Mouthpiece—I have found that the most neglected and dirtiest part of the saxophone is the mouthpiece. The reason is that students often do not remove the reed from the mouthpiece after playing and never clean the mouthpiece. The number of mouthpieces that I have seen that are just loaded with mineral deposits and scum is unbelievable. It is hard to believe that any student would want to place such an object in his or her mouth. All students should be taught that the reed is never to be stored on the mouthpiece. When finished playing, the reed should be removed and wiped dry. The mouthpiece should be swabbed out with a clean cloth and the ligature and cap placed over the mouthpiece.

As a matter of routine, the mouthpiece should be washed out in warm soapy water about once a week using a reed mouthpiece brush to clean thoroughly. Swabbing and washing will keep the mouthpiece clean indefinitely. If you have some mouthpieces that are already crusted with minerals, washing will not remove this material. In order to clean these mouthpieces see "How to Clean the Saxophone Mouthpiece," p. 205.

The Body and Keys—Most saxophone keys are nickel plated and will remain quite clean by simply wiping them with a soft cloth. These keys should never be cleaned with silver polish as the polish can gum up the key mechanism. After a long period of time the plating will wear off on some keys of the saxophone. Not much can be done to improve the appearance short of replating, which is an expensive job.

In time the body of the saxophone will begin to accumulate dirt and lint under the keys and rods. It is a good idea to remove this lint before it gets into the mechanism and slows the key action. Use a small modeler's paint brush or pipe stem cleaner and reach under the keys to brush away any dirt or lint that has collected. Care should be taken to avoid catching the springs; this might change the spring tension and affect the adjustment of the keys. This job is easy to do if done slowly and carefully.

MAINTENANCE PROCEDURES FOR THE SAXOPHONE

The Neck Cork—A new neck cork is fitted tightly to the mouthpiece and then a light coating of cork grease is applied to ease the assembling of the mouthpiece to the neck. This cork grease will, in time, attract dirt which begins to build up on the cork thus making the fit tighter. The player will add more cork grease, and the cycle continues, with layers of grease and dirt slowly building up on the neck cork.

Once a month, use a clean cloth to wipe the cork until it is free from all grease and dirt. After it is completely clean and dry, apply a *small* amount of cork grease, By following this procedure, you will not only lengthen the life of the cork but also avoid having excessive grease and dirt on the cork and in the mouthpiece.

As the cork gets older, it will begin to dry out and become compressed from the mouthpiece. As tbe cork compresses, the player is forced to push the mouthpiece further on the neck to insure a tight fit. As a result, the player is placing his mouthpiece on the instrument at the point where it will have a good fit rather than where the instrument plays in tune. The neck cork should hold the mouthpiece tightly regardless of where it is placed on the neck. If this is not happening, it is time to replace the cork (see How to Re-cork the Neck, p.196).

In an emergency you can expand the cork temporarily by holding it over some heat. Use a match, alcohol burner or bunsen burner and rotate the cork over the heat. Care should be taken to avoid getting it too hot as the cork will burn quite easily. This is not a permanent solution because the cork will quickly compress again after it is used.

The Neck Tenon—The saxophone neck has a metal tenon which is tightened down in the receiver by means of a screw. These need to be cleaned just like the flute head joint. Dirt will accumulate on the tenon; it can be kept clean by using a piece of paraffin (canning wax), available at any grocery store. Rub the paraffin on the tenon, then insert the tenon into the receiver and twist back and forth. When you take it apart, you will notice that a black film has formed. Wipe both the tenon and receiver with a dry cloth and repeat the process until no dirty film appears. Wipe both the tenon and receiver once again to remove all traces of wax. This joint should *never be greased* as then the screw will not be able to hold the neck firmly in place.

If the neck cannot be held firmly in place after tightening the screw, send the instrument to the repair shop for the repair technician to expand the neck for a proper fit.

Oiling the Keys—The keys of the saxophone should be oiled about once a month to keep them working freely and to prevent the screws and rods from becoming rusted. If the rods and screws do rust, the key action can bind up which will require a repair technician to correct. Key oil is available from your music dealer. Use a pin or toothpick and place a small drop of key oil at the end of each key and between all moveable keys which share the same rod. Work the keys to circulate the oil then wipe off any excess oil on the rod. If oil is left on the keys, it will attract dirt which will mix with the oil to slow the key action.

MONTHLY MAINTENANCE CHECK LIST—SAXOPHONE FAMILY

Chart 20 is a check list to use to help maintain the saxophone. By following this chart, you can keep the instrument in good playing shape and also be alert to any possible repairs needed before they become too severe. With some training, your students should be able to utilize this check list also.

Chart 20
Monthly Maintenance Check List—Saxophone Family

INSPECT THE FOLLOWING:

Saxophone _____ Is the neck cork clean, intact and lightly greased?

_____ Is the metal neck tenon clean and fitting properly?

_____ Are there any hard, dry pads?

_____ Are there any torn pads?

_____ Are there any loose pads?

_____ Are all the keys moving freely?

_____ Are there any missing screws or rods?

_____ Is the upper octave key working properly?

_____ Is there a mouthpiece cap?

_____ Are there any posts, guards or braces which are unsoldered?

Case _____ Are the latches working properly?

_____ Are the hinges tight?

_____ Is the handle secure?

_____ Is the case lining in place?

_____ Are all accessories stored in the proper compartment?

_____ Is the storage compartment secure?

_____ Are there any pins or medals which will lay against the instrument when the case is closed?

_____ Are there any loose objects in the case?

_____ Is the instrument held tightly in the case when closed?

_____ Is there a set of swabs with the instrument?

_____ How is the wet reed stored after playing?

DO THE FOLLOWING:

1. Clean dirt and lint from under the keys and rods.
2. Clean the neck cork and grease lightly.
3. Oil the key rods and screws.
4. Wash the mouthpiece (should be done weekly).
5. Clean the metal neck tenon with paraffin.
6. Thoroughly wipe the instrument with a soft cloth to remove fingerprints.

HOW TO REPAIR THE SAXOPHONE

DIAGNOSING INSTRUMENT MALFUNCTIONS

Before you can repair the saxophone, you need to understand the problem. Listed below are some of the more common problems that occur on the saxophone. For each problem I have suggested some possible causes. Although this list can hardly be complete, it can serve as a good guideline.

1. *Problem:* Saxophone blows hard, will not play all notes clearly.

   Possible Causes: Pads are leaking (look for torn pads, missing pads or those not

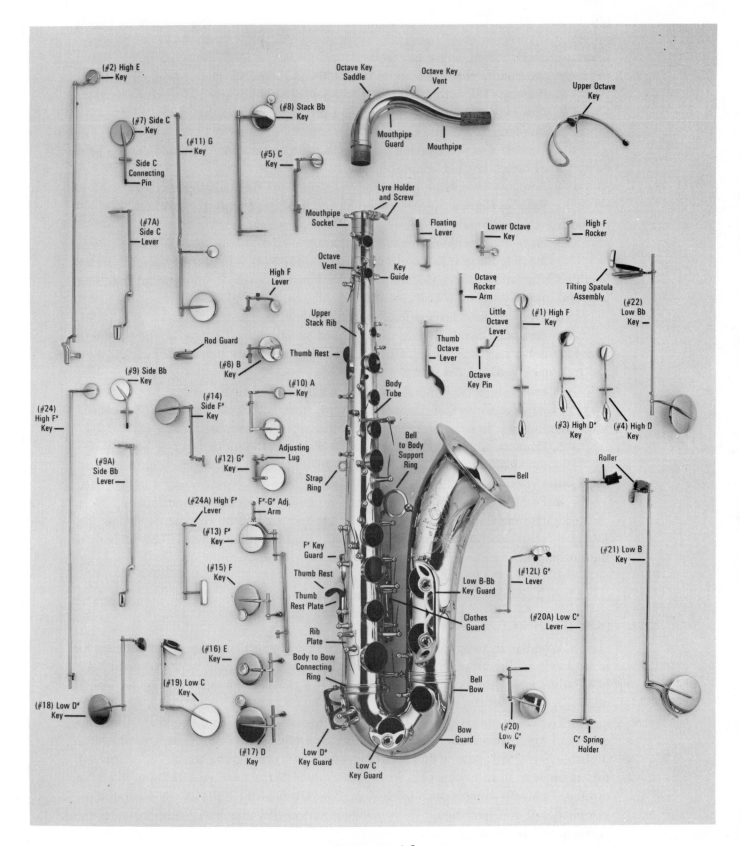

Illustration 6-2

Photograph courtesy of The Selmer Co.; Elkhart, Indiana

seating properly). Tone holes may be bent and no longer level. Keys are not regulated properly (particularly check the upper octave key at the neck). Old or broken reed.

2. *Problem:* The note "G" (high or low) will not play clearly and tends to "warble."
Possible Causes: Same as number 1 above.

3. *Problem:* Saxophone squeaks.
Possible Causes: Leaking pads, especially in the upper keys and/or side palm keys. Upper octave key not adjusted properly.

4. *Problem:* Saxophone plays the wrong pitch for the fingering used.
Possible Causes: Springs are unhooked from the key. Broken springs. Key may not be regulated correctly.

5. *Problem:* Saxophone plays out of tune.
Possible Causes: Key corks missing resulting in an incorrect key height. All key heights set incorrectly. Player's embouchure and/or reed need attention. Mouthpiece not matched properly with the instrument (try a different mouthpiece).

6. *Problem:* Keys are not functioning properly.
Possible Causes: Broken or unhooked spring. Upper octave key not properly aligned. Bent keys, rods or posts. Unsoldered post. Pivot screws too tight or rusted. Keys and rods may be dirty or rusted.

7. *Problem:* Neck does not stay tight when screw is tightened.
Possible Causes: Neck screw may be stripped. Neck screw is in backwards. Metal tenon needs to be expanded (a job for the repair technician).

8. *Problem:* Mouthpiece is loose when placed at the proper spot to be in tune.
Possible Causes: Neck cork needs to be replaced as old one has compressed and dried out.

9. *Problem:* Saxophone is "noisy" when played, keys click and rattle.
Possible Causes: Key felts are missing. Bumper felts on key guards are missing. Key guards are loose or missing completely. Key guards are unsoldered from the body of the saxophone.

10. *Problem:* Saxophone bell is loose.
Possible Causes: Bell brace has become unsoldered.

HOW TO CHECK FOR LEAKS

When your saxophone does not play properly, the first thing to do is check for leaks. Leaks in the saxophone can be the result of a missing, torn or worn pad, bent keys, loose adjustment screws or dents in the body of the instrument. Finding the leak is necessary to correct the problem.

Generally speaking, all the notes on the saxophone should produce the same quality of tone. If you have a note or notes that sound "stuffy" or are hard to blow, you probably have a leak. Also, if there is a tendency for the note "G" to "warble" when played, this is an almost sure sign of a leak. Remember that a poor embouchure, reed, or insufficient breath support can also cause problems, especially in the lowest register of the saxophone. If you have doubt, have another person play the instrument to see if the problem still persists.

Tools Needed: Leak light
Soft rubber ball (to plug the end of bell)

Procedure:

1. Check the neck. Place the palm of your hand against one end of the neck to plug and blow *gently* into the other end. If there is a leak, you should hear air escaping and feel a lack of resistance. Unless there is a crack in the neck (highly unlikely) only the upper octave pad could be leaking.

2. Check the saxophone body. Find a soft rubber ball which will fit into the bell of the saxophone. This ball should be pushed firmly into the bell to seal this end completely and not allow any air to escape. The ball should not go into the bell past the low Bb tone hole. (Somebody will need to hold this ball in place while you are checking.) Place your fingers on the keys as though you were playing the Low Bb and hold them down with the normal amount of playing pressure. Place your mouth around the receiver of the saxophone and blow gently into the instrument. (*NOTE:* Most saxophones have a slot in the receiver, so your mouth will have to go past the slot to avoid having air leak out at this point.)

Do not blow too hard, as you may blow open some keys that would normally remain closed. If there is a leak, you will hear the air escaping and may feel the lack of resistance. Be very critical when listening for the escaping air; it may not be a very loud sound. It is also possible that the air will be leaking from around the rubber ball as this is not a "fool proof" method of sealing the instrument.

Once you have located the leaking pad or pads you will have to replace the pad (See How to Install New Leather Saxophone Pads, p.192), readjust the keys (See How to Regulate the Keys, below) or have the tone holes leveled.

3. Place the neck into the receiver of the saxophone. Check to be certain that when assembled the upper octave key on the neck is completely closed. If it is not closed, bend this key slightly until the pad does rest firmly against the tone hole on the neck.

4. Since the above method is not always the most effective means of finding leaks, you may want to double check the instrument with a leak light. Most pads on the saxophone are quite visible and it is relatively simple to use a leak light. Place the light under each key, then close slowly and watch to see if the pad seals the tone hole completely. You should look at both the front and back of the pad, so close the pad a few times as you observe the tone hole from various angles. If the pad is not sealing completely, the keys may not be regulated properly; they may be bent or the pad might be hard and dry. To correct the problem see How to Regulate the Keys, below, or How to Install New Leather Saxophone Pads, p.192.

HOW TO REGULATE THE KEYS

Correct regulation of the saxophone keys is important for proper instrument performance. By following the instructions below, you should be able to locate and correct any problems. Any difference in regulating the soprano, alto, tenor or baritone saxophone will be noted in the instructions. Although the regulation of the keys is just one step in the complete adjustment process of the saxophone, it is sometimes all that you will need to get the instrument playing again.

Tools Needed: Leak light

Small screwdriver

Duck bill pliers
Round nose pliers
Pad slick
Emery paper
Materials Needed: Sheet cork as needed in sizes ¹⁄₆₄″, ¹⁄₁₆″, ³⁄₃₂″ or ⅛″
Felt discs or bumpers
Contact cork cement
Procedure: (Refer to Illustration 6-2 for key names and numbers.)

1. Check the pad seats. Before you attempt to regulate any keys, check all the pads to be certain that they are sealing properly. If the pads do not form a level seat with the tone holes, it will be virtually impossible to regulate the keys. To check the seat, place a leak light under each pad and close the key slowly using a very light pressure. It is important to be very critical during this checking procedure. The pad should close simultaneously around the entire tone hole. Often you will find that a pad is hitting the front, back or one of the sides *before* it seals the tone hole. If this is happening, visually check to see if the *key* is level with the tone hole. Sometimes, a key will be bent, causing one side of the pad to strike the tone hole before the other. If this is the case, use the large duck bill pliers to gently bend the key back to a level position and check again. Any pads that are torn, loose or not sealing properly will need to be replaced. (See How to Install New Leather Saxophone Pads, p.192.)

Also the tone hole may be uneven, making it impossible for the pad to seat properly. Place the leak light under the tone hole, then sight across the top of the tone hole (the key should be open at this time). If it appears uneven, it will need to be taken to the repair shop for leveling.

2. Starting at the top of the instrument, press the B key (#6). This should close at the same time as the C key (#5). Use a leak light to check this by placing the bulb under the tone holes and observing whether they close together. If they do not, the adjustment is made at the point where the foot of the B key makes contact with the bar of the C key. There should be a piece of ¹⁄₆₄″ cork at this point of contact. If not, add a piece and check again. If the B key is closing before the C key, add more cork on the *top* of the foot of the B key (where it contacts the C key bar) until the two keys close together. If the C key is closing first, remove some of the cork until they close together. You should not remove all the cork, however, and if the C key is still closing too soon, you will need to bend the foot of the B key down toward the body slightly with small round nose pliers, then re-adjust with cork.

3. Check under the lever of the A key (#10) to be certain that there is a round felt disc at the point where the lever makes contact with the Stack B♭ key (#8). If not, glue a piece in place using contact cement. Now press the A key (#10). This key should close at the same time as the Stack B♭ key (#8). If they do not, it is corrected by the bending the *lever* of the A key (#10). If the A key is closing first, bend the lever *down* slightly. If the B♭ key is closing first, bend the A key lever *up* slightly and recheck. (To bend the A key lever down, place a large pad slick under the pad of the A key, then press gently on the lever. To bend this lever up, hold the pad firmly against the tone hole and pull gently up on the lever.)

4. Again close the A key (#10). Along with closing the Stack B♭ key (#8) this should also close the C key (#5). If they do not close together, make the adjustment on the *foot* of the A key where it makes contact with the bar of the C key. The procedure is the same as described in step 2 above.

5. **For Baritone Saxonphone Only**—Check the G key (#11). If your saxophone has two pads for this key, be certain that they close together. Press the lever of the G key gently and, with a leak light, check to see if the two pads close simultaneously. If they do not, adjust by bending the key. Place a large pad slick under the pad which seals the tone hole first, then press firmly on the other pad. If you over-correct, reverse the process until the two pads close together.

6. Press down on the F♯ key (#13). This should close at the same time as the Stack B♭ key (#8). If they do not, the adjustment is made by regulating the cork on the arm of the F♯ key as it extends over the arm of the Stack B♭ key. Adding more cork at this point will close the Stack B♭ sooner. If neither the F♯ key (#13) nor the Stack B♭ key (#8) will close, remove the cork from the arm of the F♯ key where it extends over the G♯ key (#12). (This will be re-adjusted in step 7 below.)

7. Press down the G♯ lever (#12L). This should open the G♯ key (#12). While holding the G♯ lever down, press the F♯ key (#13). This should close at the same time as the G♯ key (#12). If the G♯ key does not close, add cork to the arm of the F♯ key (only at the point where it extends over the G♯ key) until they close together.

8. Press down the F key (#15). This key should close at the same time as the F♯ key (#13). (The Stack B♭ key will also close with the F♯ key, but this adjustment is already complete.) If they do not close together, the adjustment is made on the *foot* of the F key (#15). If the F key is closing first, add some cork to the *top* of this foot at the point where it contacts the bar of the F♯ key. Add cork until they close together. If the F♯ key is closing first, remove some of the cork until they close together. Do not remove all of the cork from this foot. If the adjustment is still not correct and you have removed as much cork as possible, you will need to bend the foot of the F key down toward the body slightly with round nose pliers and re-adjust with cork as described.

9. Press down the E key (#16). This key should close at the same time as the F♯ key (#13). If they do not close together, make the adjustment on the foot of the *E key* as described in step 8.

10. Press down the D key (#17). This key should close at the same time as the F♯ key (#13). If they do not close together, make the adjustment on the foot of the *D key* as described in step 8.

11. Press down the lever of the Low B♭ key (#22). This key should close at the same time as the Low B key (#21). If they do not, make the adjustment by regulating the thickness of the cork located between the Low B♭ key lever and the Low B key lever. The thicker this cork, the sooner the Low B key will close.

12. Insert the neck into the receiver of the saxophone and line up correctly. There are as many different octave systems as there are brands of saxophones, so it is virtually impossible to tell you exactly how to adjust this section of the instrument. Described below is what should happen. I'm certain that most of you will be able to figure out how these keys operate on your brand of saxophone.

Without touching any keys, the Upper octave key (on the saxophone neck) should be closed. If it is not, bend this key slightly until it does close. Now press the Thumb octave lever (register key). This should open the Upper octave key. While holding the Thumb octave lever down, press the G key (#11). This should close the Upper octave key while at the same time open the Lower octave key. If the keys do not operate properly, check the spring tension on all the keys involved to be certain that these keys are moving freely.

13. This completes the regulation of the saxophone. All other keys on the instrument are independent of each other and do not have to be regulated to work with other keys.

HOW TO INSTALL NEW LEATHER SAXOPHONE PADS

In your repair supplies, you should have an assortment of saxophone pads. There are a number of styles of saxophone pads available, but it is best to use a riveted leather pad. (This style pad will not be riveted in the smaller sizes.) You can use this style pad in any saxophone; however, if your saxophone has either plastic or metal resonators on the pad, it is better to replace this with the same style pad. If you have a large number of saxophones with resonators you may prefer to stack this style pad in your supplies.

Tools Needed: Leak light
Pad slick (size to fit tone hole)
Small wood or cork wedges
Alcohol or bunsen burner
Small screwdriver
Materials Needed: Leather saxophone pad
Stick shellac

Procedure:

1. Remove the old pad. Leather pads are held in place with shellac or a similar type of substance. You may need to remove the key in order to get at the pad. Use a small screwdriver to remove any pivot screws or rods needed to free the key, but be certain that you remember where the screws belong when you reassemble the key. Heat the key as shown in Illustration 6-3. (*Warning:* The pearls on the saxophone keys will burn very easily. If the key you are heating has a pearl on it, keep the flame away from this area. It is even better to cover the pearl with a small piece of metal to protect it from the direct heat, but remember that this metal will also become quite hot to hold.) Always heat the key at an angle so that the main concentration of heat will not burn the lacquer on the body of the saxophone. When the shellac is soft, remove the old pad. Some Buescher saxophone pads are held in place with a snap-on resonator which needs to be pried off with a screwdriver. It is not necessary to heat this style pad to remove it.

2. Find the correct size replacement pad. The pad should fit snuggly into the empty key cup. If it is too large, the pad will not go all the way into the cup or will bend, wrinkling the leather. If the pad is too small, there will be a space between the pad and the side of the key cup, allowing the pad to slide around in the key cup.

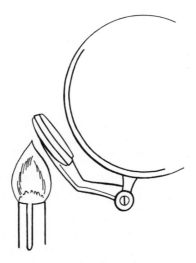

Illustration 6-3

3. Hold the end of the stick shellac in the flame of your burner and, when soft, spread over the back of the pad. Place the pad into the key. If you have Buescher style snap-on pads, see step 5 below.

4. Seat the pad. Heat the key as shown in Illustration 6-3 until the shellac softens and the pad settles into the key cup. (*NOTE:* See warning about burning the key pearls in step 1.) Place a pad slick between the pad and the tone hole. Close the key over the pad slick and, while the shellac is still soft, rotate the pad slick slightly. This will spread the shellac and level the pad with the tone hole. Remove the pad slick and close the key firmly over the tone hole. Hold firmly by wedging shut with a small wedge until cool.

5. *For Buescher Snap-On Pads Only:* After you have completed step 2, punch a hole in the center of the pad, place the pad into the key cup, place the pad slick between the pad and the tone hole, and close the key firmly over the pad slick. Rotate the pad slick slightly to level the pad with the tone hole. Then place the snap-on resonator in place to hold the pad. To seat the pad, heat the key as shown in Illustration 6-3 and close the key firmly over the tone hole. Hold firmly closed by wedging shut with a small wedge until cool. (*NOTE:* See warning regarding burning key pearls in step 1.)

6. After the key has cooled thoroughly, remove the wedge and check the pad with a leak light. Be certain that the pad is level with the tone hole. If the seat is not tight, repeat the process starting with step 2.

7. Adjust the key. It will be necessary to re-adjust the key if it works in conjunction with other keys on the saxophone (See How to Regulate the Keys, p.189).

HOW TO REPLACE KEY CORKS

Key corks on the saxophone are used not only to provide quiet key action but also to regulate the keys and adjust the key heights. For this reason the thickness of the cork used on each key is extremely important. Listed in Chart 21 is the most common size cork which is used on each key of the saxophone. In many cases, you will have to use emery paper to reduce the thickness of this cork to achieve the proper key height or adjustment.

Tools Needed: Single edge razor blade
Emery paper
Materials Needed: Sheet cork as needed in sizes ¹⁄₆₄″, ¹⁄₁₆″ and ³⁄₃₂″
Contact cork cement

Procedure:

1. Remove any old cork which may be left on the key.

2. Select the correct thickness of cork as indicated in Chart 21 and spread contact cement on a small section of this cork.

3. Spread contact cement on the proper place of the key as indicated in Chart 21.

4. Allow the contact cement to dry thoroughly, then place the cork in position. Trim off excess with a razor blade.

5. Check the height and regulation of the key with other keys on the saxophone and emery the cork if needed. (See How to Regulate the Keys, p. 189, or How to Check the Intonation of the Saxophone, p. 202.) To emery the cork, place a small strip of emery paper between the cork and the saxophone body or key with the rough side against the cork (see Illustration 6-4). Hold the cork against the emery paper and pull. This will remove a small amount of cork and shape it to the body or key of the saxophone at the same time.

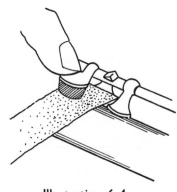

Illustration 6-4

HOW TO REPLACE KEY FELTS

The saxophone will have about six felts on the instrument. There are two types of felts used on the saxophone: (1) the felt disc, a flat, round circle of felt, and (2) the felt bumper, a small cylinder of felt.

The felt bumpers are used to regulate the height to which the following keys open: Low D♯ key (#18), Low C key (#19), Low B key (#21) and Low B♭ key (#22). The larger the felt bumper, the less the key will open (see Chart 23, page 203, for proper key heights). The bumpers are either mounted in the key guard which is above each key or on the top of the key.

The felt disc is used under the lever of the A key (#10) and under the High F lever (located above the C key (#5)). Select a disc which is the same diameter as the pearl of the lever. After installing a new felt disc, it is necessary to regulate those keys (see How to Regulate the Keys, p. 189).

Saxophone felts are glued in place with the same contact cement used for key corks.

Chart 21
Saxophone Key Corks

Refer to Illustration 6-2 for key names and numbers. Only those keys listed require cork.

Key #	Key Name	Location of Cork*	Size of Cork**
—	Floating lever	Back of top pin	1/16"
—	Register key	Under lever	3/32"
—	High F rocker	Top of each end	1/64"
—	High F lever	Under foot	1/16"
		Under lever	felt disc
1	High F key	Under foot	1/16"
2	High E key	Under foot	1/16"
3	High D♯ key	Under foot	1/16"
4	High D key	Under foot	1/16"
6	B key	Under foot	1/16"
		Top of foot	1/64"
7L	Side C lever	Under arm	1/16"
		Top of arm	1/64"
9	Side B♭ key (or)	Under lever	3/32"
	Side B♭ lever	Under arm	1/16"
		Top of arm	1/64"
10	A key	Under foot	1/16"
		Top of foot	1/64"
		Under lever	felt disc
11	G key	Under top arm	1/64"
12	G♯ key	Under foot	1/64"
12L	G♯ lever	Under foot	3/32"
		Top of spatula	1/64"
13	F♯ key	Under arm	1/64"
14	Side F♯ key	Under lever	3/32"
15	F key	Under foot	1/16"
		Top of foot	1/64"
16	E key	Under foot	1/16"
		Top of foot	1/64"
17	D key	Under foot	1/16"
		Top of foot	1/64"
18	Low D♯ key	Under lever (or)	3/32"
		Under key guard	felt bumper
19	Low C key	Key guard	felt bumper
20	Low C♯ key	Top of arm to key cup	3/32"
21	Low B key	Key guard	felt bumper
22	Low B♭ key	Key guard	felt bumper
		Under lever	1/16"

*Term "lever" as used in this chart refers to the portion of the key which is touched by the finger while playing.

**In most cases this is the starting size cork to be used. Usually the cork will need to be made thinner by using a piece of emery paper to reduce the size. To determine the correct thickness, see the following: How to Regulate the Keys, p.189; How to Check the Intonation of the Saxophone, p.202; The Complete Adjustment, p.205.

HOW TO RE-CORK THE NECK

When the neck cork of the saxophone begins to tear, fall off or become too loose, it should be replaced. Use your mouthpiece to determine if the neck cork is too loose. The mouthpiece should slide snuggly onto the neck and be held firmly in place at *ANY* position. Often the mouthpiece will be quite loose when first put on, but will fit tighter the further the mouthpiece is pushed on the neck. You will want the neck cork adjusted so that the mouthpiece will be tight in any position of the neck.

Tools Needed: Ruler
                Small screwdriver
                Single edge razor blade
                Rawhide hammer
                Pliers or scraper
                Emery paper

Materials Needed: Sheet cork ($\frac{1}{16}''$ thick)
                    Contact cork cement
                    Cork grease

Procedure:

1. Remove the upper octave key. This will make it easier to work on the neck without fear of bending the key.

2. Remove all particles of the old neck cork. This is most easily done with a regular pair of pliers. Grip the neck cork loosely with the pliers and turn them back and forth around the tenon to tear off all the old cork. Do this carefully as it is essential that the tenon be completely clean before proceeding if the job is to be successful. Check to be certain that all cork is gone and all trace of either cement or shellac, which was holding the cork in place, is removed. You may also use a metal scraper to clean the neck.

3. Cut the new tenon cork from a sheet of $\frac{1}{16}''$ cork. This cork is usually available in 4″ x 12″ sheets. The proper widths for neck corks are as follows:

           Soprano Saxophone—$1\frac{1}{4}''$ wide
           Alto Saxophone—$1\frac{1}{2}''$ wide
           Tenor Saxophone—$1\frac{3}{4}''$ wide
           Baritone Saxophone—$2''$ wide

The neck cork can be cut across the narrow portion of the sheet so that the final piece will be 4″ long and the width as indicated above. This size piece will give you a bit of waste, but it is much easier to work with the larger piece.

4. Cut a beveled edge on one end of the cork strip (see Illustration 6-5).

BEVEL

SIDE VIEW

Illustration 6-5

5. Soften the cork. Because the cork will be bent in a tight circle, soften the cork to help prevent it from cracking. Pound the cork thoroughly on both sides with the rawhide hammer to make it more pliable.

6. Apply the contact cement. The cement should completely cover the end of the neck (you can easily see where the cork is to be placed), also the entire *bottom* of the cork and the top portion of the cork which is beveled (see Illustration 6-6). Allow the cement to dry thoroughly as indicated in the directions on the container.

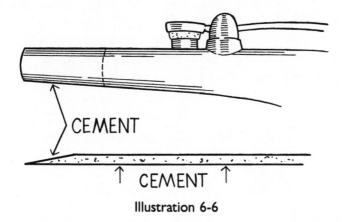

Illustration 6-6

7. Glue the new cork in place. When the cement is dry, place the *bottom* of the *beveled* end of the cork on the tenon. This step of replacing the cork is the most difficult because of the tapered neck. Take care to start the cork so that the edge is straight with the neck and extending over the edge about ½″. Work around the neck, carefully pressing the cork to make good contact and avoid any gaps. When you have completed the circle around the neck, the cork should lap on top of the beveled end which is already in place (see Illustration 6-7). As you wrap the cork around the neck it will not end evenly because of the taper. This unevenness will be corrected in step 8.

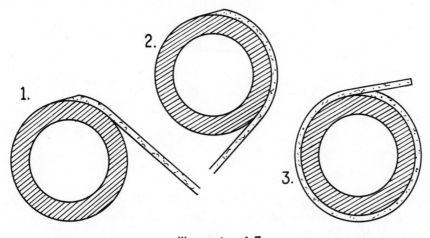

Illustration 6-7

8. Trim the cork. The cork should now be firmly in place on the neck and needs to be trimmed. Use a single edge razor blade for this job. After trimming, you may find that the cork did not completely cover the end of the neck because of the angle it took when

wrapped around the neck. If this is the case, begin again at step 3 and this time have greater amount of cork extend over the edge of the neck before starting to wrap.

9. Emery the cork. Using a strip of emery paper which is about 1″ to 1½″ wide, first emery the overlap in the neck cork so that it is level with the rest of the cork. Use the strip of emery paper as shown in Illustration 6-8. Because the neck is tapered, the cork will also be tapered as you start to emery. You must emery more cork from the wider end so that the finished cork will have a cylindrical shape. Take care to remove equal portions of cork from around the circumference of the neck. *Stop emerying* when the mouthpiece just begins to fit on the cork but is still rather tight. Apply some cork grease to the cork and push the mouthpiece in place. The cork will compress at this point and give you a good fit. (*NOTE:* If you emery until you have a good fit with a dry cork, the fit will become too loose once grease has been applied and the neck cork compresses.)

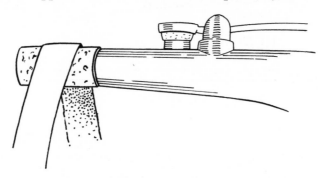

Illustration 6-8

10. Bevel the edge of the neck cork. Many repair technicians will bevel the edge of the cork slightly so that the mouthpiece will not tear the edge of the new cork. Illustration 6-9 shows how the cork should be beveled.

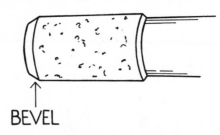

BEVEL

Illustration 6-9

11. Replace the upper octave key and the job is complete.

HOW TO REPLACE A NEEDLE SPRING

A broken needle spring is not difficult to replace. By doing it yourself you can save considerable time and keep your saxophone playing rather than sitting in a repair shop. The blue steel needle spring is the proper type of spring to use on the saxophone. You should have an assortment of these springs in your repair stock; they are used on all woodwind instruments except the flute and the piccolo.

Tools Needed: Small round nose pliers
Wire cutter

                Small hammer
                Alcohol or bunsen burner
                Steel or metal block
                Large blue steel needle spring
                Spring hook

Materials Needed: Blue steel needle spring

Procedure:

1. Remove the keys from around the broken spring to make it accessible.

2. Remove the old spring. Usually the spring will break, leaving a small stub in the post. This stub must be pulled out from the same end that it went in (see Illustration 6-10). If the flattened end of the spring is extending out from the post, grasp this firmly with the wire cutter and pull it out (see Illustration 6-11). If the other end of the spring is extending beyond the post, use the round nose pliers to squeeze the spring out of the post (see Illustration 6-12). If the spring is flush in the post, use a large needle spring as a driver to tap the spring out with a hammer. When doing this, be sure to rest the post against some object to prevent it from bending or breaking (see Illustration 6-13). It is also possible that the old spring has already fallen out of the post.

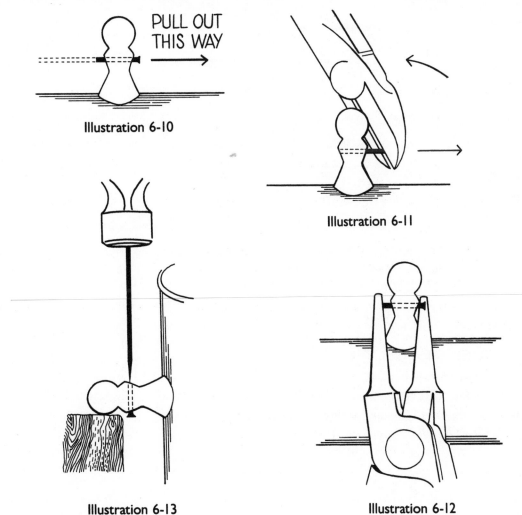

Illustration 6-10

Illustration 6-11

Illustration 6-13

Illustration 6-12

3. After the old spring is removed, find the correct size needle spring which will fit snuggly into the post but will slide all the way through. Slide the spring into the post so that the correct length will extend beyond the post, allowing the point of the spring to catch in the spring hook on the key. Mark the length of spring needed. Remove the spring and cut with a wire cutter to the correct length as marked. Be sure that you cut off the "butt end" and not the pointed end.

4. Hold the spring with a pair of pliers and heat the "butt end" of the spring in the flame of the burner until the *end* starts to turn red. Take care that only the very end of the spring turns red, for if too much is heated, it will loose its "spring." When the end is red, hold the spring against a solid metal block (vice, piece of steel, etc.) and with a small hammer tap the end to flatten slightly. Allow the spring to cool.

5. Insert the spring into the post with the pointed end going in first. Squeeze the flat end into the post with round nose pliers (see Illustration 6-14). This should hold the spring in place. If the spring does not go in far enough, you have flattened the end too much and must try again with another spring. If the spring goes in easily and is not tight, repeat step 4 and flatten the end a little more.

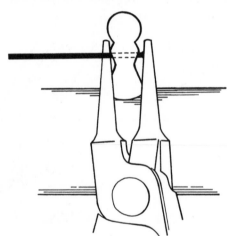

Illustration 6-14

6. Bend the spring slightly in the post. If the key affected is normally in the open position, then the spring should be bent *toward* the tone hole. If the key is usually closed, the spring should be bent *away* from the tone hole.

7. Re-mount the key and check the spring tension. (See How to Adjust the Spring Tension, p.201.) Replace all keys which were removed to make the spring accessible.

HOW TO REPLACE A FLAT SPRING

There are a few keys on the saxophone that utilize a flat spring instead of the needle spring. Unlike the needle spring, the flat spring is attached directly to the key and is held in place with a small screw.

Tools Needed: Small screwdriver
                         Wire cutter

Materials Needed: Correct size flat spring
                              Flat spring screw (if missing)

Procedure:

1. Remove the key. It may be necessary to remove other keys in order to reach the key with the flat spring. Be sure that you keep track of all screws and rods which are removed, so they can replace them in the same position when you reassemble the keys.

2. Remove the broken piece of flat spring.

3. Select a new spring which is the correct size. Flat springs come in a variety of lengths and strengths. First determine the correct length needed for the key, by examining where the end of the flat spring is to rest on the instrument. On most saxophones, there will be a little metal box on the instrument upon which the end of the spring is to rest. If your saxophone does not have this box, there will probably be either a groove in the instrument or wear marks on the body from the previous spring. The new spring must have the same length as the old spring.

4. Install the spring with the flat spring screw and mount the key to test for strength. If the key pushes too hard or too easily, replace this spring with another of the same length which will be either thinner or thicker. If the flat spring screw is missing, replace with a new screw. These screws are uniform in size and you should have a small supply of them in the repair stock.

5. Mount the spring back on the key and replace the key in the proper position. Check the tension again and adjust if necessary (see How to Adjust the Spring Tension, below). Return any other keys that had to be removed.

HOW TO ADJUST THE SPRING TENSION

The adjustment of spring tension on the saxophone is important in order to provide correct finger resistance. In Chart 22 I have listed the tension that should be set for each key.

The tension of a spring is increased or decreased by bending the spring gently in one direction or the other. Bending the spring too far will cause it to break, so only do a little at a time. Use a spring hook for this job and be sure to unhook the spring from the key before attempting to bend it. Those keys that are *normally open* need to have the spring bent *toward* the tone hole to *increase* the tension. Those keys that are *normally closed* need to have the spring bent *away* from the tone hole to *increase* the tension.

If you need to adjust the tension of a flat spring, remove the key first so that you have better access to the spring. Use small round nose pliers and bend about half the spring. If you wish to *increase* the tension of this spring, bend the end *away* from the key and toward the body of the saxophone. If you wish to *decrease* the tension, bend the spring *toward* the key and away from the body of the instrument. After the spring has been bent, replace the key and check the tension by comparing with other keys that have the same tension. If this bending action does not solve the spring tension problem, you may have to replace the flat spring with a different strength spring (see How to Replace a Flat Spring, p.200).

Chart 22
Saxophone Spring Tensions

Refer to Illustration 6-2 for key names and numbers.
The following keys should be set with a very *light* tension:*

    — —Upper octave key

    — —Lower octave key

    #5—C key

    #8—Stack B♭ key

    #12—G♯ key

The following keys should be set with a *medium light* tension:*

    — —Floating lever

    #6—B key

    #10—A key

    #13—F♯ key

    #15—F key

    #16—E key

    #17—D key

The following keys should be set with a *medium* tension:*

    #18—Low D♯ key

    #19—Low C key

    #20—Low C♯ key

    #21—Low B key

    #22—Low B♭ key

The following keys should be set with a *medium heavy* tension:*

    ——Thumb octave lever

    #1—High F key

    #3—High D♯ key

    #4—High D key

    #2—High E key

    #7—Side C key

    #9—Side B♭ key

    #14—Side F♯ key

The following key should be set with special tension:

    # 11—G key—The tension should be equal to that experienced when you push the A key (#10) which activates the Stack B♭ key (#8) and the C key (#5).

---

*When checking the tension, push one key at a time. For example, when you check the tension of the B key (#6), hold the C key (#5) down so that you are not pushing two keys down when you check one key. When the key is operated by a lever, check only the pad, not the lever. Those levers which also have spring tension should be set so that the lever tension is twice as strong as the key which it operates.

HOW TO CHECK THE INTONATION OF THE SAXOPHONE

The intonation of the saxophone is determined by a number of factors:

1. The breath support and embouchure of the player.
2. The hardness of the reed.

3. The placement of the mouthpiece as the instrument is assembled.

4. The cut of the mouthpiece used.

5. The open heights of the saxophone keys.

Item 5 is particularly important if the saxophone is to play in tune with itself. The height of the key is measured at the front of the pad and is the distance from the top of the tone hole to the bottom of the pad when the key is fully opened. Chart 23 shows the acceptable heights to which the saxophone keys should open.

If you find an individual key which is not at the correct height, it has probably lost a cork on some point of the key. These individual key heights can usually be corrected by replacing the cork (see How to Replace Key Corks, p. 193). Remember that whenever you add a cork you will have to re-check the adjustment of that key with any other keys that are activated at the same time (see How to Regulate the Keys, p. 189).

If, in checking the saxophone key heights, you find that all or many of the key heights are incorrect, it will take a complete adjustment to correct the problem.

Chart 23
Saxophone Key Heights

Refer to Illustration 6-2 for key names and numbers.

Key #	Key Name	Soprano & Alto Saxophone height	Tenor & Baritone Saxophone height
1	High F key	$3/16''$	$3/16''$
2	High E key	$3/16''$	$3/16''$
3	High D♯ key	$3/16''$	$3/16''$
4	High D key	$3/16''$	$3/16''$
7	Side C key	$3/16''$	$3/16''$
9	Side B♭ key	$3/16''$	$3/16''$
14	Side F♯ key	$3/16''$	$3/16''$
17	D key	$1/4''$	$5/16''$
18	Low D♯ key	$1/4''$	$5/16''$
19	Low C key	$1/4''$	$5/16''$
20	Low C♯ key	$1/4''$	$5/16''$
22	Low B♭ key	$1/4''$	$5/16''$

When the saxophone is regulated correctly, all the other keys will be at the correct height.

HOW TO CORRECT NON-FUNCTIONING KEYS

A non-functioning key can be defined as any key on the saxophone which is not operating properly. For the most part, when this occurs, you are going to have to send the instrument into the repair shop to be corrected. There are, however, a number of things which you can check before sending the saxophone to be repaired. These are common problems which cause key malfuntions that can easily be corrected by you.

1. **Check the spring**—Is it broken off? Perhaps the spring is just unhooked from the key. If the spring appears O.K., push against it with your spring hook. If there is no tension in the spring, it is broken and will need to be replaced (see How to Replace a

Needle Spring, p.198 or How to Replace a Flat Spring, p.200).

2. **Check the pivot screws**—These screws, which are located at the ends of the keys, go through the post and hold the key in place. It is possible that the screw is tightened down too far and is binding the key action. On the other hand, if the pivot screw is not tight enough, it will permit extra motion in the keys. This will cause the key adjustment to be inaccurate and the pads to seat poorly over the tone holes. Use a small screwdriver and move the pivot screw both ways to see if the action of the key improves.

3. **Check the key**—If the key does not close all the way, use a leak light to see if the pad is still level on the tone hole. If not, your key may have been bent. You will then need to bend the key back to a level position and probably replace the pad (see How to Install New Leather Saxophone Pads, p.192). Another possibility is that an adjustment screw is regulated incorrectly, thus preventing the key from closing.

HOW TO FREE KEY ROLLERS

On most saxophones, some keys have small rollers to facilitate finger action. These are usually found on the keys which are activated by the little finger of each hand. These rollers, when working properly, make it easier for the player to move from one key to the other. If these rollers do not move freely, the player has a more difficult time than necessary in playing those notes. It is relatively easy to correct the problem.

Tools Needed: Small screwdriver
Emery paper
Pipe stem cleaner
Alcohol

Procedure:

1. Remove the key. It will be much easier to work on this roller if you remove the key from the instrument.

2. Remove the roller. All rollers are held in place by a small threaded rod which goes through the center of the roller. To remove the roller, simply unscrew the rod and pull out. If the roller won't move because the rod has rusted, you may not be able to unscrew the rod. If this is the case, leave this repair to the repair technician. He will cut the rod and make a new one and might also have to supply a new roller. If you are able to remove the rod, proceed to step 3 below.

3. Clean the roller. In most cases, the roller is stuck because of dirt. With a clean cloth, wipe off all grease from the rod, roller and key. Take a piece of pipe stem cleaner and dip into alcohol (from your alcohol burner). Push this through the roller to clean out all grease from inside the roller. Follow up with a dry end of the pipe stem cleaner to dry out. Alcohol will also help remove grease from the rod that won't wipe completely clean.

4. Check the rod. If the rod has any signs of rust or tarnish, it should be cleaned at this time. Use a piece of very fine emery paper (crocus cloth) to gently smooth the rod. Be sure to remove all grit after doing this.

5. Place the roller over the rod and check the action. The roller should be free at this time. If the action is not better, it is possible that the rod is bent; then your repair technician will need to make a new rod for you. If the action is good, place a small drop of key oil on the rod and replace the roller on the key. Replace the key and the job is complete.

HOW TO CLEAN THE SAXOPHONE MOUTHPIECE

If the saxophone mouthpiece is cleaned regularly as described in the beginning of this chapter you will not need to do anything further. The regular cleaning with soap and water, using a mouthpiece brush, will remove all dirt and traces of minerals which begin to gather on the mouthpiece.

In reality, however, we will occasionally find a mouthpiece which has not been cleaned and is coated with a hard crust. Normal washing in warm soapy water will not remove the crust. This unsightly and distasteful mouthpiece can be cleaned quite easily.

Tools Needed: Mouthpiece brush

Small hook made from piece of wire

Muriatic acid (available from druggist)

Baking soda (mixed in water)

Procedure:

1. Place the dirty mouthpiece in a jar of muriatic acid so that it is completely submerged. The acid should be stored in a wide mouth jar which is large enough to hold the largest woodwind mouthpiece. Leave the mouthpiece in the acid about 10-15 minutes. No harm will come to the mouthpiece if left in the acid too long. (*NOTE:* The acid will corrode metal, so the jar should have a plastic cover. The science department in your school might have an old jar you could use.)

2. Lift the mouthpiece out of the acid with the hook you made from the wire so that your hand does not have to contact the acid. Immediately place the mouthpiece into the solution of baking soda and water to neutralize the acid. You will notice a bubbling action when the mouthpiece is placed in the soda solution.

3. Remove the mouthpiece from the baking soda and water solution after the bubbling stops and rinse thoroughly under clean running water. Brush out all loose material with the mouthpiece brush. The mouthpiece will now be clean. (*NOTE:* If the mouthpiece is made of hard rubber, a slight green tinge may develop. This discoloration is the result of the acid and water, but does not harm the mouthpiece.)

THE COMPLETE ADJUSTMENT—
HOW TO MAKE THE ADJUSTMENTS NECESSARY FOR PROPER
INSTRUMENT PERFORMANCE

The complete adjustment of the saxophone is a complex matter. The many adjustments needed within the key mechanism can be confusing. By carefully following the instructions below you should be able to do a thorough job of adjusting the saxophone. If, however, you are not sure of the procedures described, you might do more damage than good in attempting to repair or adjust the instrument. In this case a good rule to follow is: "When in doubt, send it out." Be sure to read completely through the procedure before beginning.

Tools Needed: Leak light

Small screwdriver

Spring hook

Alcohol or bunsen burner

Pad slicks
Ruler
Emery paper
Small round nose pliers
Single edge razor blade
Materials Needed: Leather saxophone pads
Sheet cork in sizes ¹⁄₆₄″, ¹⁄₁₆″ & ³⁄₃₂″
Stick shellac
Contact cork cemet
Felt discs and bumpers
Procedure: (Refer to picture 6-2 for key names and numbers.)

1). Using a leak light, check all pads to be certain that they have a level seat which will form a tight seal with the tone hole. You can check each pad as you adjust it in the procedure to follow or check them all at once before you begin the adjustment. If any of the pads are uneven, loose or torn, they will have to be replaced before you can continue with this adjustment (see How to Install New Leather Saxophone Pads, p. 192).

2). Check the height of the D key (#17). There should be a piece of ¹⁄₁₆″ cork on the bottom of the foot of this key and a piece of ¹⁄₆₄″ cork on the top of the foot. When open, this key should measure ¼″ (on alto or soprano) or ⁵⁄₁₆″ (on tenor or baritone) from the top of the tone hole to the bottom of the pad. If the height is not correct make the adjustment by bending the foot of the key slightly. Bending the foot toward the body of the saxophone will close the key slightly.

3). Press down on the F♯ key (#13). This key should close at the same time as the G♯ key (#12). Use a leak light to check. If they do not close together, make the adjustment by regulating the thickness of the cork on the adjustment arm which extends over the G♯ key. Adding more cork will cause the G♯ key to close sooner. Some arms will have an adjustment screw at this point, and you regulate by turning this screw.

4). Press down on the D key (#17). This should close at the same time as the F♯ key (#13). Use a leak light to check. If they do not close together, the adjustment is made by bending the bar of the F♯ key where it extends over the foot of the D key. Use round nose pliers to bend this bar slightly *toward* the foot if you want the F♯ key to close sooner. Bend the bar *away* from the foot if you want the F♯ key to close later.

5). Check the E key (#16). Be certain that it has a piece of ¹⁄₁₆″ cork on the bottom of the foot and a piece of ¹⁄₆₄″ cork on the top of the foot. Close the E key and the F♯ key (#13) should close at the same time. Use a leak light to check. If they do not close together, make the adjustment by bending the *foot* of the E key slightly. Use round nose pliers to bend the foot *toward* the body of the saxophone if you want the E key to close sooner. Bending the foot *away* from the body will cause the E key to close later.

6). Check the F key (#15). Be certain that it has a piece of ¹⁄₁₆″ cork on the bottom of the foot and a piece of ¹⁄₆₄″ cork on the top of the foot. Close the F key and the F♯ key (#13) should close at the same time. Use the leak light to check. If they do not close together, the adjustment is made by bending the *foot* of the F key slightly. Use round nose pliers to bend the foot *toward* the body of the saxophone slightly if you want the F key to close sooner. Bending the foot *away* from the body will cause the F key to close later.

7). Press on the D key (#17). This key should activate the F♯ key (#13) immediately. If the D key moves first before activating the F♯ key, then either the *E key* (#16) or the *F key* (#15) need to be adjusted. One of these two keys (or possibly both of them) will be holding the bar of the F♯ key (#13) up off the foot of the D key. Determine which key is holding the bar, then emery the cork on the bottom of the foot of that key until the bar of the F♯ key settles against the foot of the D key (#17).

8). Press the E key (#16). This key should also activate the F♯ key (#13) immediately. If the E key must move before activating the F♯ key, add cork to the bottom of the E key foot until the top of the foot touches the bar of the F♯ key. (*Caution*: If you add too much cork, you will create "play" in the D key which was just checked in step 7.)

9). Press the F key (#15). This key should also activate the F♯ key (#13) immediately. If the F key moves before activating the F♯ key, add cork to the bottom of the F key foot until the top of the foot touches the bar of the F♯ key. (*Caution*: If you add too much cork, you will create "play" in the D key which was just checked in step 7.)

10). Check the height of the Low D♯ key (#18). When open, this key should measure ¼″ (on soprano or alto) or ⁵⁄₁₆″ (on tenor or baritone) from the top of the tone hole to the bottom of the pad. The height of this key is regulated in one of two ways. Some saxophones have a key guard over the key which has a felt bumper in the guard or on top of the pad cup. The size of this felt bumper will regulate the height to which the key opens. On other models, the lever of the Low D♯ key will have a piece of cork under it. The thickness of this cork will regulate the open height of the key. The thicker the cork or felt, the less the key will open.

11). Check the height of the Low C key (#19). When open this key should measure ¼″ (on soprano or alto) or ⁵⁄₁₆″ (on tenor or baritone) from the top of the tone hole to the bottom of the pad. If the height is incorrect, make the adjustment by regulating the thickness of the felt bumper which is located between the key and the key guard. The thicker the bumper, the less the key will open.

12). Check the height of the Side F♯ key (#14). This key should measure ³⁄₁₆″ from the top of the tone hole to the bottom of the pad. If the height is incorrect, make the adjustment by regulating the thickness of the cork under the lever of this key. The thinner the cork, the farther the key will open.

13). Check the height of the Side B♭ key (#9). This key should measure ³⁄₁₆″ from the top of the tone hole to the bottom of the pad. If the height is incorrect, make the adjustment by regulating the thickness of the cork under the lever of this key. The thinner the cork, the farther the key will open.

14). Check the height of the Side C key (#7). This key should measure ³⁄₁₆″ from the top of the tone hole to the bottom of the pad. If the height is incorrect, make the adjustment by regulating the thickness of the cork under the lever of this key. The thinner the cork, the farther the key will open.

15). Check the height of the High E key (#2). This key should measure ³⁄₁₆″ from the top of the tone hole to the bottom of the pad. If the height is incorrect, make the adjustment by regulating the thickness of the cork under the lever of this key. The thinner the cork, the farther the key will open.

16). Check the height of the High F key (#1). This key should measure 3/16″ from the top of the tone hole to the bottom of the pad. If the height is incorrect, make the adjustment by regulating the thickness of the cork under the lever of this key. The thinner the cork, the farther the key will open.

17). Check he height of the High D♯ key (#3). This key should measure 3/16″ from the top of the tone hole to the bottom of the pad. If the height is incorrect, make the adjustment by regulating the thickness of the cork under the lever of this key. The thinner the cork, the farther the key will open.

18). Check the height of the High D key (#4). This key should measure 3/16″ from the top of the tone hole to the bottom of the pad. If the height is incorrect, make the adjustment by regulating the thickness of the cork under the lever of this key. The thinner the cork, the farther the key will open.

19). Regulate the Stack B♭ key (#8). Close the F♯ key (#13). This key should close at the same time as the Stack B♭ key. Use a leak light to check. If they do not close together, the adjustment is made by regulating the thickness of the cork under the arm of the F♯ key where it extends over the arm of the stack B♭ key. The thicker the cork, the sooner the Stack B♭ key will close. (Do not change that portion of cork under the arm of the F♯ key which extends over the G♯ key (#12) as this has already been regulated in step 3.) Some saxophones have an adjustment screw at this point for the regulation.

20). Check the A key (#10). There should be a felt disc located under the lever of this key where it makes contact with the Stack B♭ key (#8). If not, replace the felt disc, then check the adjustment. Close the A key and the Stack B♭ key should close at the same time. Use a leak light to check. If they do not close together, make the adjustment by bending the *lever* of the A key.

If the A key is closing first, bend the lever *down* slightly by placing a large pad slick under the pad of the A key then pressing gently on the lever to bend. If the Stack B♭ key is closing first, bend the lever *up* slightly by holding the pad of the A key firmly against the tone hole and pulling gently up on the lever.

21). Check the foot of the A key (#10). Be certain that it has a piece of 1/16″ cork on the bottom of the foot and a piece of 1/64″ cork on the top of the foot.

22). Check the adjustment of the C key (#5). Press down on the A key lever. The A key (#10) and the Stack B♭ key (#8) should close at the same time as the C key (#5). Use a leak light to check. If they do not close together, make the adjustment by bending the bar of the C key where it passes over the foot of the A key. Use round nose pliers to bend the bar slightly down toward the foot of the A key, causing the C key to close sooner.

23). Press down on the B key (#6). This key should close at the same time as the C key (#5). Use a leak light to check. If they do not close together, check to be certain that there is a piece of 1/64″ cork on the top of the B key foot, If not, replace the cork and check again. If the two keys still do not close together, make the adjustment by bending the *foot* of the B key. Bending the B key foot *down* will cause the B key to close sooner than the C key. Just a small amount of bending will affect the adjustment, so go slowly.

24). Press down on the A key (#10). This should activate the Stack B♭ key immediately. If the A key must move before making contact with the Stack B♭ key, correct this by adding cork to the *bottom* of the A key foot until the A key lever touches the Stack B♭ key.

25). Press down on the F♯ key (#13). This key should activate the Stack B♭ key (#8) immediately. If the F♯ key must move before making contact with the Stack B♭ key, correct this by making the cork under the foot of the *A key* thinner. Use a piece of emery paper to thin the cork until the arm of the Stack B♭ key just touches the arm of the F♯ key.

26). Press down on the A key (#10). This key should activate the C key (#5) immediately. If the A key must move before making contact with the C key, correct this by making the cork under the foot of the *B key* (#6) thinner. Use a piece of emery paper to thin the cork until the two keys move at the same time.

27). Press down on the B key (#6). This key should activate the C key (#5) immediately. If the B key must move before making contact with the C key, correct this by adding cork to the *bottom* of the B key foot until the foot of the B key touches the bar of the C key. Be certain that there is a piece of ¹⁄₆₄″ cork on the top of the B key foot before checking this adjustment.

28). Press the High F lever. This lever should close the B key (#6) and C key (#5) pads while at the same time open the High F key (#1). There should not be any "play" in the key action at this point. If this adjustment is not correct, bend the High F rocker arm which extends under both these keys until the proper action is achieved. If there is "play" in the keys, the arm or arms of the High F rocker will need to be bent up. Before making this adjustment, be certain that there is a piece of ¹⁄₆₄″ cork on the top of both arms of the High F rocker.

29). Press down on the G♯ lever (#12L). The lever should touch the body of the saxophone at the same time that the G♯ key (#12) touches the arm of the F♯ key (#13). If it does not, the adjustment is made on the foot of the G♯ *lever*. Removing cork from the foot of the G♯ lever will permit the G♯ key to open further. Adding cork will cause the lever to stop moving sooner.

30). Press down on the Low B♭ key lever (#22). This should close both the Low B♭ key and the Low B key (#21) at the same time. Use a leak light to check. If they do not close together, make the adjustment by regulating the thickness of the cork between the Low B key *lever* and the Low B♭ key *lever*. The thicker this cork, the sooner the Low B key will close.

31). Press down on the Low B♭ key lever (#22). Both the Low B♭ key and the Low B key (#21) should *begin* to move at the same time. If they do not, make the adjustment by regulating the bumper felts located on both the Low B♭ key and Low B key (or key guards). Set the bumper felts so the keys will open to a height of either ¼″ (for soprano or alto) or ⁵⁄₁₆″ (for tenor or baritone). When the bumper felts are regulated correctly, the keys will move together.

32). If the G♯ lever (#12L) has a spatula which extends under the Low B key lever (#21) and the Low C♯ key lever (#20), these should be regulated so there is no extra "play" in the keys. Adjust the thickness of the cork on the top of the G♯ lever spatula so that it is in contact with the Low C♯ key and the Low B key. Be certain that there is not *too much* cork here, or the G♯ key (#12) will be held in an open position. Check this with a leak light.

33). Press down on the Low C♯ key (#20). This key should open to a height of ¼″ (on soprano or alto) or ⁵⁄₁₆″ (on tenor or baritone). If the open height is not correct, make the adjustment by regulating the thickness of the cork on the arm of the Low C♯ key. This cork bumps against the body of the saxophone. The more cork, the less the key will open.

34). Check the height of the G key (#11). This key should open to the same height as the A key (#10). If it does not, adjust the height of the G key by bending the arm of this key which extends over the Lower octave key. Be certain that there is a piece of 1/64" cork under this arm before adjusting. Bending the arm toward the lower octave key will lower the open height of the G key.

35). Some baritone saxophones have a double pad for the G key (#11). If this is the case on your saxophone, check to be certain that both pads are closing at the same time. Using a leak light, close the key slowly to see if they seal simultaneously. If they do not, adjust by bending one of the pads. Place a large pad slick under the pad that closes first, then push against the pad which closes second, thus bending it down slightly. Re-check and continue to adjust in like manner until the two pads close together.

36). Check the Upper octave key. When closed, the bottom of this key should be touching the floating lever which extends up from the body of the saxophone. If this adjustment is not correct, bend the Upper octave key slightly until the two points of contact are made. Pulling up on the pad of the Upper octave key will cause the key to move toward the floating lever. Pushing down on the pad of the key will cause the pad to seal the tone hole sooner.

37). Check the Thumb octave lever. This lever should be level with the thumb rest on the body of the saxophone. As there are many different styles of octave mechanisms, it is difficult to say how the adjustment would be made if this is not correct. If you check the mechanism, you will be able to find the point of contact which regulates the height of the Thumb octave lever. The thickness of cork at this point will regulate the key.

38). Check the octave mechanism. Because there are so many different styles of mechanisms, it is not possible to describe exactly how each one should be adjusted. However, when you press just the Thumb octave lever, the Upper octave key should open. If you hold the Thumb octave lever down then press the G key (#11), the Upper octave lever should close while at the same time the Low octave lever will open. If you hold the G key down and release the Thumb octave lever, the Lower octave key should close.

39). This completes the adjustment of the saxophone.

REPAIRS TO BE SENT TO THE REPAIR SHOP

Many of the repairs that need to be done to the saxophone are relatively easy to accomplish as you follow the instructions given in this chapter. You can best determine after reading this chapter which repairs you feel capable of doing and which should be sent to the repair shop. A good rule to follow is: "When in doubt, send it out." If you are not sure about how to do a repair, more harm than good can result from your "experimenting."

There are some repairs which require specialized tools or special skills. Below I have outlined some of the more common saxophone repairs that will need to be done at a repair shop. It is hoped that this will give you a better understanding of the repair procedures.

REMOVING BODY DENTS

The tools required for effectively removing a dent in the body of the saxophone necessitates that this work be sent to the repair shop. There are really two types of dents that need to be considered. One is cosmetic; it does not affect the playability of the instrument but does detract from the appearance. The other type of dent affects the mechanical operation of the instrument and therefore needs to be dealt with immediately. If the instrument is hit against the posts (most common), the resulting dent will often cause the tone hole (which must be perfectly level) to cave in on one side. If this happens it will not be possible to have the pad seal the tone hole until the dent is removed. A dent may also cause a post to shift from its original position, causing the keys to bind.

When removing dents, the repair technician will use a large variety of long and short rods which have different size balls attached to one end. He will insert the rod into the bore of the instrument and push the dent up from the inside. In many cases it is also necessary to remove some of the keys. Great care must be taken so that the raising of the dent does not go too far, thus producing a "hump" which produces the same problem. The repair technician has become skilled at knowing how much pressure must be exerted and which size rod and ball needs to be used. In almost all cases, except for cosmetic dents, the keys in the area of the dent will need to be readjusted after the dent has been removed.

RE-FITTING A LOOSE NECK

A loose neck can cause problems in playing and adjustment. If the saxophone neck has become so loose that it is no longer possible to tighten it in the receiver of the instrument, it needs to be re-fitted. For the repair technician, this is a relatively easy task. He has a special tool called a metal tenon expander. With this tool he can actually increase the diameter of the neck. Care must be taken to avoid expanding it too much, or the tenon will then need to be reduced to the correct dimension. Because this repair is so simple, there is no reason why any of your saxophone players should have an instrument in which the neck is always loose.

TIGHTENING LOOSE KEYS

If the saxophone has a lot of "play" in the keys (that is, they move sideways on the rod or between the pivot screws) you may have a problem getting the pads to close on the seat. This "play" is usually found on older saxophones as the metal of the key eventually wears down. If the key is mounted on a rod and slides sideways along the rod, then there is too much room between the posts. The repair technician will have to stretch the hinge tube of the key to fill the gap (a process called "swedging").

It is also possible that the diameter of the key's hinge tube has enlarged through wear and is now bigger than the diameter of the pivot rod. This can be recognized if the key wiggles back and forth but does not slide on the rod. In this case, the repair technician will squeeze the hinge tube slightly to tighten, but not so much as to bind the key action.

If the loose key is held in place with pivot screws, the repair technician will check to see if the screws have backed out or are worn. Sometimes on older saxophones, the screws are worn down on the ends and cannot hold the key firmly in place. In this case the screw can be replaced with a new screw for the same brand and model saxophone. It is also possible that the hole in the post will also be worn larger, causing the screw to be loose. It is then necessary to fit the post with a different style (larger) pivot screw that can be adapted to the saxophone key.

LEVELING TONE HOLES

As mentioned earlier, it is absolutely essential that all the tone holes on the saxophone be completely level for proper seating of the pads. Tone holes become uneven by dropping or bumping the instrument causing minor (or major) dents in the body. These dents must be removed as mentioned earlier, then the repair technician must level the tone hole. To do this, he will remove all keys that are in the way and, with the use of a special tone hole file, carefully file across the top of the tone hole until it is flat. Care must be taken that the tone hole file is held level during *all* of the filing as a slight tipping of the file can cause an uneven tone hole.

After the tone hole is level, the keys are replaced and usually it will be necessary to replace the pad. The newly level tone hole will be slightly lower than the original, thus the key will have to be regulated.

REPAIRING BROKEN KEYS

If a saxophone key actually breaks in half, this can be repaired in the shop. Save the pieces and send them along with the entire saxophone. The repair technician will braze the two pieces together will silver solder. When done correctly, this will bond the two sections of the key together as securely as the original piece. It is important to send the entire instrument, so the repair technician can be certain that the key is brazed at the correct angle and re-adjusted to the instrument.

If you should loose one of the broken pieces, most repair shops will either order a new key or fashion a key from an old part of a discarded saxophone. In either case, this is usually more expensive and time consuming.

SOLDERING LOOSE BRACES AND KEY GUARDS

If you examine your saxophne carefully you will see that every post, key guard and brace is soldered in place. If these should come loose, they need to be re-soldered in exactly the same place for the instrument to function correctly. It takes a bit of experience in soldering *band instruments* to be able to do this job correctly.

The repair technician will use a gas flame for soldering, not a soldering iron. With this he is able to control the location of the heat much more accurately. A basic rule in soldering is that the solder will flow to the hot spot. The skill needed in soldering a post, for example, is to have the hot spot under the post so that all the solder will be under the post and not around the sides and top of the post. Many places on the saxophone have a number of posts, etc., located very close to each other. If the repair technician should apply too much heat, it is likely that other posts could come loose. Great care must also be taken to avoid burning the lacquer finish on the saxophone.

If you have an item which breaks off the saxophone, *DO NOT* attempt to re-attach this with glue, tape or liquid metal. None of these will work, and it will increase the cost of the repair because it will take longer for the repair technician to clean the area to be soldered.

REFINISHING THE BODY AND KEYS—THE COMPLETE OVERHAUL

If your saxophone is gold in color, it has a lacquer finish. The saxophone is made of brass and this brass is buffed to a high gloss finish, then lacquered. The lacquer prevents the brass from tarnishing. Through use, however, the lacquer will wear off at points of high contact with the hands, and also will chip off where small dents occur. Wherever the lacquer comes off, the instrument will begin to tarnish and turn a dull dark color. This tarnish in no way affects the playability of the saxophone but does eventually distract from its appearance.

Silver saxophones are also made of brass, but they are then silver plated. This silver plating is usually not lacquered so that silver does begin to tarnish and the instrument begins to look more gray than silver. This appearance can be renewed with silver polish. Have the repair technician do this job, as too much damage can result from silver polish in the wrong places.

The keys on the saxophone are usually nickel plated and this finish will last much longer than the lacquer finish. The nickel plating, however, will eventually wear off, although the points of greatest finger contact on the saxophone are usually protected by small pearl buttons.

The body and keys of the saxophone can be re-lacquered and re-plated to look like new, but this procedure should only be done as a part of a complete overhaul. Your repair technician can best advise you as to the practicality of this job (it is expensive), as older saxophones wear out and are not worth the investment.

Not all repair shops can do this type of work, although most of them have another company to which they can send it. To replate any type of instrument or key requires having the chemicals necessary to strip off the old finish and the equipment for electroplating. To re-lacquer the body of the saxophone, the keys must be removed. The instrument usually will have all the dents removed at this time, although this is not entirely necessary. The old lacquer is stripped off and then the instrument is buffed to a high gloss. The buffing is quite difficult because posts could come loose and tone holes could be worn down during this process. After buffing, the instrument needs to be completely de-greased to remove all dirt and grease. It is then sprayed with a lacquer finish. Both the lacquer booth and de-greasing equipment are very expensive; that is why not all shops have this equipment.

After the refinishing is complete, the instrument will be completely re-assembled, using all new pads and corks. Often excess plating must be removed from the keys so that they function properly on the rods. All keys must be tightened, as they will sometimes be loose because of the buffing process.

When this job is complete, your saxophone will have a "like new" appearance and playability.

THE COMPLETE RE-PAD

Even though you may do a good job of maintaining the playing condition of the saxophones in your band, there will come a time when most of the pads are starting to tear, or turn hard and dry. Many of the corks will be compressed, dried out or missing altogether. This is the time to consider having the saxophone completely re-padded. A complete re-pad in most shops will consist of replacing all the old pads, corks and felts, installing a new neck cork, and cleaning and re-fitting the metal neck tenon. Loose keys are usually tightened as a part of this job, and all tone holes are checked and re-leveled if necessary. When re-assembling, all the pads will be seated and the springs will be adjusted to the proper tension. The instrument will then be regulated for proper action. In short, the instrument should *play* like a new saxophone. Check with your repair shop for exact specifications of what work is included with a complete re-pad.

7

The Valve Brass Family

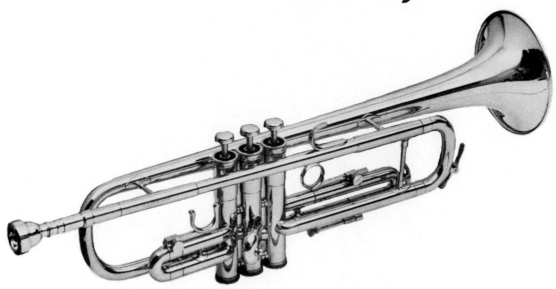

Illustration 7-1: Trumpet

Courtesy of C. G. Conn, Ltd; Elkhart, Indiana 46516

HOW TO TAKE CARE OF YOUR VALVE BRASS INSTRUMENTS

Taking proper care of the valve brass instruments should be the first, most important step in your instrument maintenance plan. By following the suggestions given here, you can avoid many of the problems which may cause the valve brass instrument to malfunction. Although this might be a review for you, it is suggested that you share this information with your students, so they will also understand proper instrument care. When the student understands the reasons for the maintenance procedures outlined below, there is a better chance that he or she will follow them.

STORE THE INSTRUMENT CAREFULLY

Valve brass instruments should always be stored in a case when not in use. An instrument left lying about on a chair, table or music stand is easily bumped or dropped to the floor. Serious damage can be done to a brass instrument if this happens. Denting is likely and this will often cause a malfunction in the valve or slide operation.

215

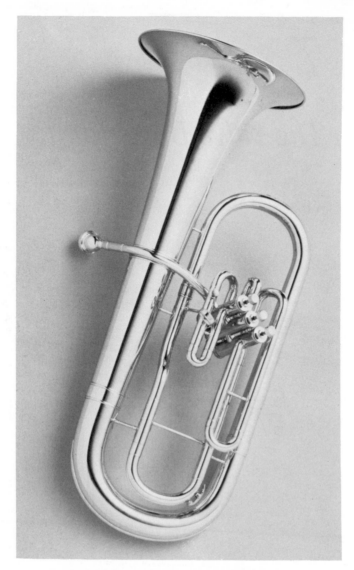

Illustration 7-2: Baritone (Euphonium)

Courtesy of C. G. Conn, Ltd; Elkhart, Indiana 46516

Sousaphones and tubas do not often have a case. These instruments, however, should have a place reserved for them for proper storage. There are a variety of sousaphone storage racks available which will hold the instrument quite securely. These are recommended over the common practice of leaving the instrument on the sousaphone chair. These chairs are often in the center of student traffic patterns and are very susceptible to being bumped or knocked over.

If tubas are used in your school they should have a case. Although large, these cases could be located in an out-of-the-way place in the room, and students should be instructed to place the tuba in the case when not in use.

The sousaphone mouthpiece, mouthpipe and mouthpiece bits should be removed when the instrument is stored. This will insure that these pieces will always be moveable and, at the same time it discourages other students from blowing on the instrument while

Illustration 7-3: Tuba

Photograph courtesy of the Getzen Company, Inc.; Elkhorn, Wisconsin 53121

it is in the storage rack. When the mouthpiece and bits are not removed, they eventually become frozen in place, making it impossible to clean the instrument properly.

Never attempt to transport any instrument without a case. I can't begin to count the number of times that I have seen sousaphones without any case loaded into the back of a truck to take them to a performance. One can hardly imagine a band director loading *all* his band's instruments into a truck without cases and hauling them to another town, yet it is done all to often with sousaphones and tubas. It is well to remember that the *large* brass instruments are just as easily damaged as are the other brass instrument.

Before storing the brass instrument, always be sure that you have drained all saliva and condensation from the instrument. Never store an instrument without draining, as

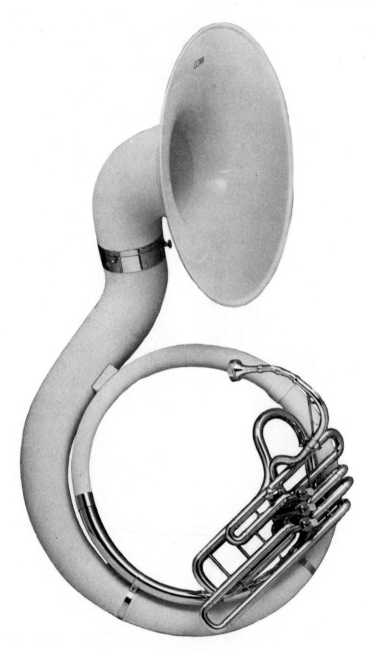

Illustration 7-4: Sousaphone

Courtesy of C. G. Conn, Ltd; Elkhart, Indiana 46516

saliva contains acids which will corrode the brass. This is the major "wear" problem that brass instruments have.

The instrument case should be designed to hold the instrument securely. Most cases have a storage section to hold the mouthpiece and other accessories. The mouthpiece of any valve brass instrument should be stored in its proper location. A loose mouthpiece can be the source of many valve problems caused by dents to the valve casings. Extra accessories such as a lyre, valve oil, cleaning brushes and mutes should also be stored in the case storage compartment. If your cases do not have a special storage section for the accessories, it is unwise to force these items against the instrument; this will contribute to denting and scratching.

Instrument cases are not designed to serve as a display area for medals and pins or to carry lesson books and music (unless there is a special compartment). This over-packing of the case can cause excessive pressure on the instrument when the cover is closed and may bend some of the tubing out of alignment. Dangling medals can scratch the finish and can also catch in the valves when closed, causing damage when the case is opened.

Unfortunately, there are many cases which do not protect the instrument very well. Check your case to be certain that it is holding the instrument securely. Place the instrument in the case, remove all accessories and close the cover and latch it. Hold the case handle (or handles) and shake the case. If you hear the instrument bouncing inside, the case is not providing the protection that it should, and it needs to have padding added.

The quickest, cheapest way to correct the problem is to lay a piece of towel on the top of the instrument. This cloth will fill up the excess space inside the case yet will not damage the instrument. Shake again and add more toweling if necessary. If the cover becomes hard to close, you have added to much toweling. Also check to see if the instrument slides around in the case. Sometimes the blocking in a case is not placed correctly and some padding needs to be added.

You can also remove the lining from the cover of the case, add more padding and then re-glue. Additional blocks can also be added. This will take more time and skill but will look better when finished.

Inspect the case periodically to be certain that it is in good condition. Prompt attention should be given to broken or loose latches, hinges or handles. Be certain that the lining is not loose. If the case has straps inside to hold the instrument, have them repaired or replaced as soon as they break. Loose linings can easily be corrected with some glue, but broken case hardware will need to be sent to the repair shop for correction. Unfortunately, this type of repair is often overlooked and, in the end, the instrument suffers the damage from this lack of attention to protection.

CLEAN THE INSTRUMENT REGULARLY

Cleaning a brass instrument is extremely important as the moisture which accumulates in the instrument from condensation and saliva will contain acids which begin to corrode the brass tubing from the inside. The corrosion will develop slowly and will not be noticeable until suddenly little dark tarnish and pit marks appear on the outer finish. At this point the metal has been completely eaten through and will soon be in need of replacing.

An instrument, which is cleaned regularly, should last for a long time with little maintenance needed. In general, all brass instruments are much easier to clean than are the woodwind instruments.

The Mouthpiece—If the mouthpiece is not cleaned, an accumulation of dirt will begin to plug the bore and hamper the flow of air through the instrument, making it harder to play. A few minutes a week will keep your mouthpiece clean and free from dirt for a long time. Use a moutnpiece brush and wash the mouthpiece once a week in warm soapy water. Be certain that the brush is designed for brass instrument mouthpieces to insure a proper fit.

The Mouthpipe—The mouthpipe on any brass instrument is the first brass tube into which the mouthpiece fits. This tube is most susceptible to acid deterioration as the greatest amount of moisture will collect in the area closest to the mouthpiece. Because of this, it is very important that the mouthpipe be cleaned as regularly as the mouthpiece. There are flexible bore cleaning brushes made for each of the brass instruments, and these should be used regularly to clean the mouthpipe. Flush the tubing out with clear water and use the flexible bore brush to remove all particles and acid residue left in the instrument. Taking the time to do this will go a long way in preventing premature brass corrosion. On most baritones, tubas, sousaphones and some cornets, the mouthpipe will lead directly into the first valve casing. In order to clean these mouthpipes, you will need to completely remove the first valve. Then wash with a slow stream of water and it will drain out the first valve casing and not get into any other part of the instrument.

The Bore—About once a month it would be advisable to clean the entire instrument bore. This is done in the same manner as described for the mouthpipe, except that it will take a little more time. In order to flush out the entire bore, you will first have to take the instrument completely apart. If you have been doing this regularly, you should not have any problems in removing the parts. If this has not been done, and you have some frozen slides or valve caps that will not come apart, see the appropriate section later in this chapter under How To Repair the Valve Brass Instruments, p. 222.

Remove all the slides from the instrument and place them in some manner so that you know how to reassemble. Generally this isn't confusing, as there are usually only four slides on a brass instrument (some models may have an extra slide). Each valve has its own slide plus the main tuning slide. The valve slides range in size with the 2nd valve slide being the smallest, 1st valve slide next and 3rd valve slide the largest. You should also remove the valves and both the top and bottom valve caps. Check to be certain you know which caps go on top and which on the bottom (some models have caps which look very similar). Also remove the valve springs if they are separate.

After the instrument is completely apart, wash each slide and the main body of the instrument with clear running water. (A little baking soda can help reduce the smell of the instrument and will neutralize any acid in the bore.) Run water into the bore and brush with your flexible bore brush. You may need a couple of different sizes to accommodate the different size tubing on some brass instruments. When all parts are clean and dry, reassemble the valves first. Place a little drop of Vaseline on the thread of each valve cap to help prevent these from corroding and place a few drops of valve oil on the valve before putting back in place. Each slide should have a light coating of either Vaseline or lanolin. Lanolin is heavier making the slides work harder, but will last a much longer time than vaseline. This lubrication will help insure that all slides work freely until the next time you need to disassemble.

The Valves—The valves should be cleaned about every two weeks. The valve oil tends to attract dirt, causing the valve action to become sluggish after a while. Usually the student will oil the valve to improve the action. Valves that are sluggish because they are dry will improve with oil, those that are dirty will improve for only a short period of time or not at all.

To clean the valve, remove it from the casing and remove both the top and bottom valve caps as well. Also remove the valve slides so that they do not fill up with water when cleaning. Flush the valve casing with clear running water and brush thoroughly with the valve brush. Rinse the valve as well and run the valve brush through each porthole to remove any dirt which has accumulated. Use a dry, lint free cloth to wipe the valve dry, then run the cloth through the valve casing and dry this also. Re-assemble when all parts are completely dry. Place a small drop of Vaseline on each valve cap thread to prevent corrosion, and use a few drops of valve oil on the valve.

The Body—The outside finish on a "gold" colored brass instrument is lacquer. The best way to clean this is to use a soft clean cloth and wipe off all fingerprints. I found that spraying the instrument with a small quantity of furniture polish will give an added sheen to the instrument while helping to remove greasy fingermarks. A brass polish will not be effective because of the protective lacquer finish which covers the brass.

Most silver colored brass instruments are silver plated, and this does begin to tarnish after while. The only way to clean this is by using a fine grade liquid silver polish. The less abrasive the polish, the better the finish will look when done. Polishing can be quite time consuming and you will find that liquid polish is much easier to put on than it is to wipe off. Leave the valves in place as you polish to help prevent any polish from getting into the valve casings.

An occasional brass instrument is nickel plated; this should be cleaned in the same way as the lacquered finish.

MAINTENANCE PROCEDURES FOR THE INSTRUMENTS

The Slides—Slides need to be lubricated regularly. This prevents corrosion which can cause slide to stick. If the student will grease the slides and move them regularly, he will never have a problem with frozen slides. It is especially important to lubricate and move the valve slides, as these are usually not regulated as often in the daily playing of the instrument.

The best lubricant for a slide is lanolin which can be purchased rather inexpensively from your druggist. This product does not disintegrate easily and will offer the most protection for the slide. The only problem with lanolin is that it is thick and, therefore, the slide will not move as easily as it would with a lighter lubricant. Vaseline is a good lighter lubricant which also works well and is more readily available. If you do use Vaseline, you should lubricate the slides more often. There are also some commercial lubricants available which work quite well, but they are more expensive.

Before lubricating the slides, you must first clean them. Use a cloth and wipe all grease from each slide. The receiving tube of the slide must also be wiped clean. To do this you will need a small cleaning rod (like a flute cleaning rod). Wrap a piece of cloth around the rod and swab out the tube until all traces of grease are removed.

Place a small drop of lubricant on the end of *one* slide tube and insert just this one tube into the correct receiver. Slide this tube in and out and rotate around to distribute the lubricant evenly. Repeat the process using the other slide tube, then assemble the slide in its correct position. By doing each tube separately, you will be able to distribute the lubricant more evenly around the slide.

The Valves—Valves should be oiled whenever the player begins to sense a slowing down in the valve action.After a few days, the valve oil will evaporate and the valves become dry.

The valve caps should be greased each time you grease the slides. This helps prevent the beginning of corrosion which would freeze the caps, making them difficult to remove. For the valve caps, you can use the same lubricant that you are using on the slide.

Corks and Felts—Check the water key corks regularly and replace them when they begin to appear water logged (see How to Replace a Water Key Cork, p. 230).

The corks and felts on the valve stem are there to control the alignment of the valve ports. Felts on the valves will eventually become compressed and oil soaked. When this happens they are no longer serving their purpose and should be replaced. The corks inside the valves will last for a long time, as the oil coating they accumulate actually helps preserve the corks. Check for crumbling corks, however, as these should be changed.

MONTHLY MAINTENANCE CHECK LIST—VALVE BRASS INSTRUMENTS

Chart 24 is a check list that you can use to help maintain the valve brass instruments. By following this chart, you can keep the instrument in good playing shape and be alert to any possible repairs needed before they become too severe. With some training, your students should also be able to utilize this check list.

HOW TO REPAIR THE VALVE BRASS INSTRUMENTS

The construction of a brass instrument is less complex than that of any of the woodwind instruments. As a result, the valve brass instruments are relatively maintenance free. There are only a few moving parts to any brass instrument, and these are the areas to which you must direct your attention in the maintenance procedures on the instrument. The repairs on a brass instrument are either so simple that they can be done with a minimum of tools and supplies, or they require such specialized tools and skill that they are best sent to the repair shop.

DIAGNOSING INSTRUMENT MALFUNCTIONS

Before you can begin to repair the valve brass instruments, you need to diagnose the problems. Listed below are some of the more common problems that occur on a brass instrument. For each problem I have suggested some possible causes. Although this list can hardly be complete, it should serve as a good guideline.

1. *Problem*: Instrument hard to blow, sounds stuffy.

Possible Causes: Valves not completely up or down. Valves in wrong casings or not properly aligned. Water keys are leaking air. Foreign object stuck in the bore of the instrument. Joint between tubing has come unsoldered causing a leak. Mouthpiece dented and/or dirty. A hole has corroded through the mouthpipe tubing.

2. *Problem*: Slides stuck.

Possible Causes: Slides are not greased properly. Slides have not been cleaned

Chart 24
Monthly Maintenance Check List—Valve Brass Instruments

INSPECT THE FOLLOWING:

Instrument _____ Do all valves work freely?

_____ Do all slides move easily and have a light coating of lubricant?

_____ Are water keys intact and the cork sealing the holes?

_____ Do all valve caps move freely?

_____ Is the mouthpiece clean?

_____ Are all braces tight?

_____ Do the valves click? (Need corks and/or felts?)

_____ Are open valves all the same height?

Case _____ Are the latches working properly?

_____ Are the hinges tight?

_____ Is the handle secure?

_____ Is the case lining in place?

_____ If there are straps in the case, are they functional?

_____ Are accessories and the mouthpiece stored in the proper place?

_____ Are there any pins or medals which will lay against the instrument when the case is closed?

_____ Is the instrument held tightly in the case when closed?

DO THE FOLLOWING:

1. Wash the mouthpiece and mouthpipe with proper brushes.
2. Flush the bore of the instrument.
3. Clean and oil the valves.
4. Grease the slides.
5. Thoroughly wipe the instrument with a soft cloth to remove fingerprints.

---

regularly and corrosion has started. Dent in slide tubing.

3. *Problem:* Valves sticking.

Possible Causes: Valves are dry, need oil. Valves are dirty, need cleaning. Valve springs may be losing tension. Valve may be dented or out-of-round. Valve casing may be dented. Valves are corroding because plating has worn off (need to be cleaned and buffed). Foreign object is stuck in the valve casing or valve port.

4. *Problem:* Instrument produces a "buzzing" sound on certain notes.

Possible Causes: Brace on the instrument has come unsoldered. Loose valve cap, lyre screw or third valve slide stop. Loose bell ring (located inside the edge of bell).

HOW TO CHECK FOR LEAKS

When the brass instrument is hard to blow or has a stuffy sound, you can suspect that there is a leak in the instrument. Leaks can come from a number of sources on the brass instrument. It could be a water key not sealing properly, a soldered joint in the instrument coming apart, or worn or damaged valves. Finding the leak is a prerequisite to fixing the instrument.

Sometimes, especially with young players, the embouchure has not yet developed and the tone will sound "stuffy." Before you begin to search for a leak, have another player blow the instrument to see if it sounds "stuffy." If so, then the problem is with the instrument and not with the player.

Tools Needed: Soft rubber ball (to plug the end of bell)

Procedure:

1. Hold the rubber ball firmly in the bell to plug that end completely. This ball should be a soft rubber one, so that it can effectively seal the end of the instrument.

2. Blow (not buzz) into the instrument, filling it with as much air as possible. Do not press any valves down; listen for a leaking air sound. Depending on the size of the leak, this sound might be very apparent or hardly noticeable. You might need the help of another person to find the leak.

If nothing seems to be leaking, press the valves down one at a time, and continue to blow into the instrument. Pressing down a valve will include that bit of tubing so that any leak which appears as you press down a valve will have to be in that valve's extra tubing or in the valve itself.

3. If nothing is still apparent at this time, you could try blowing smoke through the instrument. This is easily done if you smoke. If not, find a friend who does smoke to help you. Plug the instrument as before, but now exhale smoke into the instrument. Check with and without valves as before. The smoke will show up at the point of the leak. If the smoke begins to come from the bottom of the valve, then your valves are leaking and this will be an expensive repair job (See Repairing Leaky Valves, p. 236). You should note that, given enough time, the smoke will *eventually* leak through the valves. This is not a sign of leaking valves. So this has to be somewhat of a judgment call to determine how soon the smoke appears as to whether or not the valves actually need repair.

If, after all this testing, you find a leak, it is best to send the instrument into the repair shop. The repair of leaks requires special skills and/or tools. If you found no leak, and the tone is still stuffy, I would search for a foreign object in the bore of the instrument.

HOW TO PULL A STUCK MOUTHPIECE

Stuck mouthpieces are very common occurrences for the band director, especially when working with younger students. My advice is to invest in a mouthpiece puller. There are many models on the market. Generally speaking, the more solidly built the puller is, the more effective it is in pulling those really stuck mouthpieces.

If you do not have a mouthpiece puller, order one, and if a mouthpiece becomes stuck while you are waiting for it try the following. This does not work all the time, but might get you by.

Tools Needed: Small rawhide hammer

Procedure:

1. Cradle the instrument firmly in your arms, while holding the mouthpiece with one hand. Use the rawhide hammer to tap gently around the mouthpiece receiver while you pull and twist the mouthpiece. If the mouthpiece is not too tight it will probably come free during this process. If not, wait for the mouthpiece puller, or send the instrument to

the repair shop. Any further attempt to remove the mouthpiece will most likely result in more serious damage to the instrument and/or mouthpiece.

HOW TO STRAIGHTEN A DENTED MOUTHPIECE SHANK

As an instrument is used, it is likely that some time the student is going to drop his/her mouthpiece. Whenever a mouthpiece is dropped, there is the possibility of denting the shank. With a few inexpesive tools, you can keep all your mouthpieces straight and round, permitting the instruments to blow easily.

Tools Needed: Small dent hammer

Steel punch

Procedure:

1. The most important step in this repair procedure is that of selecting the correct size punch. Most hardware stores have various size punches. Select one which is long with a very gradual taper to it. Before you ever need the punch take a French horn and a tuba mouthpiece to the store and fit a punch to these. The punch needs to be small enough at the end to fit into the shank end of the French horn mouthpiece but should taper sufficiently so that the shank end of the tuba mouthpiece will be snug against the punch.

2. When you want to straighten a mouthpiece shank, place your punch into a bench vise (your school shop will have one) in a horizontal position. Place the shank of the mouthpiece over the punch as far as it will go, then tap lightly on the shank with the dent hammer while slowly turning the mouthpiece. As you tap, the end will round out and the mouthpiece will slip a little further on the shank. Use a light pressure and a light tapping so that you do not force the opening of the mouthpiece (see Illustration 7-5).

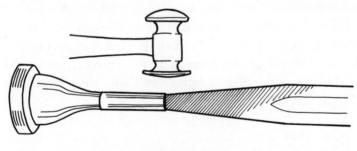

Illustration 7-5

HOW TO REMOVE FROZEN VALVE CAPS

If your students are oiling and cleaning the valves regularly, the valve caps should not stick. However, students will often only oil the valves and never clean them. Thus they will only remove the top valve caps and not the bottom caps. If you are going to start a program of regular cleaning of the valves, you may have to free up a few of these caps before you begin. Also, instruments which sit over the summer and are not used will often have valve caps which are stuck. The removal is simple.

Tools Needed. Rawhide hammer

Pair of pliers with expandable grip

Strip of leather

Procedure:

1. Tap lightly around the circumference of the stuck valve cap with the rawhide hammer. The cap will probably loosen up as you tap so then try to turn. Repeat the process a few times if necessary.

2. If step one did not free the cap, use the pair of pliers and lightly grip the valve cap with the expanded jaws of the pliers. Hold firmly and try to turn very gently. Once you feel the valve cap come loose, stop using the pliers immediately and continue to remove the valve cap with your fingers. If you do not hold the pliers firmly during this job, or attempt to turn with a lot of force, you stand a good chance of having the pliers slip on the cap, thus gouging the soft brass cap.

3. If the above method still has not loosened the cap, you will need to use more force. To prevent damage to the valve cap as described above, place a strip of leather around the circumference of the cap and then grip with the pliers and try again with more force.

4. In most cases, you will find that the valve cap will come free with either step 1 or step 2. If you are still unable to free the cap, send it to the repair shop, as any further attempts on your part will only result in damage to the instrument. Remember that brass is a very soft metal and it takes remarkably little pressure to cause dents, gouging or twisting to the various parts of a valve brass instrument.

HOW TO ADJUST THE VALVES

Adjusting the valves is probably the most important and basically the only part of a valve brass instrument that needs any type of regulating. A valve which is out of adjustment will make the instrument more difficult to play and cause the sound to be little more "stuffy." Due to the compression of the corks and felts that are used in the adjustment of the valves, all brass instruments are going to have the valves go out of adjustment. If the felts are oil soaked, the corks disintegrating, or there are clicking sounds when the instrument is played, it is time to re-adjust the valves.

> *Tools Needed:* Leak light
>   Valve mirror
>   Measuring rod (made from old lyre shaft, see Illustration 7-6)

> *Materials Needed:* Valve stem corks
>   Valve stem felts

Procedure:

1. Remove all three valves. Remove finger button from each valve and discard the cork and felt located around the valve stem on the top of the valve. Also remove the felt and cork located inside the finger button.

2. Using the measuring rod (see Illustration 7-6) to measure the amount of new cork and felt needed on top of the valve. Insert the measuring rod into the *2nd valve* casing and hook the angled end into the *lowest* port in the casing. Mark on the measuring rod with a pencil or your finger the place where the top of the valve casing is located. (If your instrument has valve caps which are recessed into the valve casing, then you must note where the threads for the valve cap begin.) (See Illustration 7-7 or 7-8).

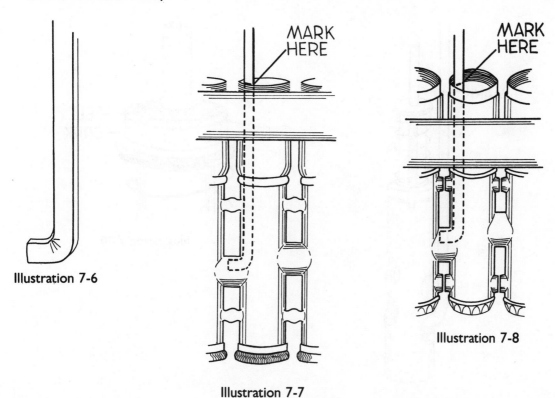

Illustration 7-6

Illustration 7-7

Illustration 7-8

3. Hook the measuring rod into the *lowest* port on the *2nd* valve. The distance that the mark on the rod extends *past* the valve piston is the thickness of cork and felt that you must add. (See Illustration 7-9). When adjusting the valve, place the cork on the valve first, then cover that with a thin piece of felt. You will have to experiment with a variety of thicknesses of cork and felt until the correct total thickness is achieved. (See Illustration 7-10).

4. Insert the 2nd valve into the valve casing and replace the top valve cap (and the bottom cap only if necessary to hold the valve spring in place). Turn the instrument upside down and check the alignment using the valve mirror and leak light. The valve mirror is a small mirror mounted on a shaft which is set at a 45° angle. Place the lighted bulb of the leak light into the 1st valve casing and the valve mirror into the 3rd valve casing. If your 2nd valve is adjusted correctly, you will be able to see the port hole in the valve line up with the port hole in the valve casing. To get a sense of perspective, move the 2nd valve slightly. If you measured correctly, the adjustment will be correct. If it is not quite right, you will need to either use a little thicker or thinner cork or felt. Adjust these items until the adjustment is correct.

5. Install cork and felt on the 1st and 3rd valves, using the exact same thickness of materials as determined when you adjusted the 2nd valve in step 4.

6. Place a thin felt washer over the valve stem or in the top valve cap. Replace the finger button and remove the 2nd valve slide. Push the valve down all the way to push the felt into position. Look into the 2nd valve through the open slide tube and see if the valve ports are lined up correctly. If the valve does not go down far enough, you will need to use a thinner piece of felt in the finger button. If the valve goes down too far, then you should add a thin cork washer. (The felt washer should make contact with the top valve cap when the instrument is played.)

MARK→

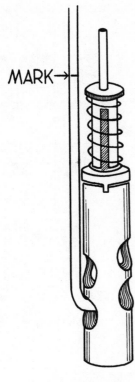

Illustration 7-9

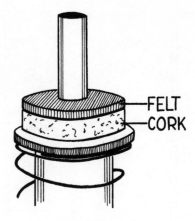

FELT
CORK

Illustration 7-10

7. Add the same amount of cork and felt to the finger buttons of the 1st and 3rd valves. The valves are now adjusted.

HOW TO PULL STUCK SLIDES

If your slides are lubricated regularly as indicated in the beginning of this chapter, you will have no problem with sticking slides. Slides that are stuck have begun to corrode in place as a result of not having been moved. On occasion, a slide will stick because of a dent in the tubing caused by a blow to the instrument.

Some corroded slides can be pulled by you, but if it has been stuck for a long time or is caused by a dent, the job will have to be done in the repair shop (see Freeing Badly Frozen Slides, p. 234).

Tools Needed: Piece of clothesline or lantern wicking
Drumstick
Penetrating oil
Rawhide hammer

Procedure:

1. Loop the line or wicking through the crook of the frozen slide a few times (see illustration 7-11). Hold the instrument carefully in your hands, cradling and supporting it as much as possible in your hands and arms. Have an assistant hold the line and give a few short snaps while you hold the instrument. The slide will often break loose this way. Care must be taken to hold the instrument firmly so that it is not pulled out of your hands when the line is pulled.

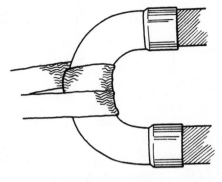

Illustration 7-11

2. If the above failed to loosen the slide, try tapping lightly on the stuck slide tube with a rawhide hammer while pulling. Be sure that this tapping is done lightly, to loosen some corrosion, not to put dents in the tubing.

3. If the stuck slide is a small slide (i.e., the 2nd valve slide) you could use a drumstick to drive the slide out. Place the drumstick in the crook of the slide (it should be tight in this position. Tap on the drumstick with your rawhide hammer. This should loosen the slide. If the crook is too large and the drumstick is not tight, this method is likely to result in denting the slide crook.

4. If this fails to free the slide, use a few drops of penetrating oil on the stuck slide and allow the instrument to sit overnight. Then pull the slide as described in step 1 above.

5. If none of the above methods has loosened the slide, it is best to send the instrument to the repair shop for further work.

HOW TO ADJUST THE SLIDES

A slide, while not frozen in place, can still be very difficult to move. This can be caused by a dirty slide, the beginning of corrosion, or a dent in the slide. If there is a dent, you will have to send the instrument to the repair shop. Otherwise, you can free the action of the slide as described below:

Tools Needed: Drumstick
Bench vise
Large round nose pliers
Fine emery paper
Crocus cloth
Vaseline or lanolin

Procedure:

1. Clamp an old drumstick in a bench vise and place one of the slide tubes over the drumstick. Take a strip of fine emery paper and clean the slide tube as shown in Illustration 7-12. Turn the slide to insure that the entire slide tube is cleaned.

2. Repeat the above with the other tube of the slide.

3. Repeat the above using a piece of crocus cloth on each of the slide tubes. The crocus cloth has an extremely fine grit and will, in effect, polish the slide tubes.

4. Wipe the tubes clean with a cloth. Apply a small amount of lubricant on the end of one slide tube (either Vaseline or lanolin), insert the slide tube into the receiver and

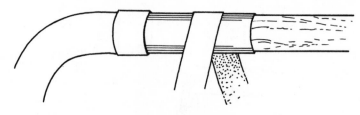

Illustration 7-12

rotate thoroughly to distribute the lubricant. Do the same with the other slide tube.

5. Replace the slide in the instrument. As you re-assemble, check to see that the two inner slide tubes are lined up with the two outer slide tubes. If they are not aligned, the slide will not move easily and your repair technician will have to realign the slide.

HOW TO REPLACE A WATER KEY CORK

Replacing a water key cork is probably one of the most common jobs needed on a brass instrument. It is easy to do and will only take a few minutes.

Tools Needed: Single edge razor blade

Small screwdriver or scraper

Materials Needed: Assorted sizes of pre-cut water key corks or cork sticks

Pad and cork cement

Procedure:

1. In most cases it is not necessary to remove the water key in order to replace the cork. With your small screwdriver (or scraper) clean out the key cup to remove all traces of old cork and glue.

2. Select a pre-cut water key cork that will fit into the water key cup. The fit should be snug so that the cork will have to be forced into the cup slightly. When in place, check for leaks by blowing into one end of the slide, while holding the other end closed with your finger. If there is a leak, shift the position of the cork so that it will be level with the water key nipple. When the seal is correct, remove the cork, place a small drop of pad and cork cement into the key cup and replace the cork in the same position. Apply pressure to the water key to press an impression of the water key nipple into the cork. This will help to insure a tight seal.

3. If you do not have pre-cut water key corks, use a cork stick. These sticks come in various diameters. Select a diameter which will fit firmly into the water key cup and cut off a piece which is approximately the correct thickness. Place the piece into the cup and check for leaks as described above. Trim the cork with your razor blade until it is level with the water key nipple. Check for leaks and if none exist, remove the cork, place a small drop of pad and cork cement in the cup and replace the cork in the same position. Apply pressure to the water key to press an impression of the water key nipple into the cork. This will help to insure a tight seal.

HOW TO REPLACE THE WATER KEY SPRING

Replacing a water key spring is not very difficult, although you will need a large variety of spring sizes.

Tools Needed: Needle nose pliers
Small screwdriver
Wire cutter
Materials Needed: Correct size water key spring
Procedure:

1. Remove the water key and old spring. Most water keys are held in place by a small rod. This rod is usually threaded, and you will need to use either a small screwdriver or a needle nose pliers to unscrew. Sometimes the rod is not threaded and can be pulled out with the needle nose pliers.

2. Select a water key spring which is made for your brand instrument or is the same size as the old one which you removed. Slide the spring over the hinge tube of the water key (see Illustration 7-13).

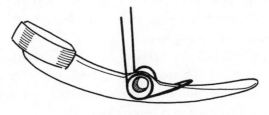

Illustration 7-13

3. The part on the instrument which holds the water key is called the "saddle." When you put the key back in the saddle, you must be certain that the open ends of the spring will be on the same side of the saddle as the closed end of the spring (see Illustration 7-14). It is sometimes quite difficult to hold these ends in place; this may take some practice. Once the spring and the key are in place, insert the rod to hold in place.

Illustration 7-14

4. If your water key is designed without a hinge tube, the spring will need to rest inside the water key in a position so that the rod will be able to slide through the water key and the loops of the spring. This style spring is much more difficult to install; the spring tends to slide away as the tension increases while installing.

5. After the key is in place, wrap each end of the spring around the post of the saddle so that the spring ends will be pointing toward the water key cork (see Illustration 7-15). Use a small wire cutter to cut off any excess spring.

Illustration 7-15

HOW TO REPAIR THE "AMADO" STYLE WATER KEY

The "Amado" style water key is used on the Getsen band instruments (see Illustration 7-16). As the style of the water key is quite different than a conventional water key, its repair and care need to be explained.

The most common problem that you will encounter with this style water key is that as it gets dirty it tends to stick. When the action begins to slow down, try lubricating. Place a drop of key oil in the hole and push the plunger back and forth. If this does not free the action, take the water key apart and clean thoroughly.

Tools Needed: Two blue steel needle springs

Small rawhide hammer

Materials Needed: Replacement parts for water key (only if needed)

Procedure:

1. The back plate of the water key is held in place with a small spring. Using the two blue steel needle springs, pinch the two ends of the spring together and remove. The back plate will then come out, followed by the coil spring which is inside the water key. Finally the main piston of the water key can be removed. If the piston is frozen and will not move, use a small rawhide hammer to gently tap the piston out.

2. Clean the piston and the water key casing with a soft cloth and some alcohol. Place a light drop of key oil on the piston and replace in the casing. Push the piston back and forth to be certain that it is moving freely.

3. When the piston action is free, replace the coil spring, back plate and the back plate spring which will hold all parts together.

REPAIRS TO BE SENT TO THE REPAIR SHOP

Most brass instrument repairs are relatively easy and they can be done by you by following the directions in this chapter. You can best determine, after reading this chapter, which repairs you feel capable of doing and which you feel should be sent to the repair shop. A good rule to follow is: "When in doubt, send it out." If you are not sure if you can do a repair as described, more harm than good can result from your experimenting.

Some brass instrument repairs require many specialized, expensive tools. It is not practical for the band director to own these tools, thus the repair must be sent out. Other repairs may seem easy enough to perform, but really require a special skill which only an

Illustration 7-16

Photograph courtesy of the Getzen Company, Inc.; Elkhorn, Wisconsin 53121

experienced repair technicial possesses. Outlined below are some of the more common valve brass instrument repairs that will need to be done at a repair shop. It is hoped that this will give you a better understanding of the repair procedures.

FREEING STICKING VALVES

Many times a sticking valve is the result of dirt or lack of oil. You can determine this by simply cleaning the valve (see Clean the Instrument Regularly—The Valves, p. 220) or oiling them. If the problem is more severe, you will notice this when you try to remove the valve. Most sticking valves are a result of a blow to the instrument causing a dent in the valve casing or a change in the alignment of the valve casing.

The repair technician has specialized tools to use to correct the problem. A dent in the casing will cause the valve to rub. The repair technician will remove the dent by using a special reamer designed for this purpose. The reamer will scrape off the protruding metal inside the casing and round it out. Care must be taken not to enlarge the casing too far, or a leaking valve will result. After the reaming process is over, the repair technician does a final fitting of the valve to the casing by working the valve with a combination of pumice and oil (or water). The pumice smooths and polishes the valve casing.

Sticking valves can also result if the valve itself has been dropped or otherwise damaged. The resulting dent is then on the valve rather than the casing. This dent forces the valve to go out of round and, therefore, will not fit correctly into the valve casing. The repair technician will use a dent hammer and tap down the high spots in the valve so that it is again round. This is a very difficult and delicate process as permanent damage to the valve can occur. This work will also be followed by a fitting of the valve to the casing with pumice and oil (or water). In addition, the valve itself is often pumiced in a special jig, to help insure its roundness.

FREEING BADLY FROZEN SLIDES

If, after you have done all the items suggested to remove a frozen slide (see p.228) it is still stuck, you need to send the instrument to the repair shop.

The repair technician will first attempt to remove the slide in the same way that you tried. Having experience in the procedure, he can better judge the amount of pressure that can be applied to the instrument.

If this does not work, he will apply heat to help loosen the corroded portion of the slide tube. Heating the outer slide tube causes it to expand, and this will often be enough to break the slide free. The trick is to use enough heat to expand, without burning the lacquer finish. If it still does not come free, he will add some penetrating oil and more heat. If these techniques do not free the slide, he must then unsolder the tubing and take the slide apart.

Usually the crook of the slide is unsoldered and removed. This will leave the two inner slides (sometimes only one) stuck in the outer slides. He will place a piece of rod or a steel ball inside the inner slide tube, then grasp that tube with a large pair of pliers (the rod or steel ball prevents the tube from collapsing when being squeezed with the pliers). With the pliers, and the additional application of heat, he is able to rotate the inner slide tube slightly and this will eventually break free.

When the parts are free, the repair technician will clean the slide. He will emery the inner slide tubes and polish with crocus cloth. He will then re-align and solder the slide back together if it was necessary to unsolder. This soldering job must be done very carefully, as the two inner slides must line up exactly with the two outer tubes. A light coating of Vaseline or lanolin as a lubricant is applied and the slide will work freely again.

REMOVING BODY DENTS

The tools required for effectively removing a dent in the body of a brass instrument necessitate that this work be done in a repair shop. There are really two types of dents that need to be considered. One is cosmetic; it does not affect the playability of the instrument but does detract from the appearance. The other type of dent affects the mechanical operation of the instrument. This type includes dents to the valve or valve casing (already discussed above) and to the slide, thus preventing the slide from moving.

When removing dents, the repair technician will use a large variety of long, short and angled rods which have different size balls attached to one end. He will insert the rod into the bore of the instrument and push the dent up from the inside. Great care must be taken so that the raising of the dent does not go too far, producing a "hump." The technician has become skilled at knowing how much pressure must be exerted and which size rod and ball needs to be used.

The dents that cannot be reached with the rod need to be removed with a "dent ball" set. This tool is actually a set of graduated size brass balls (usually about 100 balls to a set). A ball that will fit under the dent is dropped down into the tubing. This ball is driven into place with a smaller brass ball called a "driver." By shaking the instrument, the driver taps against the dent ball, slowly pushing it under the dent. When it is under the dent, the repair technician uses a dent hammer to tap on the dent. Tapping on the dent ball with the dent in between will cause the dent to lift lightly. Next, a large size dent ball is placed under the dent and the process is repeated. This continues until the dent is removed. Each time it is time to remove a dent ball another "driver" must be used to push the dent ball back out the way it came in. This process is very time consuming, so it is not uncommon for the technician to spend 15 to 30 minutes on a single dent. For this reason, brass instrument dent work is expensive.

REPLACING CORRODED PARTS

As an instrument gets older, the brass begins to deteriorate, especially if the instrument has not been kept clean through the years. Eventually this corrosion will eat through the metal tubing, leaving tiny holes which allow air to escape. On most brass instruments this happens on the mouthpipe (the section of tubing which immediately follows the mouthpiece on the instrument).

In most cases, the repair technician can order (or has in stock) a replacement piece which has been obtained from the manufacturer. He will remove the old piece, solder on the new piece to fit properly, then buff and lacquer this piece to give it a "like new" appearance. This job is time consuming and the replacement parts from the manufacturer are often expensive, so this repair cost is usually quite high. If a replacement part is not available from the manufacturer, the repair technician can make a part from stock brass tubing that he has on hand. The finished product will be the same, but he must spend more time shaping the tubing to fit the instrument, so, even though the part cost may be less, the labor cost will be considerably higher.

This same procedure can be used to replace any permanently damaged portion of a brass instrument. The only exception is that if there is permanent damage to the valve casing, repair is not possible or practical.

SOLDERING LOOSE BRACES AND JOINTS

When a brass instrument is dropped or bumped, the resulting damage may include the breaking of the soldered joint between two pieces of tubing or between the tubing and a brace. A broken solder joint needs to be repaired immediately, as the instrument will leak. A broken brace should also be repaired immediately; any loose braces will make the instrument more susceptible to further bending and damage. Loose braces will often "buzz" when certain notes are played, through sympathetic vibrations. If you hear this type of sound, look for a loose brace.

The soldering process on a brass instrument is not really very difficult *when you have experience* but can be a real disaster if you are not experienced. For this reason it is best to send *all* soldering work to the repair shop. When band directors try to do their own soldering, it is usually unsuccessful and has to be sent to the repair shop because the solder will not hold. Never try to glue, solder or temporarily repair a broken joint or brace. This always adds to the labor cost of the work in the shop because of the extra time that must be spent cleaning up your work.

The repair technician first removes all traces of old solder from the point of contact. This can be quite a task if the point of contact is hard to reach. He then uses a small piece of emery paper to rough up the two surfaces to be soldered. The area is heated and a small drop of flux is added. This flux will burn the lacquer finish, so it must be added very carefully. Solder always flows to the hottest area; therefore, the technician must direct his flame to the correct point, so that the solder will flow *between* the two pieces (making the solder virtually invisible). After soldering, the area may have to be cleaned and some touch up lacquer applied, depending on how much of an area was soldered.

REPAIRING LEAKY VALVES

As valves become very old, the rubbing of metal will eventually wear away parts of the valve and valve casing. When this happens the tolerance between these two pieces becomes greater and the valve begins to leak. If this has happened to an instrument, the instrument is usually quite old and may not be worth repairing. It *can* be fixed, however, but check on the cost before you begin as it will be expensive and might not be worth it.

Most repair shops do not have the equipment to replate valves so the work is sent out. In replating, new nickel plating is electropated to the valves. The thickness of the plating depends upon the condition of the valve. After the valve is plated, it must be refitted to the valve casing. This process takes some very sophisticated, expensive equipment. When the work is completed, the valves should look and work like new.

THE COMPLETE OVERHAUL

A complete overhaul of a valve brass instrument will result in an instrument which looks like new. In this job, usually all dents are removed, all slides pulled, cleaned and adjusted, and all valves cleaned and adjusted as well. The replating of valves is usually *not* included in this job.

Any loose or missing braces are also repaired. The instrument is completey stripped of its old finish and is buffed to a high gloss finish in the same manner as new instruments are buffed. The instrument is then thoroughly cleaned and relacquered.

The complete job will produce an instrument which has a "like new" appearance.

8

The French Horn

Illustration 8-1

Courtesy of C. G. Conn, Ltd; Elkhart, Indiana 46516

HOW TO TAKE CARE OF YOUR FRENCH HORN

Taking proper care of the French horn should be the first, most important, step in your instrument maintenance plan. By following the suggestions given here, you can avoid many of the problems which may cause the French horn to malfunction. Although this might be a review for you, it is suggested that you share this information with your students so they will also understand proper instrument care. When the student

237

understands the reason for the maintenance procedures outlined below, there is a better chance that he or she will follow them.

STORE THE FRENCH HORN PROPERLY

The French horn should always be stored in a case when not in use. An instrument left lying about on a chair or table is easily bumped or dropped to the floor. Serious damage can be done to a French horn if this happens; denting is likely, and this may cause a malfunction in valve or slide operation.

Never store a French horn without first draining it, as saliva contains acids which will corrode the brass. This corrosion is the major "wear" problem that all brass instruments have.

The instrument case should be designed to hold the French horn securely and to provide a storage section to hold the mouthpiece and other accessories. Avoid having any loose objects in the case. A loose mouthpiece can be the source of many valve problems caused by dents to the valve casing. Extra accessories such as a lyre, valve oil, and cleaning brushes should also be stored securely in the case storage compartment.

Instrument cases are not designed to serve as a display area for medals and pins or to carry lesson books and music (unless there is a special compartment). This overpacking of the case can cause excessive pressure on the instrument when the cover is closed and may bend some tubing out of alignment. Dangling medals can scratch the finish and may also catch in the valves or tubing when the case is closed, causing damage when the case is opened.

Unfortunately, many cases do not protect the French horn very well. Check your case to be certain that it is holding the French horn securely. Place the instrument in the case, remove all accessories, close the cover and latch it. Hold the case handle and shake the case. If you hear the instrument bouncing inside, the case is not providing the protection that it should, so it needs to have padding added.

The quickest, cheapest way to correct the problem is to lay a piece of towel on the top of the French horn. This cloth will fill up the excess space inside the case, yet will not damage the instrument. Shake again and add more toweling if necessary. If the cover becomes hard to close, you have added too much toweling. You can also remove the lining from the cover of the case, add more padding and then re-glue. This will take more time and skill but will look better when finished.

Inspect the case periodically to be certain that it is in good condition. Prompt attention should be given to broken or loose latches, hinges and handles. Be certain that the lining is not loose. If the case has straps inside to hold the French horn, have them repaired or replaced as soon as they break. Loose linings can easily be corrected with some glue, but broken case hardware will usually need to be sent to the repair shop for correction. Unfortunately, this type of repair is often overlooked and, in the end, the instrument may suffer damage from this lack of attention to protection.

CLEAN THE FRENCH HORN REGULARLY

Cleaning a French horn is extremely important, as the moisture which accumulates in the instrument from condensation and saliva will contain acids which begin to corrode the brass tubing from the inside. The corrosion will develop slowly and will not be noticeable until suddenly little dark tarnish and pit marks appear on the outer finish. At this point the metal has been completely eaten through and will soon be in need of replacing.

A French horn which is cleaned regularly should last for a long time with little maintenance needed. In general, all brass instruments are much easier to clean than are the woodwind instruments.

The Mouthpiece—If the mouthpiece is not cleaned, an accumulation of dirt will begin to plug the bore and hamper the flow of air through the French horn making it harder to play. A few minutes a week will keep your mouthpiece clean and free from dirt for a long time. Use a mouthpiece brush and wash the mouthpiece once a week in warm soapy water. Be certain that the brush is designed for brass instrument mouthpieces to insure a proper fit.

The Mouthpipe—The mouthpipe on the French horn is the first brass tube into which the mouthpiece fits. This tube is most susceptible to acid deterioration, as the greatest amount of moisture will collect in the area closest to the mouthpiece. Because of this, it is very important that the mouthpipe be cleaned as regularly as the mouthpiece. There are flexible bore cleaning brushes made for the French horn and these should be used regularly to clean the mouthpipe. Flush the tubing out with clear water and use the flexible bore brush to remove all particles and acid residue left in the instrument. Taking the time to do this will go a long way in preventing premature brass corrosion.

The Bore—About once a year it is advisable to clean the entire French horn bore. This is done in the same manner as described for the mouthpipe, except that it will take a little more time. In order to flush out the entire bore, you will first have to take the instrument completely apart. If you have been doing this regularly, you should not have any problems in removing the parts. If this has not been done, and you have some frozen slides or valve caps, see How to Repair the French Horn, p.240.

Remove all slides from the instrument and place them in some manner so that you know how to reassemble them. Also remove the valves and the valve caps (see How to Clean the Valves, p.244).

After the instrument is completely apart, wash each slide and the main body of the instrument with clear running water. (A little baking soda can help reduce the smell of the instrument and will neutralize any acid in the bore.) Run water into the bore and brush with your flexible bore brush. When all parts are clean, dry and reassemble the valves first. Place a little bit of Vaseline on the thread of each valve cap to help prevent these from corroding and place a few drops of rotary valve oil on the valve before putting back in place. Each slide should have a light coating of either Vaseline or lanolin.

The Body—The outside finish on a "gold" colored French horn is lacquer. The best way to clean this is to use a soft cloth to wipe off all fingerprints. I found that spraying the instrument with a small quantity of furniture polish before wiping will give an added sheen to the instrument while helping to remove greasy fingerprints. A brass polish should not be used because of the protective lacquer finish which covers the brass.

Most silver colored French horns are nickel plated. These can be cleaned in the same way as the lacquered finish instruments.

MAINTENANCE PROCEDURES FOR THE FRENCH HORN

The Slides—Slides need to be lubricated regularly. This prevents corrosion which can cause slides to stick. If the student will grease the slides and move them regularly, he will never have a problem with frozen slides. It is expecially important to lubricate and move the valve slides as these are not regulated as often in the playing of the instrument.

The best lubricant for a slide is lanolin, which can be purchased rather inexpensively from your druggist. This product does not disintegrate easily and will offer the most protection from the slide. The only problem with lanolin is that it is thick and, therefore, the slide will not move as easily as it would with a lighter lubricant. Vaseline is a good lighter lubricant which also works well and is more readily available. If you do use Vaseline, you will need to lubricate the slides more often. There are also some commercial lubricants available which work quite well, but are more expensive.

Before lubricating the slides, you must first clean them. Use a cloth and wipe all grease from each slide. The receiving tube of the slide must also be wiped clean. To do this you will need a small cleaning rod (like a flute cleaning rod). Wrap a piece of cloth around the rod and swab out the tube until all traces of grease are removed.

Place a small drop of lubricant on the end of *one* slide tube and insert just this one tube into the correct receiver. Slide this tube in and out and rotate around to distribute the lubricant evenly. Repeat the process using the other slide tube, then assemble the slide in its correct position. By doing each separately, you will be able to distribute the lubricant more evenly around the slide.

The Valves—Valves should be oiled whenever the player begins to sense a slowing down in the valve action. After a few days, the valve oil will evaporate and the valves will become dry. On the French horn, use only rotary valve oil as this is especially designed for use on the rotary valve.

To oil, remove the valve slide, then squeeze a few drops of oil down each of the slide tubes so that it will reach the valve itself. Rotate the valve as you do this to help distribute the oil on the valve.

The valve caps should be greased each time you grease the slides. This helps prevent corrosion from beginning which will freeze the caps making them difficult to remove. You can use the same lubricant for the valve caps that you are using on the slide.

MONTHLY MAINTENANCE CHECK LIST—FRENCH HORN

Chart 25 is a check list that you can use to help maintain the French horn. By following this chart you should be able to keep the instrument in good playing shape and be alert to any possible repairs needed before they become too severe. With some training, your students should also be able to utilize this check list.

HOW TO REPAIR THE FRENCH HORN

The construction of a French horn is less complex than that of any of the woodwind instruments. As a result, the French horn is a relatively maintenance free instrument. There are only a few moving parts to any brass instrument, and these are the areas to which you must direct your attention in any maintenance plan. The repairs on a brass instrument are either easy, so they can be done with a minimum of tools and supplies, or

Chart 25
Monthly Maintenance Check List—French Horn

INSPECT THE FOLLOWING:

French
Horn   _____ Do all valves work freely?

_____ Do all slides move easily and have a light coating of lubricant?

_____ Do all valve caps move freely?

_____ Is the mouthpiece clean?

_____ Are all braces tight?

_____ Are the valve strings tight?

_____ Are the valves adjusted correctly?

Case   _____ Are the latches working properly?

_____ Are the hinges tight?

_____ Is the handle secure?

_____ Is the case lining in place?

_____ Are the case straps functional?

_____ Are the mouthpiece and accessories stored in the proper place?

_____ Are there any pins or medals which will lie against the French horn when the case is closed?

_____ Is the French horn held tightly in the case when closed?

DO THE FOLLOWING:
1. Wash the mouthpiece and mouthpipe with the proper brushes.
2. Flush the bore of the instrument (once per year).
3. Clean and oil the valves (twice per year).
4. Grease the slides.
5. Thoroughly wipe the instrument with a soft cloth to remove fingerprints.

they will require such specialized tools and skill that they are best sent to the repair shop.

DIAGNOSING INSTRUMENT MALFUNCTIONS

Before you can begin to repair the French horn, you must diagnose the problem. Listed below are some of the more common problems that occur. For each problem I have suggested possible causes. Although this list can hardly be complete, it should serve as a good guideline.

1. *Problem:* Instrument is hard to blow, sounds stuffy.

Possible Causes: Valves not completely open or closed. Foreign object stuck in the bore of the instrument. Joint between tubing has come unsoldered, causing a leak. Mouthpiece dented and/or dirty. A hole has corroded through the mouthpiece tubing.

2. *Problem:* Valve is sticking.

Possible Causes: Valve is dry, needs oil. Valve is dirty, needs cleaning. Valve lever is bent, causing valve string to bind. Foreign object is stuck in the valve casing or valve port.

3. *Problem:* Slide is stuck.

Possible Causes: Slide not greased properly. Slide has not been cleaned regularly so corrosion has started. Dent in slide tubing.

4. *Problem:* French horn produces a "buzzing" sound on certain notes.

Possible Cause: Brace on the instrument has come unsoldered and is vibrating. Loose lyre screw which is vibrating. Loose solder joint.

HOW TO CHECK FOR LEAKS

When the French horn is hard to blow or has a sutffy sound, you can suspect that there is a leak in the instrument. Finding the leak is a prerequisite to fixing the instrument.

Sometimes, especially with young players, the embouchure has not yet developed and the tone will sound "stuffy." Before you begin your search for a leak, have another player blow the instrument to see if it still sounds "stuffy." If so, then the problem is with the French horn and not with the player.

Tools Needed: Soft rubber ball (to plug the end of bell)
Procedure:

1. Hold the rubber ball firmly in the bell to plug that end completely. This ball should be of soft rubber, so that it can effectively seal the end of the instrument.

2. Blow (not buzz) into the instrument, filling it with as much air as possible. Do not press any valves down at this point. Listen for a leaking air sound. Depending on the size of the leak, this sound might be very apparent or hardly noticeable. You might need the help of another person in order to find the leak.

If nothing seems to be leaking, press the valves down one at a time, and continue to blow into the instrument. Pressing down a valve will include that bit of tubing so that any leak which appears as you press down a valve will have to be in that valve's extra tubing or in the valve itself.

3. If nothing is still apparent at this time, you could try blowing smoke through the instrument. This is easily done if you smoke. If not, find a friend who does smoke to help you. Plug the instrument as before, but now exhale smoke into the instrument. Check with and without valves as before. The smoke will show at the point of the leak.

If, after all this testing, you find a leak, it is best to send the instrument into the repair shop as the repair work will require special skills. If you found no leak, and the tone is still stuffy, begin a search for a foreign object in the bore of the French horn.

HOW TO PULL A STUCK MOUTHPIECE

Problems with stuck mouthpieces are very common for the band director, especially when working with younger students. My advice is to invest in a mouthpiece puller. There are many models on the market at this time. Generally speaking, the more solidly built the puller is, the more effective it will be in pulling those really stuck mouthpieces.

If you do not have a mouthpiece puller, order one; if a mouthpiece becomes stuck while you are waiting for it try the following. This does not work all the time, but might get you by.

Tools Needed: Small rawhide hammer

Procedure:

1. Cradle the instrument firmly in your arms, while holding the mouthpiece with one hand. Use the rawhide hammer and tap gently around the mouthpiece receiver while you pull and twist the mouthpiece. If the mouthpiece is not too tight it will probably come free during this process. If not, wait for the mouthpiece puller, or send the instrument to the repair shop. Any further attempt to remove the mouthpiece will likely result in more serious damage to the French horn and/or mouthpiece.

HOW TO STRAIGHTEN A DENTED MOUTHPIECE SHANK

As the French horn is used, it is likely that at some time the student is going to drop his/her mouthpiece. Whenever a mouthpiece is dropped, there is the possibility of denting the shank. With a few inexpensive tools, you can keep all your brass mouthpieces straight and round, permitting the instruments to blow easily.

Tools Needed: Small dent hammer
                        Steel punch

Procedure:

1. The most important step in this repair procedure is that of selecting the correct size punch. Most hardware stores have various size punches. Select one which is long with a very gradual taper to it. Before you ever need the punch, take a good French horn and a good tuba mouthpiece to the store and fit a punch to these. The punch needs to be small enough at the end to fit into the shank end of the French horn mouthpiece, but should taper sufficiently so that the shank end of the tuba mouthpiece will be snug against the punch.

2. When you want to straighten a mouthpiece shank, place your punch into a bench vise (your school shop will have one) in a horizontal position. Place the shank of the mouthpiece over the punch as far as it will go, then begin to tap lightly on the shank with the dent hammer while slowly turning the mouthpiece. As you tap, the end will round out and the mouthpiece will slip a little farther on the punch. Use a light pressure and a light tapping so that you do not force the opening of the mouthpiece (See Illustration 8-2).

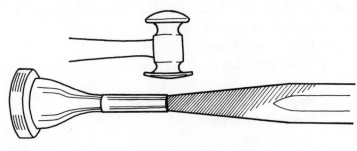

Illustration 8-2

HOW TO REMOVE FROZEN VALVE CAPS

If your students are checking the alignment of the valves regularly, the valve caps should not become stuck. In order to start a program of regularly checking the valve alignment, you may have to free a few valve caps before you begin. If the French horn sits unused for a period of time, the valve caps may dry out and become stuck. Their removal is simple.

    Tools Needed: Rawhide hammer

                  Pair of pliers with expandable grip

                  Strip of leather

Procedure:

    1. Tap lightly around the circumference of the stuck valve cap with the rawhide hammer. The cap will probably loosen up as you tap so then try to turn. Repeat the process a few times if necessary.

    2. If step one did not free the cap, use the pliers and lightly grip the valve cap with the expanded jaws of the pliers. Hold firmly and try to turn very gently. Once you feel the valve cap come loose, stop using the pliers immediately and continue to remove the valve cap with your fingers. If you do not hold the pliers firmly during this job, or attempt to turn with a lot of force, you stand a good chance of having the pliers slip on the cap thus gouging the soft brass cap.

    3. If the above method still has not loosened the cap, you will need to use more force. To prevent damage to the valve cap as described above, place a strip of leather around the circumference of the cap, then grip with the pliers and try again with more force.

    4. In most cases, you will find that the valve cap will come free with either step 1 or step 2. At this point if you are still unable to free the cap, send it to the repair shop; any further attempts on your part will only result in damage to the instrument. Brass is a very soft metal, so it takes remarkably little pressure to cause dents, gouging or twisting to the various parts of the French horn.

HOW TO CLEAN THE VALVES

    Cleaning the rotary French horn valves is a much more complicated procedure than is required on a piston valve. Because rotary valves do not simply lift out of the instrument for cleaning, this job is often completely ignored until the valve becomes so dirty that it will not move at all. The cleaning of rotary valves should be done about twice a year. It will require about 20 minutes to complete.

    Tools Needed: Large screwdriver

                  Small screwdriver

                  Valve brush

                  Short brass rod (from old lyre)

                  Rawhide hammer

                  Muriatic acid

                  Baking soda solution

    Materials Needed: Rotary valve oil

                  New valve string

    Procedure: (See Illustration 8-3.)

    1. Remove the valve string. This can be easily done by loosening the two string screws. It is a good idea to replace the string with new when cleaning the valves. Old strings do wear out and will need replacing before they break.

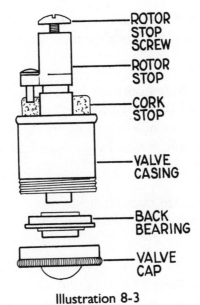

ROTOR
STOP
SCREW

ROTOR
STOP

CORK
STOP

VALVE
CASING

BACK
BEARING

VALVE
CAP

Illustration 8-3

2. Remove the valve cap.

3. Loosen the rotor stop screw (this is the large screw located on the top of the valve rotor). *Do not remove this screw completely* but rather loosen until about half way out.

4. Remove the back bearing (this is the plate which is located under the valve cap). To remove this, tap gently on the raised rotor stop screw (see step 3) with a rawhide hammer. This will drive the rotor out of the casing so the back bearing will drop out of place. Be sure to catch this bearing as it falls out so that no damage will take place.

5. Remove the rotor stop (this is the small arm on the valve rotor which swings back and forth). As you tap on the rotor stop screw in step 4, you will also be tapping to remove the rotor stop arm. Continue to loosen the screw and tap with the rawhide hammer until the screw is free and the rotor arm comes off. At this point the valve will also come out of the valve casing.

6. Both the valve and back bearing are made of brass and will show signs of corrosion and mineral deposits. These parts can be cleaned most effectively by soaking them in muriatic acid. When you place them in the acid you will notice a bubbling action as the acid works on the corrosion. Let them soak about two minutes then rinse in a solution of baking soda and water to neutralize the acid. Follow this with a thorough rinsing under clear running water, using a small brush to clean away all traces of dirt.

7. Clean the valve casing by simply wiping out with a dry cloth to remove any loose dirt and oil.

8. Re-assemble the valve as follows: Place a few drops of oil on the valve and insert into the valve casing, turning the valve to distribute the oil. Place a drop of oil in the hole of the back bearing and place this over the short shaft of the valve. The back bearing will need to be tapped firmly into place or the valve will not turn freely. Align the notch on the back bearing with the notch located on the valve casing. Use the short brass rod and tap on it lightly with the rawhide hammer to set the back bearing firmly into the valve casing. When in place, the valve should turn freely. Replace the rotor stop arm and tighten down

with the rotor stop screw. Check the alignment of the valve (see How to Adjust the Valves, p.246) and tie a new string in place (see How to String a Rotary Valve, p.248).

HOW TO ADJUST THE VALVES

Adjusting the valves is probably the most important item to check on with a French horn. A valve which is out of adjustment will make the instrument more difficult to play and cause the sound to be more "stuffy." Due to compression and the normal wear of the corks, all rotary valves will eventually go out of adjustment. Re-adjustment is a relatively simple procedure.

Tools Needed: Pliers
                 Single edge razor blade
Materials Needed: Stick cork (various sizes)
Procedure:

1. Remove the valve cap. (If this cap is stuck, see How to Remove Frozen Valve Caps, p.243.) This will expose the back bearing and also the valve shaft which fits into the center of the back bearing. If this area is dirty, wipe clean with a cloth until you can see the small line etched into the end of the valve shaft and also the marking etched into the back bearing alongside the valve shaft. These are used to align the valve. When the valve lever is up, the line on the shaft should line up with one marking; when the valve lever is depressed the line should line up with the other marking (see Illustration 8-4).

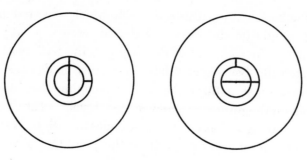

Illustration 8-4

2. If the markings do line up correctly, the valves are correctly aligned. If the markings do not line up, an adjustment must be made. Before making an adjustment, however, check to be certain that the back bearing is correctly set in the valve casing as this will affect your alignment. Along the edge of the back bearing will be a small notch. This notch should line up with a corresponding notch which is located on the edge of the valve casing. If these two notches are not aligned, correct this, then check the alignment of the valve once again as described in step 1.

3. If the valve is still out of alignment, replace the cork stops which are located adjacent to the stop arm. There are two cork stops on each valve, and each one affects how far the valve will turn in one direction. If your valve is not turning far enough, trim a little cork from the face of the cork stop to permit the stop arm to travel a little further until the correct alignment is achieved. If the valve turns too far, remove the old cork stop from the valve and replace with a new piece of stick cork.

4. To replace the cork stop, select a piece of stick cork which has a diameter slightly larger than the slot in the stop arm plate. Cut the cork to the correct length, then squeeze

the stick cork and force it into position. As the cork re-expands, it will become wedged in place in the stop plate. You will usually find that a little bit of the face of the stick cork will need to be trimmed to permit the stop arm to travel the correct distance. (If, upon checking, you find that the valve still turns too far, you will have to use the next larger diameter of stick cork in the cork stop plate.)

5. When the valve has been adjusted properly, replace the valve cap.

HOW TO PULL STUCK SLIDES

If your slides are lubricated regularly as indicated in the beginning of this chapter, you will have no problem with sticking slides. Slides that are stuck have begun to corrode in place as a result of not having been moved. On occasion, a slide will stick because of a dent in the tubing caused by a blow to the instrument.

Some corroded slides can be pulled by you, but if it has been stuck for a long time or is caused by a dent, the job will have to be done in the repair shop (see Freeing Badly Frozen Slides, p.250).

Tools Needed: Piece of clothesline or lantern wicking

Drumstick

Penetrating oil

Rawhide hammer

Procedure:

1. Loop the line or wicking through the crook of the frozen slide a few times (see Illustration 8-5). Hold the French horn carefully in your hands, cradling and supporting as much as possible in your hands and arms. Have an assistant hold the line and give a few short snaps while you hold the French horn. The slide will often break loose this way. Care must be taken to hold the instrument firmly so that it is not pulled out of your hand when the line is pulled.

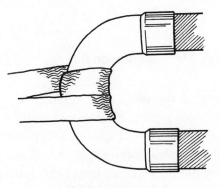

Illustration 8-5

2. If the above failed to loosen the slide, try tapping lightly on the slide tube with a rawhide hammer while pulling. Be sure that this tapping is done lightly, to loosen some corrosion, not to put dents in the tubing.

3. If the stuck slide is a small slide, use a drumstick to drive the slide out. Place the drumstick in the crook or against the brace of the slide (it should be tight in this position). Tap lightly on the drumstick with a rawhide hammer. This should loosen the slide. If the crook is too large and the drumstick is not tight, this method is likely to result in denting the slide crook.

4. If this fails to free the slide, use a few drops of penetrating oil on the stuck slide and allow the French horn to sit overnight. Then pull the slide as described in step 1 above.

5. If none of the above methods has loosened the slide, send the instrument to the repair shop for further work.

HOW TO ADJUST THE SLIDES

A slide, while not frozen in place, can still be very difficult to move. This can be caused by a dirty slide, the beginning of corrosion, or a dent in the slide. If there is a dent, you will have to send the French horn to the repair shop. Otherwise, you can free the action of the slide as described below:

Tools Needed: Drumstick
Bench vise
Large round nose pliers
Fine emery paper
Crocus cloth
Vaseline or lanolin

Procedure:

1. Clamp an old drumstick in a bench vise and place one of the slide tubes over the drumstick. Take a strip of fine emery paper and clean the slide tube as shown in Illustration 8-6. Turn the slide to insure that the entire slide tube is cleaned.

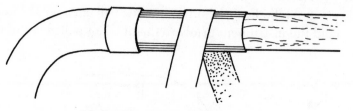

Illustration 8-6

2. Repeat the above with the other slide tube.

3. Repeat the above using a piece of crocus cloth on each of the slide tubes. The crocus cloth has an extremely fine grit and will, in effect, polish the slide tubes.

4. Wipe the tubes clean with a cloth. Apply a small amount of lubricant on the end of one slide tube (either Vaseline or lanolin), insert the slide tube into the receiver and rotate thoroughly to distribute the lubricant. Do the same with the other slide tube.

5. Replace the slide in the French horn. As you re-assemble, check to see that the two inner slide tubes are lined up with the two outer slide tubes. If they are not aligned, the slide will not move easily and a repair technician will have to realign the slide.

HOW TO STRING A ROTARY VALVE

The string on a rotary valve should be tight, thus preventing any "play" in the valve levers when operating the valve. If a valve string becomes loose, it should be tightened. If the string breaks, it needs to be replaced. A string can be replaced as described below:

Tools Needed: Small screwdriver
　　　　　　　　Single edge razor blade
Materials Needed: Rotary valve string
Procedure:

1. Remove the old string. Cut a length of new string and tie a large knot in one end. String the valve as shown in Illustration 8-7. While doing this hold the valve lever at the same height as the other valve levers. Place the stop arm in the "open" position. Be certain that the string is kept tight at all times.

2. Thread the string through the lever and as far as the string set screw. Tighten this screw after the string has been wrapped around. Then continue the rest of the threading process and tighten the string set screw on the key lever when completed.

3. After the string is tight and in place, check the height of the key lever. This should be the same as the height of the other levers on the French horn. If this height is incorrect, loosen the string set screw located on the stop arm and adjust the key lever height. Tighten the screw when the key height is correct.

4. Cut off any excess string which may be left. You should allow about one inch of excess string to permit you to tighten the string at a later date if this becomes necessary.

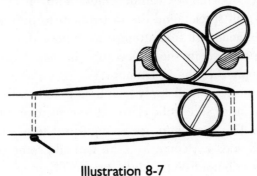

Illustration 8-7

REPAIRS TO BE SENT TO THE REPAIR SHOP

Most French horn repairs are relatively easy and they can be done by you following the directions in this chapter. You can best determine, after reading this chapter, which repairs you feel capable of doing and which you feel should be sent out to the repair shop. A good rule to follow is: "When in doubt, send it out." If you are not sure whether you can do a repair as described, more harm than good can result from your experimenting.

Some French horn repairs require many specialized, expensive tools. It is not practical for the band director to own these tools, thus the repair must be sent out. Other repairs may seem easy enough to perform, but really require a special skill which only an experienced repair technician possesses. Outlined below are some of the more common repairs that will need to be done at a repair shop. It is hoped that this will give you a better understanding of the repair procedures.

FREEING STICKING VALVES

Many times a sticking valve will be the result of dirt or lack of oil. You can determine this by simply cleaning the valves (see How to Clean the Valves, p.244) or oiling them. If the problem is more severe, send the instrument in for repair. Most sticking valves are a result of a blow to the instrument causing a dent in the valve casing or causing the alignment of the valve and casing to be changed.

The repair technician will re-fit this valve by spinning the valve in the casing with pumice and water. To do this he will completely dismantle the instrument. With a special attachment, he will spin the valve in the casing, using an electric drill. By slowly working the valve with the pumice and water he will, in essence, wear down the high spot between the valve and valve casing that is causing the valve to stick. This process can be very time consuming as the wearing down process is very slow. In addition, the cleaning up after the work is done can take almost as much time. The repair technician must be absolutely certain that all traces of pumice are out of the valve casing, adjoining valves and tubing. It is not uncommon to have the valve working freely, only to have a small piece of pumice work its way back into the valve from some adjoining tubing to completely freeze the valve again. The cleaning process, therefore, will take quite a long time, with many repeated flushings of the entire French horn tubing.

FREEING BADLY FROZEN SLIDES

If, after you have done all *you* can to remove a frozen slide (see How to Pull Stuck Slides, p.247) and it is still stuck, send the instrument to the repair shop.

The repair technician will first attempt to remove the slide in the same way that you tried. Having experience in the procedure, he can better judge the amount of pressure that can be applied to the instrument.

If this does not work, he will apply heat to help loosen the corroded portion of the slide tube. Heating the outer slide tube causes it to expand and this will often be enough to break the slide free. The trick is to use enough heat to expand, without burning the lacquer finish. If it still does not come free, he will add some penetrating oil and more heat. If these techniques do not free the slide, he must then unsolder the tubing and take the slide apart.

Usually the crook of the slide is unsoldered and removed. This will leave the two inner slides stuck in the outer slides (sometimes only one is stuck). He will place a piece of rod or a steel ball inside the inner slide tube and then grasp that tube with a large pair of pliers (the rod or steel ball prevents the tube from collapsing when squeezed with the pliers). With the pliers, and the additional application of heat, he is able to rotate the inner slide tube slightly and this will eventually break free.

When the parts are free the repair technician will clean the slide. He will emery the inner slide tubes and polish with crocus cloth. He will then re-align and solder the slide back together if it was necessary to unsolder. This soldering job must be done very carefully, as the two inner slides must line up exactly with the two outer tubes. A light coating of Vaseline or lanolin as a lubricant is applied and the slide will work freely again.

REMOVING BODY DENTS

The tools required for effectively removing a dent in the body of the French horn necessitate that this work be done in a repair shop. There are really two types of dents that need to be considered. One is cosmetic; it does not affect the playability of the French horn but does detract from the appearance. The other type of dent affects the mechanical operation of the instrument. This type includes dents to the valve or valve casing (already discussed above) and to the slide, thus preventing the slide from moving.

When removing dents, the repair technician will use a large variety of long, short and curved rods which have different size balls attached to one end. He will insert the rod into the bore of the instrument and push the dent up from the inside. Great care must be taken so that the raising of the dent does not go too far, producing a "hump." The technician has become skilled at knowing how much pressure must be exerted and which size rod and ball needs to be used.

The dents that cannot be reached with a rod need to be removed with a "dent ball" set. This tool is actually a set of graduated size brass balls (usually about 100 balls to a set). A ball that will fit under the dent is dropped down into the tubing. This ball is driven into place with a smaller brass ball called a "driver." By shaking the French horn, the driver taps against the dent ball, slowly pushing it under the dent. When it is under the dent, the repair technician will use a dent hammer to tap on the dent. Tapping on the dent ball with the dent in between will cause the dent to lift slightly. Next, a larger size dent ball is placed under the dent, and the process is repeated. This continues until the dent is removed. Each time he must remove a dent ball, another "driver" must be used to push the dent ball back out the way it came in. This process is very time consuming, so it is not uncommon for the technician to spend 15 to 30 minutes on a single dent. For this reason, brass instrument dent work is expensive.

REPLACING CORRODED PARTS

As a French horn gets older, the brass begins to deteriorate, especially if the instrument has not been kept clean through the years. Eventually this corrosion will eat through the metal tubing, leaving tiny holes which allow air to escape. On most brass instruments this will happen on the mouthpipe (the section of tubing which immediately follows the mouthpiece on the instrument).

In most cases, the repair technician can order (or has in stock) a replacement piece which has been obtained from the manufacturer. He will remove the old piece, solder on the new piece to fit properly, then buff and lacquer this piece to give it a "like new" appearance. This job is time consuming and the replacement parts from the manufacturer are often expensive, so this repair cost is usually quite high. If a replacement part is not available from the manufacturer, the repair technician can make a part from stock brass tubing that he has on hand. The finished product will be the same, but he must spend more time shaping the tubing to fit the instrument, so, even though the part cost may be less, the labor cost will be considerably higher.

This same procedure can be used to replace any permanently damaged portion of the French horn. The only exception is that if there is permanent damage to the valve casing repair is not possible or practical.

SOLDERING LOOSE BRACES AND JOINTS

If a French horn is dropped or bumped, the resulting damage may include breaking the soldered joint between two pieces of tubing or between the tubing and a brace. A broken solder joint needs to be repaired immediately, as the instrument will leak. A broken brace should also be repaired immediately; any loose braces will make the instrument more susceptible to further bending and damage. Loose braces will often "buzz" when certain notes are played, through sympathetic vibrations. If you hear this type of sound, look for a loose brace.

The soldering process on a brass instrument is not really very difficult *when you have experience* but can be a real disaster if you are not experienced. For this reason it is best to send *all* soldering work to the repair shop. When band directors try to do their own soldering, it is usually unsuccessful and has to be sent to the repair shop because the solder will not hold. Never try to glue, solder or temporarily repair a broken joint or brace. This always adds to the labor cost of the work in the shop because the repair technician must spend extra time cleaning up your work.

The repair technician first removes all traces of old solder and dirt from the point of contact. This can be quite a task if the point of contact is hard to reach. He then uses a small piece of emery paper to rough up the two surfaces to be soldered. The area is heated and a small drop of flux is added. This flux will burn the lacquer finish, so it must be added very carefully. Solder always flows to the hottest area; therefore the technician must direct his flame to the correct point so that the solder will flow *between* the two pieces (making the solder virtually invisible). After soldering, the area may have to be cleaned and some touch up lacquer applied, depending on how much of an area was soldered.

THE COMPLETE OVERHAUL

A complete overhaul of a French horn will result in an instrument which looks like new. In this job, usually all dents are removed, all slides pulled, cleaned and adjusted, and all valves cleaned and adjusted as well.

Any loose or missing braces are also repaired. The instrument is completely stripped of its old finish and is buffed to a high gloss finish in the same manner as new instruments are buffed. The instrument is then thoroughly cleaned and relacquered.

The complete job will produce an instrument which has a "like new" appearance.

has not been done, you may find that the tuning slide is frozen and you will need to refer to the instructions in this chapter entitled How to Pull a Stuck Tuning Slide (p. 261).

Once the instrument is completely apart, wash each slide and the main body of the instrument with clear running watter. (A little baking soda can help reduce the smell of the instrument and will neutralize any acid in the bore.) Run water into the bore and brush with a flexible bore brush. You may need a couple of different size brushes to accommodate the different size tubing in the trombone. When all parts are clean, re-assemble. Place a light coating of either Vaseline or lanolin on each tube of the tuning slide. This lubrication will help insure that the slide will work freely until the next time you need to disassemble. Apply a small amount of your preferred lubricant on the hand slide as well.

The Body—The outside finish on a "gold" colored trombone is lacquer. The best way to clean this is to use a soft clean cloth and wipe off all fingerprints. I have found that spraying the instrument with a small quantity of furniture polish will give an added sheen to the instrument while helping to remove greasy fingermarks. A brass polish will not be effective because of the protective lacquer finish which covers the brass.

Most silver colored trombones are silver plated and this does begin to tarnish after a while. The only way to clean this is by using a fine grade liquid silver polish. The less abrasive the polish, the better the finish will look when done. Polishing can be quite time consuming and you will find that liquid polish is much easier to put on than it is to wipe off. Care should be taken to avoid getting any polish on the hand slide of the trombone.

An occasional trombone may be nickel plated; this should be cleaned in the same way as the lacquered finish.

MAINTENANCE PROCEDURES FOR THE TROMBONE

The Hand Slide—There are a lot of opinions regarding the type of lubricant that should be used on the trombone slide. All types have value, so it will have to be a personal decision on your part. For my experience, I have found that simple trombone slide oil works as well as anything providing the slide is kept clean as described above.

Most often, students try all sorts of fancy slide creams and oils to correct a sticking slide, when the real problem is either a dirty slide or one that is out of alignment. If the slide is maintained properly, slide oil should work quite well. You should also be aware that slide creams tend to attract dirt much more rapidly, requiring the slide to need cleaning more often.

Lubricate the slide sparingly. Only the expanded "stocking" at the end of the inner slide tube needs to be lubricated; this is the only portion of the slide which will actually rub when the slide moves. The slide should be wiped dry and cleaned with a dry cloth about once a week.

The Tuning Slide—The tuning slide needs to be lubricated regularly. This prevents corrosion which can cause a slide to stick. If the student will grease the slide and move it regularly, he will never have a problem with a frozen slide.

The best lubricant for a slide is lanolin which can be purchased rather inexpensively from your druggist. This product does not disintegrate easily and will offer the most protection for the slide. The only problem with lanolin is that it is thick and, therefore, the slide will not move as easily as it would with a lighter lubricant. Vaseline is a good lighter lubricant which also works well and is more readily available. If you do use Vaseline, you will need to lubricate the slide more often. There are also commercial lubricants available which work quite well, but are more expensive.

Before lubricating the slide, you first clean it. Use a cloth to wipe all grease from each slide tube. The receiving tube of the slide must also be wiped clean. To do this you need a small cleaning rod (like a flute cleaning rod). Wrap a piece of cloth around the rod and swab out the tube until all traces of grease are removed.

Place a small drop of lubricant on the end of *one* slide tube and insert just this one tube into the correct receiver. Slide this tube in and out and rotate around to distribute the lubricant evenly. Repeat the process using the other slide tube, then assemble the slide in its correct position. By doing each tube separately, you will be able to distribute the lubricant more evenly around the slide.

The Water Key Cork—Check the water key cork regularly and replace when it begins to appear water logged or is beginning to disintegrate (see How to Replace a Water Key Cork, p.262).

MONTHLY MAINTENANCE CHECK LIST—THE TROMBONE

Chart 26 is a check list that you can use to help maintain the trombone. By following this chart, you can keep the trombone in good playing shape and be alert to any possible repairs needed before they become too severe. With some training, your students should also be able to utilize this check list.

HOW TO REPAIR THE TROMBONE

The construction of a trombone is less complex than that of any of the woodwind or other brass instruments. As a result, the trombone is relatively maintenance free. The repairs on a trombone are either so simple that they can be done with a minimum of tools and supplies or they require such specialized tools and skill that they are best sent to the repair shop.

DIAGNOSING INSTRUMENT MALFUNCTIONS

Before you can begin to repair the trombone, you will need to diagnose the problem. Listed below are some of the common problems that can occur. For each problem I have suggested some possible causes. Although this list can hardly be complete, it should serve as a good guideline.

1. *Problem:* Trombone is hard to blow, sounds stuffy.

Possible Causes: Water key is leaking air. Foreign object stuck in the bore of the trombone. Joint between tubing has come unsoldered, causing an air leak. Mouthpiece is dented and/or dirty. A hole has corroded through part of the slide tubing. The tolerance between inner and outer hand slides is too great, creating an air leak.

2. *Problem:* Tuning slide is stuck.

Possible Causes: Slide is not greased properly. Slide has not been cleaned regularly and corrosion has begun. There is a dent in the slide tubing. Slide is being pulled at an angle.

3. *Problem:* Trombone produces a "buzzing" sound on certain notes.

Chart 26
Monthly Maintenance Check List—The Trombone

INSPECT THE FOLLOWING:

Trombone _____ Does hand slide move freely?

_____ Does tuning slide move easily and have a light coating of lubricant?

_____ Is water key cork intact and sealing the hole?

_____ Does the slide lock hold the slide securely?

_____ Is the mouthpiece clean?

_____ Are all braces soldered?

_____ Does the locking nut hold the two sections of the trombone together securely?

Case _____ Are the latches working properly?

_____ Are the hinges tight?

_____ Is the handle secure?

_____ Is the case lining in place?

_____ Are mouthpiece and accessories stored in the proper place?

_____ Are there any pins or medals which will lie against the trombone when the case is closed?

_____ Is the instrument held tightly in the case when closed?

DO THE FOLLOWING:

1. Wash mouthpiece with proper brush.
2. Flush the bore of the trombone and clean with brushes.
3. Clean and lubricate the hand slide.
4. Grease the tuning slide.
5. Thoroughly wipe the instrument with a soft cloth to remove fingerprints.

Possible Causes: Brace on the trombone has come unsoldered. Lock ring is loose. Bell ring (located inside the edge of the bell) is loose.

4. *Problem:* Hand slide is sticking and hard to move.

Possible Causes: Slide is dirty, needs cleaning. Outer slide has been dented. Inner and outer slide tubes are not aligned properly. Plating has worn off the lower portion of inner slide tube. Inner slide tube has begun to corrode, causing the plating to "bubble."

HOW TO CHECK FOR LEAKS

When the trombone is hard to blow or has a stuffy sound, you can suspect that there is a leak in the instrument. Leaks can come from a water key not sealing properly, a soldered joint in the instrument coming apart, or a worn or damaged hand slide. Finding the leak is a prerequisite to fixing the instrument.

Sometimes, especially with young players, the embouchure has not yet developed and the tone will sound "stuffy." Before you begin your search for a leak, have another player blow the trombone to see if it still sounds "stuffy." If so, then the problem is likely with the trombone and not with the player.

Tools Needed: Soft rubber ball (to plug the end of bell)
Procedure:

1. Check just the bell section of the trombone. Hold the rubber ball firmly in the bell to plug that end completely. This ball should be of soft rubber, so that it can effectively seal the end of the trombone.

2. Blow into the other end of the trombone, filling it with as much air as possible, and listen for a leaking air sound. Depending on the size of the leak, this sound might be very apparent or hardly noticeable. You might need the help of another person in order to find the leak.

3. Check the slide section of the trombone. Hold the inner slide tubing with the left hand, placing your thumb over the end of one slide tube and your palm over the other end of the slide tube. With the right hand, "snap" the outer slide section out (toward 4th or 5th position). If the slide section is air tight, the outer slide will "snap" back to the original position because of suction that is formed inside the slide tubes. (*Caution:* Be prepared to catch the slide in case there is a leak in this section and no suction is formed!)

4. Check the water key in the slide section by blowing into one open slide tube while plugging the other slide tube with your finger. If the water key is leaking you will hear the air coming out (and you might even see some bubbles forming around the water key cork).

If, after this testing, you have not found a leak, search for a foreign object in the bore of the trombone.

HOW TO PULL A STUCK MOUTHPIECE

Stuck mouthpieces are very common occurences for the band director, especially when working with younger students. My advice is to invest in a mouthpiece puller. There are many models on the market. Generally speaking, the more solidly built the puller is, the more effective it is in pulling those really stuck mouthpieces.

If you do not have a mouthpiece puller, order one, and if a mouthpiece becomes stuck while you are waiting for it try the following. This does not work all the time, but might get you by.

Tool Needed: Small rawhide hammer
Procedure:

1. Cradle the instrument firmly in your arms, while holding the mouthpiece with one hand. Use the rawhide hammer and tap gently around the mouthpiece receiver while you pull and twist the mouthpiece. If the mouthpiece is not too tight, it will probably come free during this process. If not, wait for the mouthpiece puller, or send the instrument to the repair shop. Any further attempt to remove the mouthpiece will likely result in more serious damage to the instrument and/or mouthpiece.

HOW TO STRAIGHTEN A DENTED MOUTHPIECE SHANK

As the trombone is used, it is likely that at some time the student is going to drop his/her mouthpiece. Whenever a mouthpiece is dropped, there is the possibility of denting the shank. With a few inexpensive tools, you can keep all your brass mouthpieces straight and round, permitting the instruemnt to blow easily.

Tools Needed: Small dent hammer
Steel punch

Procedure:

1. The most important step in this repair procedure is that of selecting the correct size punch. Most hardware stores have various size punches. You want one which is long with a very gradual taper to it. Before you ever need the punch, take a good French horn and a good tuba mouthpiece to the store and fit a punch to these. The punch needs to be small enough at the end to fit into the shank end of the French horn mouthpiece but should taper sufficiently so that the shank end of the tuba mouthpiece will be snug against the punch.

2. When you want to straighten a mouthpiece shank, place your punch into a bench vise (your school shop will have one) in a horizontal position. Place the shank of the mouthpiece over the punch as far as it will go and begin to tap lightly on the shank with the dent hammer while slowly turning the mouthpiece. As you tap, the end will round out and the mouthpiece will slip a little farther on the shank. Use a light pressure and a light tapping so that you do not force the opening of the mouthpiece. (See Illustration 9-2).

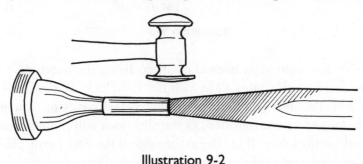

Illustration 9-2

HOW TO REPLACE SLIDE BUMPER CORKS

The section of the inner hand slide on which the slide locking ring is located is called the cork barrel. Inside this cork barrel there are small bumper corks which are used to silently stop the outer slide in first position. If your trombone has a clicking sound when brought into first position, or the slide lock does not hold the slide tight, the bumper corks are either worn or missing and need to be replaced.

Tools Needed: Small thin pick (old dentist pick)
Single edge razor blade
Ruler

Materials Needed: 1/16" sheet cork
Felt washers (optional)

Procedure:

1. Removing all the old cork (and sometimes felt) that is in the cork barrel might be the most difficult step of this procedure. Separate the inner and outer slide tubes, then place just the top tubes back together. Bring the outer tube back into what would be first position. If there is no clicking sound, there is cork in the cork barrel. Scrape around with your pick in the barrel until this piece is removed. Continue this procedure until all the

cork is removed. When the outer slide "clicks" when brought to first position, the cork barrel is clean.

2. Repeat step one with the bottom inner and outer slide tubes.

3. Measure the amount of cork which needs to go into the cork barrel for a proper adjustment. Assemble just the *lower* slide tubes and bring the outer slide all the way up as far as it will go. Make a mark on the outer slide tube with a pencil at the edge of the cork barrel (see Illustration 9-3).

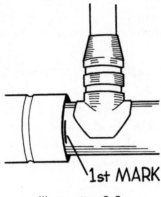

1st MARK

Illustration 9-3

4. Assemble the slide in its normal position. Bring the outer slide all the way up into first position and lock the outer slide with the slide lock. With all the cork removed from the cork barrel, the slide will be loose in this locked position. Now move the outer slide as far down (toward a lower position) as the slide lock will permit (usually about a ¼ inch). Make a mark on the lower slide tube at the edge of the cork barrel. This mark should be adjacent to the mark you made in step 3 above (see Illustration 9-4).

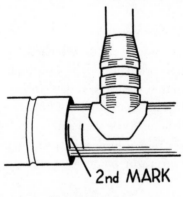

2nd MARK

Illustration 9-4

5. Measure the distance between the two marks. This is the thickness that you will need to make your bumper cork.

6. Take a piece of ¹⁄₁₆" sheet cork. (These sheets come in 4" by 12" sizes.) Cut a strip of cork 4 inches long and the width that you measured in step 5.

7. Wrap this strip around the circumference of the inner slide tube at the edge of the cork barrel. Cut to the correct length. Use the outer slide tube to push this bumper cork into place. Repeat this step with the other slide tube.

8. To check, place the slide in first position and lock. If the lock will not engage,

the cork is too thick. You can usually compress the cork enough just by squeezing the slide together until the slide will lock. Leave the slide locked for a while and the cork will compress permanently.

If the slide is still loose, the cork was not thick enough. To correct this, find a large felt washer (used for brass instrument valve caps) that will fit around the inner slide tube. Slide this washer into the cork barrel so that it fits on top of the bumper cork you just inserted. This additional thickness will usually correct the fit.

HOW TO PULL A STUCK TUNING SLIDE

If your slide is lubricated regularly as indicated in the beginning of this chapter, you will have no problem with sticking. A slide that is stuck has begun to corrode as a result of not having been moved. On occasion, a slide will stick because of a dent in the tubing caused by a blow to the trombone.

Sometimes a corroded slide can be pulled by you, but if it has been stuck for a long time or is caused by a dent, the job will have to be done in the repair shop (see Freeing a Badly Frozen Tuning Slide, p.267).

Tools Needed: Piece of clothesline or lantern wicking
Penetrating oil
Rawhide hammer

Procedure:

1. Loop the line or wicking through the crook of the frozen slide a few times (see Illustration 9-5). Hold the instrument carefully in your hands, cradling and supporting as much as possible in your hands and arms. Have an assistant hold the line and give a few short snaps while you hold the instrument. The slide will often break loose this way. Care must be taken to hold the trombone firmly so that it is not pulled out of your hand when the line is pulled.

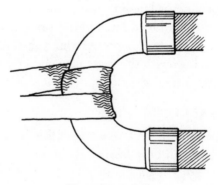

Illustration 9-5

2. If the above failed to loosen the slide, try tapping lightly on the stuck slide tube with a rawhide hammer while pulling. Be sure that this tapping is done lightly, to loosen some corrosion, not to put dents in the tubing.

3. If this fails to free the slide, use a few drops of penetrating oil on the stuck slide and allow the instrument to sit overnight. Then pull the slide as described in step 1.

4. If none of the above methods has loosened the slide, send the instrument to the repair shop for further work.

HOW TO ADJUST THE TUNING SLIDE

A slide, while not frozen in place, can still be very difficult to move. This can be caused by a dirty slide, the beginning of corrosion, or a dent in the slide. If there is a dent, you will have to send the instrument to the repair shop. Otherwise, you can free the action of the slide as described below:

Tools Needed: Drumstick
Bench vise
Large round nose pliers
Fine emery paper
Crocus cloth
Vaseline or lanolin

Procedure:

1. Clamp an old drumstick in a bench vise and place one of the slide tubes over the drumstick. Take a strip of fine emery paper and clean the slide tube as shown in Illustration 9-6. Turn the slide to insure that the entire slide tube is cleaned.

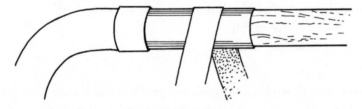

Illustration 9-6

2. Repeat the above with the other tube of the slide.

3. Repeat the above using a piece of crocus cloth on each of the slide tubes. The crocus cloth has an extremely fine grit and will, in effect, polish the slide tubes.

4. Wipe the tubes clean with a cloth. Apply a small amount of lubricant on the end of one slide tube (either Vaseline or lanolin), insert the slide tube into the receiver, and rotate thoroughly to distribute the lubricant. Do the same with the other slide tube.

5. Replace the slide in the trombone. As you re-assemble, check to see that the two inner slide tubes are lined up with the two outer slide tubes. If they are not aligned, the slide will not move easily and a repair technician will have to realign the slide.

HOW TO REPLACE A WATER KEY CORK

Replacing a water key cork is probably one of the most common jobs needed on a trombone. It is easy to do and will only take a few minutes.

Tools Needed: Single edge razor blade
Small screwdriver or scraper

Materials Needed: Assorted sizes of pre-cut water key corks or cork sticks
Pad and cork cement

Procedure:

1. In most cases it is not necessary to remove the water key in order to replace the cork. With a small screwdriver (or scraper) clean out the key cup to remove all traces of old cork and glue.

2. Select a pre-cut water key cork that will fit into the water key cup. The fit should be snug so that the cork will have to be forced into the cup slightly. When in place, check for leaks by blowing into one end of the slide, while holding the other end closed with your finger. If there is a leak, shift the position of the cork so that it will be level with the water key nipple. When the seal is correct, remove the cork, place a small drop of pad and cork cement into the key cup, and replace the cork in the same position. Apply pressure to the water key to form an impression of the water key nipple in the cork. This will help to insure a good tight seal.

3. If you do not have pre-cut water key corks, use a cork stick. These sticks come in various diameters. Select a diameter which will fit firmly into the water key cup and cut off a piece which is approximately the correct thickness. Place the piece into the cup and check for leaks as described above. Trim the cork with your razor blade until it is level with the water key nipple. Check for a leak; if none exist, remove the cork, place a small drop of pad and cork cement in the cup, and replace the cork in the same position. Apply pressure to the water key to form an impression of the water key nipple in the cork. This will help to insure a good tight seal.

HOW TO REPLACE A WATER KEY SPRING

Replacing a water key spring is not very difficult, although you will need a large variety of spring sizes.

Tools Needed: Needle nose pliers
Small screwdriver
Wire cutter
Materials Needed: Correct size water key spring
Procedure:

1. Remove the water key and old spring. Most water keys are held in place by a small rod. This rod is usually threaded, and you will need to use either a small screwdriver or a needle nose pliers to unscrew. Sometimes the rod is not threaded and can be pulled out with the needle nose pliers.

2. Select a water key spring which is made for your brand instrument or is the same size as the old one which you removed. Slide the spring over the hinge tube of the water key (see Illustration 9-7).

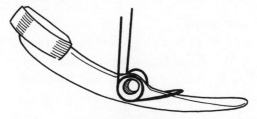

Illustration 9-7

3. The part on the instrument which holds the water key is called the "saddle." When you put the key back in the saddle, be certain that the open ends of the spring will be on the same side of the saddle as the closed end of the spring (see Illustration 9-8). It is sometimes quite difficult to hold these ends in place, and this may take some practice. Once the spring and key are in place, insert the rod to hold in place.

Illustration 9-8

4. If your water key is designed without a hinge tube, the spring will need to rest inside the water key in a position so that the rod will be able to slide through the water key and the loops of the spring. This style spring is much more difficult to install, for the spring tends to slide away as the tension increases while installing.

5. Once the key is in place it will help to wrap each end of the spring around the post of the saddle so that the spring ends will be pointing toward the water key cork (see Illustration 9-9). Use a small wire cutter to cut off any excess spring at this time.

Illustration 9-9

HOW TO REPAIR THE "AMADO" STYLE WATER KEY

The "Amado" style water key is used on the Getzen trombone (see Illustration 9-10). As the style of the water key is quite different than a conventional water key, its repair and care need to be explained.

The most common problem that you will encounter with this style key is that as it gets dirty, it tends to stick. When the action begins to slow down, try lubricating. Place a drop of key oil in the hole and push the plunger back and forth. If this does not free the action, you will need to take the water key apart and clean thoroughly.

Tools Needed: Two blue steel needle springs
　　　　　　　Small rawhide hammer
Materials Needed: Replacement parts for water key (only if needed)

Procedure:

1. The back plate of the water key is held in place with a small spring. Using the two blue steel needle springs, pinch the two ends of the spring together and remove. The

Illustration 9-10

Photograph courtesy of the Getzen Company, Inc.; Elkhorn, Wisconsin 53121

back plate will then come out, followed by the coil spring which is inside the water key. Finally the main piston of the water key can be removed. If the piston is frozen and will not move, use a small rawhide hammer and gently tap the piston out.

2. Clean the piston and the water key casing with a soft cloth and some alcohol. Place a light drop of key oil on the piston and replace in the casing. Push the piston back and forth to be certain that it is moving freely.

3. When the piston action is free, replace the coil spring, back plate and the back plate spring which will hold all parts together.

REPAIRS TO BE SENT TO THE REPAIR SHOP

The trombone requires very few repairs; many of these are relatively easy and can be done by following the directions given in this chapter. You can best determine, after reading this chapter, which repairs you feel capable of doing and which you feel should be sent to the repair shop. A good rule to follow is: "When in doubt, send it out." If you are not sure you can do a repair as described, more harm than good can result from your experimenting.

Some trombone repairs require specialized, expensive tools. It is not practical for the band director to own these tools, thus the repair must be sent out. Other repairs may seem easy enough to perform, but really require a special skill which only an experienced repair technician possesses. Outlined below are some of the more common trombone repairs that will need to be done at a repair shop. It is hoped that this will give you a better understanding of the repair procedures.

ADJUSTING A STICKING HAND SLIDE

A sticking, or badly adjusted, hand slide is probably one of the most common problems that plague both the band director and the student trombonist. Much of this problem can be avoided by following the suggested cleaning procedures and care of the slide as outlined earlier in this chapter.

The adjustment of the hand slide needs to be very precise as the tolerances are small. It is best to have an experienced repair technician handle this job; most band directors will not have the necessary skills.

One problem which can cause a slide to stick is that one of the slide tubes is slightly bent. These tubes need to be *exactly* straight or the slide action will be hampered. A slide tube which might appear to be straight to the untrained eye may have enough curve to it to cause problems. The repair technician knows how to discover this problem. If he finds that the tube is not straight, he basically will bend the tube back to a straight position. This requires great skill so as not to damage the slide further.

Another cause of sticking slides is a dent in the slide tube. An obvious dent that we all can see will, most likely, be severe enough to stop the slide from moving at all. A minor dent that can cause sticking might be difficult to see with the untrained eye. If there is a dent in the slide tube, the repair technician will remove the dent in a manner similar to that described below (see Removing Body Dents, p.267). This work must be done very carefully for, again, the slide could be damaged more if done incorrectly.

Slide tubes that are out of alignment can also cause sticking. Both the inner and outer slide tubes must be *exactly* parallel. The repair technician will either bend the slide tubes back into a parallel position or may find it necessary to unsolder the slide and resolder so that the tubes are parallel.

Dirty slides will also cause a sticking action in the slide. If the slide has not been cared for correctly, you may find it necessary to take the instrument to the repair technician for a thorough cleaning. He will have the tools necessary to clean the slide much more effectively than you could do by yourself.

If one of the slide tubes is damaged beyond repair, the repair technician will be able to replace the damaged tube with a new tube that can be obtained from the manufacturer. This work is usually expensive, but it is well worth it if the trombone is in good condition otherwise. (See Replacing Corroded Parts, p.268)

FREEING A BADLY FROZEN TUNING SLIDE

If, after you have done all the items suggested to remove a frozen slide (see How to Pull a Stuck Tuning Slide, p.261) it is still stuck, send the instrument to the repair shop.

The repair technician will first attempt to remove the slide in the same way that you tried. Having experience in the procedure, he can better judge the amount of pressure that can be applied to the instrument.

If this does not work, he will apply heat to help loosen the corroded portion of the slide tube. Heating the outer slide tube causes it to expand, and this will often be enough to break the slide free. The trick is to use enough heat to expand, without burning the lacquer finish. If it still does not come free, he will add some penetrating oil and more heat. If these techniques do not free the slide, he must unsolder the tubing and take the slide apart.

Usually the crook of the slide is unsoldered and removed. This will leave the two inner slides stuck in the outer slides (sometimes only one slide tube will be stuck). He will place a piece of rod or a steel ball inside the inner slide tube, then grasp that tube with a large pair of pliers (the rod or steel ball prevents the tube from collapsing when squeezed with the pliers). With the pliers, and the additional application of heat, he is able to rotate the inner slide tube slightly, and this will eventually break free.

When the parts are free the repair technician will clean the slide. He will emery the inner slide tubes and polish with crocus cloth. He will then re-align and solder the slide back together if it was necessary to unsolder. This soldering job must be done very carefully, as the two inner slides must line up exactly with the two outer tubes. A light coating of Vaseline or lanolin as a lubricant is applied and the slide will work freely again.

REMOVING BODY OR SLIDE DENTS

The tools required for effectively removing a dent in the body or slide of the trombone necessitate that this work be done in a repair shop. There are really two types of dents that need to be considered. One is those that are cosmetic, that is, they do not affect the playability of the instrument but do detract from the appearance. The other type of dent is that which affects the mechanical operation of the trombone. This type includes dents to the tuning slide or hand slide.

When removing dents, the repair technician will use a large variety of long, short and curved rods which have different size balls attached to one end. He will insert the rod into the bore of the trombone and push the dent up from the inside. The dent can also be "tapped" up by placing the rod under the dent and then tapping on it with a dent hammer. This will cause the dent to rise. Great care must be taken so that the raising of the dent does not go too far, thus producing a "hump." The technician has become skilled at knowing how much pressure must be exerted and which size rod and/or ball needs to be used.

The dents that cannot be reached with a rod need to be removed with a "dent ball" set. This tool is actually a set of graduated size brass balls (usually about 100 balls to a set). A ball that will fit under the dent is dropped down into the tubing. This ball is driven into place with a smaller brass ball called a "driver." By shaking the trombone, the driver taps against the dent ball, slowly pushing it under the dent. When it is under the dent, the repair technician will use a dent hammer to tap on the dent. Tapping on the dent ball with the dent in between will cause the dent to lift slightly. Next, a larger size dent ball is placed under the dent and the process is repeated. This continues until the dent is removed. Each time it is time to remove a dent ball another "driver" must be used to push the dent ball back out the way it came in. This process is very time consuming, so it is not uncommon for the technician to spend 15 to 30 minutes on a single dent. For this reason, brass instrument dent work is expensive.

REPLACING CORRODED PARTS

As a trombone gets older, the brass begins to deteriorate, especially if the instrument has not been kept clean through the years. Eventually this corrosion will eat through the metal tubing, leaving tiny holes which allow air to escape. On most trombones this will happen in the hand slide.

The repair technician can order (or has in stock) a replacement piece which has been obtained from the manufacturer. He will remove the old piece, solder on the new piece to fit properly then buff and lacquer this piece to give it a "like new" appearance. (The exception to this would be the inner slide tube which is obtained already plated.) This job is time consuming, and the replacement parts from the manufacturer are often expensive, so this repair cost is usually quite high. If a replacement part is not available from the manufacturer, the repair technician can make a part from stock brass tubing that he has on hand. The finished product will be the same, but he must spend more time fitting the tubing to the instrument, so, even though the part cost may be less, the labor cost will be considerably higher.

SOLDERING LOOSE BRACES AND JOINTS

If a trombone is dropped or bumped, the resulting damage may include breaking the soldered joint between two pieces of tubing or between the tubing and a brace. A broken joint needs to be repaired immediately, as the instrument will leak. A broken brace should also be repaired immediately; any loose braces will make the trombone more susceptible to further bending and damage. Loose braces will often "buzz" when certain notes are played, through sympathetic vibrations. If you hear this type of sound, look for a loose brace.

The soldering process on a brass instrument is not really very difficult *when you have experience* but can be a real disaster if you are not experienced. For this reason it is best to send *all* soldering work to the repair shop. When band directors try to do their own soldering, it is usually unsuccessful and has to be sent to the repair shop because the solder will not hold. Never try to glue, solder or temporarily repair a broken joint or brace. This always adds to the labor cost of the work in the shop because of the extra time that must be spent cleaning up your work.

The repair technician first removes all traces of old solder from the point of contact. This can be quite a task if the point of contact is hard to reach. He then uses a small piece of emery paper to rough up the two surfaces to be soldered. The area is heated and a small drop of flux is added. This flux will burn the lacquer finsih, so must be added very carefully. Solder always flows to the hottest area; therefore, the repair technician must direct his flame to the correct point so that the solder will flow *between* the two pieces (making the solder virtually invisible). After soldering, the area may have to be cleaned and some touch up lacquer applied, depending on how much of an area was soldered.

THE COMPLETE OVERHAUL

A complete overhaul of a trombone will result in an instrument which looks like new. In this job, usually all dents are removed, the hand slide cleaned and adjusted and the tuning slide cleaned and adjusted.

Any loose or missing braces are also repaired. The instrument is completely stripped of its old finish and is buffed to a high gloss finish in the same manner as new instruments are buffed. The instrument is then thoroughly cleaned and relacquered.

The complete job will produce an instrument which has a "like new" appearance.

10

The Percussion Instruments

Illustration 10-1

Photograph courtesy of Ludwig Industries

HOW TO TAKE CARE OF THE PERCUSSION INSTRUMENTS

Your percussion equipment should be repaired as soon as you notice any damage or wear. In this way the equipment will always be ready for use. Some schools have well-equipped percussion sections, but with the equipment damaged or in such poor repair that it does not work when needed. Most percussion repairs can be done in the school by the band director or even some responsible students. The most common repairs will be the replacement of broken heads or parts which can be attached without difficulty. Many of the smaller percussion items cannot be repaired but need to be replaced when broken.

In addition to repairing damaged or worn equipment, the director should institute a program of preventive maintenance. By utilizing regular monthly and yearly check-ups, severe damage can often be prevented. (See Monthly Maintenance Check List, and Yearly Maintenance Check List, p.275.)

Illustration 10-2

Photograph courtesy of Ludwig Industries

STORE THE PERCUSSION INSTRUMENTS PROPERLY

Storage facilities for the percussion instruments should protect the equipment from damage and keep it clean, organized and easy to find. Unauthorized playing on the percussion equipment along with poor storage facilities can account for almost 90% of the percussion damage. The director should make a point of instructing band members that all percussion equipment is "off limits" to students not in the percussion section. There is always a temptation for students to "bang around" on the "drums" and this can lead to damaged equipment. Percussion players should only be allowed to use the equipment during rehearsals and at authorized practice times.

The percussion storage facilities should be located immediately adjacent to the percussion section to facilitate the moving of equipment with a minimum of time and effort. Ideally, storage facilities should contain a number of racks for the larger instruments such as marching percussion, bass drums, snare drums, concert tom toms, etc. In addition, there should be a combination of shelves and drawers available for storing the smaller and accessory percussion instruments, sticks, beaters, mallets and slings. There are many commercially made percussion cabinets which can be used for this, although it is unlikely many would be large enough to hold all the equipment of the well-equipped percussion section. This cabinet would have to be supplemented, therefore, with additional permanent storage facilities.

The large percussion instruments such as timpani, marimbas, xylophones, vibraphones, bass drums should have larger cabinets in which they may be rolled for storage. Sometimes a small room near the percussion section will work well for this. These larger items need not be moved to storage after each use if they are covered when not in use. They should be stored, however, whenever they will not be needed for a period of time. Even when in storage, these instruments should be covered to keep them free of dust. Seasonal instruments such as the marching percussion should be in cases and stored on racks when not in use.

All storage facilities should be located away from extremes in temperature, should not be near windows or heating vents, and should have locks so that equipment may be safely stored.

CARE OF THE SNARE DRUM

Proper care of the heads and snares is of primary importance in the care of your snare drum. Heads should be cleaned when necessary. Plastic heads are far easier to maintain than the old style calfskin heads. They can be wiped regularly with warm water and a damp cloth. For stubborn stains, remove the head from the drum and scrub with a stiff brush and kitchen cleanser, rinse and dry thoroughly. Be certain to adjust the head tension when replacing the head on the drum (see How to Replace a Broken Drum Head, p.274).

Wire snares should not be pulled, plucked or strummed either individually or collectively, as this spiraled wire is easily stretched. Once a snare has stretched, it is impossible to adjust the snare for a good snare drum sound. If you have any snares that are stretched, you can either replace the entire set or cut off those particular snares (this, of course, should not be done too often).

It is best to cover the drum when not in use or store in a drum cabinet or fiber case. When storing the drum in a case, do not pack any other loose equipment into the case with the drum. Store the drum on its stand only if it is in an area which is free from traffic. It is very easy to have a snare drum knocked off the stand by a passing student.

CARE OF THE TIMPANI

The timpani should be stored with either a cardboard or masonite cover to protect the heads and a full drop cloth to protect the body of the instrument. The heads should be kept clean to help preserve the life of your sticks and maintain good tone quality. Wipe plastic heads once a month with a clean damp cloth and be sure to dry the head thoroughly.

The tuning lug threads should be lubricated lightly with Vaseline about once a year. Dents in the copper bowl can be removed by pounding carefully from the inside of the bowl with a hard rubber hammer.

If the timpani "rattle" when played, check for the following:

1. Loose screws, rods or other fittings on the timpano
2. Loose material inside the timpano bowl
3. A music stand touching the timpano and responding to its vibrations
4. Sympathetic vibrations setting other equipment or percussion instruments into vibration.

Locate the cause of the rattle, then tighten, remove or pad the offending area.

If there is a "buzzing" sound from the head when playing certain notes, the following will likely be the cause:

1. Dirt between the counterhoop and the flesh hoop
2. Dirt between the head and the rim of the bowl
3. Unequal tension of the head.

When this happens, remove the head, clean the bowl rim, clean the inside and outside of the head and counterhoop, lubricate lightly (see below), and replace the head (see How to Replace a Broken Drum Head, p.274 and How to Adjust the Timpani Head and Pedal Tension, p.277).

If the timpano "squeaks" when tuning, lubrication is needed where the head makes contact with the rim of the bowl. Remove the head, clean the rim and inside of the head and lubricate the bowl edge with Vaseline (paraffin may be used for calfskin heads). Replace the head (see How to Replace a Broken Drum Head, p.274 and How to Adjust the Timpani Head and Pedal Tension, p.277).

Many timpani have a spring tension pedal. You may find that the tension control is not set correctly. Before making any attempt to adjust this tension, read How to Adjust the Timpani Head and Pedal Tension, p.277.

CARE OF THE CYMBALS

Cymbals will tarnish after use and can never be restored to their original sheen. They can be cleaned, however, by using ordinary kitchen cleanser or copper cleaner. A metal polish can also be used if it is followed by buffing with a soft pad. It is important that the cymbal be buffed when using polish in order to remove all traves of polish which could leave stains if not removed. It is important that the buffing pads be soft if you use a power tool for this job, because the temper of the metal, which controls the cymbal sound, will be destroyed if it should be heated too much while buffing.

On occasion a hand cymbal may turn "inside out" when struck. This is usually a result of either striking the cymbal at the wrong angle or with too much power. Cymbals that turn inside out can be returned to their proper position by holding the edges of the cymbal in each hand and striking the inside of the dome against your knee. A cymbal which continues to turn inside out will weaken and eventually crack.

About once a month check the cymbal straps on the hand cymbals to be certain that the knots are secure. Re-tie the knot if it is coming loose (see How to Tie a Cymbal Strap Knot, p.279).

CARE OF THE MALLET PERCUSSION

Xylophone/Marimba—Always keep the instrument covered with a clean cloth cover when not in use. Never set other instruments or objects on top of the keyboard, as this can easily scratch the bars, causing both unsightly appearance and discrepancies in tuning. Resonators are easily dented, so care should be taken whenever moving the instrument that these are not damaged. Bars need to be cleaned and waxed periodically, and cracked bars should be sent to the manufacturer for replacement. Guideposts can bend against the bars causing a restriction in the vibration of the bars. Bent posts should be straightened and missing posts replaced. The insulators on the post will dry out after a number of years and should be replaced. Suspension cords should be secure and tight.

Tuning the bars is a job for the professional. To tune, the pitch is raised by shaving off the end of the bar and lowered by shaving off the underside. Most manufacturers will retune their own instruments and occasionally will do other brands. I recommend that all mallet percussion instruments be sent to the manufacturer for tuning.

Orchestra Bells—The orchestra bells should be covered when not in use and other instruments and objects should not be placed on top. Check periodically to be certain that the guideposts are straight and not binding against the bars. Missing posts should be replaced. Be sure the case cover is secure, especially in sets that have removable bars, and that the handles and hinges are in good condition.

Vibraphone—The vibraphone should be covered when not in use and other instruments or objects should never be placed on top of the instrument. The guideposts should be checked, with bent and missing posts corrected. The bars should be cleaned and polished about once a year. Suspension cords should be tight and replaced when wear begins to show. The damper pedal will need occasional adjustment to be sure that it is operating correctly with a minimum of foot action. The electric motor should be properly maintained with belts and pulleys kept in good condition. Vibraphones also need to be retuned occasionally; this should be done by the manufacturer.

Chimes—The chimes should be covered when not in use. The chime suspension cords are extremely important and should be checked regularly. They should be replaced at the *first sign* of wear, or you may find your chimes falling off the rack in the middle of a concert. The damper pedal should be checked periodically to be sure that it is operating with a minimum of foot action. Be sure that the rack is strong and secure at all times, but especially after moving the instrument.

MAINTENANCE CHECK LIST—THE PERCUSSION

Charts 27 and 28 are check lists that you can use to help maintain the percussion instruments. By following these charts, you can keep the various percussion instruments in good playing shape and be alert to any possibe repairs needed before they become serious. With some training, your students should also be able to utilize this check list.

HOW TO REPAIR THE PERCUSSION INSTRUMENTS

Fortunately, most percussion instruments are built to stand quite a bit of punishment and, therefore, you will encounter little need for repair. This will especially be true if proper maintenance is followed as described earlier in this chapter. On the larger percussion instruments, drum heads, snares, cord, strings and straps are about the only thing that can wear out or will need replacing. If parts of the larger drums should break, a replacement can usually be ordered and easily be put on by the director without any special instructions.

Smaller percussion accessory instruments will usually need to be replaced if broken. Fortunately, most of these instruments are relatively inexpensive.

Listed below are some of the common repairs that you will be able to do.

HOW TO REPLACE A BROKEN DRUM HEAD

Broken drum heads are probably the most common percussion repair that you will encounter. The procedure for changing a drum head is the same for all drums. If you are

Chart 27
Monthly Maintenance Check List—The Percussion

INSPECT THE FOLLOWING:

_____ Check all drum heads for holes and replace when needed.

_____ Check and replace all sticks and mallets which are cracked or broken.

_____ Check and replace or re-cover all mallets and timpani sticks that have worn-out heads.

_____ Check all snares for loose or broken strands. Cut or replace as necessary.

_____ Check all stands for loose wing nuts, screws, etc.

_____ Check all cymbal straps to be sure that knots are secure.

_____ Check chime suspension cords for signs of wear.

DO THE FOLLOWING:

1. Wipe all heads with a damp cloth to remove surface dirt.
2. Dust the bars of all the mallet percussion instruments.
3. Thoroughly tune the timpani. Balance the heads and reset pitches as required. Adjust spring tension control if needed.

Chart 28
Yearly Maintenance Check List—The Percussion

INSPECT THE FOLLOWING:

_____ Check the timpani for dents and remove.

_____ Check all cymbals for cracks. Be sure that all strap knots are tied correctly.

_____ Check the suspension cords, bumpers, posts, and bars of all mallet instruments.

_____ Check the intonation of mallet instruments and send bars to be retuned when needed.

_____ Check pedal mechanism on vibraphone and chimes for good operation.

_____ Check all accessory percussion instruments for damage.

DO THE FOLLOWING:

1. Remove all heads and clean dirt from inside head, under counterhoop and edge of shell. Lubricate rim and replace.
2. Remove all gum wrappers, paper clips, etc., that have accumulated in drum shells.
3. Clean and lubricate, with Vaseline, all tuning rods.
4. Polish all mallet instruments—wood bars with a good quality paste wax and metal bars with a good quality metal polish.
5. Polish and hand buff all cymbals.

changing a timpani head, be sure to also read How to Adjust the Timpani Head and Pedal Tension, p.277.

Replacing a drum head is relatively easy, but there are a few items that you should be aware of in order to do the job correctly.

Tools Needed: Drum key
                 Screwdriver
Materials Needed: Replacement drum head
Procedure:

1. Remove the old drum head. Most of the smaller drums have tuning lugs which use a standard drum key. Some models might require the use of a screwdriver instead of the drum key. Larger drums such as the bass drum and timpani have T-handle lugs. Some timpani use a special size drum key for their lugs. To remove the head, loosen and remove all the tuning lugs, then lift off the counterhoop followed by the drum head.

2. Check the old drum head to be certain that you have the correct size replacement. Plastic drum heads come in various thicknesses which are appropriate for the various types of drums. Most catalogs describe which drum heads are suitable to what type of drum. Measure the diameter of the drum *shell* (after the old head has been removed) to determine what diameter drum head is needed.

3. Before placing the new head on the drum, clean out any dirt or articles that might be inside the drum shell. Also check, and tighten, the nuts (or screws) that are located inside the drum shell.

4. Clean the rim and counterhoop. These two areas often become quite dirty over the period of time that a drum head is in place on a drum. Before placing the new head, wipe the rim of the drum thoroughly with a clean cloth. Also wipe out the inside of the counterhoop. (This is the metal or wood hoop that is placed over the drum head.)

5. Place the head on the drum, then add the counterhoop and tighten the tuning lugs evenly to eliminate all wrinkles from the head. Press down on the center of the head to set it against the shell.

6. Balance the head. It is essential that a drum head be balanced on the drum. An unbalanced head will produce a different response from each stick as they strike the head and will affect the evenness of sound which results. Also, an unbalanced head does not vibrate evenly, causing the head to counteract its own vibrations which will result in an inferior sound.

To balance the head, you must be certain that there is equal tension at all points around the circumference of the drum head. Use a stick to tap lightly at the edge of the drum head alongside each tuning lug. Each area should produce the same pitch. If not, adjust the lugs to correct. Tighten the lug to raise the pitch and loosen to lower the pitch.

On those drums that have two heads (i.e., snare drum, bass drum, etc.) it will be necessary to muffle the opposite head so that you will be able to clearly hear the pitch that is being produced on the head that you are tuning. Lay the opposite head against a soft cloth to prevent any vibrations.

7. Set the head tension. Once the drum head is balanced, you might still wish to change the tension of the head. You may do this by either tightening or loosening the

tuning lugs the same amount. Start by turning *each lug* a ¼ or ⅛ turn until the correct tenion is achieved.

HOW TO ADJUST THE TIMPANI HEAD AND PEDAL TENSION

One of the most common problems in timpani malfunctions and poor tone quality lies in improper head adjustment and pedal tension. Because students tend to turn those exposed tuning lugs, the timpani head adjustments need to be checked about once a month. The more effective you can be in instructing your students not to turn the lugs, the less adjustments you will have to make.

Procedure:

1. Balance the head. Strike the timpano head in the playing area adjacent to each tuning lug. It is likely that you will notice different pitches coming from different sections of the head. A balanced head produces the same pitch regardless of which area of the head you strike. A balanced head is essential; it will produce a richer tone and provide accurate intonation on the timpani. Also, the spring tension style pedal will not operate properly with an unbalanced head.

2. Set the pedal or tuning handle to the low note position. (If, on spring tension models, the pedal will not stay at this position, hold it in place with your foot.) Adjust the tuning lugs so that the head is at the correct lowest pitch for that particular timpano (i.e., an "F" on the 29″ drum, a "B♭" on the 26″ or 25″ drum, etc.)

3. Once the low note is set to the correct pitch, raise the timpano pitch about a fourth using the tuning pedal or handle. This need not be exact, as it is just easier to hear the pitch differences this way. Choose one tuning lug as a "master" pitch and tune all the other lugs so that the tone adjacent to them will sound the same as the one adjacent to the "master" lug. Opposite tuning lugs affect the pitch, so the pattern shown in Illustration 10-3 will work best when tuning. Remember to check the "master" lug after tuning each of the other lugs.

4. Use the tip of one finger to strike the head firmly so that the true fundamental pitch will sound. The sound which continues to resonate contains too many overtones to be used for tuning purposes. By placing a small soft cloth or mute in the center of the head, you will eliminate most of these overtones. Be sure to damp the head completely

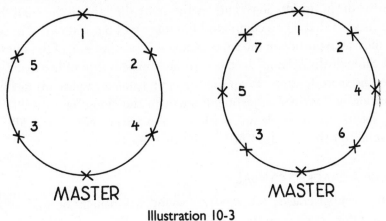

Illustration 10-3

each time before striking at the next lug. It will take some practice to learn to recognize whether a pitch is sharp or flat to the "master" pitch.

5. Once the tuning lugs have all been adjusted, re-check around the circumference of the timpano head to be sure that the head is in tune with itself. When this is achieved, the head is "balanced."

6. Return the pedal to the low note position and check to be certain that the pitch is still correct. If it is not, adjust *each lug* an *equal* amount to correct the pitch.

7. The spring tension pedal should hold at any position that you move it to. If the pedal moves *down* when released, there is not enough tension in the spring. Tighten this by turning the tension control in a clockwise direction. If the pedal moves *up* when released, there is too much tension in the spring, so turn the spring control in a counterclockwise direction. *Never make any adjustment in pedal tension until you have balanced the head and tuned the drum to the correct basic pitch!*

HOW TO REPLACE THE SNARES

The snares on a drum seem to hold a great fascination for students, and the continuous tightening and loosening, plus pulling and strumming, of the snares will eventually damage them. As the wire wound snare stretches, it will become increasingly more difficult to adjust for a nice "crisp" sound. This is the time to replace the snare.

Tools Needed: Screwdriver

Materials Needed: Replacement snare

Snare cord (optional)

Procedure:

1. Remove the old snare. When doing this be sure to observe how the snare is attached to the drum. Each model drum has its own system of attaching a snare. Most systems use a snare cord to tie the snare in place. Some drums have the snare attached directly to the snare strainer with screws. Check to see which system you have, and be certain to order the correct replacement snare for the drum. (Your music dealer should be able to help you select the correct snare.)

2. Tie the new snare in place. As most systems will require the use of snare cord to attach the snare, following is a description of how this is done.

Turn the drum upside down and lay the snare directly on the snare head. Place it on the drum head so that when completed the snare will be centered. *Tie* one end of the snare to the moveable portion of the snare strainer. The other end of the snare cord should be threaded through the "clamp" located on the opposite side of the drum shell.

3. Set the snare tension. To set the correct tension for the snare, set the strainer to the "on" position but set the adjustment screw to the "loose" position. Pull the snare tightly and secure in the "clamp" with a screwdriver. Now gradually tighten the adjustment screw on the strainer until the correct tension is achieved.

HOW TO REPAIR A CRACKED CYMBAL

When a cymbal cracks, the resulting sound will usually be undesirable because there will be a "rattle" each time the cymbal is played. This is caused by the two edges of the crack rubbing together as the cymbal vibrates. If repaired as described below, and the crack is not too severe, the cymbal should be able to give you continued use.

Tools Needed: Drill (electric or hand)

⅛" drill bit

Hack saw or coping saw

Procedure:

1. Determine the exact length of the crack and mark with a lead pencil so that it is easy to see.

2. Drill a hole into the cymbal at the end of the crack to prevent it from spreading any further into the cymbal (see Illustration 10-4).

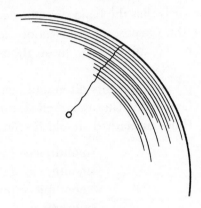

Illustration 10-4

3. Saw down the length of the crack (up to the hole that you drilled) with either the hack saw or coping saw. This will separate the two edges of the crack, thus preventing them from vibrating together. The resulting crack will be more obvious because of the space created when you saw, but the sound of the cymbal will be improved and the crack will not spread any farther into the cymbal.

HOW TO TIE A CYMBAL STRAP KNOT

All hand cymbals should have a rawhide strap which is used to hold the cymbal while it is being played. If this strap comes loose, or needs to be replaced, it should be tied with a cymbal strap knot as shown in Illustration 10-5 below. This knot will hold the cymbal very securely and the rawhide will tend to hold against itself, preventing the knot from coming untied.

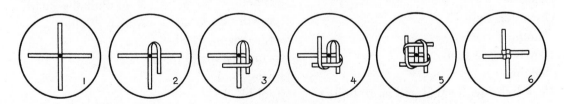

Illustration 10-5

Appendix A
Tools Needed for the
Repairs Described in This Book

Listed below are the tools that the band director needs in order to do the repairs described in this book. For the purpose of clarification, *tools* are items used to *fix* an instrument. Appendix B lists the supplies (or those items which are replaced on the instrument).

Those tools marked (*) are used less often and could be omitted if funding is a problem and purchased at a later date. Those marked (‡) are used most often and should be purchased immediately. Those unmarked should be purchased as soon as possible.

‡alcohol
‡baking soda
*ball, large soft rubber
*ball, small soft rubber
*beeswax
 brass rod (from an old lyre)
‡burner, alcohol or bunsen
‡cigarette paper (ungummed)
 clothesline or lantern wicking
*coping saw
 corks, leak testing (assorted sizes)
 crocus cloth
*drill bit (⅛")
‡drum key
 drum stick
 emery paper (220 grit)
*flute cleaning rod
 glue, super
*hacksaw
 hammer, dent
 hammer, rawhide
‡key bending tool[1]
*lanolin
‡leak light (with small and large bulbs)
‡leather (small piece)
 measuring rod[2]

‡mouthpiece brush (brass)
‡mouthpiece brush (reed)
‡mouthpiece puller
‡muriatic acid
‡pad slicks (assorted sizes)
*paint brush, small
 paraffin (wax)
*penetrating oil
*piccolo cleaning rod
‡pick, small (dental pick)
 pipe stem cleaners
‡pliers, expandable grip
‡pliers, flat nose (duck bill)
 pliers, needle nose
 pliers, round nose (large)
‡pliers, round nose (small)
‡razor blades, single edge
‡ruler, steel (6 inch)
‡scraper
‡screwdriver, large
‡screwdriver, small
 spring clamps (3 to 12)
‡spring hook[3]
*steel block
 steel punch
‡talcum powder

280

*valve brush	*vise, bench
valve mirror	wire cutter
‡vaseline	wooden wedges, small

---

[1]Cut a piece of metal (approximately $\frac{1}{32}''$ thick) into a strip about $\frac{1}{4}''$ x $4''$. Bend one end at a right angle to the rest so that the short end will be about 1 inch long and the other end about 3 inches long. Grind and buff the edges so that all roughness is removed.

[2]See Illustration 7-6. Cut a $6''$ length of old lyre shaft (square). Clamp about $\frac{1}{2}''$ to $\frac{3}{4}''$ of one end into a bench vise and slowly tap on the exposed end until it bends to form a right angle. By tapping slowly the brass will not break. This rod is then used for measuring.

[3]A good spring hook can be made out of a crochet hook or purchased commercially. File a small groove into the end of the hook to enable you to push a spring. The hook which is already a part of the crochet hook will allow you to pull the spring. The spring hook should be capable of both pushing and pulling the end of a spring.

Appendix B
Supplies Needed for the
Repairs Described in This book

Listed below are the supplies that the band director will need in order to do the repairs described in this book. For the purpose of clarification, *supplies* are items which are used to *replace* a portion of any band instrument. Appendix A lists the tools (those items needed to *fix* an instrument).

Those supplies marked (*) are used less often and could be omitted if funds are limited and purchased at a later time. Those marked (‡) are used most often and should be purchased immediately. Those unmarked should be purchased as soon as possible.

bore oil
‡cement, contact cork
‡cement, pad and cork
‡cork grease
‡cork, 1/64″ sheet
cork, 1/32″ sheet
‡cork, 1/16″ sheet
*cork, 3/32″ sheet
*cork, 1/8″ sheet
cork, stick (assorted sizes)
cork, valve stem
‡cork, water key (assorted sizes)
‡felt discs and bumpers
‡felts, valve stem
‡head joint cork, flute
*head joint cork, piccolo
key oil
pads, double skin clarinet (assorted sizes)

‡pads, double skin flute (assorted sizes)
*pads, double skin piccolo (assorted sizes)
*pads, leather bassoon (assorted sizes)
‡pads, leather saxophone (assorted sizes)
*screws, flat spring
‡shellac, stick
‡slide oil
‡snare cord
*spring, flute wire (assorted diameter)
*springs, blue steel needle (assorted sizes)
*springs, flat (assorted sizes)
springs, water key (assorted sizes)
‡string, rotary valve
*thread, heavy duty (red)
‡valve oil
‡valve oil, rotary
washers, paper flute
*water key parts, "Amado"

Appendix C
A List of Sources for the
Purchase of Tools and Supplies

1. Erick Brand
   1117 West Beardsley Avenue
   Elkhart, Indiana 46514

2. Ed Meyer Company
   3022 Pacific Street
   Omaha, Nebraska 68105

3. Ferree's Band Instrument Tools and Supplies
   P.O. Box 259
   Battle Creek, Michigan 49016

4. Parts and supplies can usually be ordered directly from the manufacturer. This is especially convenient if you wish to order a larger supply of pads, springs, screws, etc., that will fit a particular brand of instrument. Your music dealer can supply you with the current address of any of the instrument manufacturers.

5. Do not overlook the repair shop at your music dealer. The dealer will have an inventory of common supplies and parts and most will sell these to the school.